Southeast Asia

WITHDRAWN
UTSA LIBRARIES

George McTurnan Kahin was a pioneering scholar of Southeast Asian history and politics, and US foreign policy. His book offers a unique perspective on American involvement in Southeast Asia, from the 1940s to the 1970s. A biting critique of postwar American policy towards the area, it also provides an enthralling account of the author's personal experiences in revolutionary Indonesia and Vietnam, and of his attempts to bring US policy into accord with Southeast Asian realities.

Southeast Asia: A testament ranges from postwar Indonesia through the Vietnam War and the Cambodian War. Drawing both on his personal experience and on multiple archival sources, Kahin recounts the history of Indonesia's successful struggle against the Dutch down to Suharto's bloody overthrow of Sukarno in 1965. It also gives a personal view of the US involvement in Indochina, where George Kahin was an early critic of the Vietnam War and struggled to open the eyes of policy makers to the historical, political, and military realities of the Vietnamese situation. Kahin also witnessed the reluctant involvement of Cambodia in the conflict, and the 1970 coup against Prince Sihanouk, which paved the way for the Communist accession to power.

This book will be of interest to students of American diplomatic and foreign policy, Asian studies, and international relations. It is an engagingly written, often poignant, personal account of George Kahin's experiences in Southeast Asia and, as such, will also appeal to the general reader.

George McT. Kahin was Professor Emeritus of International Politics at Cornell University. His books on Indonesia include *Nationalism and Revolution in Indonesia* (1952) and *Subversion as Foreign Policy* (1995). An early and outspoken opponent of American policy in Vietnam, he co-authored *The United States in Vietnam* (1967) and wrote *Intervention: How America became involved in Vietnam* (1986).

D1707591

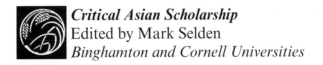

Critical Asian Scholarship
Edited by Mark Selden
Binghamton and Cornell Universities

The series is intended to showcase the most important individual contributions to scholarship in Asian Studies. Each of the volumes presents a leading Asian scholar addressing themes that are central to his or her most significant and lasting contribution to Asian studies. The series is committed to the rich variety of research and writing on Asia, and is not restricted to any particular discipline, theoretical approach or geographical expertise.

Southeast Asia
A testament
George McT. Kahin

Women and the Family in Chinese History
Patricia Buckley Ebrey

Rethinking China's History
Paul A. Cohen

Southeast Asia
A testament

George McT. Kahin

RoutledgeCurzon
Taylor & Francis Group

LONDON AND NEW YORK

First published 2003
by RoutledgeCurzon
11 New Fetter Lane, London EC4P 4EE

Simultaneously published in the USA and Canada
by Routledge
29 West 35th Street, New York, NY 10001

RoutledgeCurzon is an imprint of the Taylor & Francis Group

© 2003 Audrey Kahin

Typeset in Times by Taylor & Francis Ltd
Printed and bound in Great Britain by TJ International Ltd, Padstow,
Cornwall

British Library Cataloguing in Publication Data
A catalogue record for this book is available from the British Library

Library of Congress Cataloging in Publication Data
Kahin, George McTurnan.
Southeast Asia : a testament / George McTurnan Kahin.
Includes bibliographical references and index.
1. Asia, Southeastern–History–1945- 2. Asia, Southeastern–Foreign
relations–History–United States. 3. United States–Foreign
relations–Asia, Southeastern. 4. Kahin, George McTurnan. I. Title.
DS526.7 .K34 2002
959.05–dc21
                                                        2002067978

ISBN 0-415-29975-6 (hbk)
ISBN 0-415-29976-4 (pbk)

Contents

Illustrations

Figures

Maps

Foreword

A scholar's highest obligation, the phrase had it in the 1960s, was to speak truth to power. It turned out, however, that truth was a tragically relative term in the Cold War era. Many Americans were sent abroad to die by the tens-of-thousands, while Asians, Latin Americans, and Africans were sentenced to death by the millions, because US officials disagreed with foreign leaders about what each believed was true in terms of the needs of their own national interests.

George Kahin circumvented this problem by raising the intellectual obligation one level higher. He believed it was most important to speak knowledge to power. This obligation required work, not revelation – least of all a revelation shaped by a 1945-to-1950 world that did little to explain the rising nationalisms that tore the two superpowers' policies apart in the post-1950 era. George, to understate, did not trust preaching and revelation.

Because of his pursuit of the facts on the ground, a pursuit so disciplined that even two heart attacks after age 38 could not limit it, he became a towering figure, especially during the era of America's longest war. As Jayne S. Werner has noted, "Virtually all the arguments he made at the time have since been accepted by both academics and journalists, including many who once supported or quasi-supported the US position. Even former government figures have acknowledged the foresight he had at the time."[1]

This testament tells of George's life-long search for both the facts on the ground and the complex historical background that shaped what he studied. It also reveals the immense personal risks he took and the traumas he suffered, including continuing nightmares after visiting Vietnamese hospitals during the war. It contains a highly detailed, compelling, first-person account of the 1948–9 Indonesian revolution against Dutch colonialism. As he understood at the time, and elaborated in his landmark 1952 study, *Nationalism and Revolution in Indonesia*, the upheaval marked a crucial turn in the great historical process of anti-colonialism that shaped the next half-century. This view of Asian anti-colonialism, sharpened by the Dutch who arrested him because of his work, intensified George's determination to create the systematic study of nationalisms for the foreign policies of a nation that acted as a superpower while also acting, as it turned out, in considerable ignorance of half the world's population. As this final recounting reveals, the same determination drove him to be among the first public voices to oppose the war in Vietnam and to understand how the US involvement in Cambodia helped lead to one of the century's great catastrophes.

This testament, however, is not only a first-person account of how Washington's policies misshaped Southeast Asian politics and societies during the Cold War. It more importantly demonstrates how and why the peoples and governments of Southeast Asia shaped their own destinies, regardless of the superpowers.

George's unbending commitment to these great historical themes that shaped his life was encased in a personality that was modest and under-stated, but unrelenting; intensely disciplined, yet with a wonderful, sly, and at the right times, cutting sense of humor; committed to involvement with the largest causes, while equally involved as a friend on the personal level; and determined to accomplish what he believed to be a citizen's, especially a scholar's, responsibility to speak out, yet always bound by his extraordinary knowledge that was given backbone by an unsurpassed personal integrity. These were rare combinations of the kind that could lead the less observant into misjudging George. They were also traits that led those who knew him to respect and admire him deeply.

Born in Baltimore on 25 January 1918, he was raised in Seattle, graduated with a major in history from Harvard College in 1940, served with the US Army from 1942 to 1945, obtained an MA from Stanford in 1946, and then a PhD from The Johns Hopkins University in 1951. That year he joined Cornell's Government Department where, along with Professor Lauriston Sharp of the Anthropology Department, he shaped a pioneering Southeast Asia Program that made Cornell the world's leading depository for research materials relating to this vast area. In 1954, Kahin established the Cornell Modern Indonesia Project. It attracted both Indonesians and non-Indonesians who did some of the most important work on the history and contemporary policies of that nation. He directed the Indonesia Project until his retirement in 1988. Four years later, Cornell's Board of Trustees named a fine, nineteenth-century mansion – into which the Southeast Asia program moved – the George McT. Kahin Center for Advanced Research on Southeast Asia. Other honors included election to the American Academy of Arts and Sciences, Cornell's Clark Teaching Award, Honorary Fellow of the School of Oriental and African Studies at London University, and, in 1973, the Presidency of the Association for Asian Studies. After battling with often severe heart problems for nearly 45 years, he died on 29 January 2000.

At Johns Hopkins he studied with Owen Lattimore, who had become fascinated by rising Asian nationalisms. With his support, George went to Indonesia for dissertation research. This testament reveals not only the fasci-nating complexities of that anti-colonial struggle, but something of the personal dangers George faced in befriending leaders of the independence movement, above all Sukarno, who would lead the country until 1965.

When Cornell considered appointing George to teach new courses in Southeast Asia, opposition arose. Senator Joseph McCarthy (R-WI) had smeared Owen Lattimore as a Communist. Kahin stood by his doctoral adviser. Mario Einaudi, a distinguished member of the Cornell Government Department, and others strongly supported George, and they were backed by Cornell President Deane Malott. George thus began teaching, only to encounter "the gentleman in the back," as he called the unenrolled visitor who took notes, and, as the campus newspaper, *The Cornell Sun*, discovered, was paid by a McCarthy financial supporter. The Wisconsin Senator finally went down to failure, alcoholism, and the Senate's censure in 1954. George meanwhile had lost his passport in 1950 because of his support of Lattimore and criticism of pro-Dutch US officials in Indonesia. The passport was finally returned the same year McCarthy was censured by the Senate.

Also that year, the Geneva Accords ended the long war of the Vietnamese against French colonial rule. As France withdrew in defeat, the United States, under the direction of President Dwight D. Eisenhower and Secretary of State John Foster Dulles, stepped in – contrary to what the Accords provided – to replace the French and prop up a new South Vietnamese government led by Ngo Dinh Diem. George knew something of Dulles because he had become acquainted with Dulles's son, Avery, and had visited with the family. George also knew Diem, invited him to Cornell, and concluded that the new South Vietnamese leader, who had remained a safe distance from the long war against the French, was neither sufficiently nationalist nor competent.

In these memoirs, George writes that he paid little attention to Vietnam until early 1965, and consequently was not an expert on the country when the US commitment accelerated. His activities and lectures during the previous three years do not support that modesty. By 1962, Americans gave little attention to Vietnam, but President John F. Kennedy was raising the number of US "advisers" from about 400 to over 1,600 and giving them expanded responsibilities in trying to prop up Diem's regime. Drawing on his Harvard Business School and corporate background, Secretary of Defense Robert McNamara announced in 1962 that "Every quantitative measurement we have shows we're winning this war." That same year, George undermined McNamara's assumption in a 10 July speech at Maxwell Air Force Base. The only place to begin understanding "the present political situation in Vietnam," he began, was to realize that in both North and South "nationalism is more important still than Communism," and that Ho Chi Minh, not Diem, was seen as the leading nationalist who drove out the French. Diem's people "are either anti-Communist refugees from the North without roots in South Vietnam, or Southerners of whom the preponderant majority collaborated with the French and thereby often alienated themselves from the local population." Thus George explained "the weaknesses of [Diem's] government and its lack of mass support." That statement shaped Kahin's and other critics' conclusion that, despite McNamara's public optimism, Diem was doomed.

In 1963, Diem, a Roman Catholic, cracked down on protests led by Buddhists who comprised 90 per cent of Vietnam's population. George always considered Diem's repression one of the great mistakes in a conflict filled with them. Diem not only persecuted revered Buddhist leaders, but, in George's eyes, attempted to destroy a third force that could act as a bridge between the North and South governments so the war could be ended and the country reunited. US Ambassador to Vietnam Henry Cabot Lodge privately came to a similar assessment of those around Diem: "They are essentially a medieval, Oriental despotism of the classic family type." But Lodge's, and the Kennedy administration's, analysis then ran in quite a different direction to George's. US officials gave the South Vietnamese military the green light to overthrow Diem. Military leaders did so, then killed Diem and his brother. Three weeks later, Kennedy was assassinated. Lyndon Johnson suddenly rose to the presidency. In his first hours in office, Johnson found the United States had become responsible for supporting a new military regime in a South Vietnam that grew more chaotic by the day.

It was not pre-ordained that colleges and their faculty would react to these events with an antiwar movement. The overwhelming majority of students were not taken up with great causes. Some well-known faculty had moved into the Kennedy administration to make the world safe for the President's "New Frontier." Other faculty took large amounts of governmental funds to conduct investigations, and sometimes even experiments, about how best to "modernize" newly emerging societies before those societies might lapse to the left. Between 1955 and 1959, for example, CIA agents had worked in Vietnam behind a cover provided by a Michigan State University project. (Later, some of the professors involved with the government-supported projects perhaps not unnaturally strongly opposed Kahin's more detached view of why the US involvement was a needless tragedy.)

The conflict was also, in part, a liberals' war – a commitment, as certainly Johnson saw it, not only to defeat communism, but to raise living standards in Southeast Asia as liberals had at home under the New Deal. At the same time, these liberals, especially of the Truman–Kennedy variety, were known for being "realists" in foreign affairs, tough-minded sophisticates who knew how to measure and use power. As one of Kahin's later colleagues in the Cornell Government Department noted, however, liberal realists could be stunningly ignorant about what they were doing in Southeast Asia. "Liberals had put such a high value on hardheaded practicality," Theodore Lowi wrote in his influential book, *The End of Liberalism* (1969), "that they held rigidly to the belief that we were really fighting China in Vietnam." A one-thousand-year history of Vietnamese–Chinese hatred could not convince them otherwise.

George did not fit easily into these categories, even though he was an academic and a liberal. He certainly knew Southeast Asia too well to believe it was any Westerner's frontier. George repeatedly declared that the

Vietnamese, and other Southeast Asians, could better determine their future than the American "modernizers" who had, after all, by their own lights not been all that successful in Latin America, especially in Fidel Castro's Cuba. In many ways, Kahin fitted the realist mold in foreign affairs, but, again, his faith in knowledge, rather than ideological categories, made him aware of how a narrow realism, based on state-controlled military power, had little to offer in explaining the motivations of the Vietnamese and their victory over the French.

He was a proud liberal of the New Deal variety. George saw himself, accurately, as a man of the left. But his confidence in, as well as love for, the United States was so great that he believed reason and knowledge, accrued by hard digging, could produce constructive American reform – at home. He was not a political radical. In the 1965 national teach-in, George learned he would work with another leading antiwar voice, William Appleman Williams of the University of Wisconsin. Knowing I had been at Wisconsin, George asked what Williams was like. I said he was a Naval Academy graduate who had been wounded in the Pacific during World War II. George seemed to welcome that news. I next said Williams saw himself as a Christian Socialist and was thought of by many as a leading Marxist scholar. George was not as pleased about that information. He liked what he had read of Williams's writing, but given the audience he was trying to win over, he was not certain he wanted to be paired on this particular public occasion with someone known as a Marxist. In the end, the two men got along well, and Williams especially grew to admire Kahin.

A massive number of liberals (and even a few radicals, given that Barry Goldwater was the Republican alternative), supported Johnson in 1964 as he ran to win the presidency in his own right. George had his doubts. During the campaign the President remarked, "I regard it as wise for the flame of learning to be applied occasionally to the seats of power." George had been fanning that flame for some years, and now tried to move leading members of Congress to reverse Johnson's policy and stop the war. In September 1963, before the military coup against Diem, he had written to Senator Frank Church (D-ID), a leading member of the Foreign Relations Committee. "I was one of Ngo Dinh Diem's earlier supporters in this country," Kahin informed the Senator, but Diem could not now win the war. He remained in power only because of Washington's support. By this time, George apparently hoped the military would take over, stabilize the worsening situation, then, with Buddhist involvement, negotiate an end to both the war and US intervention. In early 1964, after Diem had been replaced by a military government which carried on the war, he warned the chair of the Foreign Relations Committee, Senator J. William Fulbright (D-AK), about "the deteriorating situation in Vietnam."

Six months later, Fulbright, devoted to his long-time friend in the White House, shepherded through the Senate the Gulf of Tonkin resolution which Johnson believed gave him a blank check to act in Vietnam. Colleges organized ever larger teach-ins to educate listeners about Southeast Asian realities. Kahin became deeply involved in these at Cornell and elsewhere. While public opinion polls showed mass support for Johnson's policies, a number of experts on Asia and US foreign policy joined Kahin in questioning the President's policies. By 10 May, 1965, Secretary of State Dean Rusk had had enough: "I sometimes wonder at the gullibility of educated men and the stubborn disregard of plain facts by men who are supposed to be helping our young to learn – and especially to learn how to think."

Five days later, Kahin answered Rusk and, more importantly, recent speeches by Johnson, in a nationally broadcast teach-in held in Washington. It was the highlight of all-day teach-ins on the war conducted before large audiences at over 100 colleges. George's debating opponent was to have been Johnson's acerbic National Security Adviser, McGeorge Bundy, who had helped guide Kennedy and LBJ ever deeper into Vietnam. At the last minute the President sent Bundy on a mission to the Dominican Republic. It was no doubt Johnson's way of trying to denigrate the teach-in and keep his adviser from those "wild men," as he supposedly called Kahin and his colleagues. If so, it failed. The affair was highly successful in getting both sides' views before the public, and especially in giving George a national audience to rebut the President's arguments point by point.

Johnson had declared in January 1965 that "the problem of Vietnam is the refusal of Communist forces to honor their agreement of 1954." George now pointed out that the 1954 Geneva agreement specified that Vietnam was "one country," that US diplomats at Geneva had spoken "only of Vietnam," not of a North and South, and said they would "seek to achieve unity through free elections" – only to go back on those commitments over the next two years. Eleven days before the teach-in, Johnson declared it was a Communist-caused war, "not civil war. It is sustained by power and resources from without." Kahin replied that, to the contrary, the "most consistent failure [of US officials] has been an inability both to appreciate the importance of Asian nationalism and to work with, rather than against that powerful force."

Johnson and his advisers believed they were fighting in Vietnam to contain China and prevent Southeast Asian nations from falling like dominoes before Beijing's power. "For over all Asia," he had declared a month earlier, "is the deepening shadow of Communist China" whose success in Vietnam could produce a "Red Asia." Kahin thought the conclusion illogical and ahistorical. "Our major aim in Asia is to contain China" so Southeast Asia can develop independently, he observed, but "if we are to salvage anything in Vietnam" it required a ceasefire and negotiated settlement (not "the futile infusion of more and more American military power"), so we could take advantage of "the historic Vietnamese fear and antagonism towards China." Moreover, Kahin added in an interesting prophecy, "Those who are still impressed by the simplistic domino theory must realize that the non-communist governments of Asia will not automatically collapse if the communists should come to control all of Vietnam."

The alternative could be stark and bloody. Johnson had said eleven days earlier, "We will not use our great power in any reckless ... manner. We have no desire whatever to expand that conflict." But Kahin believed decisions were in train to do exactly that. "Our current policy of brinksmanship," he warned, could lead Ho Chi Minh to send 300,000 soldiers south. George quoted the estimate of Hanson Baldwin, the *New York Times'* military analyst, that "as many as a million [US] men" would have to be sent in response. "A full-scale confrontation ... even if no Chinese forces were also involved," Kahin predicted, "would probably exact a toll of American lives at least as great as that suffered in Korea." The Korean war finally cost the lives of over 54,000 Americans. Vietnam was to take more than 58,000, nearly all of them after the spring of 1965.

As the bloodshed deepened, Kahin feared Johnson would retreat behind a wall of secrecy. The President had said the month before the national teach-in that "in the Congress and in the press," as well as in the public, "we are united on the need to resist aggression." At the teach-in, however, George noted that already "essential information has been withheld from the American public, and crucial policy decisions on Southeast Asia have been made before the public has even been aware that a problem exists." For someone who had the increasingly old-fashioned idea that the American public deserved full factual disclosure of the reasons why their sons and daughters were being sent to fight a highly debatable war, Kahin throughout his life believed that the hottest flame in hell was reserved for the seats of government officials who subverted democracy by hiding information behind "Top Secret" stamps. Especially in his later years, he devoted enormous amounts of time prying documents from the cold hands of State Department, CIA, and other officials who believed they best protected their own interests by keeping Americans ignorant.

George consequently drew on his knowledge of, and contacts in, Southeast Asia to provide the facts and background knowledge that Johnson and Nixon administration officials did not know or refused to recognize. A notable example occurred over Washington television in August 1965, when Kahin and Senator George McGovern debated with Senator Gale McGee (D-WY) and Assistant Secretary of State William Bundy (the State Department official responsible for overseeing day-to-day policies in Asia, and the brother of McGeorge). The debate occurred several weeks after Johnson began the rapid escalation of the number of US troops sent to Vietnam. As the documents later revealed, Johnson made this watershed decision not out of strength, but from legitimate worry that the South Vietnamese regime was so weak it would collapse unless it had a major infusion of American soldiers. It is not clear how much George knew about the President's decision. In any case, he again urged a political settlement, one that would inevitably "recognize the facts that confront us at that time." The Communist Vietminh were "not about to surrender everything at the conference table that they won over ten or eleven years of rather painful fighting since 1954."

Bundy slid over this with generalizations. McGee, however, who had a PhD in American diplomatic history, challenged George. McGee made light of "a vote of the people. This [Vietnam] is not a sophisticated area." Kahin shot back, "You don't impose an American decision on them. This seems to me a very arrogant attitude." "Not at all," McGee responded. "All that we're seeking is a chance for them in the slow processes of change among peoples who have been in a colonial existence all too long, to grow up to responsibility for the kind of government they want." It was rather difficult, Kahin replied, to exercise any kind of democratic responsibility under the South's "military dictatorship ... which squelches anyone who undertakes to talk about negotiations. Peace is a dirty word to the South's regime."

McGee, whose views were not uncommon in Washington, was beyond educating, but George carried on a correspondence with an interested William Bundy. As George tells with relish and humor in these memoirs, Bundy made him a member of a State Department consulting group which had access to top-secret documents. George quickly exploited the contact to make government-arranged trips to South Vietnam. Bundy was sophisticated, but rejected Kahin's pleas for bypassing the South Vietnam military regime and negotiating a political settlement because, in the Assistant Secretary's words, such an approach had "two basic flaws": since the North would not allow "supervised 'free' elections," it would put us "at a most colossal disadvantage" and, "more basically," real elections could not be held in a nation immersed in a war. Only the 1864 election during the US Civil War was an exception, in Bundy's view. George knew, however, the question no longer revolved around the possibility of flawless elections, but around a recognition that Ho had long ago won the battle for Vietnamese nationalism. The South's government was a badly ripped balloon into which Johnson and Bundy tried to pump increasing amounts of air. A negotiated settlement was preferable to the loss of tens-of-thousands of lives in a losing or, at best, stalemated cause that could drive the Vietnamese closer to China for military help.

The 1965 military takeover in Indonesia, the resulting bloodbath suffered by Communists and former anti-Dutch revolutionaries whom George knew, and the Johnson administration's spin that a Communist takeover in Indonesia had not only been averted, but that the result vindicated the American anticommunist effort in Vietnam – all this deeply angered and frustrated George. As this memoir reveals, his students discovered at the time that the cause of the 1965 upheaval was quite different than US officials and newspapers led Americans to believe. In their 1995 book, *Subversion as Foreign Policy*, George and Audrey declassified thousands of pages of documents (and utilized such usually overlooked sources as ship logs) to demonstrate how a CIA effort to overthrow the Indonesian government failed in 1958, but set in motion events leading to the military's seizure of power seven years later. The authors carefully concluded that the US government sympathized with the military rulers and never uttered an objection to its massacre of Indonesians. Later, in the 1960s, to George's disgust, William Bundy announced "that had we not stood firm in Vietnam in 1965," Communists could well have taken power in Indonesia. George and Audrey, who specialized in Indonesia, demonstrated that any links between the US commitment to South Vietnam and events in Indonesia existed largely in the minds of Johnson officials intent on rationalizing their beleaguered position in Southeast Asia. As George continued to dig out the facts about the 1965 military takeover, the Indonesian government finally retaliated in 1976 by not allowing Audrey and him to enter the country. Since both were scholars of Indonesia, the blacklisting severely set back their research. The ban lasted for fifteen years.

George realized that if policy were to be changed it would have to be through Congress. That conviction grew exponentially when Richard Nixon came to power. In a privately circulated paper of 1965, George emphasized that "No matter how much military power the US employs in South Vietnam, the Saigon government simply does not constitute a sufficient political base ... to provide American military power with effective political leverage." At best there can only be a stalemate, but the cost "would be tremendous – in terms of both lives and economic cost." This was the basic message he repeatedly sent to congressional leaders over the next eight years. By March 1966, Fulbright had broken with Johnson over foreign policy. Pushed in part by letters from Kahin, the Senator arrived at George's position: "de-escalation aimed at negotiation and an accommodation among the parties." The consequences would not be pretty for the President's policies, but much worse would be avoided. Powerful senators, including Senate Majority Leader Mike Mansfield (D-MT) warned the United States had to seize "the very slim prospect of a joint settlement by negotiations or ... a continuance of the conflict in the direction of a general war on the Asian mainland."

George's testimony in January 1966, the same month Mansfield's report appeared, laid out an eight-point agenda before the more hawkish House Subcommittee on the Far East and the Pacific. His points emphasized that "indigenous nationalism is the strongest barrier to" foreign subversion; dependence on Americans was destroying, not helping, South Vietnam; a Vietnamese settlement and an arms control agreement were the paths to reducing tensions with China; and "de facto policy-making of the CIA and the Pentagon" must be replaced by State Department and Congressional voices if general US policies were to succeed. Above all, he implored Congress to obtain information and expertise by rapidly increasing its qualified staff: the "common denominator" of the eight points "is the need for a much greater body of reliable information about the countries of Asia."

By 1967, US officials began to argue that the corner had been turned, the war was being won. Kahin believed this to be untrue. As he wrote, the increasing number of people under the South's control are "refugees," and "one can hardly regard them as the supporters of the Saigon government."

His skepticism proved to be correct. South Vietnam's elections returned the military rule of Nguyen Van Thieu and Nguyen Cao Ky, (who, as George repeatedly pointed out, had fought for the French against the Vietnamese). But their electoral victory was narrow. The election was, as George understood, a mere fig leaf to cover the South's political deterioration. An anonymous US policy maker essentially agreed when he told the *New York Times* that the elections "did not produce an organized political base for the government."

But, as the military side seemed to be improving, the specter of McCarthyism reappeared. A report by fourteen scholars issued through Freedom House warned that a Communist victory in Vietnam would result not in peace, but a larger war. It attacked antiwar voices for pushing the United States toward unilateral withdrawal or massive retaliation. The Freedom House group claimed to represent unheard, moderate academic voices. The response by Kahin, several of his colleagues at Cornell, and twenty-three other scholars was withering: "Nothing in their [Freedom House] statement conflicts with the basic tenets of the Johnson Administration's policies in Southeast Asia, and we would not describe those policies as moderate. Their statement also fails the test of moderation by alleging that domestic criticism of those policies sustains Hanoi's war effort." The central issue was not such diversions, but whether US policies were "realistic and wise." Kahin and a co-author of the response, John Lewis of Cornell, had buttressed their attack on these policies in 1967 by publishing *The United States and Vietnam*. Emphasizing the largely unknown (for American audiences) Vietnamese and Chinese backgrounds of the war, it became a widely used, highly influential textbook outside, as well as inside, classrooms.

In late January 1968, the Communists' Tet offensive cost their forces thousands of lives, but by moving into cities, even the US embassy compound in Saigon, before being driven back, the offensive disproved to many Americans that the war was being won. George entered into an even more intense period of activity as he briefed senators, traveled hurriedly to Paris to talk with Communist and US negotiators sparring over a possible peace, spent long hours advising the antiwar presidential campaign of Senator Eugene McCarthy (D-MN), worked with Senator Robert Kennedy (D-NY) until Kennedy's assassination in June, and wrote articles, notably in the *New Republic*, to inform the larger public debate. Nixon won the presidency, in part because he partially neutralized the Vietnam issue by claiming to have a mysterious plan to end the war. Kahin doubted such a plan existed. He believed that Nixon's election was a disaster because it would mean more war and thousands more lives lost, as, indeed, it did.

There was also a more personal cost for George. The heart disease that had struck him fourteen years earlier, reappeared, probably as a result of his packed schedules and extensive travel. He nevertheless continued to publish about the war for both scholarly and wider audiences. He also entered into a time-consuming friendship with Senator George McGovern (D-SD), a leading antiwar voice and a contender for the 1972 presidential election. Often briefing McGovern, Kahin especially gave him what turned out to be accurate advice about the Paris peace talks. They would not succeed "until we stop our offensive military operations and begin the systematic with-drawal of all our forces." The reasons for his support of McGovern went well beyond Vietnam. Kahin had grown deeply concerned over the views of many students in his classes. He believed McGovern could "help overcome the dangerous divisions that have developed in our society, and encourage these many groups – young and old – that have grown cynical and nihilistic towards the American political system to return to it, return with the belief that there is a place and scope within it for them to work constructively."

This was the Kahin who was confident, despite all that had happened in the 1960s, that politically involved people could make the system work, as long as they had the knowledge and the system was not corrupted by the likes of Joseph McCarthy. George's faith received a severe test in April 1969. Cornell was paralyzed by a crisis that had race and free-speech issues at its core. The faculty sharply divided. George's own Department of Government splintered (with one member later committing suicide), and the university's very future seemed to be in doubt. In what turned out to be perhaps the defining speech of the crisis, Kahin declared that the central issue was free speech, a principle that had to be at the very center of a university's purpose. He recounted for the 10,000 students who had gathered, and who had little memory of the early 1950s, how his career had been threatened by McCarthyism, and how Cornell had protected his right to speak and write. Indeed, without universities where speech was free, informed, and safe from the physical violence that now threatened Cornell, there would be no place for those who spoke knowledge to power. "For almost eighteen years now this university has given me a base, a sanctuary, a fortress from which I have been free to criticize as strongly as I wished whatever aspect of the Establishment's policies I chose," Kahin told the students, "and I have chosen to be very strong in my criticism." Now this "fortress" was gravely endangered by self-styled radicals who honored not free speech, but violence.

Before this huge gathering, most of whom supported the African-Americans' leader, Tom Jones, who now also was a leader among the white radicals, Kahin minced no words. Jones, who had publicly threatened members of Kahin's department, had accused Cornell's Center for International Studies of working against people of color in the Third World, especially "the Vietcong," to deprive them of their freedom. Kahin called the charge "hideously false," "the height of social and moral irresponsibility." He then instructed Jones to talk to knowledgeable people before making "other such preposterous allegations." A newly knowledgeable crowd cheered Kahin's speech. George's involvement, especially with influential alumni, was a major reason why the university's administration was changed, the campus quieted, and the values he believed in were reasserted by Cornell officials.

By mid-1973, Nixon had finally vindicated Kahin's assessment by pulling out US troops. The President reached an agreement with the Communists and de-escalated the involvement so he could more easily make a break-through to normalize US–China relations. His path to these results, however, was hardly Kahin's, especially Nixon's massive bombing of Vietnam during Christmas 1972 which merely delayed, not changed, the final agreements. As George told Fulbright, the bombing was "nothing less than a premeditated slaughter of civilians." It made it even more urgent, he added, that Congress complete what Kahin, a number of senators, and others had long worked on: a cut-off of funding to stop "the President's mad ventures in Indochina." Congress finally did so in 1973, many years too late.

For Americans, the war itself was ending, although its lessons, for those who valued historical knowledge, would never end. Kahin immediately urged termination of the Southeast Asia Treaty Organization. Set up by Dulles in 1954 to protect the region from communism (and, as a corollary, to replace bad British and French colonialism with American leadership), it had become irrelevant because so few of its members would have anything to do with the US effort in Vietnam. But George knew its "seemingly dormant quality could be changed very quickly," as he told McGovern, "on the initiative of a willful chief executive" who needed an excuse to deploy US troops. Congress finally ended SEATO in 1977. He also campaigned in Congress to expand its staffs, or create a Washington center of "academic area specialists" so the legislature would never again be at the mercy of the executive branch for information. Much of his hope was realized in 1974 and after when Congress greatly expanded its committee staffs.

By the early 1980s, George understood that the US-supported Philippine dictatorship of Ferdinand Marcos was melting. Filipinos, he believed, would soon demand that Americans leave their two huge air and naval bases on the islands. Kahin's frequent visits to the region convinced him both of Marcos's corruption and that the two bases were no longer needed by American forces. The question again, as in Vietnam, was "political viability," as he told his friend, Congressman Matthew McHugh (D-NY). On that subject, the Pentagon too often "reflects a sophomoric immaturity." "I have tried to spell out the folly of our present course – one that a few years from now will surely invite incredulity," Kahin concluded. Three years later, the Filipinos drove Marcos from power, and in 1991 the United States bowed to the pressure and pulled out of its two Philippine bases.

George was also vindicated, although in a different fashion, in Indonesia. In 1991, he and Audrey (then managing editor of publications in the Southeast Asia Program), flew to Jakarta. They were being allowed back in. On 19 January, in a nationally televised ceremony, Foreign Minister Ali Alatas conferred the Medal of Merit, First Class, on George for his work as a "pioneer and precursor of Indonesian studies in the United States." Alatas especially noted that Kahin "tried to see things and evaluate events from the perspective of the Indonesian people themselves" – a "rare but welcome specimen" when compared with some other Western researchers.

The former Indochina, however, continued to preoccupy him. George was deeply concerned about, and worked against, the causes of the catastrophe that overtook Cambodia in the 1970s. The memoir has a compelling, succinct account of the Cambodian tragedy and the US role in it. George also started what turned out be his master work on Vietnam. He analyzed the US slide into that conflict, with detailed attention given to the critical 1964–6 years. Audrey and he declassified piles of documents while conducting extensive personal interviews. According to many reviewers, the result was the definitive treatment of the war's causes. Timothy Lomperis of Duke University, an expert on the conflict, began his review in the September 1987 *Journal of American History* with this paragraph:

> At a recent conference on the literature of the Vietnam War, the participants still awaited the Messiah of the war's definitive Novel. In the social sciences, however, with George McT. Kahin's Intervention, it can almost be said the Messiah has arrived.

Lomperis and other reviewers believed no one had better dissected the pivotal 1963–6 events in South Vietnamese society and politics, or explained how the South became disastrously dependent on the United States. George placed special blame on Johnson's advisers, most of whom had been Kennedy appointees. Kahin had never been seduced by Kennedy's Camelot. He had studied it too closely. George possessed, moreover, a modesty, a disdain of the glamorous, that cut to essentials. Power was to be informed, not envied.[2]

George never stopped trying to impart the knowledge he had gathered, often at considerable personal risk, to other scholars and Washington officials. In his last years, he endured a highly risky, experimental heart operation so he might have more time to work. He laughed that "the surgeon said he would never perform *that* operation again," but George survived for several more years and gained time to complete most of this memoir. Just months before he died, he called a Cornell professor to ask for fax numbers of several Clinton administration officials so he could inform them about the United Nations' operations in the East Timor crisis. One of the leading UN officials, not surprisingly, was a long-time friend.

The Cornell professor knew these US officials would welcome George's information. They had been in his undergraduate classes during the late 1960s and had publicly testified, most recently in *Washington Post* stories and also in David Halberstam's writings on the 1990s, how their world views had been formed, above all, by George's lectures. Those Kahin-influenced policies helped shape the successful US handling of the Bosnian and Kosovo crises after 1995. The professor called ahead to tell these officials that

George would contact them, but they should know that while he was certainly sharp, his strength was noticeably ebbing, and he was home-bound. Several weeks later, the professor heard that George had boarded a plane in Ithaca to speak at a conference in Washington. The professor was astounded, but should not have been surprised. George never gave up trying to educate us and speak knowledge to power. We shall not see his like again. And for that, we, and debates over American foreign policy, shall be the poorer.

Walter LaFeber
Cornell University

Acknowledgements

When George died, on 29 January 2000, he was in the midst of completing this memoir, which had occupied much of his time and energy over the previous four or five years. He had finished good drafts on the countries with which he had been most involved – Indonesia, Vietnam and Cambodia – but had hoped also to include sections on US relations with the Philippines and Burma. He did not have time to complete his plan.

I promised him I would bring the draft chapters he had prepared to publication, and I would like to thank the following people who helped me in this task: Ben Anderson, Coeli Barry and Sharon Kahin all read the draft manuscript and provided encouragement and useful comments; David Chandler read the Cambodia section for accuracy and provided reassurance and many helpful suggestions; Frances Gouda and Elsbeth Locher-Sholten provided essential material regarding financial aspects of the Dutch–Indonesian negotiations in 1949. I would also like to thank Robert Cribb, for skillfully preparing the first three maps, and Walter LaFeber for setting the stage in his excellent foreword. I am also particularly indebted to Mark Selden for his encouragement and sensible advice, and to Craig Fowlie, Emma Howarth, Jennifer Lovel and Mary Warren for their help in the final stages of preparing the manuscript for publication.

The work, as all who knew George will recognize, is essentially as he wrote it, and reflects not only his knowledge, understanding and love for the peoples of Southeast Asia with whom he interacted for over half a century, but also the courage, humanity and self-deprecating sense of humor that colored and influenced his relationship with all those he met.

Audrey Kahin

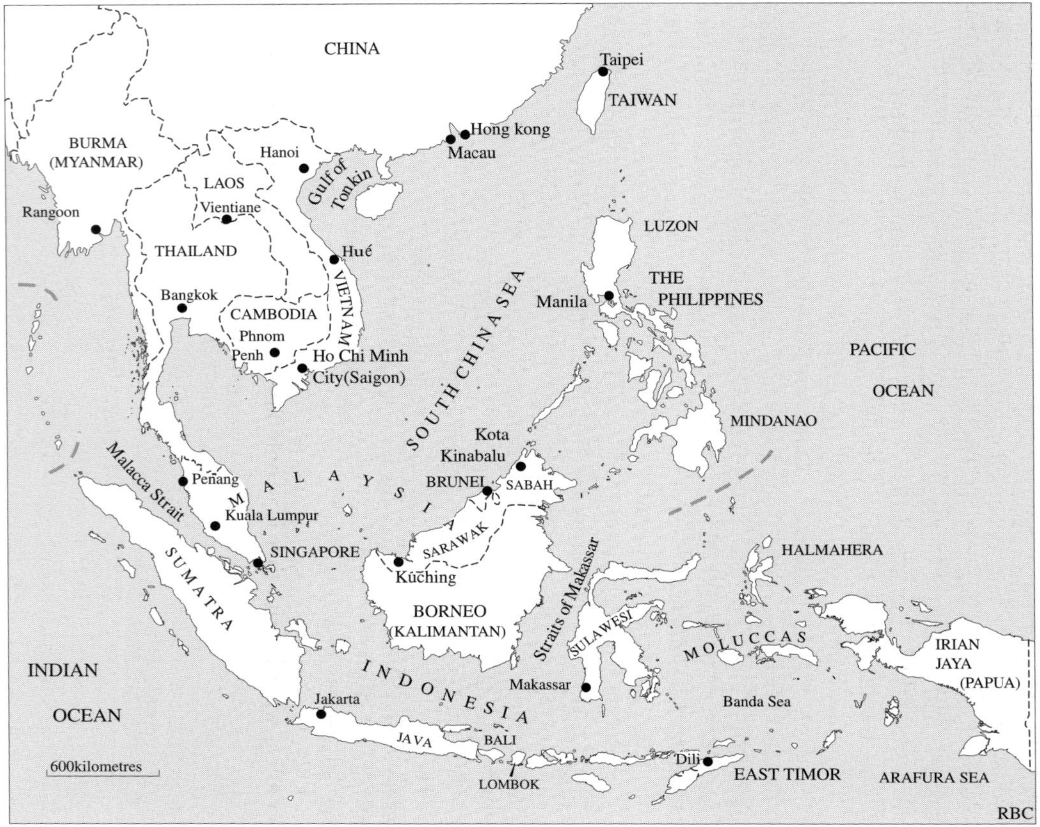

Map 1 Contemporary Southeast Asia

Source: (Map by Robert Cribb).

Introduction

The main reason for my writing this book is the realization that much of what I directly experienced during the half century since I first visited Southeast Asia, or have subsequently found in American and British archives, does not accord with what is generally accepted as constituting the historical record. All too much of significance, it seems to me, has been consciously or unconsciously swept under the rug, or tailored to fit with perdurable and broadly accepted myths as to the past roles of the American government. These myths, small and large, have served so to camouflage the reality of the often crucial actions of the US government in Southeast Asia as to leave Americans with little appreciation of how considerably these have affected the political and socioeconomic landscape of that area and conditioned the attitudes of its peoples.

For many years I expected that unchronicled developments of any significance which I experienced would subsequently find their way into the writings of others, even though assessed through somewhat different lenses. After several decades I find that this has often not been the case, and it is because I still see what I regard as important gaps in the coverage of significant events, or distorted assessments of them, that I now feel it appropriate to record my own version of some of them. For a long time I didn't think that these direct experiences, together with insights garnered through scrutiny of relevant holdings of American and British archives, would add up to enough to warrant my attempting a separate book. But I am now persuaded that perhaps they do.

I am, of course, aware that my own lens of observation must necessarily so affect what I write that it is only fair to acquaint the reader with some features of my background which I assume may affect my interpretation and evaluation of the events I describe and the import of documents I cite. Or to put it in a modern parlance that did not exist when I first visited Southeast Asia, I feel an obligation to let readers know "where I'm coming from."

There is, I guess, nothing like a serious operation, hospitalization, and the dreary process of recovery to induce one to pause and look back over the terrain that has been traversed. Having had the good fortune now to have spent a little over eight decades on this journey, I recognize that there was more luck than logic to my having emerged with a specialization on the politics and international relations of Southeast Asia – or, at least most of its countries, all of which I have at least visited. Certainly my path to this final destination has been circuitous. A great deal of luck – mostly benign – determined the route I have taken, or, perhaps more accurately, brought to bear the circumstances that nudged or prodded me along it.

I don't know much about my family background, all my grandparents having died too young for me to have ever met them, except that like most Americans it was a mixture – as best as my parents could make out approximately half Irish, a quarter Basque and a quarter English. I learned that my father's grandfather had left County Antrim in Northern Ireland during the potato famine and emigrated to America where he had finally become moderately successful in raising horses and mules in Indiana. My mother, who was descended from French Huguenot refugees who had fled to Ireland, had little patience for people interested in genealogies, and thought it nonsensical for people to spend so much time on this preoccupation. I always admired her for nonplussing those who embarked on such discussions by eventually ending them with the observation that her father being an Andrews meant that he was a descendant of the Merry Andrews, the court fools of England. When her audience found this a little bewildering, she would proceed to recount how her sister, who for a time was seriously interested in the family background, had given up probing upon discovering that in 1640 an Andrews ancestor had been known as the town fool in Taunton, Massachusetts.

I do remember well that both my parents were independent thinkers, and that on those rare occasions where I showed any suggestion of this quality they applauded. The first such instance was when at the age of six I broke with the Presbyterian Church. Neither parent was religious, and indeed they could never seem to decide whether they were agnostics or atheists. But when my peers were all attending Sunday school, I did not want to be left out, and my parents somewhat reluctantly sanctioned my attending a Presbyterian Sunday school, even though as adults they had cut any connection with that church. For me the defining moment came less than a year after I had begun going to this Sunday school, when our teacher took us on a picnic. We all were asked to take along a dish, and with no small amount of pride I brought my mother's delicious chocolate cake. It was with a sense of mounting outrage that I witnessed our teacher cutting the cake into wedges, leaving by far the biggest piece for himself. In high dudgeon I told him he wasn't acting like a Christian should, and I left the picnic, never to return to the Presbyterian Church. I reported this to my parents, who I thought would be angry, and I never forgot my sense of relief to find that they enthusiastically approved of my decision.

So far as my adult life is concerned, I certainly didn't start out with a focus on Southeast Asia. Indeed, initially I sought to be a Latin American specialist, early experiences in Mexico having kindled my interest in the area and later a project of Eleanor Roosevelt having almost made realization of such specialization possible. A year in Mexico in 1934–5 when I was in my late teens made a powerful impression on me. Seeing at first hand the wretched condition of the country's peasantry just at the time when its courageous, newly elected president, Lazaro Cardenas, sought to ameliorate their condition through his iconoclastic system of *ejidos* (a sort of self-sufficient peasant cooperative on communally held land) strongly affected me. Utopian or not, I thought his program of land reform had real promise, and I admired him. And I did so even more later, after I better understood the strength of the entrenched reactionary socioeconomic forces arrayed against his efforts.

Another experience in Mexico pushed me further into thinking that Latin America should be my beat. For during my year there I became fascinated with the archeology of its pre-Columbian heritage, and, free from parental oversight, I enjoyed brief but exhilarating trips pursuing that interest through parts of the states of Oaxaca, Guerrero and Yucatan. And so when I went to college I was bent upon studying Middle American archeology. There I found that archeology was subsumed under anthropology, which accordingly became my first major. Initially I was lucky in being assigned to Harvard's brilliant Clyde Kluckhohn as my tutor, but unfortunately his main interest was in North American Indians and he therefore concluded that in view of my interests I should be assigned to the department's only pre-Colombian archeologist, Professor Alfred M. Tozzer. Attempting to study with him was for me – and I later gathered for a good many other students – a very cold shower. Arrogant and patronizing, he abruptly and condescendingly dismissed, without any flicker of interest, what I in my youthful enthusiasm believed to be fresh insights into the nature of pre-colonial Miztec and Zapotec cultures that had existed in what was now the Mexican state of Oaxaca. He soon drew me aside to inquire how much private income I had. My answer being "none," he made clear that in that case he would have to discourage my aspirations to enter the field of archeology.

And so I moved over into Far Eastern history where I found myself the first honors applicant of the young and newly arrived China specialist, Assistant Professor John K. Fairbank. At that time he was very shy and reserved, but generous in spending time with his students and encouraging them, and I liked him. Through a bit of luck I impressed him more favorably than I deserved. In the course of gathering material for my undergraduate honors thesis on the Sino–Japanese war of 1894–5 he mentioned that one of the most knowledgeable people on that subject was Dr Hu Shih, China's highly respected scholar and ambassador to Washington. Sensing my interest, Fairbank promptly interjected that I shouldn't expect to interview him, since he was extraordinarily busy and rarely found time to see even well-established scholars. Nevertheless I persisted, for I was interested in Hu Shih as a man as well as an expert on my thesis topic, and, I suspect, also because I wanted an excuse to see Washington, which I'd never before been able to visit.

I had no idea of where in that city I would stay, but on the way down in the train I did what many people those days did, I looked through the red hotel guide that on every coach was lodged in a rack opposite the restrooms. In leafing through its coverage of Washington I found listed "Hotel Cass – Two and a half for a room and a bath." Given my modest budget, that seemed like a pretty good deal. In taking a taxi to the hotel from Washington's railroad station, I was impressed to find that the driver knew exactly where the Cass was and didn't need me to tell him the address. I was even more impressed when on arriving there I found several attractive young women in the lobby all wearing evening dresses. In my naiveté I thought nothing of this, accepting their choice of afternoon apparel as simply customary in the nation's capital.

After arriving in my room I telephoned Ambassador Hu Shih's secretary, stating the topic of my research and requesting an interview. She responded pleasantly, but firmly, that the ambassador's appointment book was full but that if by any chance there were a cancellation of any of his existing appointments she would call me back. She sounded anything but encouraging, but when I returned from lunch I found a message asking me to call her. To my great surprise – and it seemed to hers as well – the ambassador suggested I come by to see him the next afternoon. No one had previously been so audacious as to try to arrange an appointment from my "hotel" – or at least to acknowledge that they were staying there. This, Hu Shih, his face enveloped in an impish smile, conveyed as I settled down in a chair by his desk. "I just had to see what you were like," he said after having in an avuncular fashion explained to me that the "hotel" in which I'd chosen to stay, though once quite respectable, had during recent years become notorious as one of the most elegant upper-scale bordellos in Washington. Perceiving my embarrassment, he graciously turned to a full hour-and-a-half's discussion of the pertinent developments leading up to the outbreak of the 1894–5 war between China and Japan. He particularly emphasized, I remember, the importance of Korea's nationalist Tong Hak rebellion – a factor, he said, that those who had written about the war had underestimated. Armed with that insight, I returned to Cambridge and learned about and incorporated into my thesis more about the Tong Hak's rebellion than I'm sure Fairbank ever wanted to know. But, thanks to Hu Shih, my thesis turned out to be reasonably good. Fairbank continued to marvel that I'd been able to get the interview, but I never explained how I'd managed this.

As Fairbank's student I was invited to tea once a week at his house at 41 Winthrop Street together with his one graduate student in his first years of teaching, a southern lady of great charm and intellectual brilliance, Mary Claybaugh. Later she married Arthur Wright, both of them ultimately becoming professors of Chinese history on Yale's faculty. I'm not sure whether it was because of being overawed by her intelligence or the realization that graduate study in Chinese history would require learning that difficult language that most dissuaded me from trying to enter graduate study in this field. Anyway, events soon made it unnecessary for me to agonize over that decision.

While studying Far Eastern history I had also begun, like many of my classmates in the years before America's entry into World War II, to become intensely interested in the broader field of international relations. Because of that I became an initially rather passive head of the small Foreign Affairs Committee of the college's Student Union. That passivity ended, however, when the head of the union took it upon himself to pronounce that the union fully backed the Soviet Union's decision to enter the 1939 pact with Nazi Germany. Though I'd previously been supportive of Moscow's role in the war, I was keenly disillusioned with what I perceived to be its unprincipled expediency in entering into this arrangement with the Nazis. And so I protested the union's stand on this issue and with a few of my friends pulled our little Foreign Affairs Committee out of the Student Union to form our own organization, which became the Harvard Foreign Relations Club. Since I was willing to do most of the work, I became its president, with two close friends, Avery Dulles and Eric Johnson, respectively, vice-president and secretary. Professor Heinrich Bruening, the former Christian Democratic leader who had been Germany's last democratically elected chancellor before he fled from the Nazis and who had been kind enough to admit me into his graduate seminar, agreed to be our faculty adviser.

Our organization's most notable accomplishment was to mount a conference, "Peace Through a New International Order," in the spring of 1940, just a couple of months before the fall of France. In our idealism and naiveté we thought we could help demonstrate that the ominous tensions in Europe and the Far East might still be susceptible to resolution through negotiation. Seeking to make the conference as realistic as possible, we prepared our agenda carefully, in the process consulting closely with Bruening, several other supportive faculty and Avery Dulles's father, John Foster Dulles, who struck us as having valuable ideas in the sphere of political economy.

The university's president James Bryant Conant declined our invitation to attend the conference but designated the Secretary of the Harvard Corporation Jerome Davis Greene to represent him and give a welcoming speech. Each of some twenty eastern colleges and universities sent delegations of students representing a particular country. In our attempt to make the conference more realistic we also invited the ambassadors of numerous countries, including those of Germany and Japan, to participate by making brief presentations.

Several developments at that conference are still vivid in my memory. The German and Japanese ambassadors almost immediately accepted our invitation, and registered their decision to attend before we could be assured of countervailing presences from Britain, France or China. President Conant called me to his office to tell me that, while sympathetic to our aims, he would be obliged to leave town if either the German or Japanese ambassador attended. Protocol, he explained, demanded that he receive any ambassador who visited the campus on an official basis. He urged me, therefore, to try to disinvite them as quickly and discreetly as possible. I did my best to carry out this uncomfortable assignment, advising them that in the interest of informality it had been decided not to invite anyone of ambassadorial status from any country. We ended up with quite a few consul generals – though none from either Japan or Germany – whose diplomatic missions understandably thought my explanation pretty lame. Conant didn't have to leave town. His representative Jerome Green walked out on us, informing us no more than an hour before he was due to give his welcoming address that he was ill and couldn't attend. In suddenly being called upon to pinch hit I quickly discovered that I was anything but an acceptable extemporaneous speaker.

The main component of the conference, however, was the interaction of the student delegates representing different countries. This went reasonably well except that the Yale delegation, led by Sumner Welles's son, playing the pivotal role of France, was unabashedly sloshed. But the positions taken by most of the student delegations were sober and realistic. Students from none of the colleges or universities could be prevailed upon to represent Germany. And so Avery Dulles magnanimously volunteered to do so. His performance in that capacity guaranteed the conference's success. At least it injected – albeit quite inadvertently – a sudden burst of humor and boisterous laughter that served to offset the many somber realities that the conference laid bare. To appreciate this it must be recalled that Germany, at this time, was bent on gaining access to Romania's strategically valuable Ploesti oil fields. And it must also be understood that the girl from Vassar, representing Romania, was pretty, very shapely and clad in a brazenly red dress. Very realistically, Germany, wishing to gain access to the only significant source of petroleum in Western Europe, asked for a bilateral meeting with Romania. After over a half hour of private discussion Germany emerged to report to the plenary session of the conference that it had negotiated a non-aggression pact with Romania calling for her total disarmament and the demilitarization of all her frontiers. In soberly reporting this agreement, Avery showed the most serious mien and no trace of a smile. There was a pause and then the whole assembly broke out into uncontrollable laughter. Whether inadvertently or not (I was never sure), Avery had injected some sorely needed humor into our generally bleak proceedings. The strain of trying to keep our little conference from collapse did much to help persuade me that I should abandon my long nourished plan of trying to enter the US Foreign Service.

In the months before graduating from college in mid-1940 I tried desperately to find a job having some relationship to international relations, but in the end was unsuccessful. It is sometimes forgotten that in the year before World War II the United States was enveloped in a mini-depression, but in any case my credentials for such work were anything but strong. The only offer of a job I received in this field I ultimately felt obliged to turn down.

At first blush it seemed perfectly suited to my interests and I was elated. It came about as a consequence of a somewhat iconoclastic article, "Soviet Foreign Policy," I had written for the *Harvard Guardian*, an interdisciplinary journal of the social sciences, then in its second year. While hostile to Nazi actions in Europe, the article was also critical of British expediency (Czechoslovakia) and Soviet imperialism (annexation of the Baltic states and half of Poland). This combination appealed to an independent-minded maverick Porter Sargeant, a wealthy Bostonian best known for publishing an annual guide to private American secondary schools. Recently he had also developed a keen interest in international affairs, and on his own had launched a weekly pamphlet that enjoyed a surprising circulation and seemed to appeal primarily to an audience that was both anti-Fascist and opposed to American entry into the war. He seemed to think that my views suited me to become editor of a new journal he had been planning to publish that would in fact be an expanded version of this newsletter. And so I was invited to join him at dinner in his Brookline mansion.

A splendid meal with his secretary attending – and mightily impressing me by taking down every banal statement I made – was most agreeable. It was evident that the conversation – so far at least – had confirmed him in his decision to offer me a job as editor of his projected international affairs journal. But after dinner we retired to his den for a brandy and to discuss details. To assure himself that I was the right man, he had one final question. "What did I think of Roosevelt's plan to turn over surplus American destroyers to escort shipments of war supplies to Britain?" We had been in full agreement in our opposition to British colonial policy, particularly in India and Burma, and it was a clear disappointment to him that I differed strongly with him on this point and applauded Roosevelt's plan. Patiently he sought to change my view, but was unsuccessful. He seemed really saddened when he ushered me to the door for his son to drive me home, and it was clear to me that neither from his standpoint nor mine would it be possible for me to work as editor for the journal he had planned.

That was the only job possibility in the international field that I found, and I now had to content myself with work as claims adjuster for an auto-mobile insurance company at $110 per month. That was just enough for food, lodging and tuition to commence part-time graduate study back at Harvard, enrolling again in one of Bruening's seminars. Being provided a company car for my work meant that I could arrange my work schedule of interviewing accident witnesses to accommodate the seminar and use of Widener library; and it also permitted me to scour areas some distance from the company's office in Boston to look for inexpensive lodgings. And thus I ended up in a wood-stove-heated summer cottage on Lake Cochituate, not far from Thoreau's Walden Pond, for which I paid rent of only $12 per month to the octogenarian lady who owned it and claimed to be Daniel Webster's granddaughter. That low rate was possible once I promised to take her once a week to her doctor's office and the adjacent cocktail lounge in nearby Uxbridge. I did develop greater respect for Thoreau. But aside from the use of the car, I had a clear advantage over him. For while I could not easily wait to build a fire and heat warm water to shave and wash in my cabin each winter morning, I could stop by on my way to work in Boston and slide unobtrusively into the vacant men's room of Stone Hall on the nearby Wellesley campus where undisturbed I could shave and wash with abundant hot water. Later I discovered that my early morning surreptitious entry for these ablutions had earned me the name of "the phantom of Stone Hall."

In the late spring of 1941 prospects began to look up, with the possibility of becoming a Latin America specialist revived, when I was awarded a fellowship in the just-launched Inter-American Field Studies program. Sponsored by Eleanor Roosevelt, the genesis of this modest program stemmed from her disillusionment with many of those visitors to the White House who purported to be Latin America specialists. She felt it important to compensate for this deficiency by providing for the training of a fresh group of young specialists, and to this end secured most of the first year's funding from the son of ex-president Garfield. She interviewed all the applicants and chose ten of them to be supported for a summer's training at Harvard to be followed by a year's research in one of the Latin American countries. The project I proposed was a study of Haya de la Torre's Aprista movement in Peru aimed at ameliorating the lot of the Indian peasant populations of the Andean area roughly congruent with the old Inca empire. I admired Haya de la Torre, seeing in him and his objectives something of a parallel with Mexico's Lazaro Cardenas. I remember all too vividly my embarrassment in my interview with Mrs Roosevelt, a lady whom I greatly admired. Noting that in my projected field research I would, whether I liked it or not, be regarded as something of an ambassador from the United States, she asked what would I respond if someone asked me to explain the Roosevelt administration's Agricultural Adjustment Act. I stumbled miserably, but she then kindly shifted the conversation to the nature of my proposed research and what I thought of Mexico's *ejido* system. Fortunately my discussion of it satisfied her, and she told me at the end that this compensated for my woeful lack of knowledge of the Agricultural Adjustment Act. I later found that I had passed this test and one demonstrating a satisfactory knowledge of Spanish.

But despite this lucky break, it was soon evident that I was not destined to become a Latin America specialist. Just as I was finally about to leave for Peru, having purchased my steamship ticket and had all my inoculations, I found that my draft board refused to grant me permission to leave the country, a requirement set in place even well before America's entry into the war. (My official residence having shifted from Seattle, where I'd grown up, to Cochituate, I was now in the jurisdiction of the Concord draft board, one that apparently had scant empathy for an outsider who chose to spend the year in a run-down summer cottage, one that I later learned was adjacent to that of a well-known bootlegger.) So with my Latin American fellowship no longer tenable, I managed to get a tuition scholarship at the Fletcher School of Law and Diplomacy (run jointly by Harvard and Tufts, and on the latter's campus). Studying there during the fall term of 1941 until Pearl Harbor, I was able to take my third seminar with Heinrich Bruening. I also wrote a substantial seminar paper for the political economist Professor Eugene Staley in which I, probably foolishly, confronted his ego by criticizing his recently published conclusion that Japan's war economy was on the ropes and due imminently to collapse.

Reports of the Pearl Harbor attack precipitated my joining hundreds of others in the Boston area at the local Navy Recruiting Office. Here I learned that because of glasses and poor eyesight I would have to secure a waiver to join the service, and was advised to proceed to Seattle to await the outcome of my request. There I waited for over five months, with no such waiver coming through, until I was drafted into the army. During that period I volunteered to work with the American Friends Service Committee (AFSC), which seemed to be the only organization concerned about the fate of the unfortunate Nisei (Japanese Americans) and prepared to help them during the desperate period while they awaited shipment to concentration camps in California and elsewhere. Although I could understand the fear of many local citizens who expected Japanese air attacks (my father was among those many who dug an air-raid shelter on his property), it seemed to me that the Nisei had the same right to be treated as fully fledged American citizens as German or Italian Americans, or indeed my own Irish-American ancestors. As my area of responsibility I was assigned Bainbridge Island, an area of about 20 square miles, close to both Seattle and the Bremerton Navy Yard, heavily populated by Nisei farmers engaged in the back-breaking work of strawberry and vegetable growing. Upon learning that these truck farmers were soon to be sent away, many local merchants had decided not to pay the bills owed the farmers for their produce. My main job, a rather unpleasant one, was to collect these debts. I was reasonably successful and in the process managed to antagonize many of these merchants. I was deeply touched by the gratitude of the Nisei, who on the eve of their departure for the unknown could be made a little bit relieved if they had a little cash in hand. I remember especially an old man with a tiny house on the beach who had been accused of spying on the ships which had to pass it on their way to the Bremerton naval base. Like many of the Nisei he preferred something close to a Japanese diet, but as a token of his appreciation for my having collected what was due him from the merchants, he insisted upon honoring me with what he described as a "typical American meal." I would have much preferred Japanese fare, but what he pressed on me, with evident pride, was a meal of hot dogs and marshmallows!

The waiver for poor eyesight that I had sought to get into the navy never came through, and I was inducted into the army in mid-May 1942 and sent directly to a camp in a desolate area on the central Texas plain to begin the normal three-month period of basic training. In the midst of this I was summoned to the office of the camp intelligence officer who, after some discussion, raised my spirits by informing me that, on the basis of my records and our discussion, he was persuaded that I was well suited for intelligence and that he was prepared to arrange for my transfer to that branch and admission to an intelligence school. I was delighted and told him I was prepared to sit out the extra month in the camp which he thought might be necessary while the usual background check was made. Meantime I was to be officially "frozen" in place while that investigation was being conducted.

I settled back into the routine of a second round of basic training, periodically checking in with this intelligence officer to see how matters stood. He seemed increasingly puzzled at how long my background check was taking, but encouraged me to continue waiting, despite the long limbo of frozen status I was in. Finally, well into my third round of basic training, he called me in to tell me that he had just been informed that my background check indicated that I was "pro-Japanese" and therefore unsuitable for an intelligence assignment. He appeared to be as astonished and incredulous as I was and said he was determined to follow up and discover how this conclusion had been reached. Finally, after my fourth period of being "frozen" in basic training, he called me in to tell me, his sympathy and indignation evident, that upon pressing he had been told that the sources of the accusation were the very food wholesalers from whom I had collected debts owing to the Bainbridge Island Nisei. Though he shared my disappointment, he indicated that, given the nature of the army's bureaucracy, there was nothing more that he could do.

And so, after completing a fourth period of basic training, I was shifted by that same army bureaucracy, along with a group from the same camp whose records had also reportedly been "lost," to Stillwater, Oklahoma. After all that basic training, which must have been something of a record, I was in excellent physical condition, albeit lighter by about fifteen pounds and a bit dehydrated by forced marches under the Texas sun. This, plus the fact that during my substantial sojourn in Texas I had attained the rank of Buck Sergeant (Figure 0.1) and become a platoon leader, apparently made me qualify, in the eyes of the Stillwater army clerks, as just the right person to become calisthenics instructor for a full company of other abandoned souls who had all been left, outraged and helpless, by the loss of their records. Without adequate records we were in a sort of bureaucratic limbo whereby we could not easily initiate efforts to get ourselves moved into some meaningful branch of the army. This condition was so stultifying that a group of us volunteered to help local farmers as field hands – first being assigned to the back-wrenching labor of cotton pickers, and, following our revolt from that, being moved to the much gentler occupation of picking pecans.

Then, happily returning to a regimen of only early morning calisthenics, I spent much of the rest of my six-month stay in Stillwater searching for possibilities for getting out. Finally I found a bulletin board announcing openings in Army Specialized Training Programs involving intensive language and area study. The choices still open were limited, and I

Figure 0.1 As Buck Sergeant, 1943

volunteered for training in Indonesian. I was a bit anxious about my chances, recognizing that this country was at the time occupied by the Japanese, and worried lest the charge of being "pro-Japanese" might limit my chances. But apparently the charge had not been included in my records, or else the army was desperate enough for men willing to volunteer for an Indonesian assignment that it didn't matter. In any case, to my delight my application was quickly accepted and soon afterwards I was even happier when I found that the locale for the Indonesian program was the campus of Stanford University – certainly a much pleasanter place to be stationed than central Texas or Oklahoma.

There were sixty GIs enrolled in this special nine-month program. For the first month we studied the Indonesian language intensively, but at the beginning of the second were abruptly informed that it had been decided that for the next eight months we would study Dutch rather than Indonesian. This shift puzzled us, and we were not fully satisfied with the explanation that in the envisaged campaign against the Japanese occupation forces in Indonesia, Dutch would be more useful since we would have to liaison with Dutch officers and non-coms who could not speak English. This was, of course, patently untrue since almost all Dutch officers had gone to secondary school, where they would have been required to learn English. We later learned that Dutch intelligence had reported – correctly – that most of the GIs in our group had anticolonial attitudes and that apparently it was considered dangerous to equip them with a language capacity that would enable them to talk directly to the Indonesian population. And so for the remaining eight months we intensely studied Dutch, with a few hours per week being devoted to study of the peoples who lived in what was still referred to as the Netherlands East Indies.

The poor guy who taught us area studies – an anthropologist named Felix Keesing – had an awful assignment. He had been told by Washington to get us familiar with the terrain on Sabang island off the north-western tip of Sumatra, as that was where we would probably attack. So we went through exercises, map-reading, studying the terrain of Sabang island as best we could. Keesing's assignment was supposed to be for a month, but no new instructions came through, so he had to continue focusing on Sabang for nine months. He implored Washington for something else to do, but they just told him to keep on attacking Sabang Island. So week after week we attacked it from every possible angle. Thirty years later, in 1971, when visiting Indonesia with my wife Audrey, I finally went there. As we landed I was still able to tell her everything about Sabang's geography, pointing out every ridge and stream and route across the island.

Towards the end of our course we were interviewed by an OSS colonel to ascertain among other things whether we would agree to go wherever they wanted to send us. Those of us who did were told we would next be sent for parachute training. It was our understanding that, in his expected invasion of Indonesia, General MacArthur planned to drop parachutists just prior to the sea-borne assault of his main forces. These parachutists would have the responsibility of blowing up bridges and doing whatever else could be done to impede the Japanese troops from contesting the American coastal landings. Apparently it was believed that the native Indonesian population would happily welcome us, even if we had to work through the accompanying Dutch, whom, as we later discovered, MacArthur was bent on reestablishing in at least temporary authority. In retrospect it is clear that, even if we had managed to float down in our parachutes without being shot by the Japanese and their Indonesian auxiliary troops (the Peta on Java and Giyugun on Sumatra), we would have had a most uncomfortable time once on the ground. We would have had to rely on Dutch officers as intermediaries, and our own half-baked knowledge of the Dutch language would not have been much of an asset in interacting with most of the Indonesians we were likely to encounter.

Fortunately for us, and for the United States, Allied plans changed. After occupying only the western tip of Netherlands New Guinea, General MacArthur and his American troops were ordered to bypass the rest of Indonesia and go directly to the Philippines. (Australian troops under his command did occupy limited areas of Borneo, Celebes (Sulawesi) and some of the Lesser Sunda islands, and helped the Dutch regain control there.)

And so, after our course finished in September 1944, none of the sixty hard-working American soldiers trained at Stanford went to Indonesia. Being of no further use to MacArthur's operations, members of our little group were sent to perform a variety of jobs in Europe for which they were mostly untrained. The top man, whose Dutch was near perfect, was sent to Italy to become a company cook in the mule-born 10th Mountain Division. Because of my rank of Buck Sergeant I wound up in a motor pool in France where I was initially put in charge of servicing large trucks I did not know how to drive. I was very lucky – enough so to feel guilty – for I did not get to Europe until January 1945 and just missed the Battle of the Bulge; and then I found that German artillery consistently shot over my little unit at more important elements behind us – leading us to believe that their intelligence had established that we were in fact an "administrative roadblock" and were not worth wasting ammunition on.

But even though the army never sent me to Indonesia, the training it had given me certainly kindled my interest in the country – deeply enough to ensure that I would try hard to learn more about it and, if at all possible, visit it. I had nurtured a deep interest in its people's ongoing struggle for independence, and, upon being discharged from the army in October 1945, decided I would undertake graduate study wherein to the extent possible – at least in a dissertation – I could focus on modern and contemporary Indonesia.

Like other recently demobilized American soldiers, I qualified for the educational support provided by the GI Bill of Rights. But so many of

America's Asia specialists were either still in the Far East or Washington that it was not easy to find a suitable graduate school in which to enroll. John Fairbank was still in Chungking and Harvard's Rupert Emerson, one of the few American political scientists who had worked on Indonesia, was still in Washington. Stanford was willing to give me a semester's credit for my army training there and was generous with respect to my prewar part-time graduate study at Harvard and the Fletcher School. And there was an able China historian there, Meribeth Cameron. So it was to Stanford I returned for six months to complete an MA in political science and write a rather simple thesis on the political history of the Chinese in Indonesia. In the meantime, I had become attracted to Johns Hopkins, to which an eminent China specialist, Owen Lattimore, had just returned. His presence and the proximity of the Library of Congress in Washington, which had holdings on Indonesia far superior to Stanford's, decided me to try to transfer to Johns Hopkins to continue graduate study for a PhD in political science. Thanks, I think, primarily to a strong letter of support from Heinrich Bruening, I was admitted as doctoral candidate there with a modest fellowship augmenting my GI Bill support. I enrolled in several of Lattimore's very interesting Asia seminars where most of the work was on China, Mongolia and Sinkiang – which he knew extremely well, but while he was interested in Indonesia he made no pretense as to a capacity to direct a dissertation dealing with it.

Fortunately Johns Hopkins permitted outside specialists to serve on its graduate committees, and after I returned from research in Indonesia in mid-1949, Harvard's Rupert Emerson was kind enough to join mine and serve as dissertation director. He was rigorous in his criticisms but generous with his time and very helpful. My Dutch and French were adequate enough to meet the university's language requirements, but what I really needed to prepare for field research was a good bit more than the single month's study of the Indonesian language I'd had in the army. I found myself pressured by two professors, one an eminent Sanskritist and the other a specialist in Tagalog – both hungry for even one student – who assured me that by studying these languages with them I would have a necessary foundation for Indonesian. It was soon clear that study of these languages would be only very marginally helpful and in desperation I scoured possibilities in Washington where, through the kindness of my recently made friend in the Department of State, Claire Holt, I found a tutor in Indonesian. This was seventeen-year-old Sapin Binali, one of many destitute Indonesian seamen who had been stranded in the United States during the war and was as yet unable to return home. Claire, an extraordinarily generous person, had rescued him and given him a place to stay in her tiny Georgetown house. My weekly trips to Washington to learn Indonesian from Sapin had the additional reward of stimulating talks with Claire, who opened my eyes to the richness of Javanese culture and was clearly supportive of Indonesian independence.

And so I embarked on an effort to specialize on Indonesia. The voyage turned out to be fascinating, but it was anything but easy. From the outset I was handicapped by my lack of training in the Indonesian language. The Dutch I'd learned in the US army was useful, but only marginally so. And then, soon after my first year of research there a vindictive American ambassador to that country, who was angered by my criticism of his policies, had my passport lifted so that for five years (1949–54) I could not return to Indonesia, or go anywhere abroad. Later my criticism of General Suharto's government made it impossible for me, or my wife, to get a visa to enter the country officially for fifteen years – 1976 to 1991. I was fortunate enough to have some excellent graduate students at Cornell who were interested in Indonesia, most of whom were able to enter the country for their research, though several of them briefly found it difficult to secure visas. (One of the very best, Benedict Anderson, was kept out even longer than I was.) Being able to rely on these students and other friends who were Indonesia scholars and on correspondence with and visits from some of my old Indonesian friends I was partially able to compensate for my own continuing lack of access to the country, but I was certainly seriously crippled by this. However, even before the 1965 coup in Indonesia, my opposition to American involvement in the Vietnam war had led me to shift my attention away from Indonesia to a more general concern with American policy on the mainland of Southeast Asia.

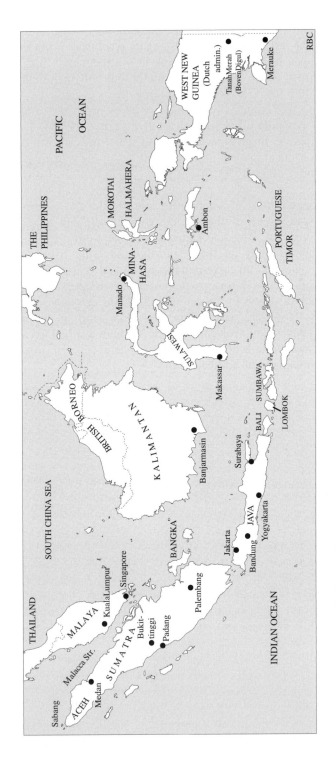

Map 2   Indonesian Archipelago, 1950
Source: (map by Robert Cribb)

1 The Indonesian revolution

The Indonesia that emerged in the late 1940s stretched west to east across an area the breadth of the United States and incorporated a land area equal to that of Mexico, or three times the size of Texas. Known as the Netherlands East Indies until its brutal occupation by the Japanese during World War II, it ranked together with British India as one of the world's two richest colonies. Soon after the end of the war the Netherlands began an all-out effort to reestablish control over the 70 million people who inhabited this jewel in the Dutch crown.

At the Potsdam Conference of July 1945 the task of recovering the East Indies from Japan was formally transferred from General Douglas MacArthur to Britain's Admiral Louis Mountbatten. Thereby the United States was able to avoid the difficult and thankless task of disarming the Japanese armed forces in Indonesia and dealing with the government of the Indonesian Republic, which had asserted its independence from Netherlands rule on 17 August 1945. The shift in strategic planning also saved the United States from the travail and embarrassment that might well have attended General MacArthur's initially scheduled plan to reestablish Dutch government in the Indies[1] – an undertaking that would have locked American troops in combat with Indonesian nationalists, as Britain's troops were for over a year, and would presumably have resulted in casualties on the same scale.

Thus, only in July 1945 – and unfortunately accompanied by the transfer of an all too slender body of relevant intelligence as to conditions in that area – was Britain's Admiral Mountbatten vested with that onerous responsibility, as was also the case for Burma and the southern half of Indochina.

It was against the background of Japan's impending defeat that on 17 August 1945, Indonesia's two paramount nationalist leaders, Sukarno and Mohammad Hatta, proclaimed their country's independence and launched the Republic of Indonesia before a small and hastily assembled group of nationalists. The statement then read out by Sukarno, with Hatta standing by his side, is worth quoting in *full* – as has generally not been the case.[2] A translation of it was given to me by Haji Agus Salim, foreign minister of the Republic of Indonesia, on 17 October 1948, during the course of a discussion I had with him about the beginnings of the Republic. Sukarno's full statement reads:

Brothers and Sisters All!

I have asked you to be in attendance here in order to witness an event in our history of the utmost importance.

For decades we, the People of Indonesia, have struggled for the freedom of our country – even for hundreds of years!

There have been waves in our actions to win independence which rose, and there have been those that fell, but our spirit still was set in the direction of our ideals.

Also during the Japanese period our efforts to achieve national independence never ceased. In this Japanese period it merely appeared that we leant upon them. But fundamentally, we still continued to build up our own powers, we still believed in our own strengths.

Now has come the moment when truly we take the fate of our action and the fate of our country into our own hands. Only a nation bold enough to take its fate into its own hands will be able to stand in strength.

Therefore last night we had deliberations with prominent Indonesians all over Indonesia. That deliberative gathering was unanimously of the opinion that NOW has come the time to declare our independence.

Brothers and Sisters:

Herewith we declare the solidarity of that determination.

Listen to our proclamation:

PROCLAMATION
WE THE PEOPLE OF INDONESIA HEREBY DECLARE THE
INDEPENDENCE OF INDONESIA. MATTERS WHICH
CONCERN THE TRANSFER OF POWER AND OTHER THINGS
WILL BE EXECUTED BY CAREFUL MEANS AND IN THE
SHORTEST POSSIBLE TIME. DJAKARTA, 17 AUGUST 1945
IN THE NAME OF THE PEOPLE OF INDONESIA
SUKARNO–HATTA

So it is, Brothers and Sisters!

We are now already free! There is not another single tie binding our country and our people!

As from this moment we build our state. A free state, the State of the Republic of Indonesia – evermore and eternally independent.

Allah willing, God blesses and makes safe this independence of ours![3]

During the year that followed it was primarily with British military power that the nascent Republic of Indonesia had to contend. After a year of bruising military operations and substantial casualties, and recognizing the clearly anticolonial sentiment of the Indian Army troops upon whom they were heavily dependent, the British made clear to the Dutch that they were no longer willing to continue their fight against the Republic's forces. But although British military commanders had been much less partial to the Dutch in Indonesia than they were to the French in Vietnam and Cambodia, by the time their troops withdrew from Indonesia at the end of October 1946 they had managed to shoehorn into the country approximately 91,000 Dutch soldiers armed with modern American equipment, a substantially larger force than they had introduced into Indochina.

In taking over the battle against the Republic's forces from the British, the Netherlands' objective was not merely to disarm and repatriate any remaining Japanese troops, but also to reestablish Dutch administrative authority to a much greater extent than the British had permitted.

The United States had quietly acquiesced to the year-long British military operation in Indonesia, supplied some of the shipping to bring her troops there and raised no objection when Britain, in fighting the Indonesians, used the American Lend–Lease military equipment originally provided for employment against Nazi or Japanese forces. Nor did Washington object when, on their departure, the British turned over this American military equipment to the incoming Dutch forces.

Sporadic Dutch military actions culminated in mid-1947 in an all-out operation – euphemistically termed a "police action" – to subdue the Republic and reimpose Dutch administrative authority over the entire archipelago. Over the next three months, defying the United Nations Security Council's call for a cease-fire, Dutch troops, spearheaded by modern US military equipment – including tanks and airplanes – penetrated deeply into the richest parts of Java and Sumatra. As a result, the Republic's residual areas on the densely populated island of Java, despite normally being significantly deficient in food, now had to support over a million refugees who fled from the areas overrun by the Dutch army.

The UN Security Council's designated Committee of Good Offices finally managed,[4] in January 1948, to broker an agreement between the Dutch and the Republic. This "Renville Agreement" called for an end to the Dutch blockade and for a cease-fire, heavily favoring the Dutch. Although temporarily ending the fighting, this in effect froze the military positions of the two adversaries, separating them with a truce, or "Status Quo" line connecting up the areas where the Dutch tank columns had penetrated. The Republic was required to withdraw some 35,000 of its troops behind this line, which meant evacuating them from large pockets of territory bypassed by the Dutch armored spearheads into the rump areas left in Republican hands. In return for this withdrawal the Dutch promised that plebiscites would be held in the territories newly occupied by Dutch troops to ascertain whether their inhabitants chose governance by the Republic or by the Dutch. The Republic's leaders felt confident of success in these plebiscites. But the Netherlands was not only unwilling to lift its blockade of the Republic, it also refused to allow preparations for a plebiscite to proceed. Instead it unilaterally set about erecting a congeries of small and large puppet states in the areas overrun by its forces. Its ultimate goal was to establish a federal Indonesia that would be made up of these "states" together with the Republic of Indonesia. In this federation each of these Dutch creations, despite its usually miniscule size, was to have a representation equal to that of the Republic. Thus the Republic would be politically swamped. This "federation" was to be tied to the Netherlands crown in a way whereby the Dutch could expect to preserve their control over Indonesia. Though the United States had not indicated approval of such a federal order, it had grudgingly acquiesced to the Netherlands' military campaign of mid-1947 and for at least several months supported an interpretation of the Renville Agreement that accorded considerably more closely with that of the Dutch than with that of the Republic.

So far as American public opinion was concerned, the Netherlands began with a considerable advantage over the Republic of Indonesia. The folklore with which most Americans grew up had cast the Dutch in a very favorable light – images of the boy at the dike, Hans Brinker and the Silver Skates, and Dutch women scrubbing their porch steps every morning were commonplace. Indeed, physical cleanliness was always seen as a hallmark of the Dutch people. There was no equivalent Indonesian mythology incorporated into American culture, even though the Dutch in the Indies themselves marveled at the discovery that Indonesians generally washed more often than they did. And while many Americans were sympathetic towards the Dutch for the suffering they endured under the Nazi occupation, few were even aware of the hardships suffered by Indonesians under the heel of Japan's occupation of their country.

Though there was still a considerable reservoir of anticolonial feeling in the United States, the first Truman administration's view of the Indonesian–Netherlands dispute favored the Dutch by a considerable margin. Any anticolonial sentiment by American policy makers was still heavily outweighed by their tendency to accept Dutch propaganda that, after initially depicting the Republic's leadership as pro-Japanese Quislings, had since at least early 1946 convinced many Americans in Congress and the Truman administration that the Republic was dangerously pro-Communist and ran the risk of ultimately developing into a Communist-dominated government. The official US tilt in favor of the Netherlands became all the more pronounced between 1946 and 1948 as Cold War calculations persuaded American policy makers that US strategic and economic interests in Western Europe – especially as plans developed for the building of NATO – should not risk offending the Netherlands by pressing her to adjust to the demands of Indonesian nationalists for independence.

Thus, the Indonesia which I sought to visit in mid-1948 to study its revolution and postcolonial political order was a divided one – with major areas of the country militarily and politically controlled by the Dutch and an equally extensive area governed by the newly independent Republic, each part headed by a political leadership dedicated to a distinctly different agenda. And the revolutionary Republic of Indonesia which was the major focus of my study had moved from early expectations of American support to extreme disillusionment and, among many of its politically conscious inhabitants, a sense of betrayal. This perception of the United States not unnaturally produced an atmosphere of suspicion towards me that, as the only American resident in the Republic, I initially found difficult to overcome.

It had not proved easy for me to get to Indonesia, especially that part of it which in 1948 was controlled by the revolutionary Republic of Indonesia. In January of that year I was elated to learn that I had been awarded a $3,000 fellowship (later increased by $1,350 for support of my wife and child) from the Social Science Research Council (SSRC) in New York to conduct research on the government and politics of the Republic of Indonesia. That provided the financial means of getting to the Netherlands East Indies, but I also needed visas for the Dutch-controlled areas and for the Republic. The Indonesian Republic had no diplomatic relations, embassy or consular offices in the United States, but its ex-prime minister, Sutan Sjahrir (Figure 1.1), visited New York briefly during a few weeks in the spring of 1948 to deliver a speech to the United Nations General Assembly. I took the opportunity to call on him in his apartment there and talk over my research plans with him and his very bright young assistant, Soedjatmoko Mangoendiningrat (Figure 1.2), who stood about a foot taller than Sjahrir. This was the beginning of friendships with both that lasted until their deaths. Our long discussion in New York was amicable, frank and, for me, very interesting – especially as it pertained to Dutch–Indonesian relations and conditions within the Republic. Towards the end of our meeting Sjahrir excused himself for a few minutes and returned bearing a letter he had written on my behalf to Haji Agus Salim, the Republic's minister of foreign affairs. Presentation of this to the consular office of the Republic in Batavia would, he assured me, get me the visa I would require to be admitted to the Republic.

But, as many people had warned me, getting a visa from the Dutch authorities for the Netherlands East Indies – the territory that I had to pass through on my way to the Republic – proved a more formidable undertaking. On the advice of Owen Lattimore and Rupert Emerson I did what I could to equip myself with press credentials and was fortunate enough to get them from a very small news bureau in New York, the Overseas News Agency (ONA). It was clear that ONA did not regard me as a terribly promising correspondent, since they only gave me authority to cable stories of no more than 100 words. (I could, of course, send them longer pieces by airmail.) The Dutch in Washington were apparently well aware of the minor stature of this

Figure 1.1   Sutan Sjahrir   *Figure 1.2*   Soedjatmoko (Koko)

organization, so that its sponsorship and that of the SSRC proved far from sufficient to induce their embassy to grant me a visa. What finally did bring them around, some three months after I submitted my application, was a letter from Isaiah Bowman, president of Johns Hopkins University, supporting me and my research plans. He was a man of high standing in international circles, having been Woodrow Wilson's geographer at the Versailles Conference. Nearly half a century later, in going through the Dutch archives, I found reference to his letter in my behalf as coming from a man with "impeccable credentials." I hardly knew him, but since he had brought Lattimore to his university to head its Walter Hines Page School of International Relations, he was inclined to be supportive of Lattimore and his students and pleased to have scholars from his university engaged in field research abroad. Though in my one discussion with him I made clear my anticolonial feelings, they did not appear to disturb him. At any rate it was apparently because of his intervention that I was finally informed in late May that I had a visa to visit the Netherlands East Indies.

An Atlantic passage was easy to secure, but shipping between Europe and Indonesia was very tight. Only by paying for an upscale first-class cabin was I able to get a ticket on the three-week voyage from Europe to Batavia on the *Oranje*. Though that ticket cost me a large chunk of my fellowship funding, my first-class passage probably contributed to my later being given access to the lodgings in Batavia that the Dutch East Indies government's Regerings Voorlichtings Dienst (RVD – Government Information Office) reserved for the press.

Figure 1.3   Cornelis (Kees) Van Mook, June 1948

But my real stroke of luck occurred on the first leg of the trip, crossing the Atlantic in tourist class aboard the Holland America Line's rather more ancient *Veendam*. Soon after it sailed out of New York on 11 June, I met a friendly young Dutchman, Cornelis (Kees) Van Mook (Figure 1.3), who had just finished his degree in marine engineering at the Massachusetts Institute of Technology (MIT) and was now on his way home to Holland. He had spent his youth in Indonesia, was sympathetic towards the independence movement there and keenly interested in my projected research. He kindly volunteered to help me learn a bit more Indonesian, and we walked the pleasant summer decks together practicing the language and talking about the country.

The ship was full of middle-class Dutch, mostly returning from a summer vacation and/or visiting relatives in America. I soon began to notice that as we approached groups of them spread out in their deck chairs we rarely encountered a smile and most of them simply turned away. Indeed, as I mentioned to Kees, even when by myself I had begun to feel something of a pariah. Grinning broadly, Kees chuckled and said to me: "It's all my father's fault." It was only then that he disclosed that his father was the acting governor general of the Netherlands East Indies, Hubertus Van Mook (Figure 1.4). And it was then, too, that I began to appreciate that, while I had come to think of Governor General Van Mook as a rather conservative

Figure 1.4 Acting Governor General H.J. Van Mook

colonialist, many middle-class Netherlanders regarded him as politically radical and too accommodating to Indonesian nationalism. Although word had spread that the governor general's son was aboard the ship, it was not expected that he would be traveling tourist class and very few passengers actually recognized him. But as we walked the deck together we sometimes overheard whispers: "There goes the son of Van Mook." Kees found this amusing, for, as he told me, I looked much more like his father than he, and as a consequence by the end of the Atlantic crossing I was being regarded as the son of the "radical" governor general by even more of the Dutch passengers than he.

Indeed, as I later discovered, the fact that Hubertus Van Mook was never given the title of full-fledged governor general – without the slightly demeaning qualifier of "acting" – was because his political objectives in Indonesia struck many members of the Dutch political establishment as simply too radical and inclined in favor of ultimate Indonesian independence (a schedule which, of course, was regarded as much too slow and conditional for most Indonesian nationalists). At any rate, the cold shoulder that I received from many of these Dutch passengers awoke me to a more realistic appreciation of the constraints that Dutch domestic politics imposed on those relatively liberal Dutch politicians and officials who dealt with their country's relations with Indonesian nationalism. I was reminded of the frustration and helplessness of that substantial minority of liberals in the American Congress and public who fifty years before had vainly opposed the brutal US military campaign against the Philippine independence movement, and the annexation of that country as a colony.

For me it was an unusual stroke of good fortune that Kees was kind enough to volunteer to write a letter of introduction to his father and urged me to call on him after I reached Batavia.

When the *Veendam* docked at Southampton I switched over to the Netherlands Steamship Company's *Oranje*, then one of the most beautiful ships sailing to the Far East. Despite the luxury of my first-class cabin the three-week voyage to Batavia was not easy. It must be understood that most senior Netherlands Indies officials were then being flown out, under top priority, to take up their duties in Indonesia, while their wives and children followed separately by ship. Thus, the ratio of women to men among my fellow passengers was heavily skewed in favor of women – mostly middle-aged or older. My recently-made friends, Lauriston and Ruth Sharp, who, with their two children, had also been passengers on the *Veendam*, were aboard, as well as a few British officials and their families bound for Singapore, where the ship docked shortly before reaching Batavia. The head steward in the *Oranje*'s dining room, realizing that I was an English-speaking American, naturally seated me at a table with these British passengers. I found them congenial enough, but recognized that such a seating arrangement would not be conducive to realizing my plan of taking advantage of the voyage to practice my still underdeveloped knowledge of the Dutch language. And so after that first meal I went up to the head steward to request that henceforth I be seated at a table where the passengers were all Dutch. "Young man," he beamed, "I will surely take care of you!" And at the next meal I found myself seated at a table with four eager women in their fifties whose husbands were being sent out to Indonesia by air. The steward informed them that I'd requested a table where only Dutch was spoken. I went on to explain that, since I wanted very much to improve my Dutch, I would appreciate it if they would limit all discussion to that language, even though I realized they could probably all speak English better than I could Dutch. After a few minutes of whispering among themselves they expressed their agreement, saying that they had but one condition: I must agree to go up to the salon each evening and dance with them. Being all too aware of what a terrible dancer I was, I initially balked. But they persisted, and I finally agreed, little realizing at the time what avid dancers they were and how insistent they would be about holding me to my promise. The only concession I was able to exact was that I would be expected to dance with no more than one of them per evening, but as I grimly calculated there were at least twenty evenings ahead before we reached Batavia.

The women were all nice enough and did maintain their end of the bargain, though we soon found the topics we could discuss were decidedly limited. They were understandably embittered over the harsh experiences they had endured during the Japanese occupation and blamed the government of the Indonesian Republic for tardiness, heavy handedness and inefficiency in the process of their release. In none of these women could I detect the slightest inclination to sympathize with Indonesian aspirations for independence.

And, despite my clumsiness and lack of appetite for it, we did dance. Indeed every evening, even in rough weather, except during a heavy monsoon in the Indian Ocean, we took to the floor. But the heavenly reprieve of that monsoon lasted only three days. With tables and chairs lashed down because of the size of the swells, one of the ladies, the powerful six-foot Mrs Suurenbroek (which my quite unscientific Dutch translated as "Sourpants") was game to try. The intrepid persistence of my four dancing partners and me during even very rough weather attracted notice from the other passengers. It may also perhaps have reinforced the impression that, because of my prominent first-class provenance, I must be an important correspondent, even though most Dutch officials on board had probably never even heard of the Overseas News Agency.

At any rate I counted myself very lucky when a day after landing in Batavia (Jakarta) on 14 July I was accepted as a bona fide correspondent, given accreditation and assigned a room in the correspondents' mess in a house at #93 Javaweg, later renamed HOS Tjokroaminoto. (A good description of that house and the pleasant and helpful Dutch couple who ran it, Herman and Hennie Buiten Huijs, appeared in the 10 January 1948 edition of the *Saturday Evening Post*.) In the mess and at the office of the Government Information Office (RVD), I soon met most of the handful of foreign correspondents assigned to Batavia. The de facto doyen of the foreign press corps, Quentin Pope, and I soon became good friends. Highly intelligent, very hard working and skilled at dealing with officials, he was grudgingly respected by the RVD even though they hated his paper, the *Chicago Tribune*, which had recently called for the Netherlands queen to be hanged because of Dutch efforts to suppress the Indonesian Republic. He was also respected by the other correspondents, in part because he had left the *New York Times* for a better paying job on the Chicago paper, making him by far the best-paid journalist stationed in Batavia. I also developed friendships with Dick Applegate and Arnold Brackman, respectively correspondents for the Associated Press and United Press, and two young Dutch correspondents, Chris Scheffer and Henk Van Maurik, respectively of the *Groene Amsterdammer* and the *Gelderlander Pers*. Both of them were of a liberal orientation – sympathetic to the Republic and especially to the conscripted Dutch boys who, they felt, had for the most part been dragooned into fighting for a colonial cause in which they did not believe. The Dutch journalists distinguished between these conscripts and the regular soldiers in the Royal Dutch army and in its sister organization, the KNIL (the Royal Netherlands Indies Army – the old colonially recruited force). I also came to know several Indonesian journalists, including Sanjoto and B.M. Diah, as well as some of the members of the local Chinese–Indonesian press, including Injo Ben Goat, editor of the middle spectrum *Keng Po* and chairman of the All Chinese Labor Association, and Chen Tey Sue of the progressive *Seng Hwo Pao*. Though there was sharp competition between all these journalists, there was often also a remarkable degree of solidarity among them whenever it was clear that officials of the RVD or other Dutch Indies officials were not being sufficiently forthcoming – hardly an infrequent phenomenon.

On 2 August 1948, a little over two weeks after my arrival in Batavia, I called on Governor General Van Mook in his marble-floored office in the center of the town. The kind letter of introduction from his son paved the way for a cordial reception and a long and interesting discussion. It was abundantly clear that this man really loved the Indies, felt a part of it and saw his own destiny closely linked to it. His attitude towards Indonesian nationalists was a bit paternalistic, but certainly not condescending. He said that he wished to give the Indonesians their independence as soon as possible, but that he wanted to be sure that, when they departed, the Dutch left behind an Indonesian government that was strong enough to control and guard the country against the local Chinese and Indians and "possibly the Communists as well." The Republic of Indonesia was far too weak to do this, he contended, as had already been demonstrated before the Dutch military action of mid-1947.

We discussed at length his concept of a federal United States of Indonesia tied to the Dutch crown. He expressed confidence that once this was established and it was clear that the Netherlands was transferring real power, this polity would ultimately exert sufficient political attraction to bring the Republic into its fold – if not as an entity, then at least many of its individual leaders. I asked him whether the establishment of a Dutch-sponsored United States of Indonesia would not be seriously hampered by the fact that the vast majority of Indonesian intellectuals were in the Republic. On the contrary, he said, an increasing tendency was already under way for individual Republicans to join the federalist camp. Moreover, he continued, non-Republicans were already gaining much political experience and general administrative know-how by their work in the present Dutch-sponsored provisional federal government. He would like, he said, to have come to a political agreement with the Republican leadership two years earlier but Holland had first to be educated to this idea. Van Mook said that he had always gotten his instructions from The Hague, and what initiative he could take was limited to the latitude of discretion permitted by his instructions.

A little over a week later, thanks to an introduction from Van Mook, I had a long discussion with the head of his cabinet, P.J. Koets, a man who evidently admired and sympathized with Van Mook. Like Van Mook, Koets gave the clear impression of genuinely wanting to grant real independence to Indonesia. But, as with Van Mook, the Republic was not to be the repository but rather a Dutch-sponsored federal Indonesia. He felt that once "responsible people" in the Republic saw that the Dutch were sincere and actually granting real power to the Indonesians then these "responsible people" would "come over to and join the federation." The great stumbling block, he said, was that there were too many people in the Republic with "vested interests in the present political set-up." Also "the political outs will always make political capital of any concessions made to the Dutch scheme by the present leaders." Within the Republic, he continued:

> There are too many people anxious for power and too many with guns and the power that goes with them ... Those people know that under a Dutch-sponsored federation they would lose their arms and thus their power. [This would make it difficult for] people in the Republic presently in positions of political power to be able to take steps towards bringing the Republic into the federal fold, and if they should attempt to do so they would undoubtedly find themselves in a position so compromising that the political outs would benefit, while the armed groups would certainly actively oppose such steps ... The only solution short of force would be a Dutch policy towards the federation that would generate a politics of attraction that would win over to the federal side the present most important Republican leaders – at least most of those in the present Republican government.

He went on to say that the military campaign (he used the official term "police action") mounted by the Netherlands against the Republic a year before, in July 1947, had been intended to disarm semi-independent groups within the Republic and "put under control" those who would not cooperate with a Dutch-sponsored federal solution. Among the Republican leaders for whom he appeared to have a high regard were Vice President Hatta and former Prime Minister Sjahrir. He did not appear to want to discuss Sukarno and he was clearly negative in his appraisal of former Prime Minister Amir Sjarifuddin, who was now leading a left-wing political coalition.[5]

At the United Nations' urging the Dutch had permitted the government of the Republic of Indonesia to operate a liaison office in a small house at Pegangsaan Timur in Batavia. (Ironically it had been at the front of this house that three years earlier Sukarno and Hatta had proclaimed Indonesia's independence.) The house also contained a room designated as the Consulate of the Republic of Indonesia. Soon after my arrival in Batavia I went there armed with the letter of introduction to Haji Agus Salim, the Republic's minister of foreign affairs, that Sjahrir had given me in New York. It immediately produced a friendly reaction from Consul Surjotjondro and the promise I could pick up a visa valid for residence and travel within the territory of the Republic whenever I was ready to go there.

But as for getting into the Republic – whether Yogyakarta, its capital, 200 miles to the east, or any of its territory – Surjotjondro had no suggestion other than the pious hope that the United Nations Good Offices Commission (GOC) might be prevailed on to give me a seat on one of their irregularly scheduled flights to Yogyakarta reserved for their own personnel. But even that tenuous possibility required not only a visa from the Republic but also permission from the government of the Netherlands East Indies – an altogether more difficult proposition unless one were a member of the GOC or an acceptable member of the press. In any case, my objective was to remain in the Republic for at least six months and if possible longer, and journalists who could manage to get on the UN's infrequent plane for Yogyakarta were given permission by the Dutch for only very brief visits – usually for no more than a week. Though earlier, on a few occasions, the UN delegation had been able to get sufficient cooperation between the Dutch and Indonesian Republic's armed forces to enable a train to get through to Yogyakarta, this was no longer possible. A few cars could be rented in Batavia for an exorbitant price, but correspondents were unable to find drivers willing to take them further east than Bandung. In any case, I would first have to secure permission from the Dutch to cross the Status Quo Truce Line, or Van Mook Line as it was more widely known, that under the UN's directive (based on the Renville Agreement of January 1948) separated the Dutch and Republican military forces in central Java.

Because of my earlier contact with Van Mook it seemed logical to return to the acting governor general to seek his support for crossing into the Republic. But this required authorization not only from his civilian branch of the government, which he was willing to give, but also from the Netherlands Indies military. I only then learned how strong the differences and tension were between Van Mook and the Dutch military chief in Indonesia, General Simon Spoor, and especially Spoor's intelligence chief, Lt Col Van Lier. Sullen, surly and exceedingly arrogant, Van Lier made it evident from the outset that he was unlikely to do me any favors. But since Van Mook had indicated that his civilian government had no objection to my crossing the Status Quo Line, Van Lier apparently felt it incumbent to give me a long interrogation before pronouncing his verdict. He concluded this by telling me that neither on the basis of my press credentials nor my doctoral research was he prepared to endorse my request for a seat on the United Nations plane to Yogyakarta. "Of course," he concluded smugly, giving me a malicious grin, "so long as you can find your own transportation we have no objection to your crossing over." He was, of course, safe in assuming that I was in no position to hire an airplane or rent a car and driver in Batavia willing to chance the long drive to Yogyakarta.

Van Mook did not seem surprised at Van Lier's attitude, and, greatly discouraged, I began to accustom myself to the conclusion that I would be unable to visit the Republic, and my research would have to be confined to Dutch-controlled areas of the Indies. The other correspondents sympathized with me, especially those who had run up against Van Lier, but none could come up with a workable suggestion. Those who had visited the Status Quo Line explained to me that one couldn't just step across it, and that the line actually was straddled by a sort of no-man's land about 10–15 km wide wherein one ran the risk of being shot by soldiers from either side. In any case they convinced me that, even if I were foolish enough to try to cross on my own, I'd not be able to find a rental car and driver in Batavia willing to take me.

Suddenly, however, something of a miracle occurred that was finally to solve my problem. The American consulate general in Batavia announced that outstanding US Lend–Lease military equipment – specifically vehicles – whether provided to the Dutch or the British, had to be promptly turned in. British and British/Indian forces operating in the Indies in 1945–6 had been provided with a considerable amount of such war material. Most of it had apparently been taken over by the Netherlands Indies armed forces as the British left, but there was still a bit scattered about, and the Dutch military felt that at least a token amount had to be returned. Apparently very little was, but one tired old jeep that had been in the hands of an Indian army sergeant was reluctantly surrendered by him, as required, to the American consulate. (I was told that as many as 600 soldiers of the British Indian army had defected to the Republic's side in 1946, some of them with their vehicles.) US consulates were required to auction off whatever material was turned in to the highest bidder, with priority going to ex-members of the US armed forces. Apparently I was one of the very few such ex-GIs who showed up at the consulate to bid. Spotting the battered old jeep brought in by the British Indian Army sergeant, I lifted up its hood to discover that he had kept the engine in very good shape. So I placed my sealed bid for the jeep at $502. There were very few, if any, other qualified bidders, and to my delight I won the jeep. I now had my own transportation!

Even so, Van Lier reneged, refusing to endorse Van Mook's permission for me to cross into the Republic. He insisted that the Republican army would take over my jeep if I brought it in. "If you take it in," he said half mockingly, "you'll have added 5 per cent to the transport capability of the Republic's army." He finally granted me permission only after Van Mook pointed out to his superiors that, since the other more important foreign correspondents knew of Van Lier's promise that I could go if I could find my own transportation, it would provoke unnecessary friction with them if he now reneged.

So finally the Dutch as well as the Republican government gave me the necessary permission to cross the Status Quo Line if I could get there. I now needed to discuss my plans with the American representatives in Batavia.

As I've already noted, in the years just after World War II the active role of the British in Indonesia had initially tended to shelter the United States from assuming any position of responsibility in the Netherlands–Indonesian dispute. But following the withdrawal of British and British/Indian forces at the end of 1946 this proved increasingly difficult. After having held to a public posture of neutrality in the dispute, the United States finally at the end of June 1947 took a stance unequivocally supportive of the Netherlands' legal position when it dispatched an aide-mémoire to the Republic calling upon it to "cooperate without delay" with the Dutch in the immediate formation of an interim federal government for the whole of Indonesia, a demand that was reluctantly accepted by Sutan Sjahrir, the Republic's prime minister. This American note, however, went on to state that an earlier agreement, signed at Linggajati under the aegis of the British shortly before their departure, had stipulated that there should be an interim period running until 1 January 1949 "during which the Netherlands is to retain sovereignty and ultimate authority in Indonesia." Since no such provision actually appeared in the Linggajati Agreement, the Republic's leaders could only conclude that the United States was backing the Dutch against them. This clearly weakened Sjahrir's position, and his government quickly fell, to be succeeded by one headed by Amir Sjarifuddin, that was, at least at first, even less disposed to compromise with the Dutch.

By the time I arrived in Indonesia in August 1948 the belief was widespread that the Netherlands was being critically supported by the United States in its effort to reestablish its control over the East Indies. Thus, a CIA report of 14 November 1947 had concluded:

> Already in Indonesia and Indochina the native population tends to regard Dutch and French efforts to reestablish their control as having been made with U.S. support. To the extent that the European Recovery Program [Marshall Plan] enhances Dutch and French capabilities in Southeast Asia, native resentment will increase.

And it is uncontestably clear that, just as in the case of France in Vietnam, the Netherlands' effort to reestablish control over Indonesia was critically dependent upon American financial support and military supplies. Indeed, during the period I was in Indonesia the American economic aid being provided the Netherlands was approximately equivalent to the financial support being pumped out of that country to support Dutch military operations in Indonesia.

Moreover, a peasant did not have to understand bookkeeping to realize that the United States was backing the Dutch or the French with military equipment in their efforts to subdue the local independence movements. It was plain for all to see, for the Netherlands, like France, largely ignored the request by US Secretary of State James Byrnes that all US insignia be removed from the military equipment the United States had provided it.

In addition to the American aide-mémoire of 28 June 1947, and the belief that the US was providing crucial financial and material support to the Dutch effort of military reconquest, trust was further eroded by American actions after the United Nations-sponsored Renville Agreement of January

1948. In subsequent months the United States was seen, with considerable justification, as pressuring the Republic to live up to the concessions it had made under that agreement while being unwilling to induce the Dutch to live up to their end of the bargain. The central quid pro quo of the Renville Agreement had called for the Republic's withdrawal of approximately 35,000 of its troops from their still intact residual concentrations bypassed by Dutch armored spearheads, back into the truncated area it still held in Java following the Dutch military campaign; and for the Dutch to end their blockade of the Republic and permit plebiscites in the areas their troops had seized to determine whether their inhabitants preferred to live under Dutch or Republican administrations.

When I arrived in the Republic in late August 1948 – some seven months after the Renville Agreement had been signed – the Republic's troops had marched back from the Dutch-penetrated areas into what was left of the Republic. The Netherlands, however, had neither lifted its blockade nor permitted preparations for a plebiscite in the areas its army had overrun. Instead, there, as well as in the other parts of Indonesia they held, the Dutch unilaterally proceeded to establish numerous large and small puppet states. Their cavalier action in establishing this highly artificial order had long-term consequences. It strongly tarnished the idea of federalism and thereby seriously undermined prospects for adoption of significant administrative and fiscal decentralization in the years after Indonesia secured full independence, even though it was clear that for a country as large and differentiated as Indonesia this might well have been best.

The American representative on the UN Good Offices Committee, Frank Graham, had led the Republic's prime minister, Amir Sjarifuddin, to believe that the United States would pressure the Dutch to live up to their end of the Renville Agreement. When the United States refused to honor this commitment, Amir, together with politically conscious Indonesians in general, saw this as an American betrayal. This interpretation was strongly underscored when Graham was recalled soon after shepherding the agreement through to signature, and was replaced with a Foreign Service officer, Coert DuBois, widely known at the time for his pro-Dutch position. Frank Graham shared Amir's perception that American acquiescence to the Dutch position on Renville was a betrayal. Indeed, when many years later I discussed this matter with him, he stated that the State Department cut off the limb that he had, in good faith, persuaded Sjarifuddin to stand on. He bitterly complained that there had been a *double* betrayal – that he had been betrayed by his superiors in the State Department who had led him to believe they supported his compromise position, and he in turn had betrayed Sjarifuddin whom he had in good faith led to believe that his position was endorsed by the State Department. Although a reading of relevant US documents, subsequently declassified, indicates some ambiguity in the Department's position, Graham's grievance appears valid.

Sjarifuddin's acute sense that he had been betrayed by the United States, together with the support the Soviet Union gave to the Indonesian position in the United Nations Security Council, helped induce him in August 1948 to join in a coalition with the Indonesian Communist Party. Graham's successor, Coert DuBois, also soon lost patience with the Dutch and moved to a position more favorable to the Republic, but when he did so the State Department removed him as well. In mid-August 1948 he was replaced by a Eurocentric senior US Foreign Service officer, Merle Cochran, known to be strongly partial to the Netherlands position in its dispute with the Republic. But even Cochran soon underwent the same metamorphosis as DuBois and within a few months had moved much closer to the Republic's position, albeit not so close as his predecessor.

With the successive recalls of Graham and DuBois, Sjarifuddin had no reason for believing there would be any change in American policy away from its heavy tilt in favor of the Netherlands, nor any reason to expect it would honor the understanding of the Renville Agreement that had induced him to sign it.

Having obtained permission from both the Dutch and Indonesians to enter the Republic, I had sensed that the American consul general in Batavia, Charles Livengood, though not keen about my trip, was not inclined to try and stop me. He proved to be considerably broader-minded than the Consulate's political officer, Glen Abbey, whose generally poor reporting he apparently balanced off with that of three very able junior members of his staff, all of whom I came to know well, Donald Davies, Harold Nelson and Richard Stuart. The last of these had come out to Indonesia as early as October 1945 as a member of the OSS and was clearly the best informed man in the consulate. (In my judgment, both then and in retrospect, the only official American in Indonesia whose political grasp approximated Stuart's was one of the younger members of the US delegation on the UN Committee of Good Offices, Charlton Ogburn.) However, it was Abbey, not Stuart, whom Livengood designated to call me in for an official briefing when it was learned that I'd finally gotten permission to cross the Status Quo Line into the Republic. I'd already met Abbey and was not keen on seeing him again. But I told myself it was important to learn more of the views held by that influential minority in the State Department that most clearly shared the pejorative official Netherlands' view of the Republic's leadership. It should be noted that within the State Department during most of the immediate post-World War II period the European desks were much more influential than the newly born Southeast Asia Division, whose senior staff were initially nearly all recently added temporary personnel seconded from American universities, rather than the usually very Eurocentric senior Foreign Service officers such as manned the Netherlands and French desks in the Department. (The only Southeast Asian country where those who worked in its Southeast Asia Division had

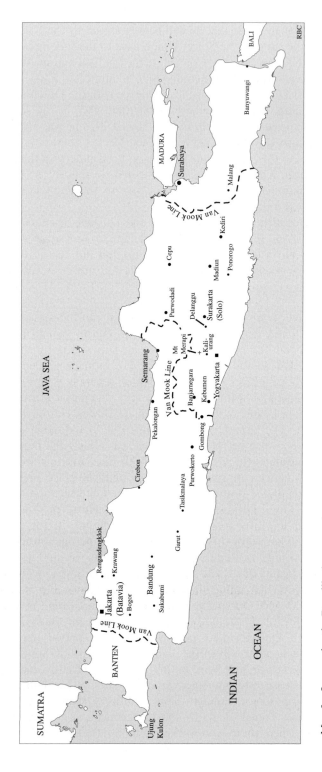

Map 3   Java under the Renville Agreement
Source: (map by Robert Cribb)

a major influence on US policy was Thailand, unique, of course, because it had never been a colony.)

Clearly displeased with my plans to visit the Republic, Abbey warned me that I would be entering what was essentially a pro-Communist country. He stressed that I should be especially on my guard against the puppeteer (*dalang*) behind the Communist movement there, the "dangerous" Molly Bondan, an Australian "Communist" who, he alleged, was married to a well-known Indonesian "Communist." In fact neither Molly nor Bondan, her husband, were any more Communist than Abbey, and their actual backgrounds provided a revealing insight into the propensity of a good many Dutch officials to smear as "Communist," or "Communist sympathizer" anyone who was critical of the Netherlands' position and favored the Republic's independence – as I was soon to discover pertained to myself.

Bondan, a close friend of the Republic's vice-president, Mohammad Hatta, had been arrested by the Dutch in 1933 and then sent, like him and Sutan Sjahrir, to the notorious fever-ridden concentration camp of Tanah Merah at Boven Digul, deep in the interior of Netherlands New Guinea (Irian Jaya, West Papua), where he languished for eight years until he was transferred to Australia with other nationalist prisoners immediately before the Japanese overran the Indies. Though only a minority of the Indonesian nationalists interned at Boven Digul were Communists or Communist sympathizers, the Dutch tended to give them all that label. This they had done to Bondan, even though Hatta, now also the Republic's prime minister and known by the Dutch to be anti-Communist, only about a year before had appointed Bondan to a politically sensitive senior position in the Ministry of Labor. As for Molly, she earned her "Communist" credentials not only by virtue of having married Bondan but because, when she was arrested with him in Semarang in 1947 on their way from Australia to the Republic, her baggage was searched and yielded a couple of records of the composer Stravinsky – a Russian!

In the meantime I had learned of the terrible state of the roads I would have to traverse to make the over-200-mile trip to Yogyakarta. And upon closer inspection of my venerable jeep at a reputable garage I was convinced that it could not make it all the way. It was one of the mechanics, as I recall, who suggested that I put it on a freight train to the railhead at Purwokerto and then drive it the remaining ninety-odd miles to Yogyakarta. So I went to the railroad office where I found personnel very different from Col Van Lier – pleasant and anxious to help. A few days later I supervised the loading of my jeep atop a flat car on the same train I would take to Purwokerto. The railroad personnel insisted that I attach one or more American flags to it so that Republican guerrillas still operating in the mountains of West Java would not shoot it up. And so very early on the morning of 24 August the train, with my flag-decked jeep on a flat car and me in a coach, left Batavia for Purwokerto.

We arrived there without incident late that night, with the local railroad officials giving me dinner in their mess and a cot in their dormitory. Some of them told me that they would soon be proceeding on to Yogyakarta with the Dutch army to "free the Sultan of Yogyakarta," and after looking at my jeep good naturedly assured me that, even if they had to lay some new track, they expected they'd get there before me. (It was surprising how many of the Dutch accepted the official line that the Sultan of Yogyakarta was a captive of the Republic and cut off from inhabitants of his principality, when in fact he was a dedicated supporter of the Republic and, unlike his counterpart the Sunan of Surakarta and many of the surviving aristocracy in and outside of Java, strongly opposed to any reassertion of Dutch power. That such a hereditary feudal leader would not welcome the sheltering return of the colonial administration simply did not fit the picture Dutch officials sought to project. In fact, it was the Sultan of Yogyakarta who even then was pioneering the Republic's progressive program for peasant empowerment in local administration.)

The next morning I reported to the office of the local Dutch army commander. He had heard from Batavia about me and lost no time in making clear that if I elected to drive my jeep the remaining ninety miles to Yogyakarta it would be at my own risk. Regulations required, he said, that I be provided with an armed escort to accompany me as far as the Dutch post on the Status Quo Line at Gombong, after which I would be on my own. In telling me that I only merited a corporal, the lowest possible rank for this purpose, I sensed he was trying to convey that he regarded me as of the least possible importance. But he was thoughtful enough to advise me to keep the three small American flags on my jeep fully visible, especially when traversing the approximately nine-mile stretch of uninhabited no-man's land lying to the west of Gombong.

My escort turned out to be a stocky and very feisty Ambonese corporal who had apparently already done some fighting and relished the opportunity for more. It should be noted that in the Netherlands Indies Colonial army, the KNIL, the Ambonese, and secondarily the Menadonese – both largely Christian – were regarded as the most martial and dependable by the Dutch, occupying a position roughly analogous to the Gurkhas in the British Indian army.

After I'd driven for about an hour we could hear gunfire off to the left and the corporal urgently indicated I should stop. He clambered out with his rifle and ran off through the wooded terrain towards the sound of the rifle fire. I felt very foolish sitting there alone in the jeep on this deserted road waiting for the corporal to return. In about a half hour he came back, breathing heavily, sweaty and grinning with satisfaction. He'd clearly used his rifle and seemed very pleased with himself. We drove on for about another half hour into the area that I reckoned must be the buffer no-man's land and heard another burst of firing, more sustained than previously. Again he ordered me to stop and disappeared into the foliage at the side of the road. I sat and sat most uncomfortably waiting for him to return and feeling very much abandoned on that quiet, empty road.

Finally, after what seemed to be an hour, but which was probably much less, he returned as before, again very sweaty and dusty, but brimming with satisfaction.

Again we encountered no traffic until we were close to the town of Gombong. He took me to a Dutch sentry post near the end of a bridge that spanned a small river, which here itself formed the Status Quo Line. A Dutch officer took the corporal's place and accompanied me to the middle of the bridge, at the other side of which was a post of the Republican army, the TNI (Tentara Nasional Indonesia). Walking quickly from the Republican side was a TNI officer, Lieutenant Sutrisno, who had clearly been expecting me. Meeting at the middle the two officers saluted and the Dutch officer yielded his seat to Lt Sutrisno, a pleasant and serious young man who fortunately had a fairly good command of English.

Sutrisno and I drove on into the territory of the Republic of Indonesia towards Kebumen, the largest town on the way to Yogyakarta. We were entering what in 1948 was the heartland of the Republic on Java. It was an area that stood physically isolated from the rest of Indonesia, for following their military campaign of mid-1947 the Dutch, in defiance of the United Nations-sponsored Renville Agreement, had erected a tight blockade around the area, as well as around Banten (at the extreme western end of Java) and the areas on Sumatra still controlled by the Republic. The military truce line (Status Quo Line) established by that agreement had become a carefully guarded Dutch barrier, not only to travel, but also to the import of food, cloth and medicine. With the Republic's residual territory in central Java normally severely deficient in the food it produced, and with many thousands of refugees having fled into it to escape the fighting and Dutch occupation of their areas, living conditions had become much harsher.

Many of the Dutch officials whom I'd met believed that maintenance of the pressure of this blockade would undermine the Republic's will to survive. Most of them seemed convinced that genuine nationalist feelings were limited to only a small proportion of the Indonesian population and were for the large majority weak and superficial. They argued that what they referred to as "the extremists" who ran the government of the Republic would soon be repudiated once the populace realized how the independence they championed had in practice translated into greater suffering.

When on 25 August we arrived at Kebumen, Sutrisno suggested we have lunch at a small Chinese restaurant on the edge of the town's *alun alun* (open central square). Parking the jeep a short distance from the door, we settled down to eat the rather modest fare available. As we ate, we could hear a growing clamor outside. A large and angry crowd had assembled, and Sutrisno began to look concerned. Then there was a pounding on the door of the restaurant, and he went out to talk to leaders of this rapidly swelling and increasingly vociferous multitude that had collected around my jeep and occupied the space between it and the restaurant. After a few minutes he came back in, looking very worried. The crowd, he said, thought that I was a Dutchman. He'd tried unsuccessfully to convince them otherwise, and they'd pointed to the flags on my jeep as proof of their contention. It was imperative, Sutrisno said, that I go outside and address this crowd to convince them before they became violent that I was American and not Dutch. As Sutrisno and I moved rapidly towards the door he explained that though the Republic's army through whose territory we had just passed knew what an American flag looked like, the populace in general did not. They had been taught that the double striped red and white flag of the Republic meant freedom, but that adding the blue third represented the Netherlands flag and Dutch control of their lives. They had seen that the flags on my jeep were red, white *and blue*, and for them that was proof that the jeep and I were Dutch intruders.

We opened the door and faced at least 500 obviously angry people who began to press closer. I had just told Sutrisno that my knowledge of Indonesian wasn't at all adequate to address a crowd, but I was now sufficiently frightened that my adrenaline surged and to my surprise I was able to summon up more of the language than I thought I knew. Stumbling through an attempt to differentiate the Dutch and American flags, I pointed out the crucial difference of the stars on the American flag, and then moved on to a simplistic, but rousing comparison of the American and Indonesian anticolonial revolutions.

The crowd now became attentive and much quieter, its angry face soon softening. When I concluded my desperate speech, arm outstretched in the revolution's Merdeka (Freedom) salute and loudly pronounced that powerful word, the transformation was complete. Providentially the crowd's hostility vanished and there was loud applause. Sutrisno, who apparently had been just as worried as I was, beamed at me in congratulatory approbation. Feeling very lucky, but weak and shaken, I hoisted myself into the jeep and we continued on the way to Yogyakarta.

The road passed by the massive ninth-century Buddhist monument, the Borobudur, where the custodian was so pleased to see a visitor that he sent his son up a coconut tree to fetch us two of its nuts and lopped off the tops so we could quench our considerable thirst. Driving on we passed only one automobile, but as we came closer to the city soon began to encounter an increasing number of the ox carts and bicycles that constituted its almost exclusive means of transport. As we were entering the city there was increasing pedestrian traffic. Most of the people looked thin and undernourished, with many clad in rags or burlap cut from gunny sacks. They stopped and stared in sheer disbelief at this jeep-borne foreigner with his strange flags flying. Soon there was the wail of sirens and two planes flew low over the main road we were on, and we dutifully pulled over to the side until the sirens stopped. Sutrisno seemed unconcerned but a little annoyed, explaining that this had been one of numerous irregularly held air-raid exercises designed to prepare the public for possible Dutch air attacks. Chuckling softly, he told me that these mock raids made use of almost the entire viable Republican airforce – namely three old Japanese Zeros.

We drove close to the center of Yogyakarta past its main thoroughfare, Malioboro (a corruption of "Marlborough," the name given it by Britain's Sir Stamford Raffles early in the nineteenth century), until we came to a quiet little street, Terban Taman. Here at number 8a was a government guest house containing three bedrooms, one of which had been reserved for me. Next door was a house of similar size reserved for the infrequent visits of United Nations personnel to Yogyakarta, mostly military observers largely concerned with noting truce violations, especially across the ceasefire line. (Most United Nations personnel who entered the Republic were housed in bungalows in the more salubrious climate of the old Dutch hill station of Kaliurang at an elevation of about 3,000 feet on the slopes of the largely dormant Merapi volcano some twenty miles to the north.)

My arrival in the Republic roughly coincided with that of Merle Cochran, the new American representative on the UN's Good Offices Committee, who had arrived in Batavia on 9 August 1948, and that of Musso, the prewar Communist leader, who reached Yogyakarta from Moscow on 11 August.

Active in the Indonesian Communist party in the early 1920s, Musso fled to Moscow at the time of the 1926–7 Communist uprising. After eight years of exile in the Soviet Union he had returned briefly to the Netherlands East Indies in 1935 where he sought rather unsuccessfully to establish a Communist underground movement in Surabaya. Since then he had lived rather uneventfully in Moscow with no apparent contact of any significance with what was left of the Indonesian Communist movement. Now, in August 1948, the Soviet leadership presumably thought the time ripe to send him back once more to Indonesia. He flew back via Prague, where he met up with Suripno, a young member of the Indonesian Communist Party, who ostensibly served as his secretary. Together they then flew on to New Delhi where they took a plane, recently purchased by the Republic, to Padang in Sumatra, from where after a stay of about a week they continued on to Yogyakarta.

Musso's return, it should be noted, also followed Moscow's shift from the 1935 Dmitrov Doctrine, with its emphasis on Popular Front anti-Fascism to the new, 1947, "two camp" Zhdanov Doctrine. Though arguing that socialist and capitalist systems could co-exist, Zhdanov held that the world was divided between two camps: an "imperialist anti-democratic camp" led by the United States, and a "democratic anti-imperialist camp" led by the Soviet Union. The new doctrine was still largely Eurocentric in orientation, often being regarded as a Soviet riposte to the Marshall Plan. As Ruth McVey notes in her classic study, *The Soviet View of the Indonesian Revolution*,[6] "The implications of the two camp doctrine for the Asian situation were not worked out authoritatively" until the appearance of an article by E.M. Zhukov in the December 1947 official Soviet party journal

Bol'shevik. This was no call for revolution in colonies or ex-colonies, but it did argue for broad fronts of revolutionary elements led by local Communist parties. Zhukov bracketed Indonesia with Vietnam as places where Asian Communist parties were already embarked on this course.

In any case, this formula of a broad national front fitted well with the political organization that former prime minister Amir Sjarifuddin had sought to establish seven months before Musso's arrival, the Front Demokrasi Rakjat (People's Democratic Front). The two largest political parties, the Muslim Masjumi and the PNI (Partai Nasional Indonesia) had resigned from Amir's cabinet, together with the Sjahrir-led right wing of his own Socialist Party in protest over his having signed the Renville Agreement. In the face of these defections, Sjarifuddin concluded in mid-January 1948 that the only feasible coalition offering him a chance for recapturing the prime ministership lay in the building of a left-leaning national front based on a coalition of that majority of the Socialist Party that had not defected with Sjahrir and the then only slightly further left Communist and Labor parties, together with whatever other minor parties he could attract. It was Sjarifuddin's hope that the moderately left-leaning nationalist front (Front Demokrasi Rakjat, or Peoples' Democratic Front) that he now sought to build would marshal enough support to supplant the presumably temporary "business cabinet" that Sukarno had appointed Hatta to lead just after the January 1948 fall of Sjarifuddin's government. That this was not an unreasonable expectation is suggested by the fact that both Sjarifuddin's outgoing cabinet and its two immediate precursors led by Sutan Sjahrir had been *Sayap Kiri* (Left Wing) coalitions.

Following Indonesian disappointment with the United States over its partisanship in favor of the Dutch in the implementation of the Renville Agreement, there is no doubt that the actions of the Soviet Union on the Security Council of the United Nations – in general strongly favoring the position of the Republic over that of the Netherlands – significantly reinforced the tendency of many Indonesians to look more favorably on the Soviet Union and, for increasing numbers of them, on the Indonesian Communist Party (PKI) as well. And it is clear that this tendency was accelerated when the PKI moved during the spring of 1948 from its erstwhile relatively moderate variant of nationalism (certainly more willing to compromise with the Netherlands than parties at the center and on the right of the political spectrum) to a much less compromising stance similar to that previously taken by the independent nationalist communist Tan Malaka and his followers. For the more Soviet-oriented PKI this involved a clear repudiation of the same Renville Agreement it had originally supported. In making this shift, the Communist Party and its ally the smaller Labor Party had associated themselves with the vanguard of a broad shift in popular political sentiment that by mid-1948 had swelled into a mounting tide. And as the Republic's population endured the increasingly harsh consequences of the economic blockade that the Dutch maintained in defiance of the terms of the Renville Agreement, the power of this tide increased. Despite the generally poor quality of their intelligence on Indonesia, Soviet leaders could scarcely miss the magnitude of this development and fail to realize that if there were to be a propitious time for them to risk involvement in Indonesia this was it. And thus it was not simply fortuitous that Moscow should decide that this was the appropriate time to send Musso (Figure 1.5) back to Indonesia.

When I myself arrived in Yogyakarta, I was fortunate to be quartered in the government guest house, for while I lived there the other two bedrooms were occupied by a series of very interesting people representing a whole range of political positions, and I could not help but learn a lot from most of them. Indeed, we could not easily escape one another, for we all ate breakfast, and most of our other meals, at the little house's single dining table. The provenance of my house- and table-mates ranged widely. The two that were already ensconced when I arrived I overlapped with longest and came to know particularly well.

The first of these was Raden Suripno (Figure 1.6), soon to become a member of the Indonesian Communist Party's Politbureau. Suripno had arrived in Yogyakarta shortly before me, escorting Musso from Prague in his return journey from the Soviet Union. Suripno had just initialed on behalf of the Republic a consular treaty with Soviet representatives in Prague. He was clearly something of an independent maverick among Indonesian

Figure 1.5 Musso

Figure 1.6 Suripno

Communists, taking evident pride in this, and he was surprisingly open with me in discussing long-term Indonesian Communist expectations. Like most leaders of the still rather small Indonesian Communist Party, he was from an aristocratic family, his father having been Bupati (Regent) of Klaten, a town between Yogyakarta and Surakarta. He was well educated and had served in the underground in Holland during the war. A man of slight and graceful figure, Suripno's aristocratic mien was enhanced by an attractive birthmark in the middle of his forehead that looked very much like a slightly elongated Indian caste mark.

My other housemate was John Coast, a highly intelligent British socialist who during the war had been imprisoned by the Japanese in Singapore and obliged to work on their "Railway of Death," connecting Siam and Burma, and had written a book about that experience, with that title. After a short postwar stint with the British Foreign Office, he had returned briefly to Siam and then gone on to Indonesia to work on English language materials for the Republic's Ministry of Foreign Affairs. Later he was to write a book about his experiences in the Republic, *Recruit to Revolution* (published by Christopher's in London in 1952). Regarding himself as a social democratic member of the Labour Party, he had while working in the Foreign Office been a good friend of the redoubtable Irishwoman, Dorothy Woodman, the genial, motherly head of the anticolonial Union of Democratic Control. It was under her wing that he had met and begun friendly debates with Suripno and had developed his interest in Indonesia. It has occurred to me that Coast may have been a British intelligence operative; if so they could not have picked an abler man. But they also could not have picked a man truly dedicated to that career, for a few years after the revolution he emerged as a successful London impresario and arranged for the first postwar tours of Balinese dancers to England and the United States.

When I arrived, Suripno and Coast had already been engaged for several days in good-natured, though sometimes a bit heated, exchanges at the dinner table over their not too great ideological differences and had clearly come to respect each other. Sitting between them at the table as they debated their ideas was a fascinating experience for me.

Since my main purpose was to write a doctoral dissertation, it had been decided that my housing arrangements should be made through the Ministry of Education, headed by Ali Sastroamidjojo, one of the leaders of the PNI (Indonesian Nationalist Party). About my height but heavier, and with a mustache, he was of a sober and serious mien. He had received his university education in the Netherlands and though regarded as a bit vain and prickly was generally well respected. He had a protégé, Raden Suwanto, who had received a fellowship for a year's graduate study at Yale through the sponsorship of Raymond Kennedy, a professor of sociology there with an interest in Indonesia. The fellowship was primarily for tuition and Ali Sastroamidjojo, correctly concluding that the small sum available for Suwanto's living expenses would be inadequate, asked me by how much it would have to be supplemented per month to ensure that Suwanto would be able to live tolerably comfortably. I thought that another $150 would be sufficient, and Ali promptly suggested that if I would supply that amount it could be used to pay for my room and board at the guest house. This seemed reasonable to me, and that was the bargain that quite amicably we struck.

After escorting me to Yogyakarta, Lt Sutrisno remained worried by our experience at Kebumen, and, wanting to keep me out of trouble, asked me whether now that we were inside the Republic I would mind relinquishing one of my jeep's American flags and flying a Republican one in its stead. I readily agreed, and the next morning we set out to buy the cloth necessary to construct a small Indonesian flag. We needed just two small pieces of red and white cloth, Sutrisno's wife having volunteered to sew them together. But so severe was the shortage of cloth that, even though I was prepared to pay a premium price, we had to scour most of the Chinese shops and the market before we could find the necessary pieces of red and white cloth, each a little larger than a man's handkerchief. Sutrisno's wife kindly stitched them together, and that afternoon we set out to find a blacksmith who could mount small steel poles on each of the jeep's two front fenders to serve as staffs for the American and Indonesian flags we wished to mount (Figure 1.7). Though it was Friday afternoon we were soon able to find a blacksmith willing to do business.

Figure 1.7 Sutrisno with my jeep

And so right on the heels of my adventure in Kebumen I encountered a second example testifying to the fact that Indonesian nationalism was anything but superficial and confined to a small elite. The wizened old blacksmith was prepared to get to work promptly on the jeep, and for a price that Sutrisno thought was reasonable. But he attached two conditions: the Indonesian flag would have to occupy the place of honor on the right front fender, with the flag staff for the American flag relegated to the left fender; moreover, he insisted that the staff bearing the Indonesian "red-and-white" flag would have to be ten centimeters taller than that flying the American "stars and stripes." I readily agreed, appreciating that there could hardly have been a more precisely calibrated measure of Indonesian nationalist sentiment.

As I later drove around inside the Republic with my two fraternal flags flying it soon dawned on me that, whether I liked it or not, my old jeep was serving as a vivid symbol of American backing of the Republic – though regrettably much less than actually existed. I later learned that this symbolism was not appreciated by senior American officials in Batavia, especially Merle Cochran, the US member of the United Nations Committee of Good Offices (and a little over a year later the first US ambassador to Indonesia after it had won its independence). And this flag flying, understandably, angered Dutch officials and helped account for the speed with which they arrested me and confiscated my jeep when they attacked Yogyakarta four months later. Also angering them, as I later discovered, were the stories I began cabling to Overseas News Agency beginning about a month after my arrival. For the conditions I found within the Republic were very different from what the Dutch were describing to the outside world and it was inevitable that my reporting reflected this.

The evidence of a severe cloth shortage in the Republic was reinforced a few days after I arrived in Yogyakarta when I called on Mohammad Natsir, Minister of Information, to register as a correspondent and discuss my research interests. He seemed genuinely pleased in my having been able to get into the Republic and seriously interested in my proposed research. A prominent leader of the progressive "Religious Socialist" wing of the Republic's largest Islamic political party, the Masjumi, this modest, soft-spoken, and very serious cabinet minister wore a shirt that was eloquent testimony to the severe cloth shortage in the Republic, scrubbed clean but mended in more places than I could count. His reputation for personal integrity and incorruptibility was well represented in that shirt, which I learned was the only one he possessed and had to be washed daily. That this was the case was driven home for me about a week later when I arrived at his office in the midst of a small celebration centered on his being presented with a new shirt, his second, for which his little office's staff had taken up a collection. They explained to me that he was the only cabinet minister who was down to only one shirt, and that, for the sake of his dignity and that of the office, they had pooled funds to get him a new shirt. I doubt very much that anyone else of cabinet rank had been reduced to a single shirt, but that was also the case with Professor Djokosutono, head of the Political Science and Law Faculty at the Republic's nascent Gadja Madah University. A confidant of Sukarno, renowned for being able to quote verbatim long passages from the writings of a multitude of Western political philosophers, he had a single shirt, which he reserved for important occasions, and always received me, as did some others, in his pajamas.

The reports I sent back to the United States were influenced by a force to which the Dutch had been largely oblivious – the depths and spread of nationalist feeling among the Indonesian population, both within and outside the Republic. That it was widespread even in the Dutch-controlled areas became clear to me when, after my stay in the Republic, I visited them. But within the area controlled by the Republic it was prevalent and strong, as my experience with the crowd in Kebumen and with the old blacksmith had demonstrated. Dutch wishful thinking tended to minimize its force, but it was much too strong for their military and economic power to break.

My appreciation of the power of this nationalism and the effectiveness of the Republic's leaders in awakening it was reinforced when a few weeks after my arrival in Yogyakarta I witnessed President Sukarno speak before a huge crowd in the city's large public square. I had been unaware until shortly before that he would make this address, for I don't recall any notice in the local papers. But the people knew about it and streams of many thousands were making their way to the field as I approached it. I had heard that Sukarno was an eloquent orator, but I was totally unprepared for the extent of his rapport with that crowd. He had a sort of magnetic charisma that quickly established a bond with it. He modulated his voice skillfully, used gestures at just the appropriate places in the rhythm that he developed, and within a few minutes the crowd seemed silently to interact with him. He spoke of self-respect, dignity and independence from the Dutch and seemed to direct a current of electricity into the crowd, which responded as if it were a magnetic field. As he spoke he developed a rhythm which rose into a powerful ultimate crescendo. I later learned that he traveled through much of the Republic making such speeches and, in the process, giving his audiences the feeling that they were part of an historical enterprise predestined for success. It was as if he was a heart pumping oxygen into and animating the Indonesian body politic. This was a capacity that only partially diminished as he grew older. I well remember the last time I heard him speak. It was in Manila in August of 1963 before a colloquium of approximately a thousand initially blasé and cynical University of the Philippines students. Following the same technique I had witnessed before the citizens of Yogyakarta and peasants from the surrounding countryside fifteen years earlier, he swept those Philippine students along into an exuberant standing ovation, that afterwards I discovered had been a stunning and somewhat incomprehensible surprise for them.

Though Sukarno was clearly pre-eminent in his ability to engage the Indonesian populace in a nationalist orientation, there were, of course, other Republican leaders as well who contributed importantly to this process. Amir Sjarifuddin, head of the Socialist Party and prime minister after Sjahrir, being regarded next to Sukarno as the ablest orator. (Hatta was known as a relatively pedestrian public speaker except when he became angry, as during the Madiun rebellion.) Indeed, arousing of nationalist sentiment by the country's political leaders, whether through their writings or oratory, had been going on for some four decades, despite persistent, and often very harsh, Dutch efforts to control the process. These cumulative efforts had prepared the soil well for the culminating post-World War II phase of the struggle for independence. Without this perduring political engagement of the Indonesian populace by the nationalist leadership and the essential political foundation this constituted, the Indonesian revolution could not have succeeded.

All this renders rather absurd the specious retrospective dichotomy, so prominent in the discourse of later years, of diplomacy versus armed struggle as the factor paramount in the success of the revolution. It was, of course, both, and these two factors were mutually complementary and inter-dependent. But this simplistic dual focus – later argued so vigorously by some scholars and especially by spokesmen of the Indonesian army – tended to obscure or trivialize a crucial third factor upon which each was depen-dent: namely, the political awakening and engagement of the populace by several generations of nationalist leaders culminating with Sukarno and his political colleagues in the immediate postwar years. It was this factor to which proponents of both schools often tended to attach too little weight, or, especially in the case of some proponents of the priority of military struggle, take for granted or even dismiss. Especially was such an attitude true of Suharto and his supporters in their blatant rewriting of history and their effort to build up his legitimacy while denigrating that of Sukarno.

The nationalism that was so widespread in the Republic was not simply political in orientation. And it certainly could not be understood as being confined to a forceful assertion of independence from the Netherlands. The power of that river that the Dutch had for so long attempted to dam, channel and control was also infused with a powerful urge for socioeco-nomic reform. This and the goal of political independence were complementary and intertwined. But the strength of Indonesian nationalism and the sense of shared purpose that underlay it cannot, I believe, be under-stood without greater attention to its goal of social justice than has usually been accorded it by both Indonesian and Western chroniclers.

Here it should be noted again that the political cast of almost the whole spectrum of Indonesian political parties during the struggle for indepen-dence was in varying degrees socialist. For most politically conscious Indonesians, capitalism was equated with colonialism. The widespread antagonism to capitalism engendered by the weight of Dutch colonial economic exploitation had done much to prepare the way for socialist orientations among most nationalist leaders. A majority of them espoused some variant of socialist philosophy, and many, whether conscious of it or not, were influenced by elements of Marxism. Even more regarded Lenin's simple and easily grasped concept of imperialism as applicable to colonial economies such as the Netherlands had run in Indonesia.

Only a small minority of the Republic's socialists regarded themselves as Communists and they were split between the relatively small Soviet-oriented Communist Party that had been a minor member of the Left Wing (Sayap Kiri) coalitions and the more strongly nationalist followers of the veteran nationalist communist Tan Malaka, whose followers were mostly members of the equally small, socioeconomically more radical Murba (Proletarian) party. The large generally politically left-of-center PNI (Partai Nasional Indonesia) incorporated a widely variant group of socialists, with its eclectically Marxist-leaning left wing constituting its strongest component. The Islamic Masjumi, the Republic's largest political party, was during the revolution most strongly influenced by its modernist wing whose most prominent leaders, Sjafruddin Prawiranegara and Mohammad Natsir, regarded themselves as "religious socialists."

Although, during the revolution, I felt that some leaders' professions of egalitarianism were often heavily paternalistic in character, nevertheless to one degree or another that idea did seem to inform the concept of independence that all the Republic's leaders held. To be sure some leaders, such as Tan Malaka, were much more strongly wed to egalitarian goals than others, but never did I find it absent from leaders, at whatever level, that I encountered. And, as in other exploited colonial economies, it was almost inevitable that there would be among most Indonesian nationalists a strong reaction against the capitalist system through which that exploitation was carried out. The pattern of Dutch colonial rule, though immensely profitable to the Netherlands, gave little scope for the indigenous population to benefit from its process – considerably less than, for instance, British rule in India or American rule in the Philippines. Certainly the Dutch system of economic exploitation left a relatively much smaller proportion of the native population beneficiaries of their system, and only a very few Indonesians could be said to have had or been given scope to develop a vested interest in capitalism.

Dr Sukiman Wirjosandjojo was the Masjumi's chairman, then serving as minister of interior in Hatta's cabinet. In a long discussion I had with him on 7 November he emphasized that the Masjumi's social program was in consonance with the teachings of the Koran. The party was "against capitalism," but private property was to be protected – though within limits. "No one is to be allowed a plot of land when his neighbors have none," and

> to ensure social justice the Islamic laws of charity must be lived up to. In agriculture, social justice is to be achieved through *Zakat* (alms tax,

tithe). The means of credit should be in the hands of the state. Small-scale enterprises should be left in private hands, but basic industries as well as the means of transportation and communication should be nationalized, and what capitalist enterprise remains should be in the hands of the state.

Sukiman then proceeded to analyze the composition of the Masjumi's leadership. There was the "progressive wing" of the party made up of intellectuals (among whom he numbered himself, a medical doctor) and which included those who identified themselves as "religious socialists." And there were the "religious leaders," incorporating the *kiayi* (religious teachers). He went on to say that

> these religious leaders mostly come from what might be termed the indigenous middle class, and thus in the same representatives there tend to be associated the interests of the religious leader and the small trader and larger landowners, comprising together a group that is in a social sense the least progressive.

Dr Sukiman felt that with respect to social objectives the Masjumi could best cooperate with other parties that had a religious basis, the Christian (Protestant) and Catholic parties. But, he said that there was also "a strong basis for cooperation with Sjahrir's Indonesian Socialist Party – certainly with its leadership," though he recognized that "there is a tendency with its rank and file membership to be somewhat anti-religious."

Musso's sudden and quite unheralded arrival in Yogykarta on 11 August had meant that Amir Sjarifuddin, then heading the coalition of left-wing organizations making up the Sayap Kiri (Left Wing), had had to decide almost immediately whether to invite Musso to team up with him or run the risk of having to compete with a man who, whatever his limitations, had a reputation as a prominent nationalist and came with the apparent blessing of the Soviet Union – a perception which Musso certainly did not deny. Musso was, after all, a seasoned Communist, who, despite some errors of judgment in the past, still enjoyed considerable prestige as a nationalist leader. In any case, apparently Musso and Sjarifuddin felt the need of each other to advance their own political fortunes, and soon after Musso's arrival they moved towards a marriage of convenience, working together to shape into one powerful political party the majority remnant of Sjarifuddin's Socialist Party, the Communist Party and its ally the Labor Party.

Musso lost no time in denouncing the Renville Agreement, and this meant that Sjarifuddin was under even more pressure to abandon it himself. Especially was this so because he saw no prospect of any change in American policy towards the Netherlands–Indonesian dispute, particularly given the initial clearly evident partiality towards the Dutch position adopted by the new American appointee to the UN's Good Offices Committee, Merle Cochran. Indeed, Cochran's arrival in Indonesia in mid-August 1948 strongly reinforced the feeling of most of the Republic's leadership that reliance on the United States was futile and made the Soviet Union, and its pro-Republic stance in the United Nations, look all the better.

The conversations I'd had with Sjahrir in New York and Batavia had apparently given him confidence in me that he had passed on to some of his lieutenants in Yogyakarta – especially Ali Budiardjo, Subadio Sastrosatomo and Dr Sudarsono – with all of whom I quickly developed a friendly relationship. Apparently because of this and the reputation I was gaining as a "progressive American" sympathetic to the Republic in its struggle with the Dutch, I found myself within a few days of my arrival in Yogyakarta thrust into the tense matter of possible fusion between Amir Sjarifuddin's Socialist Party and the Indonesian Communist Party (PKI).

Despite Sjahrir's having withdrawn his supporters from the Socialist Party (PS), still headed by Amir Sjarifuddin (Figure 1.8), to form his own Indonesian Socialist Party (PSI), his major lieutenants, Subadio Sastrosatomo, who was to become one of my close friends, and Ali Budiardjo, apparently still felt considerable warmth towards Amir. They

Figure 1.8   Amir Sjarifuddin

believed that his bitterness over what he saw as an American betrayal over Renville was pushing him unnecessarily close to Musso and a fusion of his Socialist Party with the Communist Party (PKI). These young adherents of Sjahrir were deeply worried over the fact that Amir was known to be in the process of deciding whether or not to fuse his large Socialist Party with the relatively small PKI, now headed by the recently arrived Musso, and the even smaller pro-PKI Labor Party led by the Communist Setiadjit. They seemed to think that having the credentials of a "progressive American" I might be able to help convince Amir that belief in the prospect of a more even-handed American policy need not be abandoned and that he should not take the plunge of fusion with the Communist Party and implicit reliance on the Soviet Union. Although I certainly did not feel adequate to even attempting this mission, I agreed to try. And so on 27 August I went to Amir Sjarifuddin's house to meet him in his office there.

I'd never before met Sjarifuddin and was surprised at the warmth of the reception he gave me. He was relaxed and friendly. I declined the cigar he offered me (no other Indonesian ever offered me one), and on his initiative we immediately began a most intense discussion about American politics – a subject in which it was evident he was very seriously interested and surprisingly knowledgeable. It was clear that he had been hugely disappointed at the American role in the non-implementation of the Renville Agreement. He gave me the impression of hoping against hope that the United States would shift its position back to the one more supportive of the Republic that he had counted upon, but that he didn't regard this as likely. He had been closely following the upcoming American presidential election, and on the basis of what he'd read and heard had concluded that Thomas Dewey, the Republican candidate, would win. This, he thought, portended no improvement in American policy towards Indonesia and he seemed to want me to assess his conclusion.

That Dewey was likely to win the election was, I knew, the conventional wisdom in the United States, and I had to agree with him as to this likelihood and the probability that this would not portend a shift in Washington's policy to one less favorable to the Netherlands. And on the basis of Truman's record in the Indonesian–Dutch dispute it was clear that Amir didn't think that his re-election would do anything to improve the American role, much as he clearly hoped for that. He then talked of his great admiration for Franklin Roosevelt and asked me when I thought that the progressive forces for which he stood could be expected to come back to power. Believing full well this would not be possible before the succeeding election four years hence, I told him that. I vividly remember the drawn look on his face and the helpless gesture he made with his hands, as he indicated that had been his own assessment and concluded: "That will be too late."

Two days later, on 29 August, Sjarifuddin made a public pronouncement that he had evidently been moving towards during the previous week – his

Socialist Party would merge with the Communist and Labor parties. In publicly teaming up with Musso, Sjarifuddin announced that he himself had been member of the underground Communist Party since 1935 when he had returned to Indonesia and joined the Communist underground organization in Surabaya.

This latter claim, I was soon to find, was not believed by many politically knowledgeable Indonesians, including Hatta, Sjahrir and Sukarno. When I queried them about it in 1948 and 1949, none of them believed that Sjarifuddin had ever been a Communist. They pointed out that in the prewar years many non-Communist nationalists had at various times worked together with the Communists, whether pro-Soviet or those refusing alignment with Moscow, such as Tan Malaka's strongly nationalist Communist group. A willingness to work with Communists towards the common goal of national independence, they insisted, did not transform non-Communists into Communists. And they quite appropriately pointed to the example of anti-Fascist national front governments in years just before the outbreak of World War II in Western Europe. They believed Amir had been shaken by the unexpected outcome of his reliance on Renville and the loss in his political stature this had entailed. And they saw him as panicked by the unexpected arrival of Musso and the challenge he represented to Sjarifuddin's own leadership of the left wing in the Republic's politics – an ascendancy, it should be noted, that had already been diminished by the defection of Sjahrir and his followers from the Socialist Party. In their view, protection of his leftist credentials from the competition of Musso and the sudden change of events, combined with political expediency calculated to deny Musso too strong a competitive advantage, prompted Sjarifuddin to make this public claim.

In my talks with Hatta, he insisted that Sjarifuddin was "too religious to be a real Communist." If he was to be considered a Communist, "it must be a new kind of communism," Hatta said. I later found that Dr Frank Graham, the previous US representative on the UN's Committee of Good Offices and the American who had come to know Sjarifuddin best, would not tolerate the proposition that he was a Communist. In buttressing this conviction Graham mentioned, among other things, his experience during the Renville negotiations of pacing the deck of the ship of that name aboard which the negotiations were conducted. One night about 2 a.m., he recalled, he had observed light coming from one of the cabins he passed. Upon quietly looking through the window he saw Sjarifuddin reading from a Bible open before him. Sjarifuddin, he insisted, though often seen with his Bible during the day could hardly have expected a curious deck stroller looking in his window at that time of night.[7] Hatta, who during this period saw Sjarifuddin as his major political rival, was subsequently bitterly angry at General (then Colonel) A.H. Nasution for what he regarded as his responsibility, along with Colonel Gatot Subroto, in having Sjarifuddin executed during the Madiun rebellion without benefit of a trial.

Of all the senior leaders with whom I discussed Amir, it was Sukarno who seemed to me to be most empathetic and to appreciate best the relevant past background and immediate context that now shaped his actions. This was consistent with Sukarno's actions during the Japanese occupation when at some risk to himself he intervened with the Kempeitei to have Sjarifuddin, who had played some role in the anti-Japanese underground, released from prison.

On 5 September several of the university students whom I'd met dropped by to ask me whether I'd like to accompany them to the hall where the Indonesian Federation of Students had invited the recently arrived Musso to speak. The hall was overflowing with students anxious to hear for the first time from this controversial and semi-mythical Communist nationalist from the prewar period. The students were very attentive and polite and keenly followed what he had to say. He spoke with a strong voice and exuded a warm and avuncular personality. But he was no Sukarno. And though he had serious things to say, most of his speech struck the students as rather pedestrian. And from time to time he was discomfited by the subdued laughter of a few of them, for the Indonesian he spoke was well out of date and flawed by a number of expressions that betrayed his vintage. But he certainly held their attention, especially during the question period at the end.

Musso began with a long eulogy of Soviet Russia, particularly emphasizing what he claimed to be increasing Soviet economic production in comparison to that of Britain and the United States. He maintained that frequent economic crises in the United States had diminished production. This, he said, was a key to understanding present Russian foreign policy. It did not want war and was confident that in a war with the United States it would win, but it preferred that if war came it would come later, for every day Russia through the Communist system became economically stronger and its production increased. On the other hand, he said, the United States, because of production based on profit and recurring economic crises, would suffer a steadily decreasing production.

Musso then went on to urge that Indonesia consummate the consular treaty that Suripno had just initialed while both were in Prague. "This would mean Russian recognition of the Indonesian Republic and would make Indonesia's international position much stronger." He said he couldn't say exactly what Russian material help would be forthcoming, but was certain that it would be important. In the present world, he said, a country cannot stay neutral; it must choose between the United States and Russia. "Obviously a nation, such as Indonesia, that is fighting imperialism cannot side with an imperialistic power; it must align itself with the forces fighting against imperialism, and that means Russia."

Then moving on to conditions within Indonesia, he said: "The social revolution in Indonesia must be accelerated; in particular all vestiges of feudalism must be liquidated." Then, referring to the fusion of the Communist Party, Labor Party and Amir Sjarifuddin's larger Socialist Party six days before, he went on to say that the Communist Party, of which he had now emerged as chairman, and these affiliates were now convinced that the Renville Agreement and its predecessor the Linggajati Agreement had both been mistakes. He said that if concrete advantages could be obtained he was willing to negotiate with the Dutch, but that it now appeared obvious that negotiations were a waste of time. "Freedom can only be won by fighting for it."

The present Hatta government, he concluded, should yield place to "truly representative, responsible government." The Communist Party was "not planning any coup d'état, but plans to gain power legitimately through organization," and "will not resort to force unless other groups begin such a course of action." He concluded by acknowledging that the Communists alone could not win the revolutionary struggle; other parties were necessary too, and that "above all students must participate in politics."

In the question period at the end of his speech it became clear that the students were well informed, and Musso was clearly taken aback by the probing he was subjected to. It was soon evident that the majority of students were not sympathetic to communism, and those that had heard him before or had read his statements were very much alert to inconsistencies in his arguments. (Thus, in a speech a few days before he had stated that only the Communist Party alone could win the revolutionary struggle.) He was hard put to give satisfactory answers relating to Tito's confrontation with the Cominform and the status of religion in Russia.

The effect of the United States' reneging on the interpretation of the Renville compromise that Indonesian leaders had been led to expect has generally been greatly underrated. There is no doubt that it significantly affected the course of a critical period in Indonesia's history. Not only did it bring about the collapse of Amir Sjarifuddin's government and convince him he had been betrayed by the United States, it could, I believe, be plausibly posited that, without this, the Communist-led Madiun rebellion might not have occurred.

2   Communism and the Republic

I arrived in Yogyakarta on 25 August 1948 during a period of considerable tension within the Republic produced by a number of factors, including the return of Musso and the alliance between him and Amir Sjarifuddin. Certainly the fusion of the Socialist and Communist parties at the end of August 1948 changed the political landscape, presenting the Hatta government with a more formidable challenger on the left. The consequent increase in political polarization together with the steadfast Dutch blockade, with its attendant mounting food shortage, and the Netherlands' continued intransigence against permitting the Renville-sanctioned plebiscite to take place in the areas overrun by Dutch forces the previous year, produced an atmosphere of increasingly palpable uneasiness within the Republic.

But the most important factor in this increasing strain was the unease induced by the continued unfolding of the "rationalization program" that Mohammad Hatta, Sjarifuddin's successor as prime minister, had introduced a few weeks after taking office on 31 January of that year. Hatta's fundamental purpose in initiating the program was to reorganize and streamline both the economy and armed forces into much more efficient entities in order better to confront Dutch power.

Inexorably advancing during the months after it was launched in March 1948, the rationalization process made sense for supporters of Hatta's government in terms of strengthening the Republic for a final struggle with the Dutch; but for Amir Sjarifuddin and his followers the program spelled a loss of power and influence within the military forces, and to a lesser, but significant, degree among the ranks of skilled labor as well. There is no doubt that by mid-September 1948 this program was leading to an increasing erosion of the strength of Sjarifuddin's Socialist Party and its allies within the military establishment – forced retirements, or their prospect, precipitating anxiety and finally a mounting alarm among their adherents. Although only modest progress had actually yet been made in the process of military rationalization, there was already great unease both in the few units that were actually undergoing demobilization and in those units rumored to be slated for imminent dissolution.

The second prong of Hatta's rationalization program focused on the civilian economy and the bloated and inefficient bureaucracy. The economy was clearly in desperate straits, having been further weakened as a consequence of the Dutch blockade and the necessity to support several hundred thousand refugees from the areas overrun by the Netherlands' military forces in mid-1947. Consequently for many in the Republic, especially among Hatta's supporters, it made good sense to reduce an unbearable economic burden, including a rapidly mounting monetary inflation, by trying to eliminate redundancy and inefficiency even if alternative jobs were not available for the displaced workers. This situation – even though it involved a process still largely on paper, or in Hatta's mind – was seriously unsettling for those likely to be affected, especially the politically conscious members of SOBSI (Sentral Organisasi Buruh Seluru Indonesia, or Central Organization of all Indonesian Labor), the Republic's major labor union federation, and one in which Sjarifuddin's Socialist Party and its ally the Labor Party held dominant influence.

During the spring of 1948 there had already been stirrings of discontent among cotton-field workers and processors in the Delanggu area of central Java, and it was believed that oilfield workers in Cepu and the railroad repair workers at the major repair yards in Madiun were apprehensive and restive. Indeed, by mid-September rationalization of the 6,000 man force of railroad workers living in the Republic's third most populous and largest industrial city (with certainly the largest concentration of skilled labor in the Republic) had been slated to get under way. Whether or not any members had actually been laid off by then is unclear, but it is reasonable to assume that some were worried and restless at the prospect. For civilian workers in general, the announcement by General Sudirman, commander-in-chief of the armed forces, that, if necessary, not only would the oil operations at Cepu and railroad operations at Madiun be militarized, but that this process might be extended to postal and telegraph workers, undoubtedly increased their level of anxiety.

Given this situation, especially among military units anticipating rationalization, it is understandable that when I asked the officer whom I regarded as the most politically knowledgeable member of the UN's small group of military observers stationed within the Republic what he regarded as the major cause for the Madiun rebellion, which broke out in mid-September, he unhesitatingly affirmed that he and his handful of colleagues saw it as the reaction to the rationalization program within the military.

During the first week of September 1948 I had three long and informative talks with my housemate, Suripno. I had the impression that he had been pleased to learn of my meeting with Sjarifuddin and was more comfortable in discussing matters with me as a consequence. In any case, it was evident that he wanted to. John Coast was absent, so that just the two of us sat at the table of the little house we shared. When we talked on 1 September,

Suripno briefly gave me an account of his diplomatic mission to Prague to meet with Soviet representatives in order to open up diplomatic relations with Moscow and of his trip back to Indonesia with Musso. Then he focused on the history of the Communist movement in Indonesia, stating among other things that Musso as well as Tan Malaka had opposed the abortive rebellion of the Communists in 1926–7. He was apparently aware of the dispute as to whether Sjarifuddin had previously been a Communist, and he emphasized that indeed he had been, and had joined the so-called "Illegal Communist Party" established in Surabaya by Musso on his brief return to Indonesia in 1935. Sjarifuddin, he claimed, had worked as a leader of the Communist underground from then on through the period of Dutch and Japanese control.

Suripno then stated that, following Japan's capitulation, the newly established Socialist Party which Sjarifuddin headed was in effect the Communist Party. It had been a mistake for it to fuse with Sjahrir's "revisionist Socialists" in November 1945, but when the pro-Sjahrir members defected in February 1948 to form the Indonesian Socialist Party, then the larger group making up Sjarifuddin's residual Socialist Party became once more Indonesia's authentic Communist Party. Its members, he said, infiltrated and took control of what was termed the "Communist Party," led by the discredited Jusuf, and, with the help of Setiadjit, a bona fide Communist recently returned from Holland, also took over the Labor Party (Partai Buruh).

With the Socialist Party of Sjarifuddin, Setiadjit's Labor Party and the reconstructed Communist Party (PKI) now all led by members of Sjarifuddin's Socialist Party, it had seemed silly, Suripno said, to have three Communist organizations masquerading as three different parties. It had therefore been concluded that it made sense to fuse them into just one Communist Party, and that process was what was now taking place. The Communists, he said, desired to keep their party small and select. Its current membership, he said, stood at only about 2,500 in Java and 500 in Sumatra, and in the fusion with these other parties the Communists desired to keep membership down. Consequently, of the approximately 60,000 members of Sjarifuddin's Socialist Party only about 30,0000 would be accepted as members of the newly constituted Communist Party. He emphasized that Indonesian Communists now recognized that the nationalist revolution – freedom from the Dutch – must be accomplished before there would be any possibility of introducing communism. "After the freedom of Indonesia has been established, then it may be that communism will take precedence over nationalism." In emphasizing this he seemed to be departing from Musso, who was advocating radical socioeconomic reform concurrent with the struggle for independence.

And I was struck the next day when I attended a session of the Working Committee of the KNIP (Komite Nasional Indonesia Pusat), the Republic's Parliament, that Prime Minister Hatta (Figure 2.1) made a major speech similarly insistent upon national revolution preceding social revolution. On

Figure 2.1 Vice President Mohammad Hatta

that occasion I had the good fortune of meeting General Sudirman, head of the Republic's armed forces, and incidentally a man opposed to military participation in this representative body (a far different position from that taken by General Suharto two decades later). Sjahrir, too, in the talks I had with him emphasized this same priority of national revolution preceding a social revolution – one which, it is interesting to note, Ho Chi Minh was concurrently holding to in Vietnam.

In this 2 September address Hatta, who had a reputation as a dull speaker, came close to an impassioned eloquence fueled by his anger at what he regarded as Musso's reckless advocacy of major socioeconomic change in the middle of a nationalist revolution. "In the present stage of our revolution," he emphasized, "we are engaged in our *national* revolution. Our present revolution is sure to break down midway if we allow elements of social revolution to creep into it." He admonished that "Even those who formerly quoted the maxims of Marx and Mao Zedong to remind us that we have not yet passed the stage of national revolution and that therefore the time had not yet come for a social revolution, these people have forgotten their own theories." Hatta also attacked Musso for advocating moving the Republic's foreign policy away from neutralist nonalignment with the great powers towards dependency on the Soviet Union, a position which Musso defended strongly in his speech to the Indonesian Student Federation just three days later. On 6 and 7 September Suripno and I continued our discussions. He first went into further detail concerning his diplomatic mission to Prague and flight back to Indonesia with Musso. He said that the Soviet government had ratified the consular treaty he had negotiated on 22 May but that the Hatta government had been dragging its feet on reciprocating. (I had learned that Hatta was doing so because he felt the Republic's ratification would infuriate the United States and bring it more solidly behind the Dutch.) I asked Suripno whether his talks with the Soviet representative in Prague had, as Musso and some other Indonesian Communists were alleging, led to a Soviet undertaking to provide material support to the Republic, even at the risk of breaking through the Dutch blockade. Without hesitation he responded that the Soviet representative had made no such assurance, and that the most he could promise was that, with a consular treaty signed, it would be possible to have trade relations, but that there had been no commitment that Soviet ships or planes would run the Dutch blockade. In effect, said Suripno, the Soviet representative had made no concrete promises regarding trade.

On 7 September, Suripno and I had our last talk. He gave no indication that he was about to join Musso and Sjarifuddin and a few other leaders of the newly fused party for a two-week speaking tour of central Java that would go as far east as Kediri and end in Madiun, some 75 miles from Yogyakarta. This time he seemed really eager to talk, as if he felt it important historically to explain to me his and the new party's position and expectations, with apparent assurance about the Communists' plans and expectations. He explained that the process of party fusion, reorganization and political education of its expanded membership would take some time – he didn't speculate exactly how long.

The party could be expected to oppose any further negotiations with the Dutch until after independence had been won. Party leaders anticipated a further Dutch military assault against the Republic in the near future and felt that this would be their great opportunity. They understood – correctly – that in the face of the next Dutch attack the Republic's leaders planned to evacuate to Sumatra, thereby abdicating, in their view, to the Communists as well as the Dutch. (The Communists were at this time believed by numerous well-informed Indonesians to have benefited from Amir Sjarifuddin's long period as minister of defense prior to the formation of the Hatta cabinet in early 1948. The Pesindo (Pemuda Sosialis Indonesia, Socialist Youth of Indonesia) troops, which were their only real military muscle, had been brought into this relationship by Amir. Some also believed that the Communists were now in a better position than the regular Republican military forces to wage guerrilla warfare against the Dutch because they knew the location of the majority of arms caches and ammunition dumps prepared in anticipation of a further Dutch attack.) The Communists, Suripno assured me, would assert a leading role in the guerrilla struggle against the Dutch, emerging more clearly as leaders of the revolution in a Java free of the Dutch.

Sometime that night or early the next morning Suripno, unannounced, left our house at Jalan Terban Taman, and I never saw him again. He had gone to join Sjarifuddin and Musso on their long-planned speaking tour of central Java.[1] This was part of the new Communist Party's effort to build up popular support and its effort to organize its now expanding membership after the fusion of the three left-wing parties. It was during this tour that the Madiun rebellion broke out, and that development, or at least its timing, clearly came as a surprise to Suripno as well as many of his colleagues, some of whom were picked up by the government very soon after the rebellion was under way. (It was because I had dwelt in the same house as Suripno that later, during the height of McCarthy's power, Merle Cochran, then America's first ambassador to Indonesia, charged that I had been close to the Indonesian Communists and therefore should be denied a passport for a return trip to Indonesia.)

I was surprised one morning soon afterwards to encounter numerous soldiers of the Republic's crack Siliwangi division, with their distinctive tiger-head shoulder patches, patrolling some of the streets in Yogyakarta, and I became increasingly aware during the second week of September that there were serious political disturbances and sporadic fighting thirty miles away in Surakarta, the Republic's second largest city. I had assumed, as apparently now did many of Yogyakarta's inhabitants, that the fighting involved primarily the pro-Tan Malaka Murba Party and other GRR – Gerakan Revolusi Rakjat (People's Revolutionary Movement) – elements, the pro-Sjarifuddin Pesindo (Socialist Youth) and the army's under-strength 5,000-man 4th (Senopati) division, the largest military unit slated for imminent demobilization under Hatta and Nasution's rationalization program. Though many in the capital at the time (and I, when writing my book *Nationalism and Revolution in Indonesia* in 1950) had thought the Senopati division and its commander, Colonel Suadi, to be on balance pro-Communist, this turned out not to be the case, and he was able to keep his unit largely neutral in this local power struggle.

The then seemingly irrational chaos in Surakarta at this time (which so far as I know has still not been satisfactorily analyzed by any scholar, whether a military or political specialist) was further complicated by the fact that Sukarno on 16 September, with Hatta's evident concurrence, had fulfilled a promise made a month earlier and released from imprisonment the most famous nationalist Communist leader, Tan Malaka, his lieutenant Sukarni, and Abikusno (head of the small Partai Sarekat Islam Indonesia), purportedly in the interest of national unity. These were three of the most important political leaders allegedly behind the political kidnapping of Sjahrir and several of his government associates in the spring of 1946, and they had been in jail ever since. (Five others charged with involvement in the plot – Dr Buntaran, Iwa Kusuma Sumantri, Subardjo, Pandu Wiguna and

Muhammad Yamin – had been released a month earlier.) Over the next few months I managed to have discussions with Abikusno, Subardjo and Sukarni, but unfortunately not with Tan Malaka. After trying to intercede on my behalf, Sukarni reported back that Tan Malaka trusted, and would meet with, no American.

What was politically most significant in their release was not, of course, that these men had allegedly led a failed coup against the government headed by Sjahrir. Rather, it was that two of the most prominent among them – Tan Malaka and Sukarni – were distinctly *nationalist* Communists with a firm record of opposition to any shade of doctrinaire alignment with the Soviet Union and thus stood in opposition to Musso and his pro-Moscow variant of communism. It was widely, and probably correctly, believed that they had been released with the expectation that, because of Tan Malaka's considerable prestige, he and these other prominent mostly non-Communist nationalists, would provide a significant counterweight to the evidently mounting popular criticism of the Hatta cabinet led by Musso and Sjarifuddin. The government did not acknowledge this, and in talking with me about the releases some seven months after the event, Sukarno merely told me that Tan Malaka and the others had been freed because there were "no grounds for prosecution. The prosecution had no case, so they had to be released. I felt it better that the government itself grant Tan Malaka his release rather than the Department of Justice say there was no case against him."[2]

Not until the morning of 19 September, while I was on a brief visit to Kaliurang to talk with some junior members of the UN's Good Offices Committee, did I learn that a rebellion had begun in Madiun on the night of 17 September, launched by what was termed "The Democratic Front Government" led by what was now being called the "PKI Musso" – the collo-quial designation of the product of the recently announced fusion of Sjarifuddin's Socialist Party and the Communist and Labor parties. I had just met for the first time with Merle Cochran, the American delegate on the UN's Committee of Good Offices for Indonesia, and was taking a walk with him, when Haji Salim, the Republic's foreign minister, fresh from an emergency meeting of the cabinet, breathlessly overtook us to report that the rebellion had broken out. Haji Salim went on to state that in Yogyakarta the army and police had been ordered to occupy the headquarters of all Communist orga-nizations and take their occupants into custody. It was evident that Cochran was every bit as surprised as I was at the outbreak of rebellion. He immedi-ately turned around and strode back, seemingly as fast as his considerable bulk would permit, to join his colleagues in the UN delegation's office.

It was apparent that Musso and Sjarifuddin and at least most other senior members of their newly amalgamated organization were equally surprised at the outbreak of the rebellion. Numerous intermediate and lower echelon members of that organization were, as Haji Salim had reported, promptly picked up by the army and police in Yogyakarta from their offices or homes there and, according to many, including Hatta, were not prepared for the Madiun coup.[3] As mentioned before, just a few days earlier, the senior members, including Musso, Sjarifuddin, Setiadjit (former head of the Labor Party) and Suripno (just appointed to head the foreign affairs section of the new Communist party's Central Committee) had embarked on a speaking tour through central Java. According to various estimates this tour was to have lasted between two and six weeks. It was regarded as the beginning of a campaign to build up political support for their new party, a process that was envisaged as lasting at least a few months. Their goal was to replace the Hatta government on the back of what they apparently believed would be a rising tide of public support.

In later discussing the matter with me, Hatta acknowledged that left-wing leaders held "key positions in the trade unions and a strong position among the peasantry," and he believed that, even before Musso's arrival, Sjarifuddin's earlier coalition planned "to put pressures on me through mass meetings and demonstrations to resign and reinstate Sjarifuddin" as prime minister. The leaders of the new left-wing coalition appeared to believe they could achieve this without resort to force, though there were some indications that they contemplated moving to rebellion if they were unsuccessful in replacing the Hatta government through peaceful means. If they were to choose rebellion, Hatta later told me, he had not expected them to act before some time in November.[4]

It must be emphasized that there was a widespread expectation in Yogyakarta, certainly not confined to the Communists, that the Dutch would soon mount an all-out military attack against the Republic, and that, for the reasons Suripno had expressed to me, the Communists would be left in a strong position to benefit from wearing the mantle of nationalist resistance. Even if the Dutch were not successful, damage to the Republic's administrative infrastructure and military capacity could advantage the new Musso–Sjarifuddin alliance.

Pending that expected denouement, whether the Communists took a peaceful route to displace the Hatta cabinet or whether they felt it necessary to resort to rebellion, they needed time, presumably at least a few months after the fusion of the three parties at the end of August, to win broader and more dedicated popular support. Everything being equal, that would seem to have been a reasonable calculation. But everything did not remain equal. Underestimated both in the Communists' plans to win power and in the expectations of the Hatta Government was the swiftness and strength of reaction to the Hatta–Nasution rationalization program – especially within the military, but also among the ranks of the small non-agrarian labor force. From the standpoint of Sjarifuddin and his supporters, the rationalization program within the military, quite understandably, seemed to have as its primary target the diminishment of their strength within the Republic's regular army and especially its allied militias (laskjars), most importantly the most reliable of them, the relatively elite Pesindo.

There were, then, three major concurrent developments that were of primary importance in precipitating the Madiun rebellion of September–October 1948. These were the rationalization program, especially within the armed forces; the escalating struggle for military ascendancy in Surakarta wherein the balance of power was being significantly affected by the military rationalization program; and the reorganization and expansion of the political bases of the tenuously coalesced parties led by Musso and Sjarifuddin – a process naturally viewed with some apprehension by Hatta and his supporters.

All of these served as triggers for the launching of rebellion, but undoubtedly the most important of these were the premature actions by military units panicked by increasing indications that they were slated for demobilization, together with pressure from labor groups threatened with loss of their relatively favorable standard of living.

Overall there is irony in the fact that the rebellion and the Republic's strong response to it constituted the major factor in shifting US backing away from the Netherlands in favor of the Republic. For once the government led by Sukarno and Hatta had put down the rebellion and shot its leaders,[5] it was no longer possible for the Dutch to make American officials and the US Congress believe – as previously many of them had – that most leaders of the Republic were under strong Communist influence and that their government was providing a bridge to an ultimately Communist Indonesia.

The Madiun rebellion had many other consequences for the Republic. Destruction of the Communists and Sjarifuddin's left wing of the Socialist Party begot a polarization and a shift to the right. This eliminated any prospects for the Indonesian revolution becoming more than a nationalist revolution, and increased the caution that Hatta, Sukarno and Sjahrir had already manifested before the rebellion broke out. Within the Republic's army, the loss of Sjarifuddin and the left-wing militias (the TNI Masjarakat and especially Pesindo) both weakened the TNI vis-à-vis the Dutch and also shifted its internal balance to the right. When Tan Malaka was murdered a few months later, this rightward tendency in both civilian and military spheres was further exacerbated. With the overall strength of its army undermined, especially its radical components, the Republic became more dependent on American support. This sapped its ability to resist Dutch pressure for negotiations, culminating in the Roem van Royen Agreement. The more that the shift in internal power grew at the expense of the left, the more the Republic's leaders felt they could not risk alienating the US by embarking on radical socioeconomic revolutionary change or resisting their pressure to reach a compromise agreement with the Dutch.

Within a couple of weeks of Suripno's departure I found the makeup and political coloration of the three-roomed government guest house in which I was staying considerable changed. My friend and housemate John Coast also departed in the single plane operated by the principal ad hoc blockade runner, rather grandly known as Pacific Overseas Airways, for that "airline's" base in Bangkok – a flight that took place without public announcement, and usually without public knowledge, every two or three weeks – and soon afterwards, his room was taken by another agreeable occupant. This was Hamid Algadri, an Indonesian of Arab descent from a prominent family of Pasuruan, a normally prosperous town some 20 miles southeast of Surabaya. A legally trained member of the Indonesian delegation to the Committee of Good Offices and a prominent member of Sjahrir's Indonesian Socialist Party, he had suddenly been brought from Batavia to be added to the Republic's office in Kaliurang at a time when its handful of cottages were already overcrowded with personnel from its American, Australian and Belgian representatives, their staffs and the committee's secretariat. The committee's venue alternated between Batavia and Kaliurang, standing at a cool elevation on the lower slopes of the 9,000 -foot Merapi volcano, less than an hour's drive from Yogyakarta. The full complement of the Good Offices delegations was now working in Kaliurang and those members who had liaison duties with the Republic's foreign office could best function if a room could be found for them in Yogyakarta. Hamid stayed on with me for about four weeks until we were captured together by the Dutch, and I came to know him well, a warm friendship that endured until his death at 86 in 1998.

The most dramatic change in housemates occurred about ten days after the outbreak of the Madiun rebellion and less than three weeks after Suripno's sudden departure. It was then that, ironically, the recently vacated room of this senior Communist Party official was assigned by the Republic's hard-pressed housing office to the man who was probably the first CIA agent to reach the Republic, Arturo Campbell, a churlish, self-important man who said he represented the US Treasury. Before being suddenly flown into Yogyakarta this squat, rotund 200-pounder had probably spent a month or more in Batavia, and it was clearly the sudden outbreak of the Madiun rebellion that had induced him to make this visit to Yogyakarta. At that time neither I nor Indonesian officials had heard of the recently launched CIA, but that he was an intelligence operative the Indonesians did not doubt. He saw a lot of Cochran while he was in Yogyakarta, my Indonesian friends informed me, and their strikingly similar obesity convinced some that they must be brothers. But he smiled less than Cochran and, by his blustering demeanor and self-important attitude, very quickly antagonized many Indonesians.

The fact that Campbell occupied a room next to mine clearly risked undermining the progress I had been making in convincing suspicious Indonesians that I was not an agent of the US State Department. Campbell had apparently come to learn while in Batavia that I had some knowledge of Indonesian politics and assumed that my fluency in the language was much greater than it actually was. And so he lost little time in informing me that he wanted me to assist him. When I declined and pointed out that I'd

Figure 2.2   Mt Merapi from Kaliurang

already had great trouble in disabusing people that I was a State Department employee he evidenced no understanding of my situation, asserting that since I was the only American in Yogyakarta I had "a duty" to assist him. When I persisted in my refusal to work with him he became visibly very angry and finally threatened to "report" me, whatever that meant. His threat was not an idle one, as I was to learn about a year later when my criticism of the policies of Merle Cochran brought him, by then the first US ambassador to Indonesia, to enlist Campbell in his successful effort to keep me from returning to the country.

I learned shortly after Campbell's departure that he'd finally had to settle for a young man from the Republic's foreign office to accompany him on his round of appointments. He was probably better off than if I'd done so, for this chap spoke considerably better English than I did Indonesian. But clearly the chemistry was no better, this interpreter telling me afterwards how much he resented Campbell's attitude of superiority and how outraged he felt when in accompanying him to Vice-President Hatta's office he witnessed Campbell offering Hatta funds in support of the Republic, which Hatta had promptly declined. I later learned that Campbell had made a similar offer to Sutan Sjahrir, which was also refused. Campbell seemed to have no appreciation of how acceptance of American financial support, especially in the overheated polarized political context then operative in Yogyakarta, would compromise the recipient.

On Campbell's second day in Yogyakarta I returned home to the house he now shared with me and Hamid Algadri to find a queue of junior officers of the Police Mobile Brigade stretching from the door of his room through the living/dining room out the front door and past the little porch. He was interviewing them, I soon learned from one of them who was a friend of mine, Male Wiranata Koesoemah, to determine their suitability to partici-pate in a special training program for police officers in the United States. He was obviously not happy at my observing this procedure, and as I walked into the house past the line bellowed out most unceremoniously: "I want to talk to you." Not long afterwards I learned why, when I found Hamid shaken and angry at a confrontation he had had a few hours earlier with Campbell when he caught the American in my room in the act of rummaging through my belongings. Campbell, he said, appeared flustered and embarrassed at being discovered, and as an excuse invoked the name of Major Brentel Susilo (in charge of intelligence for the city of Yogyakarta) as justification for his presence in my room. He said that Brentel had informed him that I was in contact with John Foster Dulles and he subjected poor Hamid to a long interrogation aimed at eliciting whatever information he might have concerning my relationship with Dulles. It was evident that the paranoid Indonesian intelligence officer had turned over to Campbell all the letters of mine he had confiscated, and these included one I'd sent to Dulles via his son who had been a close friend of mine in college.

If he'd had a better command of English and could have accurately trans-lated the letter, Brentel Susilo might have appreciated that, if it actually was read by Dulles, it could have been helpful to the Republic, for it presented the situation in the Republic very differently from what the Dutch were telling American officials. At any rate, since I'd never had occasion to mention Dulles to Hamid, he had no basis for telling Campbell about our relationship, even if he'd wanted to – which was decidedly not the case.

Many years later I learned from Male Wiranata Koesoemah's older brother Achmad that there was a second objective in Campbell's recruit-ment. In his opinion, that aim was as important, at least in the long run, as the program for flying young Police Mobile Brigade officers to the United States for police training. This was the selection of a smaller number to be flown there to study intelligence operations, with Indonesia's first post-independence intelligence organization stemming from this venture. (Then a major commanding a battalion in the Police Mobile Brigade which would soon after the Dutch attack of 19 December 1948 win fame for fighting its way back across the Status Quo Line through Dutch forces well into its old Preanger base area in West Java, Achmad was regarded as one of the most talented of the brigade's commanders.)

There was a series of other interesting transients occupying for brief periods the room where Suripno had stayed, including Dr Sudarsono, the Republic's ambassador to India and formerly minister of interior in Sjahrir's second cabinet (12 March 1946–2 October 1946) and several free-lance pilots. And, in fact, Campbell may not have been the first CIA agent to visit the Republic. I'm not absolutely sure of the date, but as I recall, the former OSS Major, Jim Thompson, preceded him. A much pleasanter and more intelligent man than Campbell, Thompson was believed by the Indonesians to be an American intelligence agent, and later he was widely regarded as having been with the CIA during his considerable postwar residence in Thailand and Laos, where he won fame for reviving the silk industry. (He disappeared and was presumably murdered in 1967 under mysterious circumstances while on a morning walk in the Malayan highlands.) He flew in through the Dutch blockade one day with a letter of introduction from my friend Lauriston Sharp, then a Cornell professor of anthropology doing research on rural Thailand. Ostensibly at least, Thompson's mission in Yogyakarta was to do for Javanese batik what he had done to revive the silk industry in Laos and Thailand, and we spent a pleasant evening together talking about the political situations in Thailand and Indonesia.

The Dutch blockade of the Republic was exercising ever greater hardship on the Indonesian population. Not only was cloth in short supply, but, of more critical importance, were medicines which the Dutch blockade rigorously shut out of the Republic. Almost directly across the street from my government guest house was the clinic of Dr Yap, Yogyakarta's only Western-trained eye specialist. (He was, I later discovered, highly regarded by his medical counterparts in Batavia.) Every morning a long queue began to form outside his door of people waiting to be treated. He explained to me that more than half of his many patients were going blind because of a dietary deficiency. Their deterioration and ultimate loss of eyesight could easily be remedied, he told me, if the Dutch would only permit him to import certain vitamin concentrates easily obtainable in Batavia. He had friends there who would be happy to purchase these, and the United Nations Good Offices Committee was quite prepared to fly these and small quantities of other medicines he needed in its occasional plane from Batavia. But the Dutch adamantly refused permission for them to be sent through their blockade. Despite his Dutch training Dr Yap had become very bitter towards them.

I, too, was bitter, not just towards the responsible Dutch officials but also towards the head of the Republic's military intelligence in Yogyakarta, the obtuse and paranoid Major Brentel Susilo. When I sought to arrange for the most critically needed medicines to be flown in by appealing to the American Friends Service Committee in Philadelphia, he confiscated my letter and refused to let me send it out. (My outgoing letter and the incoming medicines could have been carried by one of the occasional planes of freebooters from the Philippines that managed to break through the Dutch blockade every two or three weeks.) And so every day, because of this Dutch blockade of medicines more and more inhabitants of the Republic were losing their eyesight through no fault of their own other than their inability to get enough food. On a visit to a clinic I also discovered that where cotton bandaging was not critically necessary sterilized banana leaves were sometimes being substituted.

The only exception I was aware of where the Dutch permitted the import of medicines occurred about a month after I arrived in Yogyakarta when in something of a panic they suddenly themselves took the initiative and sent in inoculations against the bubonic plague which had manifested itself in Yogyakarta and which they presumably feared could easily cross the Status Quo Line into Dutch-controlled areas. I joined thousands of others assembled on successive days in a large field to await their turns to be injected by these Dutch-supplied inoculations against the plague.

There was also an acute shortage of doctors in the Republic. This was made very clear to me when, after suffering some of the usual internal upsets experienced by strangers to the tropics, I suddenly came down with a really major malady – tropical sprue. Caused, as I understood it, by a shortage of Vitamin B and B complexes in the diet, it began with a blistering of the mouth and throat that soon worked its way down into the stomach and intestines until one reached a point where it was impossible to absorb nutrition from the food one ingested. This I learned from one of the few well-trained physicians in the Republic, Dr Soetomo Tjokronegoro, a kind and caring doctor whom I'd been fortunate enough to meet soon after my arrival in Yogyakarta and who was good enough to come and see me when he had learned I was seriously ill. He explained that tropical sprue was a very serious proposition and that the Dutch usually sent cases as advanced as mine back to the Netherlands to recover. He readily perceived that I was too weak to try to drive back across the Status Quo Line to Netherlands-controlled territory, and he knew of no UN Good Offices Committee flights to Batavia due for a long time, even assuming they would be willing to evacuate me. He said that what I urgently needed was the ongoing attention of a qualified physician, but that the few in the Republic, including himself, were too fully absorbed with duties of a higher priority to give me such help. Their immediate obligation, he said, was looking after the Republic's sick or wounded soldiers, whose numbers grew every day in the sporadic fighting that continued in some areas along the Status Quo Line despite the Renville truce.

And then he made a surprising proposition: If I would be willing to be treated by a doctor who was regarded as "ideologically unclean" he could arrange for me to be attended by a highly competent internist knowledge-able of tropical medicine who, despite his ability, had earned that reputation of being ideologically tainted because of having spent many years working for a Fascist government. Dr Soetomo went on to explain that this man, Dr Faruki, was an Indian who had been well trained by the British and Germans and found employment in one of the best German hospitals where, despite Nazi racial prejudice, he was so able that he was promoted to head the hospital. At the end of the war, with his German wife, he had made his way back to India. There, because he had worked with the Nazis he had been treated as something of a pariah. He had then gone on to Indonesia where the shortage of doctors in the Republic was so acute that its govern-ment, despite his having worked under Hitler's government, welcomed him and provided him and his wife with a decent room in Yogyakarta's only modern hotel, the Merdeka (Freedom). Here his stature was better than in India, but he was still shunned by many because of his having worked in Nazi Germany.

Dr Soetomo was relieved when I told him that so far as medical help was concerned I had no ideological scruples, and so the next day Dr Faruki called, armed with a large book on tropical medicine. After examining my blistered mouth and throat he opened up one of the volumes he had brought and, perched on the side of my bed, leafed through it to show me colored pictures depicting what tropical sprue did to one's internal organs. The pictures were not pretty, and I was impressed. Concluding, as had Dr Soetomo, that I had a serious case of tropical sprue, he too told me that Dutch doctors generally sent patients in my condition back to Europe to recover. Then, after some rather pejorative observations about the abilities of Dutch doctors, he said that he accepted me as his patient and, his eyes lighting up, announced: "You are my challenge!" I was very fortunate, for not only was Faruki highly intelligent and well trained, but he also proved to be imaginative and resourceful.

After exacting my promise to abide strictly by his instructions, he proceeded to outline for me the regimen I was to follow. This stipulated a diet limited to red (unhusked) rice and eggs, with each meal preceded by my swallowing about 2 oz of hydrochloric acid (apparently to compensate for my own lack of digestive juices brought about by the sprue) and taking large quantities of vitamin B pills. Though he had little trouble in finding hydrochloric acid, he was unable to find anywhere in Yogyakarta the vitamin B concentrate that he said was essential in overcoming my sprue. But a day later he returned, gleeful at what he had accomplished. He announced that he had solved that problem by boiling up an extract from water buffalo liver, which he said contained a sufficient concentration of the vitamin. He then produced a hypodermic needle fitted with a very large cylinder filled with a brown liquid which he informed me was the liver extract. This he injected into my buttock every day. It stung like fury, but after a while, because of it and his other prescriptions, I felt better and about ten days later was able to get out of bed.

During the last days of my recovery the Madiun rebellion was being overcome, and I had an invitation from Roeslan Abdulgani, the secretary general of the Ministry of Information, to accompany him and a few members of his staff to inspect conditions in a broad area to the west of Yogyakarta where the impact of the rebellion had been heavy and the current status and attitude of the population was unclear. I was delighted at my good fortune, even though I later suspected – correctly, I believe – that my invitation stemmed primarily from the ministry's desperate need for the transport my jeep could provide. Though still weak, I implored Dr Faruki for permission to make the trip, and this kind, outwardly very stern, man finally gave way. The extent of his generosity was measured by his willingness to lend me one of his three precious hypodermic needles. On this week-long trip I had to promise to remain strictly on the diet he had prescribed. Though the area we passed through to the west of Magelang was unusually impoverished we could usually find red rice. But eggs were out of the question and unavailable after we'd left that town. The only way to supplement the rice was to settle for Chinese buried eggs. Usually considered a great delicacy, the gelatinous objects were, of course, too expensive for nearly all the local inhabitants, and therefore obtainable thanks to my relative wealth. The bottles of hydrochloric acid and water buffalo liver extract that Dr Faruki supplied me with were ample, but injecting myself with the hypodermic with its massive tube of liver-of-water-buffalo extract was a desperate battle. For the extract stung so mightily that I kept backing away from the needle, literally chasing myself around the room until at last I cornered myself and agonized as I inserted the needle into my apprehensive rear.

My jeep and the Ministry of Information's only car, each with five occupants, did make it all the way to Banjarnegara and back, passing through Magelang, Parakan, Wonosobo and Mlipak en route. As we passed though the villages and small towns we stopped briefly to talk with the people, who instantly gathered around the ministry car and my strange beflagged jeep. The crowds always increased when Roeslan and his assistants began passing out simple grainy pictures of Sukarno and Hatta, with the enthusiastic crowd occasionally fighting among themselves to be sure of getting one of these, and the children being asked to tell us which was Sukarno and which was Hatta – almost always identifying them properly – to the cheers of the enthusiastic crowd.

During the trip I had ample opportunity to talk informally with numerous local officials and political leaders holding political views across a wide spectrum. Among these was the conservative aristocrat governor of central Java, Wongsonegoro whom I met in Magelang, seat of the Republic's central Java administration on 6 December 1948. He was an impressive looking man, tall, erect and dignified, and calm and modest in his demeanor. During our talk he gave me his interpretation of Sukarno's much debated "Political Testament" of September 1945, where he and Hatta had designated the men they hoped would succeed them should they be captured or killed. Wongsonegoro was the first among the four members of the testament quadrumvirate whom I interviewed. Though he was governor, he was happy to give me as much time as I wanted, so I learned more details from him about that subject than from any of the other three. He said that he had first heard about the political testament in December 1945 after having just served as the Republic's governor of Central Java and evacuated from Semarang to Purwodadi and then to Magelang (presently capital of Central Java and his governorship). He then learned from Sajuti Malik, editor of the Yogyakarta newspaper *Kedaulatan Rakjat* that Sukarno and Hatta had selected him as the conservative member of the foursome, to represent the traditional administrative service (*pangreh pradja*), because of the widely held respect in which he was held by that body (which was just what Sukarno later told me). Sajuti Malik had further told him that it was better not to stay on as governor of Central Java (a post to which he had been appointed in September 1945) and instead make himself ready for something bigger (apparently with reference to the testament).

Later, at the meeting of the Solo session of the Republican Parliament (KNIP) in February 1946, Achmad Subardjo (who had served as minister of foreign affairs in the short-lived first cabinet of the Republic (31 August–14 November 1945)) had also informed him about the testament, stating that he was number three or four on the list of those designated there to take over power in case Sukarno and Hatta were incapacitated. Wongsonegoro emphasized that Subardjo had been Tan Malaka's intermediary in arranging for the political testament. He had refused Subardjo's invitation to accompany him to his house to see the testament, because he had no interest in becoming president or vice-president. Wongsonegoro added that he had himself not met Tan Malaka, and that Subardjo had not mentioned him at all as being a leader of such a new government. If he had accepted Subardjo's invitation and accompanied him home, he said, he would probably have learned more about the scheme. He said he had never discussed the matter with Sjahrir.

In our discussion Wongsonegoro mentioned that he had been one of the founders of the prewar Parindra party, and that in 1925 he had been chairman of Young Java and in 1930 had been one of the founders of Indonesia Muda (a fusion of youth organizations from Java, Sumatra, Sulawesi, etc.). He and Sukarno had known each other as students and had first met at a students' conference in 1926. With respect to his departure from his governor's office in Semarang on 18 November 1945, he said that earlier in September he had made the first APWI contract with Allied forces – this with General Bethell. The quid pro quo of that signed contract, he said, called for his helping to repatriate Allied prisoners in return for Bethel's promise to tolerate the entrance of no NICA (Netherlands Indies

Civil Administration) officers into Semarang Residency and to permit no Dutch troops to land there. The shooting of some Indian British army officers, however, had led to the battle of Semarang. The fighting continued thereafter and Bethell was unable to withdraw his troops, he said. It was on the 18th that Wongsonegoro had left Semarang, first for Purwodadi, and then Magelang.

We spent the first night in Magelang, where, despite my strong reservations, I was prevailed upon to give a short speech in my lame Indonesian and answer an army of questions from an audience intrigued by the fact that an American looked very much like a Dutchman. The next day we ascended to the beautiful town of Wonosobo, some 3,000 feet high, with a cool and invigorating climate. Here we visited a branch office of the Ministry of Information, housed in a modest building that might once have been a small store. This branch specialized in making revolutionary posters. Because of the paper shortage, they were obliged to make their own semi-paper substitute. Though thick and uneven, it was able to bear the black and red coloring stenciled on it. I was told that the products of this little workshop were regularly taken across the Status Quo Line and affixed to walls of buildings at night. Two of these posters especially caught my eyes, and I carried them back to the United States with me and they now adorn walls in my house and office. One which was especially popular (Figure 2.3), I gathered, was of a young boy astride a placid water buffalo bearing the caption "Merdeka untuk selama-lamanya" (Freedom forever) – perhaps a bit bucolic for a revolution, but clearly representative of a population very tired of continued fighting and uncertainty and deeply yearning for the return of peace and tranquillity.

The other poster (Figure 2.4) that I picked up was a dramatic example of the popular disillusionment with both the United States and the Soviet Union and the already well-rooted belief that Indonesia should follow a nonaligned neutralist foreign policy equidistant from the two great powers. On its left side was a jumble of small office buildings that the artist assumed looked like Washington DC, with an American flag in the background, and on the right a mélange of similar looking buildings with the Soviet flag as background. Large crosses had been drawn across these two renderings of Washington and Moscow, but between them in the middle of the poster, and unsullied by any such excrescence, stood a clear rendering of Java's most impressive monument, the eleven-hundred-year-old Borobudur – suitable as a symbol of nationalism for at least the Javanese part of Indonesia's population. In large letters underneath was the motto: "Tidak Berpedoman: Washington atau Moscow – Tetapi Republik Indonesia" (Our compass is neither Washington nor Moscow, but the Republic of Indonesia).

Our two vehicles then started out on the arduous climb up to the 7,500-foot high Dieng Plateau. We first stopped at the bare dusty little town of Parakan, which had been one of the chief places controlled by the Musso Communist Party during its recent fighting against the government's forces.

Figure 2.3 Revolutionary poster

Figure 2.4 Revolutionary poster

The area was very poor. It did have brown rice available, but no chickens were visible. That, of course, meant that no fresh eggs were to be had, and I can well remember that in trying to adhere to Dr Faruki's diet I was obliged again to settle for Chinese buried eggs, purchased at a considerable price. I later found that in Chinese restaurants these repulsive gelatinous blobs were regarded as a highly prized delicacy, but after being sated with them in Parakan, I could never bring myself to eat one again.

But in this little town I had some fascinating talks with some of its more prominent inhabitants. These included the major who had been garrison commander when the Madiun rebellion broke out and had been briefly incarcerated by the rebels, with several local political leaders. But most fascinating was Kiayi Haji Subekti, a highly regarded Islamic leader in his seventies, who had attained widespread fame for amulets regarded as capable of protecting the wearer from machine gun or rifle fire. He stood six feet tall, with a splendid white beard and the most unusual eyes I had seen – bright brown pupils circled by bright blue. I could readily appreciate how he exuded a charisma that induced people to believe in his having magical powers. In our long discussion he turned out in fact to be quite a modest man, quick to repudiate any suggestion that the amulets accredited to him had power to repel bullets or any other danger. In talking with other prominent people in the town we discovered that it had been his venal and opportunistic chief assistant who had spread the idea of his being able to bless amulets that provided invulnerability to bullets and who had made a tidy fortune in selling them to people who came from many miles around. I later was told that his amulets, despite the fact that he disowned them, had been sold by his assistants to hundreds of revolutionaries involved in fighting the Japanese and then the British in Semarang and Surabaya a few years before. But what was most striking to me in the long discussion I had with this impressive old Haji were his homespun ideas about socialism and the socioeconomic order he felt most appropriate to Indonesia's needs, which he expounded to me in simple, but compelling, language.

As we continued our trip the next day through the hills up the steep incline to the cold Dieng Plateau, the ascent was too much for the ministry car, and my doughty jeep had to pull it for several miles. I found no answer as to why the several central Javanese kings entombed in miniature temples (*tjandi*) on this little plateau should have chosen what was one of the very coldest parts of Java to be buried. People here seemed better clad than elsewhere in the Republic, because of the cold, wearing jackets and sometimes pants made of leather so durable that it did not easily wear out.

We drove on to Banjarnegara, a mid-sized town that was our final destination, en route again passing out pictures of Sukarno and Hatta to the small but excited groups that crowded around us at any village or town at which we stopped. Soon after we reached Banjarnegara we were surrounded by a large crowd and ushered into a spacious building which served as a movie theater and which evidently was the object of considerable local pride.

Apparently there had not been a movie to show for a long time, and I got the uneasy feeling that I was something of a substitute as it was made clear to me by Roeslan and others in our group that there would be keen disappointment and resentment if I didn't give a speech. Indeed, the theater was overflowing with enthusiastic people and, as I looked out over them, it was clear to me that I could not afford to disappoint them.

My repertoire of speeches was pretty thin, and I could never go very far beyond the one I had given at Kebumen a little over three months before. This time, however, I made reference to the Status Quo Line, for Banjarnegara was close to it, and to the Dutch troops that it was widely believed were poised for a major invasion. Roeslan seemed to have been caught up in the crowd's enthusiasm, and this time he introduced me not as "Tuan Kahin" (Mr Kahin), but as "Bung" (Brother) Kahin. That title, which had come in with the revolution, was generally reserved for its senior leaders, and Roeslan's applying it to me left me a bit bewildered, as it brought a roar of approval from the assemblage, for it signified my adherence to the revolution. One could say that the term "Bung" at this time in the Indonesian revolution was rather akin to "Citizen" or "Comrade" in the French and Russian revolutions. When I had completed my little talk, once again incorporating a comparison of the American and Indonesian anticolonial revolutions, the crowd got to its feet in enthusiastic approbation. In all that tumult I could not, as I mightily wished, just calmly walk off the stage. But given the excitement, it seemed to me that the only way I could becomingly end the session was to give the Indonesian revolutionary salute of "Merdeka!" (Freedom!), in the same way that an Indonesian speaker would have done. Coming from this American stranger who flew both an Indonesian and American flag from his jeep, though, the result was simply greater enthusiasm. Roeslan had told me that being so close to the Status Quo Line I should expect that the Dutch would have an agent in the audience, and indeed almost fifty years later when I was going through the archives at The Hague I found this had indeed been the case.

On our return trip, close to Wonosobo, on 5 December, we first stopped – as I recall, for some urgent repairs to the ministry car – near Mlipak, a large village, a four-kilometer walk from the highway, with a population of 1,166 people, according to the village head (*lurah*). I should note that most of the roads we were traveling had not been adequately repaired since before the Japanese occupation and, though passable by a jeep, were a long torture for Roeslan's passenger car. It was presumably because a mechanic had to be fetched from Wonosobo even before repairs on his car could begin that we found ourselves spending most of the day in this village. Whether we liked it or not, we were treated as honored guests and, after Roeslan's talking briefly with the *lurah*, I found myself once again being introduced as "Bung Kahin" and asked to give another short speech. The *lurah* was clearly pleased at being visited, even if unannounced, by a high government official, which Roeslan as secretary general of a ministry certainly was, and he and the villagers seemed to regard it as an additional honor to be visited by a Dutch-looking person who was not Dutch and came from the famous country of America – a place of which many of the inhabitants appeared to have heard. The *lurah* worked quickly to make suitable arrangements, and soon I found myself being ushered to the open space before his house through a defile between the twin ranks of the sixty-man village militia, each of whom shouldered a six-foot-long bamboo spear.

After I'd made a shortened version of my usual speech, I was free to talk to my heart's content to the *lurah* and any of the members of the village council (*dewan desa*), or indeed to anyone in sight, about conditions in the village. There was plenty of time, for Roeslan's car took much longer than expected to become roadworthy again. I was happy to have this opportunity, for the revolution's impact on the agrarian sector had been one of the subjects to which I'd hoped to give high priority, but the pace of major developments in the capital had thus far left no time for this. And so in Mlipak I made a very small beginning at looking into this matter.

The quality of the china in which the *lurah* served us tea provided a clue to a phenomenon of which I'd not previously been aware. When I remarked on the quality of the cups, I discovered that this was not peculiar to Mlipak, but that a great deal of china had shifted from the sideboards of middle-class homes in the towns to the villages. This was emblematic of a widespread shift in wealth as an indirect consequence of the revolution that benefited peasant landowners in most of Java – especially middle-level and wealthy peasants – while town and city dwellers, for the most part, suffered considerably.

Fundamental in this reverse skewing of income levels was the staggering inflation attending the three-and-a-half years of Japanese occupation and the fighting against the British and Dutch that followed. As has often been the case elsewhere, inflation benefited peasant landholders – but, of course, not landless peasant laborers – usually making it much easier for them to pay fixed land taxes and get rid of accumulated indebtedness. With peasants in Central Java receiving approximately sixty times as much for their rice per kilo in mid-1948 as in 1941, it was usually relatively easy for them to pay off their debts, and, where the government still collected a land tax, to pay it too. (The land tax had remained fixed and the government had not yet completed its efforts to introduce an income tax as a substitute.)

Moreover, a large part of peasant debt was to rural Chinese money lenders, and because in many areas there was a tendency for peasants to see the Chinese population as aligned with the Dutch in the struggle for independence, the Republic's officials were all the less disposed to intervene to help collect even the inflation-lightened monetary debts from peasants, and their debts in kind as well. And while most peasant landholders benefited from the inflation that often wiped out their indebtedness, the town and city dwellers, trying to get by on salaries that lagged far behind the inflation, were often in desperate straits. They were frequently obliged to sell their furniture and china as well as any extra clothing to get enough rice to sustain their families. And so in Mlipak the bourgeois china from which we drank tea at the *lurah*'s house and some of the furniture I saw there had probably been sold off or bartered by the small middle class – largely bureaucratic – that dwelt in the nearby town of Wonosobo.

And so, alongside the national revolution to end Netherlands rule, led from the top by nationalist leaders – civilian and military – and supported by a broad base of peasants and town dwellers, there was also a quietly moving, unplanned socioeconomic revolution resulting mainly from an unstoppable inflation that inexorably swept though the entire country. Unheralded and unguided by the Republic's leaders, who were virtually powerless to affect its course, it exerted a powerful leveling impact that significantly changed the social face of broad areas of Indonesia, especially those within the Republic. The irony was that, though most of the Republic's leaders advocated a more equitable economic order and regarded themselves as one or another variant of socialist, they had almost nothing to do with the instigation of this tidal change, one which swept them along without any real possibility of directing its course. Nor, given the power of the objective factors that were operative, was it likely that, even if they were more gifted as economic managers, they would have been able in any very significant way to have done so.

Although my little on-the-spot survey was anything but scientific, its findings were apparently close to the norm obtaining in most of the Javanese part of the Republic after the government's rural administrative reforms introduced in 1946–7. That Mlipak represented a reasonably good example was clear when, after our return to Yogyakarta, during the second week of December I visited several other villages in the company of Selosoemardjan, the Sultan of Yogyakarta's secretary. I make mention now of the situation in Mlipak in 1948, not because of any anthropological expertise, but because I have since discovered that first-hand records of the important changes introduced as an adjunct to the Indonesian revolution are unfortunately very scarce.[6]

Haji Agus Salim, the foreign minister, seemed appreciative of the reports I was sending to the Overseas News Agency (ONA) and told me that when I had important dispatches and they were brief his office could get them to the ONA in New York via radio. Just as with the Republic's own messages abroad, they would, thanks to the good offices of Nehru's government, go to New Delhi and be forwarded from there to New York. Moreover, he assured me, my dispatches would escape Dutch scrutiny because they would be sent via the Republic's secret code. Neither Haji Salim, other members of his government, nor the leaders of its army then realized that the Dutch had broken that code long before, and that as a consequence both the Republic's diplomacy and the plans and conduct of its military operations were often known in advance by the Dutch. Indeed, it was this Dutch advantage in intelligence – for the Republic had been unable to break the Dutch code – that gave the Netherlands' forces a significant battlefield advantage.

Fortunately for me, those same factors that angered the Dutch – the flags on my jeep and my ONA dispatches – increased the confidence and trust in me of numerous Republican officials and offset the suspicions of many that I was an American government agent – a theme that the powerful local Communist press maintained. The Republic's military intelligence in Yogyakarta also was highly suspicious of me, its chief, Major Brentel Susilo, going to Haji Salim to demand I be thrown out – back across the Status Quo Line. To substantiate his claim that I was a Dutch spy, he came to the foreign ministry armed with a dossier that proved, he said, that previously I had been an employee of one of the major Dutch enterprises, the East Java Steam Tramway Company (Oost Java Stoomtramweg Maatschapij). He never explained whether his files indicated I had been a member of the company's board of directors or a simple conductor or motorman. Haji Salim advised against my pursuing the matter, warning that the major, however paranoid, was venal and very powerful, and a man whom one should avoid irritating. Though I did my best to get along with Brentel, I was completely unsuccessful. He confiscated or held back for censoring most of the letters I tried to send out on the occasional blockade-running plane and was a persistent barrier to my attempts to meet senior Republican military officials.

Despite these suspicions about me, it was soon evident, and a most unexpected surprise, that I was something of a celebrity. The fact that I had been able to drive through the Status Quo Line was, I found, regarded by many as an admirable achievement demonstrating a sort of defiance of the Dutch, and there is no doubt that my flying both Indonesian and American flags from my jeep was regarded similarly. Belatedly I discovered that my jeep-borne crossing of the S.Q. lines was more hazardous than I had appreciated, and that I was credited with a courage that I had not possessed. For I learned that the few jeeps driven by the handful of United Nations military observers that occasionally probed the line to check on reported military skirmishes were all painted white, with well-defined black lettering making clear they represented the UN, and that a jeep such as mine, painted a military dark green was considered fair game by Republican forces. But I was too immodest to insist that I should be credited with foolhardiness rather than courage. (This distinction between white and dark green jeeps was brought home to me during the Madiun rebellion when I was attending a performance of Javanese dancing in the *kraton* of Hamengkubuwono IX, Sultan of Yogyakarta. The sultan was about to borrow my jeep in order to drive out and assess the situation in an area of unrest not far from the Status Quo Line, when one of his subordinates intervened to insist it would be safer for him to borrow the white jeep of a UN military observer who was also in attendance.)

And beyond this, as the only American in the Republic for much of the time I was there, I could not help but stand out. Indeed, insofar as I could ascertain, apart from the transient UN Committee of Good Offices personnel stationed mainly in nearby Kaliurang, the total number of foreigners resident in Yogyakarta was no more than half a dozen. These included the most agreeable and intelligent consul of India, Mohamad Yunus, sent as a symbol of support to the revolution by Jawaharlal Nehru, for whom he had served as one of four private secretaries; Father Zoetmulder, an eminent Jesuit scholar of Javanese culture who lived in a village about fifteen miles from the capital – probably Muntilan; my house-mate John Coast; and the bête noire of Consul Glen Abbey, Molly Bondan, who with her Indonesian husband also worked for the Ministry of Foreign Affairs. And resident in Yogyakarta for about a month while I was there was Thakin Tha-Kin, an imposing six-foot Burmese, also sent by his country as a symbol of its support of the Indonesian revolution and what was regarded as a common socialist agenda. Having been joint secretary of Burma's ruling Anti-Fascist People's Freedom League (AFPFL), he was highly regarded by the Republic's leaders who desperately sought anticolonial foreign support. We got along famously from the outset, and seven years later when I visited Burma he opened many doors for me.

Just as I was feeling some elation because of the confidence I seemed to have gained with many of the Indonesians I was meeting in the Republic, I briefly experienced what at the time seemed to be a poignant setback. By chance I discovered that some of the university students whom I had quickly gotten to know were sometimes referring to me, good humoredly, in their private conversations, as "Hanuman." Despite what Claire Holt had briefly taught me about some aspects of Javanese culture, I had forgotten that name, and so I innocently asked an older acquaintance what it meant and was told "the white monkey." I went through a few days of despondency, thinking my new friends were mocking me, until to my considerable relief I learned what I should have known, that, in the old Hindu epic of the Ramayana, which the Javanese had taken over and adapted to their own culture, Hanuman was one of the "good guys," the white monkey king who fought on the right side. The term as they applied it to me was not meant to be pejorative, but rather complimentary, and so to my considerable relief I found I was not being made fun of after all.

Being regarded as supportive of the Republic undoubtedly made it much easier to meet many of the Republic's leaders. Within my first two months in Yogyakarta I was fortunate enough to meet and have informal discussions with a whole range of political leaders. These included President Sukarno, Vice-President-cum-Prime Minister Mohammad Hatta, Haji Agus Salim, minister of foreign affairs, Dr Sukiman Wirjosandjojo, minister of interior, Sjafruddin Prawiranegara, minister of economic affairs, Dr Ali Sastroamidjojo, minister of education, Dr Johannes Leimena, minister of health, and Mohammad Natsir, minister of information, who both during and after the revolution was to be one of my closest friends. I also had many helpful discussions with junior members of their staffs. And I was also able to talk with political leaders then in opposition to Prime Minister Hatta's government, such as Achmad Subardjo, minister of foreign affairs in the Republic's first cabinets in 1945, Sukarni, Tan Malaka's chief lieutenant and head of the nationalist-Communist Murba (Proletarian) Party, Suripno, one of the top leaders of the pro-Soviet Indonesian Communist Party (PKI), and Abikusno Tjokrosujoso, head of the Partai Sarekat Islam Indonesia (which had broken off from the Masjumi). I also came to know well and had many helpful conversations with Selosoemardjan, private secretary to the Sultan of Yogyakarta, and until recently chief of staff of one of the more important militias, the Yogyakarta area's Laskjar Rakjat (People's Army), who also became one of my closest friends. And I saw more of Sutan Sjahrir, who was now out of government and with no immediate power, but still influential. He was intermittently in Yogyakarta as personal adviser of Sukarno, with whom he stayed when in town.

A couple of weeks after my arrival in Yogyakarta I had paid an initial call on President Sukarno (Figure 2.5) in what was referred to as "the palace," a large house just off Malioboro Street that had once housed the Dutch Resident. He was warmly cordial, appeared to be keenly interested in my already famous jeep, which he examined carefully and asked me some technical questions about that were beyond my ken, reflecting, I assumed, his training in engineering. My responses betrayed my layman's knowledge, and I could not even remember what its horsepower was. But he seemed to enjoy looking it over and gave it an approving pat.

Not until Sukarno invited me to visit him on 12 November, did I have an opportunity to have a serious talk with him, but it was relaxed and

Figure 2.5   President Sukarno, September 1948

unhurried, lasting the better part of the morning. He clearly wanted to talk and seemed to enjoy himself, especially when we turned to the subject of nationalism. He wondered if I had read Hans Kohn, Lothrop Stoddard and Ernst Renan, and seemed eager to discuss them all. (I could admit only to Hans Kohn.) He then went on to discuss his views on nationalism, saying that he perceived four different kinds of nationalist reactions in colonial countries, varying with the type of colonial rule that had been exercised. He defined these as

1   Liberal Colonial Rule: Exemplified by the US in the Philippines, where Philippine nationalism developed through nonviolent political means, the colonial people being given wide opportunities of education and their living standard greatly improved. This was possible because the colonizing power was chiefly seeking markets rather than a field of investment. Since markets are desired, it is beneficial to the seller to raise the living standards of, and educate, the population.
2   Semi-Liberal Colonial Rule: Exemplified by British rule in India after 1860, begetting a somewhat stronger reaction and a somewhat more militant nationalism.
3   Semi-Orthodox Colonial Rule: Exemplified by the Dutch in Indonesia. In this case the importance of the colony as a market is definitely subordinated to its importance as a field of investment. Moreover the importance of the colony to the economy of the colonial power is much greater than in the previous two types. Very meager educational facilities allowed the colonial population and their economic condition [to be] depressed, sparking a nationalist reaction that was strong and violent.
4   Orthodox Colonial Rule: Exemplified by Spanish rule in the Philippines.

In discussing why the development of government in the Philippines had tended to take on an increasingly authoritarian character, Sukarno pointed out that American rule had lasted for only about forty-five years as against a conditioning of almost 300 years of Spanish rule.

When I asked Sukarno what the term "merdeka" (freedom) meant to the Indonesian masses, he answered:

Merdeka has both a political and economic meaning for the masses. They can all see the difference between Dutch rule and the accounts of the old native kingdoms, where Indonesians ruled, that have been handed down to them. In an economic sense they [at least the rural population] remember that during Dutch rule they were able to get much less food than now under the Republic. Now, though the city population is comparatively badly off, because of the Dutch blockade – which has meant no consumer goods to trade to the peasantry for their rice and also has meant inadequate means for transportation of the rice from producing and surplus areas to the deficit areas – the peasant population eats much more now than during the Dutch times, and the old signs of malnutrition and disease are disappearing from the countryside. During the Dutch times, in addition to having to surrender a considerable part of the crop in order to pay taxes, the peasant's supply of food was limited because of the existence of Dutch sugar and tobacco estates in lowland areas that had formerly grown food for local consumption – particularly rice. Mountain estates work no real hardship on the people, as they affect the growing area very little.

Without my bringing up the question, Sukarno said that

the problem of peasant welfare cannot be met by the solution propagandized by Musso and Sjarifuddin – namely, that the area of the village reserved for paying the village officials be divided among the peasants. Such an area of approximately 1 per cent of the land of each village will help the peasantry almost not at all. The peasant, with his average of two-thirds of a hectare, can only be helped via large-scale migration to Sumatra and Borneo. Fifteen million at least should migrate. Concurrent with this migration the country should be industrialized.

He then volunteered,

It is the economic conditions brought about by the blockade that have been chiefly responsible for the attraction of communism. In addition, Musso and Amir have made political capital from the fact that negotiations with the Dutch have produced nothing. If only a reasonable political settlement can be achieved, the wind will be taken out of their sails. If a reasonable settlement can be achieved and the blockade lifted the basis of the Communists' appeal will disappear.

It was exactly a month later, on 12 December 1948, that I had my second discussion with Sukarno. He clearly wanted to talk for he invited me while I was in the midst of my week-long trip through central Java with Roeslan Abdulgani, whose office informed him that Sukarno wanted to see me again. It was at a time when there was growing apprehension in the Republic that the Dutch were about to launch a major military attack. We talked initially about that prospect, Sukarno holding that, with the United Nations Committee of Good Offices for Indonesia temporarily ensconced in the hill station of Kaliurang, a short distance outside of Yogyakarta, the Dutch would not dare attack because of the adverse international repercussions this would cause. His view then seemed reasonable to me, but it was only a week later, on 19 December, that the Netherlands loosed its heaviest attack ever against the Republic, capturing Kaliurang as well as Yogyakarta in its initial thrust.

When we met on 12 December, Sukarno was kind enough to recall that when we had last talked I had said that if ever he had time there were other questions I would like to ask him. So now he asked me to fire away, and most of my questions were designed to get his views on a number of questions pertaining to the early political history of the Republic.

Having only a few days before talked with Wongsonegoro about the controversial matter of the "Political Testament," it was very much on my mind. I found that Sukarno's view of it was very close to that of Sjahrir, with whom I'd discussed it in Batavia a couple of months earlier, and now with that of Wongsonegoro as well.

The genesis of the idea, said Sukarno, was the fact that in late 1945 he and Hatta were aware that the British were under much pressure from the Dutch to arrest them, and there was a strong chance that, if they were not arrested by the British forces, the Dutch would have them assassinated. They drew this conclusion after Sukarno's car was fired on (fortunately when he wasn't in it, but his chauffeur was wounded in the arm) and after Dutch colonial troops fired at the cars of both Sjahrir and Sjarifuddin. Because of these fears – arrest by the British or assassination by the Dutch – Sukarno and Hatta decided to write a political testament in which would be set out the names of the people they wished to lead the revolution in case they were incapacitated. These were the Communist Tan Malaka, Iwa Kusuma Sumantri, another revolutionary of the extreme variety, and also with a strongly Marxist outlook, the moderate revolutionary and revisionist Marxist Sjahrir, who could be said to be representative of the youth, and Wongsonegoro, a moderate, highly respected by the old-line civil servants.

However, Sukarno continued, Tan Malaka upon leaving Batavia shortly thereafter forged a new draft of the settlement in which he alone was indicated as the person to whom authority was to be turned over. Moreover, he indicated to people that the transfer of sovereignty was already called for since, by being in Jakarta (Batavia), Sukarno and Hatta were in reality under the control of the British and Dutch. (Sukarno did not explicitly make this last statement, but it could be inferred from what he said.) Thus, said Sukarno, by forging the new testament Tan Malaka showed himself to be a dishonest man.

Sukarno said that he first met Tan Malaka (at least for the first time since the Japanese invasion) about two weeks after the declaration of independence when Subardjo brought him around, saying that Tan Malaka wanted to see him. According to Sukarno, Tan Malaka was the intellectual author of the 3 July 1946 attempted coup d'état, but there was no way of proving it. Nor was there any way of proving the connection of Iwo Kusuma Sumantri or Subardjo with this coup. The latter two backed the affair because they felt themselves neglected and entitled to important places in the leadership of the government. "Iwo is brilliant and terribly ambitious, as is Yamin." After holding the important post of foreign minister in the Republic's first cabinet, Subardjo had been dumped by Sjahrir. (It could be inferred from what

Sukarno said that to some degree Sjahrir was responsible for Subardjo's defection.) "Then," said Sukarno, "a short time ago I gave him a job as an adviser to the foreign ministry."

"Sjahrir's greatest weakness," Sukarno added, "is that he insists upon working only with a small circle of people, his close and trusted friends. Thus his cabinets were largely limited to this circle." Sukarno had talked to Sjahrir about the matter a number of times and felt it to be the latter's great limitation. He felt strongly that Sjahrir should be willing to widen the circle of people he was willing to work with politically.

In response to my question, Sukarno said that he thought revisionist socialism and the socioeconomic objectives of Islam were very close. He was convinced that the two would be able to cooperate closely in Indonesia, even though they could not actually fuse. More specifically, he stated that he and the progressive group within the Masjumi and the Partai Sosialis Indonesia would certainly be able to cooperate closely. He seemed to feel that progressives in the Masjumi would control the party. The atheism espoused by members of the Partai Sosialis Indonesia was the chief reason why there could be no fusion between their ideology and Islam. In addition, he stated, Islam rejects historical materialism.

I then turned the discussion to the KNIP (Komite Nasional Indonesia Pusat – Central Indonesian National Committee), established on 29 August 1945 as a 135-member body appointed by him and Hatta, charged with advising them and their cabinet. With its membership increased to 514 on 29 December 1946 (probably to ensure passage of the controversial Linggajati Agreement with the Dutch), the KNIP had gradually through its continuously sitting 47-member Working Committee come to take on some of the qualities of a parliament, exercising legislative power that in effect balanced and checked the exercise of such power by Sukarno and Hatta and their cabinet. It had now become established practice that, to take effect, all legislation passed by the cabinet had to be approved by the Working Committee. The members of the KNIP were not elected, the electoral law not yet having been passed, but had been appointed by Sukarno and Hatta following their joint deliberation. In their appointments to this body these two clearly made some effort to pick individuals of standing and prestige, so that the body had a sufficiently representative character that it would be fair to characterize the Republic's government as being significantly pluralistic.

Of the KNIP's membership, 222 seats went to the political parties: 60 to the Masjumi, 45 to the PNI, 35 to the Socialist Party (then led by Sjahrir and Sjarifuddin); 35 to the Labor Party; 35 to the Communist Party (PKI); 8 to the Christian Party (Protestant) and 4 to the Catholic Party. Another 80 seats designated as "Occupational" were split evenly between "Workers" and "Peasants"; 78 seats were reserved for "Regions" (50 for Sumatra; 8 for Borneo [Kalimantan]; 10 for Celebes [Sulawesi]; 5 for the Moluccas, and 5 for the Lesser Sundas). Under the category of "minorities," Chinese were

allotted 7 seats, Arabs 3 and Dutch 3. Finally there were 121 seats under the
rubric "Individuals, minor parties, and armed organizations."

With this background in hand, I asked Sukarno how he and Hatta
decided on appointments to the KNIP. He said that the two of them had
determined party strength "after having received reports from Residents
throughout the country giving their estimates of party strength within their
residencies; these determinations are, of course, only rough estimates." The
practice was for him and Hatta to designate the number of seats a party
might have and then for the party to present them with a list of the candidates which it approved. There was no limit on how long the list presented
by the party might be. In selecting the names he and Hatta tried to give each
party "a good geographical distribution – representation from all over
Indonesia." In addition, he said, appointments were "not made entirely on
the basis of people that are apparently supporting a party." Other criteria
than mere numbers had to be followed – in particular the degree of organization and integration of the party. Strength had other criteria than mere
numbers. The Masjumi with 60 seats was certainly under-represented as far
as numbers alone were concerned. However, if more seats had been given it,
the Socialist Party would certainly have resisted this, while the Socialist
Party "was not entitled to its 35 seats on the basis of the number of its
members." Sukarno went on to say that he and Hatta made no attempt to
select a certain proportion from left, right and center of the party involved,
but did try to select "its outstanding leaders."

Sukarno had been looking forward to the holding of national elections
(for the KNIP) in April 1949, but told me he had been recently informed by
the chairman of the Election Board that it would be impossible to make all
preparations for them by that time, even though Sukarno had urged him as
strongly as he could to do so within three months if possible. The chairman,
he said, had promised to do the best he could. Sukarno went on to say that
"a number of political parties are not at all anxious to have elections and are
afraid they will show how weak their popular support is; they are afraid of
this aspect of democracy."[7]

I found general corroboration of Sukarno's view of the testament when
I called on Hatta for an interview scheduled in advance with Dr Maria
Ulfah Santoso, a most impressive woman who had secured a doctorate in
jurisprudence from Leiden and had been Indonesia's first woman to hold a
cabinet position (social affairs in Sjahrir's third cabinet, 2 October 1946–27
June 1947). Highly respected for her intelligence, good judgment and political acumen, she was rightly regarded as a very important asset to Hatta.
She was as modest as she was intelligent and seemed to have almost no
detractors. I found her reputation of being able to run Hatta's office with
an efficiency unmatched in Yogyakarta fully justified. When I called that
day and sat in the waiting room chatting with Bung Tomo of Surabaya
battle fame, we discussed this, for we could see the dispatch and understanding with which she handled the visitors who preceded us. (Bung

Tomo still had his long hair, which he had sworn he wouldn't cut until Indonesia was free.)

When I spoke with Hatta, I found him in general agreement with Sukarno as to the character of controversial "political testament" of early October 1945. He described it very much as he later did in June 1960, when Ben Anderson, Herb Feith and I queried him about it. He added that Dr Sukiman, now head of the Masjumi, had been his and Sukarno's first choice to represent Islam in the putative quadrumvirate that would replace them if they were killed or incapacitated, but because Sukiman was out of Batavia at the time, they had invited Iwa Kusuma Sumantri instead. (When I talked with Sjahrir in Batavia, on 15 February 1949, about the testament his view accorded closely with that of Sukarno and Hatta.)

3   The Dutch attack on Yogyakarta

When I returned to Yogyakarta, after my trip with Roeslan and his staff into western Central Java, things seemed normal, at least much as they'd been before we left. There was still widespread fear of a major Dutch attack, but it was less acute than during the Madiun rebellion. The UN Good Offices Committee and its staff had moved from Batavia, as they periodically did, to the pleasant mountain station of Kaliurang. My housemate Hamid Algadri, one of the few members of the Indonesian delegation who was quartered in Yogyakarta rather than Kaliurang, was convinced that, with the committee and its secretariat ensconced so close by, the Dutch would not dare attack Yogyakarta. As mentioned above, when I talked with Sukarno on 12 December he was decidedly of the same opinion.

The feeling was general in Yogyakarta that the Dutch would attack within a month or two, but no one thought it to be quite as imminent as it proved to be. Friends of mine in the Good Offices Committee secretariat warned that when the attack came I could not expect city dwellers to discriminate between a white American and a Dutchman, and that, in any case, I should understand that it was widely believed that the Dutch would not launch an attack unless they had the acquiescence of the US government. They urged me either to join them in Kaliurang, which would be regarded as neutral territory, or take advantage of one of the empty seats now available on their plane and return to Batavia.

In view of the widespread belief that an attack would take place in the near future, Hamid and I were surprised to find that the Dutch authorities in Batavia had given permission in mid-December for Mrs Earle, a husky middle-aged American woman who was a professor of geography at the University of Washington, to have a seat on the UN Good Offices' plane and fly into Yogyakarta. This strong-willed woman had persistently endeavored to secure this permission without success, and the fact that she was finally granted it only a week before the Dutch attack later led Republican officials (who had given her a Republican visa in Batavia) to speculate that the Dutch authorities did so in order to further convince Republican intelligence that no Dutch military move was imminent. Republican officials quartered her in the guest house next to the one where

Hamid and I resided. Another of its three bedrooms had just been given to James Pamoedjo, an American of Indonesian background who worked in the Indonesian information office in New York, and who had just flown in on the last flight through the Dutch blockade by the one plane operated by the shoestring Pacific Overseas Airways. The third bedroom there was reserved for, and was occupied by, the itinerant UN military observers. In our guest house the third bedroom was turned over on 17 December to a young, newly arrived, British pilot, Adrian Donati, who had just flown his small plane, representing his life savings, in through the Dutch blockade and arranged to sell it for gold in the next day or so to the Republican government.

Essential to an understanding of the stunning success of the Netherlands forces in their blitz attack against Yogyakarta on 19 December 1948 was their having broken the Republic's secret communications code. On the basis of records I found nearly five decades later in the archives at The Hague in the collection of papers of General Simon Spoor, the commander-in-chief of Dutch forces in 1948, it appears that the breakthrough had taken place by at least September of 1948. This success was of crucial importance in the Netherlands–Indonesian struggle, for it gave the Dutch an enormous advantage, of which the Indonesians were only all too belatedly aware. It imposed a crippling limitation on both the Republic's military and diplomatic efforts, which its leaders did not begin to fathom until after the Dutch attack of 19 December. Having broken the code, the Dutch were privy to what the Republic's military and civilian leaders were confident was secret. This permitted the Dutch easily to adjust to and preempt the Republic's plans in both the military and diplomatic spheres. As General Spoor's papers in the Netherlands archives testify, the Dutch were so confident of the lead-time advantage this gave them that three days before they launched their attack they were laying the groundwork for the press conference they expected to call that day in Batavia to explain why they were taking this action. Indeed, they went so far as to prime a few sympathetic reporters as to the questions they should ask when the conference was held.

The Dutch timed their attack in accordance with two important pieces of information they had learned from their access to the supposedly secret coded information transmitted over the Republic's radio network. Most important was the plan for India's prime minister, Jawaharlal Nehru, to send his private plane through the Dutch blockade to pick up Sukarno and Hatta and fly them out of Yogyakarta. Hatta would be taken as far as Bukittinggi in West Sumatra, where he would lead the Republic's government on Sumatra in the face of the anticipated Dutch attack. Sukarno and a few of his staff would then be flown on to New Delhi and from there to New York where Sukarno would address the UN General Assembly. Given his powerful oratory and command of English, it was believed he would there make a powerful impact beneficial to the Republic's cause. Probably equally disturbing for the Dutch was their receipt of reports that the Republican leadership then planned for Sukarno to set up a government in exile under Nehru's protection to carry on during the fighting.

Nehru's plane was apparently to be dispatched somewhere around the middle of December. Within those parameters knowledge of the date set for the Republican army's maneuvers refined the timing for the Dutch attack. But the desire to preempt Sukarno's and Hatta's departure on Nehru's plane was undoubtedly the major precipitating factor in establishing the date.

I knew more about Hatta's and Sukarno's plans for their trip than most, since they had agreed that I could occupy one of the seats on Nehru's plane that were to be vacant as far as Bukittinggi, where apparently one or two Sumatrans would be added to Sukarno's entourage. Sukarno and Hatta had fortunately accepted my plea that effective coverage of the revolution necessitated my spending some time in Sumatra, at least in the revolution's Sumatran headquarters of Bukittinggi. So I counted myself very lucky and was eagerly awaiting the trip. I was not sure exactly when Nehru's plane was due to arrive in Yogyakarta, and I've never been able to ascertain whether Dutch intelligence had discovered the exact arrival date. But no one expected that the plane's pilot would be foolish enough to land at Batavia's Kemayoran airport for a final refueling before proceeding on to Yogyakarta. When he did just that Dutch authorities, not unnaturally, refused to give him clearance to proceed further. The Indian government, having already strongly espoused the Indonesian cause in the United Nations, clearly lacked the leverage to oblige the Dutch to reverse this decision, and Nehru's plane never made it to Yogyakarta (and so I was never able to make it to the Republic's revolutionary capital on Sumatra).

As a result of the Netherlands' having cracked the "secret" code, the Republic's army was caught completely off balance when General Simon Spoor, the Dutch commander, picked the day for an all-out assault on the Republic. The early movements of his soldiers were advantaged because they had found out, through intercepts, about Republican plans for army maneuvers on 19 December 1948. That meant that the movements of the Dutch troops were initially camouflaged by expectations on the Republican side that their own armed forces were scheduled to go on maneuvers on that day. So on that morning the Dutch forces struck, launching by far the largest attack yet against the Republic, on Java and Sumatra. Both General Nasution, head of the Republican army's principal combat component on Java, and Merle Cochran, chairman and US representative on the UN Committee of Good Offices, were caught flat-footed and unable to respond quickly to the carefully planned lightning attack that the Dutch suddenly unleashed.

Having learned on 18 December that the Republic's army was expected to go on maneuvers the next day, I was not concerned when I was awakened shortly after midnight by what sounded like artillery fire from a great distance. These muffled rumblings continued for at least an hour, after which I fell asleep again. But at 5.30 a.m. I was awakened by a heavy explo-

sion, the concussion from which shook the house. The sound of the explosion seemed to come from the direction of Yogyakarta's Maguwo airfield,
some five miles to the northeast of the house in which I was living. I ran
outside and found many others who lived on the street there as well. There
were a number of planes in the air that we could hear but not yet see, it
being cloudy as well as dark. When there was eventually enough light to
make out the planes, we at first assumed they must be the three old Japanese
Zeros that constituted the Republic's airforce (Figure 3.1), and there was
general approbation at how realistic were the Republic's armed forces
maneuvers.

Figure 3.1   The Republic's airforce

One reason for the initial confusion regarding the provenance of the planes
was that at the very outset Dutch rockets had blown up the Republic's radio
station, and it was not until about 8.30 a.m. that we were able to hear a Dutch
broadcast from Semarang giving Dutch commander General Spoor's order
of the day to his forces to cross the Status Quo Line and capture Yogyakarta
in an assault that was officially described as a "purging action" to cleanse the
Republic of all "unreliable elements." The broadcast urged the inhabitants of
Yogyakarta to stay off the streets. As for the unpreparedness of the Republic's
army, it should be noted that at the time of the Dutch attack General Nasution,
commander of its ground forces, was not in the Yogyakarta area, but
rather, as he acknowledges, with his staff on an inspection tour of East Java.

Amongst those who had remained unconvinced that this was a Dutch
attack were the two UN military observers quartered in the house next to

mine – the American, Major Montana, and the Englishman, Commander Mather. Accordingly, they left in their jeep for the airport about 7.30 a.m. with Captain Sudarto, their liaison officer from the Indonesian army, in order to meet Merle Cochran, American representative on the UN Committee of Good Offices, who was due to arrive at 8.00 a.m. on a plane from Batavia. They did not return until about 4 p.m., well after the Dutch troops had entered the city. Sudarto was no longer with them, for despite their protests, the Dutch had taken him prisoner when they reached the airport.

Not long after the departure of the two military observers, the sky became full of Dutch planes – Mitchell bombers (B-25s), P-51s and Dakota transports. Most of the planes were engaged in dive-bombing, as they loosed cannon fire, rockets and machine guns against particular targets in the city. But some of their machine-gunning appeared to be quite indiscriminate as some planes raked streets crosswise rather than lengthwise. About mid-morning the bombing and rocketing became more intense and sustained. What appeared to be a P-51 strafed the street diagonally only fifty yards from our house. As it moved off, I ran outside and took a photograph of it.

At around 10 a.m., during a lull, Donati and I ran down the street about a block and a half to where the Republic's airforce headquarters was located and were told that the Dutch had occupied the airport, after having wiped out its defenders, who I later found had been forty-seven airforce cadets. These cadets had been armed with nothing but rifles, because some senior brass had taken away their only machine guns to Surakarta a few days before.[1] We were told that the Dutch operation began with raining down on the airport several hundred dummies which drew fire from the cadets and disclosed their location, whereupon the Dutch planes rocketed and machine-gunned them. Having secured control of the airport, the Dutch, using two waves of planes, each consisting of twenty-three Dakotas (DC-3s), brought in between 800 and 900 airborne infantry. Thereafter, they were able to maintain a steady stream of air transport from their main base at Semarang, their mid-Java capital.

Soon after we had returned to our house, and before the lull in the rocketing, bombing and machine-gunning ended, a friend of mine, Ali Budiardjo, secretary of the Indonesian delegation to the Committee of Good Offices, came briskly walking up the street, apparently after having first stopped in at the Indonesian chief-of-staff headquarters (near airforce headquarters at the bottom of our street) to see Colonel Simatupang (soon to be his brother-in-law) who had already left for the mountains. Despite his weak asthmatic condition Ali was determined to follow Simatupang's unit, and told me he was going to walk up the Kaliurang road to where it was based. I gave him a sweater and a waterproof vest to cover it and he was promptly off towards the Kaliurang road. (I later learned he was soon able to join Simatupang.)

From Ali I learned that a cabinet meeting had been called for 10 a.m. in the presidential palace, and that it was still under way. I later learned that

Vice President Hatta's car had been attacked by a Dutch plane as it was descending the road from Kaliurang to bring him to this cabinet meeting. Several bullets had hit his car, but he and his driver were uninjured. I was told that the Sultan of Yogyakarta had then dispatched his own car to pick up the stranded Hatta and brought him the rest of the way to the meeting. Hatta was undoubtedly shaken by this experience, and also because one of his principal aides, Masdoelhak Nasution, had been shot and killed in his home by Dutch soldiers, as well as by the fact that the secretary general of the Department of Education, who was husband of Hatta's private secretary, Maria Ulfah Santoso, had been pulled from his car, lined up with eight other civilians and shot to death by a Dutch major. This was an incident that I carefully investigated, being able to talk to witnesses.[2] When a report of the incident was made, a Dutch spokesman insisted that the killing could not have been done by a Dutch major, and that a mistake had been made, with the executioner only a sergeant major.

Not long after Ali had left me, the Indonesians put the torch to both the airforce and adjacent chief-of-staff headquarters, an action that triggered some of the Dutch bombers to drop large bombs on the smoldering remains of both. Soon after the heavy explosions caused by these bombs ceased, there staggered up the street, stunned and temporarily half-blinded by the blasts, another friend of mine, I.N. (Didi) Djajadiningrat, who had been living very close to these two headquarters. I ran out of the house and pulled him, stumbling, inside, where he collapsed, though he quickly recovered. I'd heard reports that the Dutch were angry that my jeep carried both an Indonesian and American flag. So I ran out to the garage next to our house where I kept my jeep and substituted a small American flag for the Indonesian one, so that the jeep now bore two American flags. About 1 p.m. the Dutch planes again stepped up their rocketing, and their planes soon were continuously flying over the city – rocketing, machine-gunning and some appearing to fire small cannon. At 1.20 p.m. there were many more bombs and my typed account ended with a handwritten scrawl: "The bombing and rocketing too heavy to continue at my typewriter." In the first lull, Hamid and I ran next door to urge Mrs Earle (the American geographer) and James Pamoedjo to join us. With the two military observers having left, they apparently felt rather lonely and accepted our invitation with alacrity.

During another brief lull in the bombing when I ran outside to inspect our shrapnel-covered roof I saw six grim-faced peasants stooping low as they ran down the shallow storm gulley alongside the street in front of our house, each carrying over his shoulder a six-foot *bambu runcing* (a sharpened bamboo spear), such as had been common in the very early days of the revolution, but I had not previously seen in Yogyakarta. They were loping straight down the street towards a position just occupied by a Dutch machine-gun squad that had worked its way up the street from near its junction with Gondoloyo boulevard. The Dutch unit had taken up its position on our street, Terban Taman, after having cleared it of the four Republican security guards assigned to protect it, whose rifle fire had held up the advance of Dutch troops up the street for about thirty minutes. None of the six peasants returned along the street, and I assumed that the burst of Dutch machine-gun fire that I heard shortly after they had passed our house had wiped them out. There was no way of knowing what fool had ordered them into battle.

Our major concern was that one of the rockets that the Dutch now appeared to be using with such profligacy might hit our house. Accordingly, we sought to arrange the furniture, beds and mattresses in a concentration in the living room/dining room that we thought would best protect us in case of a hit. Donati, who said he'd lived through the London blitz, seemed to have sensible ideas as to how to do this, so we yielded to him to be architect of this mélange. We established what we thought were places of relative safety under beds or mattresses, well bolstered with pillows and pieces of furniture. Fortunately no rocket hit our house, though as Dutch forces advanced up our street their machine guns blasted out our windows and their rifle fire shot out most of the light fixtures.

After that there was an eerie calm, and then suddenly we heard voices speaking Dutch. Donati and I, who were on the fringe of our little indoors encampment of furniture, beds and mattresses, pulled ourselves out and held our hands high in what we assumed was the requisite manner for surrender. The squad of Dutch marines that had surrounded our house was fronted by a screen of four or five very unfriendly looking Ambonese soldiers who entered it first. One pushed his Sten gun vigorously into Donati's stomach without firing it, and his companion lurched towards mine with his. At that moment the red-headed Dutch marine officer in charge of the squad, Lt Bakker, providentially yelled out "Halt ezel" (Halt, donkey) and they both ended their alarming stomach lunges.

We were then all marched outside the house where, despite the rain, Hamid was ordered to sit out on the curb, and the rest of us on the porch. Hamid and I protested at this discrimination, and the Dutch lieutenant finally consented to his joining the rest of us on the porch. Shortly after we had assembled there Haji Agus Salim ran breathlessly down from his house at the end of the block to join us, gasping "Haji Salim" as he arrived. It was evident he preferred not to be captured alone by the Ambonese troops. Lt Bakker was clearly very pleased at having garnered such an important prize as the minister of foreign affairs, and treated him with a politeness not lavished on the rest of us.

Soon afterwards the sudden rattle of small arms fire further up our street brought the lieutenant and his squad briefly to abandon us, flinging themselves flat on the ground or crouching in the parallel drainage ditch to take up positions so they could sweep the street with their heavy machine gun. After a few intermittent bursts of fire from it with no response from up the street, our red-haired marine lieutenant, now sweaty, breathing hard and chewing on his pipe, which, I learned, his teeth always clenched in battle, returned to the porch.

Apparently, he had dispatched one of his men to report to the main body of Dutch troops still further down the street near the two blasted headquarters buildings, for about a half hour later there arrived the main unit's intelligence officer, Captain Vosveld. He was visibly delighted with the capture of Haji Salim and treated him with great courtesy. He questioned us all briefly, indicating there would be further interrogations later. The questions he asked me indicated he already knew something about me, including my jeep. Vosveld told the group of us to be ready to leave imminently with no more than a single bag for the airport, when we would be flown initially to Semarang. Mohamad Yunus, the Indian consul who lived across the street, came over and kindly offered to look after the rest of our baggage while we were away, pointedly making sure that Vosveld understood that he would be doing so.

It was another two hours before we left, and shortly before we did the two military observers returned. They then officially protested, without avail, to Captain Vosveld the arrest and detention of their Indonesian liaison officer, Captain Sudarto. They seemed to think I might be able to reach their superior, Colonel Mayer, in Batavia, and asked me to get in touch with him to explain their status and that they awaited further orders from him.

At 2.30 p.m. two jeeps of the Dutch military police arrived under the command of a surly Eurasian lieutenant named O'Hearn. I marveled to myself at the provenance of his Irish name but felt it wise not to query him. Vosveld ordered me to take my jeep out of the garage and share in carrying our group to Maguwo airfield. The road had not been blocked, though within a few villages we passed we could see numerous recently felled trees, apparently hit by artillery. We encountered no soldiers nor any people at all – only a few wounded water buffalo, wandering aimlessly along.

At the airport Lt O'Hearn demanded the keys of my jeep, saying he planned to use it. I asked him for a receipt, which he refused to give me. Nor would he agree to hand it over to the UN military observers until he had finished using it, the length of which period he refused to estimate. We were finally ordered to board a Martin bomber that was to fly us to Semarang. The plane bore no markings, but as I climbed up its steps and looked back from its doorway I saw drawn up on the tarmac several other planes of American origin still bearing the US star that the Dutch had not bothered to paint over. And on the other side stood my faithful old jeep with its two American flags briskly waving in the breeze. At these sights the anger in me boiled over and quite recklessly – and probably foolishly – I turned around, descended the steps and charged over to the jeep, then being pawed over by a couple of Dutch officers. Defiantly I looked these startled men in the eyes, brazenly tore off the two flags from their fender poles and stuffing them in my pocket, turned back and climbed aboard the plane again. This was not meant to be any symbol of American patriotism, but was rather a sudden manifestation of flaming anger at what I regarded as brutal force and wanton killing against a people for whom I had developed great respect and affection.

According to the report by A.G. Pringgodigdo, head of the president's secretariat, submitted via Mohamad Roem to the UN Committee of Good Offices, Dutch troops had begun to attack the presidential palace at about 2 p.m. on 19 December 1948.

> The President's bodyguard at first resisted, but at the order of the President a party went to the Dutch carrying a white flag to inform them that the President's bodyguard would no longer offer resistance. Thereupon a Dutch officer, Lt Col. Overbeak, came to inform the President that he and all the people who were in the Palace at the time were interned and were not allowed to leave. He asked the President to give his word of honor that he would remain there, and the President agreed. On that same day Vice President Hatta and his family were also interned.

On Monday morning, 20 December 1948, Lt Bakker came to the President to inform him that he was to be taken to a meeting with General Meyer (the commander of Dutch forces in Yogyakarta). In the afternoon Captain Vosveld (top Dutch intelligence officer attached to General Meyer's command) took the President by jeep to Dutch headquarters. According to the president, he was asked to order the TNI (the Republic's army) to cease fire, but replied that as a prisoner he was not in a position to do so. General Meyer declared that the President was not a prisoner but that he was only under house arrest, whereupon the President replied that this "amounted to the same thing."

Roem went on to report that on 20 December at about 3 p.m. the Dutch army arrived at Kaliurang, where the UN Committee of Good Offices was then based, and that on the 22nd the staff of the Indonesian delegation was taken to Yogyakarta by truck, all of its archives being seized by the Dutch. On 22 December the Dutch army flew Sukarno, Hatta, Sjahrir, Assaat (head of Parliament's Working Committee), Haji Salim, Air Marshall Suriadarma and A.G. Pringgodigdo to the island of Bangka off the southeast coast of Sumatra, where they were interned behind barbed wire in a small tin-mining village. (For a brief period Sukarno, Sjahrir and Salim were separated from the others and interned at Prapat on Lake Toba in the southern interior of North Sumatra, but Sukarno and Salim were then reunited with the others on Bangka, while Sjahrir was allowed to go to Batavia.)

In later years, especially during the Suharto regime, it became fashionable among many of the Indonesian military, Nasution included, to criticize Sukarno and Hatta for lacking the courage to follow the Indonesian army into the mountains outside Yogyakarta to participate in guerrilla resistance

Figure 3.2   President Sukarno under arrest,
December 1948

Figure 3.3   Haji Agus Salim under arrest

under its protection. What protection? All the objective indications that prevailed as Hatta and Sukarno sat around the cabinet's table at mid-morning 19 December indicated that, in view of the deplorable ongoing performance of the Republic's armed forces, it was unreasonable to expect any real protection in such a venture and that to attempt to join the armed forces would be foolish and very likely suicidal. The two leaders were not athletic youths, being respectively sixteen and seventeen years older than Nasution. Hatta was ill and, with his car having just been attacked by a Dutch plane as he drove down from Kaliurang earlier that morning, had good reason to believe that Dutch planes could strike anywhere in the Republic. But air strikes apart, Hatta had calculated that if he and Sukarno went into the hills it would take at least a battalion to protect them. And by the time the cabinet met that morning it concluded that there were not enough troops left in Yogyakarta to provide this. Moreover, the events of the early morning had given them reason to believe that Dutch intelligence was so good that, even with a protective battalion to guard them, the enemy would learn where they were and bring air power against them.

And though Sukarno and Hatta didn't yet know that the Dutch had cracked the Republic's secret code, they had plenty of evidence of the superiority of Dutch military intelligence. Otherwise how could the disposition of the two military forces be accounted for, especially the fact that at the time of the Dutch attack most of the Republic's army were off on training exercises rather than in defensive positions, and its ground forces commander and most of his staff were nowhere near Yogyakarta but on an inspection tour of East Java? Equally important, as Dutch troops began to encircle the city, Hatta and Sukarno would have already heard of the stunningly rapid collapse of Republican military resistance at Maguwo airfield and the short time it had taken Dutch troops to push the five miles between it and the city. Certainly little had transpired that gave Hatta and Sukarno any reason to believe that if they did take to the hills the Republic's army could protect them. It was one thing to fight an ultimately successful guerrilla war against the Dutch and quite another to do that while having to provide protection for two middle-aged leaders.

In retrospect, however, it is clear that the Dutch blitzkrieg and their rapid capture and incarceration of most of the Republic's top leaders was seriously detrimental to the Netherlands' efforts to win favor in the court of international opinion, and in fact their move seriously backfired.

Before the Dutch troops had entered Yogyakarta, Sukarno, Hatta and Mohammad Natsir had prepared proclamations to be read over the city's radio station that called on all Indonesians to continue fighting the Dutch and never cooperate with them. Before these could be broadcast, however, rockets from Dutch planes had demolished the radio transmitter. But those statements were copied and passed hand to hand among the city's population. I learned of this, I think, from my near neighbor Mohamad Yunus, the Indian consul, shortly before I was forced to leave, and it was then impossible for me to get any of the limited typewritten copies of these statements. But I told myself that if I were ever able to return to Yogyakarta I should make it my priority to get them.

Our plane flew us to Semarang, the main base from which the Dutch were mounting their attack on Yogyakarta, and there on its large airfield I saw more American planes with their original stars undisguised, as well as several half-tracks and many trucks still bearing the same US insignia. A couple of months later when I was in Surabaya, I ran into Dutch marines brazenly wearing US combat fatigues with "US Marines" stamped in block letters above their breast pocket. When I then asked a major in the crack Dutch Marine Brigade what he was doing in a US marines uniform, he calmly replied: "I'm proud of having been trained at Quantico" (the principal US marines training camp). Presumably the inception of the training of Dutch marines in the United States had been predicated on the expectation that they would be part of MacArthur's end-of-the-war assault on the Japanese home islands, but I've never been able to ascertain the extent that training continued after Japan's capitulation.

That evening in Semarang we four foreigners were quartered in a reasonably comfortable guest house, the Pension Juliana, that was already mostly occupied by Dutch estate owners, their families and employees, who had been evacuated the day before (18 December) from the estate area south of Semarang in anticipation of the Dutch attack and possible Indonesian reprisal. After many impediments being placed in my way I was finally able that evening to get to the acting commander of the Dutch Central Java command, Lt Col. Klaprogge. He promised me that telegrams I had prepared for the American and British consulates and the Milex (military observers) Board would be sent that evening. Those to the consulates explained our whereabouts and requested that our families be notified. That to Colonel Mayer, head of the Milex Board was from Mather and Montana, the two UN military officers we had just left in Yogyakarta, stating they were staying there and asking for instructions. So far as I was able to ascertain, none of these messages was ever sent.

The next morning from about 10 a.m. to noon we were separately questioned by Dutch intelligence officers. It was during this interrogation that I got the first hint that the Republic's vaunted secret communications code had been broken by the Dutch, for early in the interview this generally low-key interrogating officer asserted that he and his colleagues had read all the news dispatches I'd written in Yogyakarta. It seemed to me quite plausible that they had, for I'd never been fully convinced that the messages I'd sent through Haji Salim's facilities at the Foreign Office to the Overseas News Agency and to certain individuals could not somehow be intercepted by the Dutch. If they had indeed bothered to read what I transmitted this way they must, of course, have mastered the Republic's communications code, and things much more important than my views would have been known to them. Some forty-five years later, when General Spoor's papers were opened in the Dutch archives, I found this to be the case, including translations of those of my dispatches they had apparently found particularly disagreeable. It was in one of the folders in this archive almost half-a-century later that I discovered that, well before the Dutch attack on Yogyakarta, these dispatches of mine to ONA alone had earned me a place near the top of the Netherlands East Indies Forces Intelligence Services' (NEFIS) list of "The Ten Most Undesirable Aliens" in Indonesia. (That select list was as I recall a mixed bag, incorporating the name of Bob Freeburg, a brave freelance blockade-running pilot, whom I'd admired, as well as the CIA agent, Arturo Campbell, who was anything but an object of my admiration.)

That afternoon the four of us were flown with a military police escort to Batavia, where we were immediately taken to military police headquarters and initially detained. The military police officer whom we were ushered in to see appeared quite unsure of himself, and the sergeant he left behind at his desk seemed even more so when, after a short period of perfunctory questioning, he suddenly excused himself and walked out of the room. Sensing this, I went up to the sergeant and, summoning as authoritative a voice as I could, ordered him to get the American consulate on his phone. I had no reason to think that the American consulate would not soon be aware of our situation, but I did not relish the idea of possibly spending the afternoon and night at the military police barracks. To my surprise the sergeant meekly obliged, put through the call and I was able to talk to a vice-consul who promised to come over immediately, and also to get in touch with the British consul on behalf of Donati.

After I was released from Dutch military police headquarters in Batavia I quickly got in touch with the foreign correspondents whom I'd previously befriended. Most of them had been tied to their desks in Batavia while I'd been away, and they were understandably envious of the experiences I'd had in the Republic. And I, on the other hand, representing what was probably the smallest news organization among them, was anxious that what I'd learned, especially about the recent Dutch attack that none of them had witnessed, be given broader dissemination than I could manage through the Overseas News Agency and a few journal articles. So I was glad to talk to them at length and help them as much as I could with regard to the nature of the Dutch attack and the intricacies of Indonesian politics as I understood them. They appreciated this, and the bonds I had previously established with them grew stronger. Their support was soon to prove crucial for me.

I had expected that some of the officials of the Dutch RVD – Regerings Voorlichtings Dienst (Government Information Service) – would not have been overjoyed at the cables and articles I had sent when I was in the Republic, so I was not surprised when I was abruptly informed that there would no longer be a place for me to stay in the correspondents' mess, such as I'd been fortunate enough to have before I'd left for the Republic. But my anxiety as to where I could stay was immediately overcome by the generous offer of Hal Nelson, a young political officer in the US consulate, and another friend, Arnold Brackman, the United Press correspondent, to share their large and rambling apartment over Batavia's Capitol Restaurant, located almost across from the central post office and alongside one of the canals that the homesick Dutch had built in the older parts of downtown Batavia. Presumably because of its proximity to the main canal and the restaurant, their apartment had what must have been one of the greatest concentrations of rats in Batavia and so appropriately they called their abode affectionately "Rumah Tikus Dalam Kali" (rat house in the Kali).

But they were agreeable apartment mates and had engaged as house boy an ex-guerrilla who turned out to be an excellent cook. And the Capitol Restaurant down below was a gathering place for all sorts of rumor-mongers, some of whom dispensed the sort of tips that journalists are willing to follow up.

While I was prepared for a chilly reception from some of the RVD officials, I still found some of the senior ones, including Van Goudover, its courtly head, friendly. But I was quite unprepared for the viciousness of the attack a few days after my return by Ritman, its brusque executive director, who evidently had been antagonized not only by what I had written but especially by the extent that I appeared to him to be influencing the other correspondents with my assessment of the Republic, its leaders and the nature of the Dutch attack. To discredit my information, he suddenly called what he termed a very important press conference, wherein he point blank accused me of being "a paid employee of the Republic" and craftily, but clearly, implied that I was a Communist. Fortunately for me I had good friends among the foreign correspondents and domestic journalists, and most of them had already been antagonized by the calculated misinformation Ritman had been feeding them. They protested angrily at his accusation and innuendoes, and then, organized and led by my good friend Quentin Pope of the *Chicago Tribune*, the acting doyen of their corps, they marched on Ritman's office, demanded he retract the accusations and disparaging innuendoes he had made against me, and refused to leave until he made a written apology and posted it on his office door. Ritman sullenly complied, and, of course, he now hated me. But several of his senior colleagues and some other Dutch officials thought he had made a fool of himself and demeaned his office, and they made clear to him that he had best repair his tattered relationship with the press corps.

With some of Ritman's senior colleagues now so critical of him, and with most of the other correspondents and journalists now solidly behind us, Quentin Pope and I realized we were suddenly in a strong position and decided this was the propitious time to request the RVD's backing to make trips back into newly Dutch-occupied areas of the Republic – Pope to Surakarta and Madiun and I back to Yogyakarta. We promptly applied for permission to make a week's trip to these destinations, and Ritman, though very much opposed, appeared to feel that if he refused he would further damage his own position. Cheered on by our colleagues, we both flew out on 7 January, managing to get into these newly Dutch-occupied interior areas several days before the first UN military observers arrived.

When we got in both of us found we had to bear the encumbrance of being chaperoned by a Dutch intelligence officer. But I was fortunate, for the young lieutenant assigned to watch me in Yogyakarta, Jan Vredeveld, turned out to be a bright and pleasant young conscript who clearly didn't have his heart in the war and seemed to be about as sympathetic towards me as was possible, given his own orders. And fortunately, as I soon discovered, his boss, the intelligence chief for Yogyakarta, Captain Vosveld, apparently most evenings had his intellect dulled by too much alcohol.

But as Lt Vredeveld readily appreciated, to be chaperoned by even so sympathetic and circumspect a person as he seriously restricted my freedom as a journalist to make contact with Republican political leaders and officials – many of whom I knew to be still at large, some above ground and a few still in hiding from the overworked and often poorly briefed Dutch intelligence service. And he realized that my trying to see them with a Dutch military escort was bound to inhibit their talking with me and could easily bring them to the attention of, and likely investigation by, the Dutch security forces.

Consequently, with Vredeveld's obvious approval, I went to see General Meyer, the Dutch commander in Yogyakarta, to request that I be accorded the freedom normally granted to accredited journalists of talking unchaperoned with any of the city's inhabitants. I was apparently the first journalist with whom he'd had to deal, and his response, though polite, was cautious. He clearly did not want to assume responsibility himself for my having greater scope for my investigations, and responded by offering what he referred to as a "compromise." He would give me freedom to see any Republican whom his chief of intelligence, Captain Vosveld, would approve. Nevertheless, he insisted that Lt Vredeveld continue to accompany me to all my meetings with people in Yogyakarta. That friendly young lieutenant was obviously embarrassed at having to continue in this role, but now, it seemed to me, he was even more discreet in maintaining a distance when I was talking with people.

And so that evening I called on Captain Vosveld in the modern and well-furnished house he had appropriated. He was, as Lt Vredeveld had predicted, already well into his cups, but I realized that, nevertheless, he was shrewd and must be reasonably well informed, so that I had to be very cautious in going over names with him as to people I wanted permission to see. Consequently I limited myself to those who were sufficiently well-known not to be endangered by my singling them out, for the most part cabinet members and party leaders. I was surprised at his lack of recognition of some of the minor party leaders whom I mentioned in our rambling conversation. Among them was Abikusno Tjokrosujoso, head of the small, but politically significant, Partai Sarekat Islam Indonesia, a faction that had two years before split off from the Masjumi to join Amir Sjarifuddin's cabinet and thereby given it at least token Islamic representation. Of more immediate importance, and something I had heard reported but wanted to check out, was a report Vosveld had evidently not yet received that Abikusno's two sons had recently been dragged from his house and shot to death by a group of Dutch soldiers well after their occupation of the city. Vosveld clearly did not know who Abikusno was, but, as I soon learned from Vredeveld, he had learned of my visit to him and been sufficiently concerned that he telegraphed his superiors in Batavia to ask about him and mentioned my interest in the matter. This I learned was one of the things that brought Vosveld's superiors to order him to stop my investigations.

Undoubtedly even more important was Vosveld's discovery that I was on the track of the speeches Sukarno, Hatta and Natsir had prepared to be read over Yogyakarta's radio station on the morning of 19 December, but which could not be delivered before Dutch planes loosed rockets against the station and destroyed it. A few copies of these addresses had been typed up and were, I soon discovered, circulating within the city. I realized their importance and so, unfortunately, did Captain Vosveld. And so much of my time during the remainder of my four days in Yogyakarta was spent in trying, undetected, to secure one of the rare copies of each address.

My quest for the carbon copies of these typewritten undelivered speeches got off to a slow and discouraging start. I had flown up with a small valise and a large suitcase which was full of baby food to deliver to the wives of incarcerated friends of mine whom I knew would be having a hard time feeding their infants. And, for these same families, I was also carrying Dutch guilders that their relatives and friends in Batavia had asked me to take to them since they would command a good exchange rate with the Republican rupiah, still the most utilized currency in Yogyakarta. Lt Vredeveld clearly approved of this baby-food mission and was happy to transport me around the city in his jeep to carry it out. Moreover, he was thoughtful enough to stay a discreet distance out of hearing range when I talked to these wives, and again when I visited the main hospital to check on whether civilian friends that I knew had been admitted there. In the course of these visits, as he was surely astute enough to realize, I was able to pick up information as to which cabinet ministers and party leaders had remained behind to go underground in the city and which ones I might have some possibility of reaching.

Presumably, so he could help out in the hospital, the authorities had not jailed Dr Johannes Leimena, a friend of mine who had served as minister of health in the last Republican cabinet. In any case he was still free, and Indonesian friends I talked to during my first day in Yogyakarta told me I would be able to contact him through a mutual friend, Jo Kurnianingrat, whom the Dutch found it useful, as they did with several other well-qualified women, to permit to work at the clinic of the Indonesian Red Cross. Lt Vredeveld and I set out to find the house where Jo was living and found her in. He had the impression, of which I did not disabuse him, that I was visiting an old girlfriend, and he stayed out in the front yard of the house, at an even greater distance than usual. What I had not realized, nor certainly had Vredeveld, was that Leimena was already in the house, but well out of Vredeveld's sight to the right and behind where Jo was sitting in plain view.

And so I was able to get across to both Jo and Leimena the urgency of my quest for the three aborted radio addresses. Leimena managed to whisper to me that I should ask to visit my old friend Bishop Sugiopranoto the day after next, and he would arrange to have copies of the speeches at his house for delivery to me. I don't know what suspicions my request to visit the bishop aroused, though I knew he had the reputation for being a strong supporter of the Republic, but at the last minute an obviously puzzled Lt Vredeveld informed me that permission had been denied.

But my request to call on Abikusno was met and, accompanied by Vredeveld, I went to his house that evening. There I found a deeply saddened and angry man. A very distraught Abikusno told me that the report of the killing of his sons was indeed true; on 25 December a group of Dutch soldiers had forced their way into his house, demanded delivery of firearms which were not there and having been told so clubbed his two sons with the butts of their pistols, dragged them out of his house and shot them. The Red Cross had identified their bodies from the identification papers still on them and had accordingly notified Abikusno, asking him to formally identify the bodies. The official explanation of the Dutch authorities, he said, was that his sons had been killed because they were out after curfew – an accusation he vigorously denied. Abikusno gave me the names and whereabouts of the Red Cross investigators, whom I was quickly able to find and who gave me a detailed corroboration of the affair.

I later inferred from what little Vredeveld was able to tell me that a report of my visit to Abikusno and plans to see Bishop Sugiopranoto had reached Lt Col. Van Lier, head of Dutch army intelligence in Batavia, the same man who had sought to bar me from entering the Republic six months before, and apparently when he learned of these contacts he was furious with Captain Vosveld. And so the day after I saw Abikusno a visibly embarrassed Lt Vredeveld came by the Grand Hotel in which I was staying to inform me that orders called for me to be kept under house arrest in the hotel until I could be flown back to Batavia under military police escort on the first available plane the next morning.

When I attempted to go downstairs to the hotel's dining room that evening I found my way barred by a Dutch corporal armed with a carbine who informed me that he had orders to keep me upstairs in my room and that if I needed to eat he was to have food sent up to me. If he had had any sympathy for me I soon dissipated it by foolishly taking pictures of him from the top of the stairs while he was performing this guard duty.

That evening of 9 January, as I was sitting at the desk in my room writing up what I'd experienced during the day, at exactly 10 p.m. I heard several

Figure 3.4   View from my place of detention, Yogyakarta, 9 January 1949

explosions and rifle fire on the periphery of the city that seemed to be near the Sultan's kraton. At 10.40 p.m. there was a very heavy explosion in that general area. The lights in the hotel all went out and I learned that a power station had been blown up. Because the hotel served as a headquarters for much of the Dutch civilian and some military personnel, it was equipped with an emergency diesel generator that soon started up and the lights came on again. As they did the hotel became a major target, and an authoritative Dutch voice on the first floor shouted: "Alle lichten uit!"

At about 11 p.m. there was shooting within the block on which the hotel was situated and I leaned out over my room's little verandah to see what was going on. But, as I did, bullets literally whistled around me and I quickly ducked back into the room. After a lull the shooting started up again, interspersed now by mortar fire. Just after midnight a mortar shell struck the roof of the Toko Oen Building just across Malioboro Street from my room. It caught fire and black smoke began to erupt through the roof. Seeing that made me suddenly very much aware that with my room being on the third and top floor of the hotel, and just under its roof, it was every bit as vulnerable to a mortar shell as the Toko Oen. So with my flashlight shining on my face I stumbled downstairs to where the Dutch corporal was still doing sentry duty. When I pointed out to him the relative safety of the inhabitants of the first floor and my desire to join them, he shrugged, told me he had his orders and grimly pointed me to go back upstairs to my room. There I spent the time until about 2 a.m., when the fighting seemed to stop, under my bed.

I learned the next morning that the hotel had been under attack from both the front (the Malioboro Street side), and the rear where an arroyo led to the back of the hotel. The hotel walls had been pocked in many places by machine-gun bullets and sappers had been in the process of laying a charge of dynamite near its rear door when they were driven off by Dutch snipers on the roof of the hotel. The Republic's troops had penetrated to the very center of the city and had only finally been driven out by the tanks and armored cars, which I had heard repeatedly charging up and down Malioboro Street during the night. The attacking force, much larger than in a previous attack on 29 December, had consisted of a heavy battalion of the Police Mobile Brigade and one or two companies of the KRIS (Kebaktian Rakjat Indonesia Sulawesi) – a militarily well-honed unit made up of soldiers from Sulawesi (mostly Minahassans who had been living on Java at the end of the Japanese occupation).

There was a postscript to my experience in the hotel which was so bizarre that I have felt to write about it would make readers doubt my sobriety, but perhaps now half a century later it is appropriate to do so. Approximately five weeks later, on 16 February 1949, I was in Bandung at the house of Wiranata Koesoemah, who was then away, having dinner with two of his sons. (Bandung was then Dutch-occupied, and they were in the process of trying to induce the father to be a more tractable head of a Dutch-designed West Java puppet government of Pasundan than he was willing to become.)

The two sons and I were in the midst of discussing the dramatic trek of the battalion headed by Ahmad Wiranata Koesoemah, which had departed from the Yogyakarta area on 20 December, and fought its way back through both Dutch and Darul Islam forces to its pre-Renville bases in West Java. A servant entered to whisper something to Male, the elder brother, who excused himself, saying someone wanted to see him on a matter of importance. He went out to the hall for a few minutes to talk to the caller, a young lieutenant in the Police Mobile Brigade, and returned with him into the dining room. The caller, Male explained, wanted to deliver a message to me. This young man, who looked no more than twenty, was obviously embarrassed and was breathing hard, but clearly determined to speak his piece. Drawing himself up he announced that he had come to offer me an apology. He went on to explain that he had been in charge of the sapper unit assigned to blow up the Grand Hotel and had actually been in the process of laying dynamite sticks at its back when driven off by the Dutch snipers on the hotel's roof.

Since the episode was well known, he said, he assumed I'd heard all about it. But what he wanted me to understand was that he had felt ashamed ("*malu*") when he later learned that there had been a pro-Republic American in the building. He wanted me to know that there was nothing "personal" about this effort to blow up the hotel, and that it had in no sense represented any hostility towards me. When the young lieutenant had left my two hosts couldn't contain their laughter, but I must confess to having been deeply touched by this chivalrous gesture.

On 10 January, the morning after the attack, I waited to be picked up and transported to the airport. I remember feeling depressed, for I had failed in what I regarded as my most important objective: obtaining copies of the addresses that Sukarno, Hatta and Natsir had prepared on the morning of 19 December to be broadcast over the Republic's radio – the calls for resistance to and non-cooperation with the Dutch. I knew that at least two carbon copies of these typewritten statements were circulating surreptitiously in Yogyakarta, but with the interdiction of my meeting with Bishop Sugiopranoto my chances of getting one seemed ended.

Remembering that the road to the airport passed the Indonesian Red Cross clinic, and that Jo Kurnianingrat who worked there was very much aware of the importance of these statements, I gambled on trying to stop off there. With the impassive military policemen, who were sitting in the back seat of Lt Vredeveld's jeep, able to hear anything I said, I ventured to say "I assume Captain Vosveld would not want to be in the position of denying an accredited correspondent the usual right to get updated casualty records from the Red Cross." Vredeveld, who clearly thought I had been treated badly, readily agreed. And so on the way to the airport we did stop at the Indonesian Red Cross office.

I went in, with Vredeveld staying a polite distance behind me in the doorway, and approached the desk to ask Jo Abdurachman, a friend of mine as well as of Jo Kurnianingrat, for the casualty figures usually dispensed to journalists. She excused herself, and I could hear muffled conversation with someone in back room, after which she re-emerged with Jo Kurnianingrat who was bearing a pile of papers. There was an exchange of banalities about how incomplete such records always were, during which one of them managed to whisper to me to look carefully inside the pile. I leafed quickly through the sheaf to discover, to my delight, copies of the three addresses. They tied it up with string, and with my new bundle I got back into the jeep. The casualty sheets were clearly visible on the outside, and neither Vredeveld nor the dour military police officer showed any interest in looking further. We drove on to the airport where I said goodbye to Vredeveld, an altogether decent and honorable young man, whom by now I regarded more as a friend than as a military chaperone.

Though, when the military police officer and I landed in Batavia, I fully expected to be detained and interrogated, I was told I was free to go and promptly took a taxi to the UN Good Offices Committee's office. There I sought out Tom Critchley, its Australian representative, who I knew was pro-Republic and whom I trusted more than Merle Cochran, the American representative. Critchley recognized the importance of the documents, expressed great pleasure in receiving them and readily agreed to have copies made for me. Soon afterwards I took copies to friends of mine in the

Republic's underground organization in Batavia, and they promptly had more copies made for distribution throughout Java. With that achieved, I felt my trip to Yogyakarta had been really worthwhile.

Still grateful to my friends among the correspondents and journalists who had made my trip to Yogyakarta possible, I soon got in touch with them to tell them what I'd learned. I, of course, reported to the Overseas News Agency as well, but I knew that these friends from the other newspapers would reach a broader audience than I could. And since my departure several new correspondents had arrived in Batavia. Among them was Robert Trumbull of the *New York Times*, whose issue of 11 January 1949 carried an account of my description of the 9 January attack on Yogyakarta, saying: "Mr Kahin's is the first outside account of the current guerrilla warfare in the interior since the Dutch 'cease-fire' order of Dec. 31 ... There have been no Dutch communiqués on major actions since the cease-fire."

Apart from the fact that in the early evening of my fourth day in Yogyakarta I was arrested, put into a guarded room in the city's main hotel and shipped back the next morning under military police escort to Batavia, things had gone extraordinarily well during the four days I was able to spend in Yogyakarta. Most importantly, I had finally been able to get copies of Sukarno, Hatta and Natsir's speeches and carry them back with me undetected to the UN Good Offices Committee and the Republic's underground organization in Batavia – from where they were distributed throughout Java.

Also, I had found that the civilian head of the Dutch economic administration for Yogyakarta, B.J. Muller, was so fed up with what he regarded as the Dutch army's foolish and heavy-handed conduct in the Yogyakarta area that he welcomed the chance to explain to me the realities of the economic and administrative situations there. One point he stressed was how few Republican officials were cooperating with the Dutch administration, and that those few were probably only working because expressly ordered to by the Sultan of Yogyakarta, who did not wish the civilian population to suffer unduly. I also learned how surprised General Spoor and his senior officers were at the sultan's unwillingness to cooperate with them. In a blundering effort to influence him, Spoor soon afterwards flew in the pro-Dutch Sultan of Pontianak, Hamid II, known to the Dutch as "Max," to reason with the Yogyakarta sultan, but Hamengku Buwono refused even to meet with him.[3]

And finally, on the last evening of my brief stay in Yogyakarta, I had witnessed what was by far the heaviest counter-attack of the Republic's army there – one that penetrated into the very center of the city. This attack, it should be noted, came well before Suharto's much ballyhooed involvement in the second major Republican attack against Dutch-occupied Yogyakarta, one actually planned by Hamengku Buwono IX, the Sultan of Yogyakarta, on 1 March 1949. (The first Republican attack against Dutch-occupied

Yogyakarta – considerably smaller than either of these, involving, I was told, a force of only about 400 men – had taken place on 29 December 1948.)

After having returned to Dutch-controlled Batavia, my main objective was to visit and assess the character of the congeries of "states" the Dutch had been establishing in the areas of Indonesia outside of the Republic as components of a new federal order. The first step in this process, as announced by Van Mook on 9 March 1948, was to be the establishment of an "Interim Federal Government" which was to function until superseded by an enduring Dutch-sponsored federal "United States of Indonesia." Although the Renville Agreement of January 1948 had stipulated that creation of such an interim regime was to be brought about by joint Dutch–Republican cooperation, and not by the unilateral action of one of the parties, the Dutch acted entirely on their own despite the Republic's protest to the UN Committee of Good Offices.

Most of the correspondents in Batavia suspected – correctly – that the new system that the Netherlands government was launching with such fanfare was fundamentally a scheme of divide-and-rule calculated to maintain Dutch hegemony in a guise more pleasing to the outside world. Van Mook and some of his supporters hoped that enough power might be transferred to the newly established states that were to make up this new federal order to attract a significant portion of their populations. Their expectations were, however, disappointed, for the Netherlands government was unwilling to countenance even as much of a shift in power as they sought, and certainly not enough to permit any significant degree of political attraction for the inhabitants of these areas.

As I was to discover during the first four months of 1949 in visiting the two largest of these Dutch-created states – East Indonesia and Pasundan (West Java) – and several smaller ones, these political entities were fundamentally elaborate façades for indirect Dutch rule and a continuing thinly disguised Dutch control of those parts of Indonesia their armed forces continued to occupy, or kept trying to subdue. That the political pattern of the federation was designed to undercut the Republic's influence and remove it from a meaningful role was soon evident to Batavia-based journalists. It would be hard to conclude otherwise when the Dutch finally divulged that in the federation they envisaged, each of its sixteen components would have equal representation, with this ultimately meaning each would have two senators. Thus, the Republic, comprising approximately half of Java and three-quarters of Sumatra and with a population of more than 31 million, would have equal representation with that of the tiny "state" of Riau, a group of small islands located just off Singapore with only about 100,000 inhabitants. The small islands of Bangka and Billiton, off the coast of Sumatra, also each constituted a "state," and the sparse population of Borneo was divided into five more states. Journalists in Batavia were quick to appreciate that this system was designed not only to swamp the Republic as a constituent state, but also to yield a divide-and-rule formula designed to ensure easy Dutch dominance of the federation.

The principal questions remaining were the degree of autonomy the Dutch would permit the component states of this grossly unbalanced and weirdly distorted "federation" and, more immediately, how representative of their inhabitants were their administrations. This was something that the correspondents and other journalists tied to their desks in Batavia had neither the time nor funds to explore – especially because of the cost of air transportation to most of these far-flung states. Neither, I thought, did I, for the money from my fellowship was now nearly exhausted. But fortunately once more my beloved old jeep came to my rescue.

At a time when financial necessity was bringing me to conclude that I would have to terminate my research without having explored the situation in the Dutch-occupied and administered areas, I learned from a friend in the American consulate that foreigners whose property had been taken over by the Dutch army could put in a claim for its return, and that he thought I would qualify with respect to my confiscated jeep. Apparently Americans with much more clout than I – rubber estate managers and others in business – were applying, and he thought it would be awkward for the Netherlands East Indies administration not to accord me similar treatment. I took up his suggestion, and to my surprise in about two weeks was informed that my jeep had been returned and that I could pick it up at the consulate. Except for three bullet holes that had hit no vital part, it was the same old jeep, and I was delighted.

The shortage of vehicles in Indonesia was acute, and within a few days the large Dutch plantation conglomerate, the Borneo–Sumatra Maatschappij (Borsumij) had learned of my jeep's return and promptly approached me with an offer to buy it. They offered me in Dutch guilders (easily converted to US dollars) well over twice what I had paid for the jeep, and I accepted with alacrity. It was enough to pay for my air passage back to the United States and for extensive air travel within Indonesia, enabling me to visit seven of the Dutch-sponsored federal states that had already been established or were in the process of being formed – East Indonesia (including flights to Makassar, Manado and Bali), Middle Java, East Java, Madura, Pasundan (West Java), Bangka and South Sumatra.

Because of several rather unique circumstances, Dutch control over their largest state, East Indonesia, with a population of about 11 million, was relatively strong.[4] Composed of Sulawesi, together with the Moluccas and the lesser Sundas (including Bali and Ambon), its scattered maritime geography allowed the Dutch to employ their naval power more easily than in other areas. And the relatively effective Australian military occupation of much of the area, following the Japanese occupation, that had preempted any early establishment of a major Republican military presence there at the beginning of the Indonesian revolution, made the road of entry easier for the Dutch troops that followed them. Moreover, two important Christian areas of East Indonesia – Ambon and the Minahassa peninsula of northern Sulawesi – had been the two major recruiting grounds for the KNIL, the Netherlands Indies colonial army. Veterans of the KNIL mostly retired to these areas, so that for economic as well as political reasons many of their inhabitants felt a special tie to the Netherlands. Furthermore, at least a sizable minority, if not a majority, of the feudal aristocrats in this vast area believed that their social and economic positions under an egalitarian-oriented Republican rule might suffer.

In visiting these "states" I was not prepared for the strength of pro-Republican sentiment there, the vigor of Republican underground organizations and the extent to which the Republican army had expanded its control in some of them – notably Pasundan (West Java) and East Java. (I also heard reports of similar military activity in South Sumatra but had less opportunity to check them.) Pasundan was the second largest "state" in the federal order the Dutch were attempting to build, having over 10 million people. Dutch military forces controlled, even loosely, no more than a third of its vast, mostly mountainous West Java terrain, and in any effective sense Dutch dominance was limited to a much smaller area. The Republic's crack Siliwangi division probably controlled at least as large an area as the Dutch, and the rest of the province was under the somewhat more shifting control of the Darul Islam – an organization that regarded the Renville Agreement as a betrayal to the Dutch and now stood opposed to both them and the Republic – and the irregular pro-Republic troops of the Laskjar Rakjat Djawa Barat, operating mostly in the Krawang delta area. And the Republican underground organization was pervasive throughout most of West Java (the same area as the putative state of Pasundan), and strong even in the heavily Dutch-garrisoned capital of Bandung. In fact, there were continuing small-scale probes by Republican forces into the outer perimeter of Dutch defenses around this town.

The "State" of East Java, despite the political astuteness of the governor, the notorious Charles Van Der Plas,[5] was still in a distinctly formative stage. (In talking with Van Der Plas I was struck by his considerable knowledge of the internal politics of the Republic. He appeared to be, as I'd heard, strongly pro-Sjahrir, but I was surprised to find him indicate his respect for Tan Malaka, of whose history he was very knowledgeable.) During my visit to Surabaya in mid-April 1949, I learned that a major part of East Java was dominated by the Republic's armed forces, and civil administration of the Republic's underground government in East Java was being directed by Dr Sukiman, the Republic's minister of interior, who had escaped from Yogyakarta before its occupation by the Dutch army.

Indonesian members of the "parliament" for the "state" of East Java, however, were critical of Dutch control of the indirect process of election and the fact that no political parties had been allowed to function. They were especially angered by the number of people jailed during the electoral process, and they were resentful that no powers had yet been transferred to their "state" by Batavia though it had been formally launched in August 1948. Some acknowledged that they were not yet sure exactly what these powers might be since the constitution had been written in Dutch and was only then in the process of being translated into Indonesian.

When I visited Semarang, putative capital of the not yet fully officially launched "state" of Middle Java, I found it to be precisely as Columbia Law School Professor Arthur Schiller described it in his subsequent study of the Dutch interim federal order: "merely an undefined political entity."[6] I found that even those apparently few local leaders who might have been disposed to try working with the Dutch were discouraged not only because they had been refused permission to hold direct elections for a local council, but that in any case they felt it useless to take a position as to formation of a local government since Batavia had not yet even made clear what the boundary might be between a Middle Java political entity and the residual state of the Republic of Indonesia. In any case, the Dutch had refused to devolve any powers on representatives of the area. Local leaders informed me that the Republican army had been actively on the offensive in the area and that 75 per cent of the regency of Probolinggo was now in its hands as against about a third two months before. They said that the railhead city of Purwokerto (where the previous August I had unloaded my jeep) was surrounded by Republican forces and they had captured several of the loco-motives based there. A most depressed Dutch marine major told me that – as had been the case when Quentin Pope reported three months before – the major city of Madiun was still critically dependent on air transport for much of its food, and that it could be reached overland only occasionally by mili-tary convoys heavily escorted by tanks.

The "state" of South Sumatra looked, on paper at least, to be second only to East Sumatra in the extent of autonomy granted it. But when I very briefly visited it in early May 1949, I encountered a smoldering discontent at how little substance of authority had actually been transferred by Batavia. That perception I found to be general among almost all those Indonesian leaders I encountered in the seven projected federal areas that I visited who had hoped that the Dutch would really devolve significant authority on them. And as I today review the rather extensive notes I took on my visits to these seven components of the putative Dutch-crafted interim federal order, I can come to no different conclusion than I did fifty years ago: "This new government represented no real change in the power structure of Dutch-controlled Indonesia. It was merely the old Netherlands Indies regime with a few anti-Republican Indonesians included to present a better facade."[7]

Nor, given the stifling impact of the omnipresent state of "War and Siege" and its attendant martial law, should one have expected much more. As Schiller has noted:

> In spite of the creation of negaras [states] in these parts of Java and Sumatra the state of siege was lifted in only one region, that of the

Negara Madura by decree of November 23, 1949. It is notable that this was only one month before Netherlands sovereignty terminated.[8]

Given the artificial nature of this federal order, and the common perception that at its most fundamental level it was a system of Netherlands divide-and-rule, it is understandable why successive generations of Indonesians were repelled by the concept of federalism – even though their country desperately needed some variant of that formula of administration.

The next-to-last component state of the projected Dutch-sponsored interim federal government that I visited was Bangka, an island slightly larger than Bali, located off the southeast coast of Sumatra. During the week in early May 1949 that I was there, I spent a couple of days in its capital of Pangkalpinang talking to Dutch officials and Indonesian leaders in an effort to learn something as to the administration and degree of autonomy of this small "state."[9] The main object of my trip to Bangka, however, was to visit the leaders of the Republic that the Dutch had interned there – especially Hatta and Sukarno. For nearly four days I stayed with them in their little compound on a hill at the edge of the tin-mining village of Muntok at the extreme northeast corner of the island.

Others interned there with whom I had a chance to talk were Haji Agus Salim, Mr Assaat, chairman of the Working Committee of the KNIP (Komite Nasional Indonesia Pusat), the Republic's parliament, Abdul Gafar Pringgodigdo, Sukarno's modest and self-effacing, but very knowledgeable chef-de-cabinet, and Mohamad Roem, head of the Republic's delegation to the UN's Good Offices Committee. (Roem was so struck with the intelligence of Norma, one of the Muntok village girls, that he and his wife later adopted her; she blossomed into a beautiful young woman and married Hamengku Buwono IX, Sultan of Yogyakarta.)

Assuming that Sjahrir would be more tractable than he was, the Dutch had permitted him to return to Batavia. The Republic's finance minister, Sjafruddin Prawiranegara of the progressive wing of the Masjumi, was in the mountains of West Sumatra heading the Republic's Emergency Government from there. (He had been sent on a mission to Bukittinggi, the Republican capital of Sumatra a few weeks before the Dutch attack of 19 December 1948 and charged by Hatta with the leadership of the Republic's government in case Hatta and Sukarno were captured by the Dutch. Since the days immediately following the Dutch attack he had been broadcasting over his radio there a line of uncompromising resistance to the Netherlands.) Dr Sukiman, a more centrist leader of the Masjumi Party who had been serving as minister of interior, was heading the Republic's underground administration in East Java. And Natsir and several other cabinet members were also presumed to be operating with the Republic's underground organization on Java.

Most of my time on Bangka was spent in relaxed and unhurried discussions with Sukarno and Hatta, and I was able to gain a much better understanding of their views and their participation in the revolution than I'd been able to in previous briefer meetings in the tense atmosphere of Yogyakarta (Figure 3.5).

By this time the Republic's mounting military successes and the increased support for it in the United Nations combined to create an atmosphere wherein its leaders could now more realistically look forward to the possibility of finally securing full independence from the Netherlands by the end of the year. And from my standpoint, the timing of my visit was perfect, since these leaders, having been incarcerated together for so long – until only about a week before in a tightly confined area behind barbed wire – had grown bored with each other's company and found my presence a refreshing change. They seemed pleased I had come and were eager to talk to me. Over the course of three days I had several much longer discussions with Sukarno and Hatta than would have been possible under normal circumstances.

Sukarno liked to take walks while talking and seemed completely relaxed while doing so. The leaders were now free to leave their restricted quarters on the hill above the village and visit the house of the local *wedana* (district head) where the Dutch officials made American films occasionally available. On the occasion I attended the showing of one of them in their company, Sukarno became understandably bored as the film was so bad and suggested that he and I go out hunting crocodiles, of which there were many in the canals that had been opened by earlier tin-dredging operations. He borrowed two very ancient muskets from the *wedana*, of a vintage that must have gone back almost to the East India Company, and we set out in the dark to look

Figure 3.5   With Sukarno, Haji Agus Salim, and their families, Bangka, May 1949

for them. Fortunately we found none – to my great relief, for I didn't think I could master my old firing piece, and in any case I bore no grudge against crocodiles.

I found both Hatta and Sukarno remarkably open in talking about many aspects of the revolution's history and their views on Indonesia's future. The following are some of the notes I took that I believe are most important.

We talked extensively about many of the more controversial aspects of the revolution – particularly its early days, the Japanese occupation, the Madiun rebellion, their political philosophies and their views on the future of the Republic. Both men were insistent that fundamentally Indonesia's national revolution had to precede its social revolution.

Sukarno saw the national phase of the revolution as continuing for at least ten years after the transfer of sovereignty from the Dutch and possibly for several decades. "The essential point must be the building up of a nation – a strong national state … As a socialist I'm first of all a nationalist." But that didn't mean, he said, that in the process of building up a strong national state social problems could be neglected. Whereas Hatta thought it would be feasible to move from a nationalist to a socialist phase of the revolution – incorporating a strong component of cooperatives – without the intermediate step of building up a strong middle class, Sukarno thought that such a transitional step was necessary. He felt that expropriation of foreign properties would be a mistake, that Indonesia needed foreign capital and should gradually buy out foreign investments. (Hatta did not express himself on this point, but I sensed that implicitly he would agree with Sukarno.) Hatta was clearly the better grounded of the two in his understanding of socialism and had a more sophisticated understanding of Marxism. It was interesting that among the few other Indonesian leaders he singled out as having a solid understanding of Marxism were Tan Malaka and the PKI's Tan Ling Djie. In his advocacy of socialism for Indonesia, Hatta saw it in the context of a mixed economy wherein the cooperative sector would run a close second, followed by a third, smaller, sector of private enterprise.

Both men were deeply concerned to maintain national unity. Hatta favored a decentralized federal arrangement and Sukarno a unitary state. Sukarno seemed to be especially absorbed with the problem of national unity and emphasized: "The work of my lifetime is building up a national state."

Another common denominator in Hatta's and Sukarno's discussions of Indonesia's future that struck me forcefully, and one which I think has been little appreciated by scholars of Indonesian history, was their view of the appropriate political role of Islam. Both were strongly opposed to the idea of an Islamic state and apprehensive that efforts to push for that objective might tear apart the country's unity. But both felt strongly that Islam and socialism were fully compatible and that in combination could form an appropriate amalgam for Indonesia (a "working synthesis" was Hatta's term).

For all of the Republic's political leaders that I met it was socialism of one variant or another that would provide the road towards greater social justice, and the vast majority of Indonesia's nationalist leaders, especially most of those who led the revolution, were profoundly anti-capitalist. That they should have been so seemed natural in view of their conditioning by Dutch colonial rule. Nevertheless, the rewriting of Indonesian history under the rule of Suharto and his army historians has been so extreme as to make nearly all of the present generation of Indonesians quite unaware of the fact that almost the entire leadership of the revolution espoused one variant or another of socialism and that a major thrust of the Indonesian revolution was strongly anti-capitalist in character. The possibility for the generation growing up under President Suharto's rule to understand this was of course seriously undermined by the fact that he and his followers undertook to root out Marxist thought as well as communism. The heavy trauma of his ruthless killing of so many Indonesians suspected of support for one ideology of the left, communism, was sufficiently brutal to intimidate most of two generations of Indonesians from searching for any progressive ideological solutions to the country's problems that might possibly be construed as Marxist, and Marxism came to be seen as the major fundament of all socialism.

Under Suharto, even that substantial portion of Modernist Islamic leaders who during the revolution were proud to identify themselves as "religious socialists" found it politically wise to distance themselves from that term. By its massacres of 1965–6 and its subsequent sporadic crackdown on independent advocacy of progressive socioeconomic prescriptions, the Suharto regime cowed many independent inquiring minds among young Indonesians and frightened them from attempting to explore even non-Marxist variants of socialism. To be known as interested in any variant of socialism, whether democratic or not, was too great a risk for nearly all intellectuals or would-be labor leaders of the Suharto period. The Suharto regime's intimidating grip was too firm and ruthless to be able to predict how soon its stultifying atmosphere would dissipate.

This ignoring of the socialist beliefs of many of the revolutionary leaders has been matched by the propensity to see the revolution as almost exclusively a struggle for political independence from the Dutch. This attitude was greatly strengthened by Suharto's entourage and by some of his foreign apologists. Even the term "revolution" was unsettling for Suharto and his supporters, who for many years insisted instead on the term "independence struggle," a term bereft of social and economic implications. This was driven home for me when in mid-1995 a major Indonesian publisher explained to me in some embarrassment that a major reason for having deferred publishing an Indonesian edition of my book, *Nationalism and Revolution in Indonesia*, for at least ten years after it had been translated was because, in view of the then-prevailing political climate, it would have been dangerous to attempt this. But in 1995 – one of a few ephemeral periods when the Suharto regime thought it good public relations with the outside world to appear more open than usual, there was an unusual window of opportunity for publications and conferences that departed a bit from the regime's official line. Given the fact that the Indonesian Council of Sciences (LIPI) had just felt it appropriate to invite me to present a keynote address at its conference marking the 50th anniversary of Indonesian independence, his publishing house thought it safe to bring out its long-sequestered translation of my book. It was explained to me that however appropriate a title incorporating the term "Revolution" had been when the book was published in English in 1952, and thereafter for the duration of the Sukarno period, it became politically no longer acceptable in the climate of Suharto's rule. If we had substituted something less politically inflammatory than the word "revolution," perhaps "economic development," which the Suharto regime preferred as its hallmark, I suppose there would have been less difficulty.

Other Indonesian friends insisted, however, on a different explanation for the deferred publication of my book in Indonesian – one that had never occurred to me, but was I thought quite plausible. This was the fact that I had there inadvertently undermined the importance of one of Suharto's proudest military achievements in the Revolution – his undoubtedly significant role as a major leader in the attack of 1 March 1949 against Dutch-occupied Yogyakarta, for which he had every right to be proud. The problem was that in my book I had noted that there had been two other such major attacks by Republican forces, 29 December 1948 and 9 January 1949, and I had devoted much more space to the latter, since I had actually witnessed it, than to the 1 March affair in which Suharto had been involved, and of whose role I had not been aware when I wrote my book.

Arguably the 9 January attack, which I observed cut right through the center of Yogyakarta, was as heavy as that of 1 March. But it was Ventje Sumual's Kris (Kebaktian Rakjat Indonesia Sulawesi – Loyalty of the Indonesian People from Sulawesi)[10] and units of the Police Mobile Brigade (Mobrig)[11] that mounted that highly successful attack of 9 January, and there is no indication that Suharto participated. While a whole chapter in Suharto's autobiography is devoted to the attack of 1 March, there is no mention of the equally powerful attack of just seven weeks earlier.

4   The Dutch transfer sovereignty

The return to the United States from Indonesia was much more rapid for me than my trip out. Thanks to the sale of my jeep to Borsumij, the big Dutch estate management company, I had sufficient money left over, even after my flights around Indonesia, to buy a ticket on British Overseas Airways that took me home in stages aboard their comfortable seaplanes. Flying from Batavia on 18 May 1949, I first made very brief trips to Singapore and Kuala Lumpur, where I visited foreign correspondent friends whom I'd met in Indonesia, and then flew on west. With my relay of BOAC planes making the essential overnight refueling stops in Calcutta, New Delhi, Rome and Southampton, I arrived in New York on 31 May and soon was united with my wife, son Brian and daughter Sharon, who had been born in early March while I was still in Indonesia.

At Southampton I had again met Dr Subandrio, the Republic's representative in London, who came down to see off Sudarpo Sastrosatomo, brother of my good friend Subadio. Sudarpo was on his way to Washington to resume his duties as press officer for the Republic's representation there – an office that some seven months later, after the United States recognized the new government of Indonesia, was to become the Indonesian embassy. One of the ablest and most energetic press officers the Republic ever had in Washington, Sudarpo deserves much credit for helping turn opinion in the US Congress, and ultimately some stubbornly pro-Dutch members of the State Department, in favor of the Republic. In this effort he had important help from his friends Soedjatmoko ("Koko") Mangoendiningrat, Nicodemus Lambertus ("Nick") Palar, the Republic's chief representative in New York, and from Sumitro Djojohadikusumo, a recent PhD from the Rotterdam School of Economics, who soon came to spend considerable time as a member of the Republic's delegation to the Round Table Conference at The Hague – the long series of meetings sponsored by the United Nations to achieve a final negotiated settlement of the Dutch–Indonesian dispute.

Sudarpo knew of my reporting from Indonesia and my friendship with Sjahrir and numerous members of his party (the PSI), of which Sudarpo, like his brother Subadio, was a member. We had plenty to discuss, and he expressed keen interest when I told him of my intention to go to Washington to talk with Frank Graham and Owen Brewster, two of a handful of senators who had indicated some interest in the Indonesian–Dutch dispute. I soon discovered that Sudarpo and I shared anxious concern over what we felt to be Hatta's overly great dependency on, and largely uncritical acceptance of, the advice of Merle Cochran, the career US foreign service officer who served as American representative on the United Nations Committee of Good Offices in the Dutch–Indonesian dispute. What worried us most was Cochran's ability to persuade Hatta that he was the only significant proponent of the Republic in Washington. Indeed, already in the negotiations during the spring of 1949 (leading to the Roem–Van Royen Agreement of 7 May 1949), Cochran had worked assiduously to convince Hatta and other members of the Indonesian delegation that the only American support they could count on was what he himself could persuade the State Department to extend.

Over the months following my departure, events in Indonesia moved rapidly. Under the Roem–van Royen Agreement, which was formally accepted by the Republic and the Netherlands on 7 May,[1] the Dutch agreed to release all Indonesian political prisoners and allow the interned Republican leaders to return to Yogyakarta. On 6 July Sukarno, Hatta and their colleagues made a triumphal entry into the Republican capital. By 1 August both sides had agreed to a ceasefire, and later that month Hatta and other delegates of both the Republic and the Dutch-sponsored Federated States (BFO) departed for The Hague where a conference was scheduled between the two sides to arrange the transfer of sovereignty from the Dutch to the Indonesians. Mohammad Hatta, still prime minister of the Republic, and, like Sumitro, one of the very few well-trained Indonesian economists, was due to lead the Republic's delegation at this crucial Round Table Conference which would run from 23 August through 2 November 1949. Cochran became US representative at the conference, where he worked hard to persuade Hatta and his fellow Republican delegates that it was only through his influence that the Republic could expect meaningful American support. Sudarpo, on the other hand, was accurately reporting back from Washington to the Indonesian delegation at The Hague that considerable backing for the Indonesian position was beginning to build in the American Congress. Cochran belittled Sudarpo's assessment and, in effect, insisted that he was the only effective channel to American policy makers concerned with Indonesia and that congressmen's views on Indonesia carried no real weight.

While following the Dutch attack of 19 December 1948 and their subsequent disregard for UN directives, Cochran's originally strongly pro-Netherlands attitude had moved closer to the Republic's position, he was apparently at the same time thinking in terms of advancing his own career in American foreign policy circles. His attitude towards the Republic's position was evidently little affected by the idealistic streak of his predecessors, Frank Graham and Coert DuBois, or of the Australian member of the

UN Committee of Good Offices, Thomas Critchley. Critchley's firm grasp of Indonesian political realities and very significant contribution to Indonesia's ultimate full independence has, I think, been all too little appreciated by both Indonesians and Australians.[2] Only gradually did Indonesian leaders come to appreciate how Cochran's calculations for his own advancement were weakening his support of the Republic during the course of the negotiations in the late spring and summer of 1949 leading up to and during the crucial conference mounted by the United Nations at The Hague. Certainly by the time that conference concluded on 2 November 1949, it appeared that Cochran now saw his own career best served by appeasing at least the minimal demands of Eurocentric elements in the Department of State and Congress, who, with an eye on the American effort to build a military counterweight to Soviet power in Europe – soon to emerge as NATO – were anxious not to antagonize the Netherlands government.

In confronting the formidable tacit alignment of American power behind the Netherlands in the Round Table negotiations at The Hague during mid- and late 1949, the Indonesian delegation did, however, hold a number of strong cards – potential if not actual – that collectively gave it greater bargaining strength than some of its members realized. Without attempting to calculate their relative importance, they can be listed as:

1   the continuing pressure of the Republic's army in its largely guerrilla operations against the Netherlands armed forces, throughout wide areas of Java and Sumatra;
2   continuing Indonesian scorched-earth operations to destroy Dutch plantations and other installations, with a resulting erosion of the confidence of Dutch and other Western business interests in being able to salvage their investments in Indonesia through continuation of a policy of military force;
3   a mounting concern in the American government that continuing delay in the transfer of sovereignty over the East Indies from the Netherlands to an independent Indonesian state would provide the opportunity for growth of both the extreme left wing and the Darul Islam among the Indonesian population;[3]
4   the unexpected willingness displayed by most of the Dutch-appointed "Federalist" members of the Indonesian delegation during the Round Table negotiations to take positions close to those of the Republic's representatives on the major issues in dispute;
5   a rising tide of criticism in the American Congress of Dutch military actions and of their refusal to abide by United Nations prescriptions for settling the dispute with the Republic, and the increasing disposition of some US senators to cut economic assistance to the Netherlands if it continued on this course;
6   an increasing weight in both the UN Security Council and General Assembly in favor of the Indonesian Republic and against the

Netherlands, with Australia, India and the Soviet Union taking the lead, and with the prospect of India's Prime Minister Jawaharlal Nehru rallying an enlarged bloc in the General Assembly in favor of the Republic.

It should be noted that all of these factors soon began to influence American as well as Dutch policy makers. Collectively they ultimately produced a bargaining strength for the Indonesian negotiators at the Round Table Conference that moderated the thrust of the tacit Cochran–Netherlands alliance.

Cochran's insistence that the Indonesian government acquiesce in deferring any agreement on the status of West Irian (western New Guinea) is well known. Thereby, after the Dutch transferred sovereignty over the rest of the Netherlands East Indies, they would continue to administer West Irian for another year before its future status would be determined through further negotiations. It may well be that yielding to the Dutch in the Round Table Conference over the immediate status of West Irian was a price that had to be paid to ensure that strongly nationalist elements in the Netherlands did not oppose relinquishing Dutch sovereignty over the rest of the colony. In the event, the Netherlands refused to honor this provision, and its continuing intransigence with regard to such negotiations, culminating in its unilateral incorporation of West Irian into the Kingdom of the Netherlands in 1952, provided the basis for the new Indonesian government's abrogation of the entire Round Table Agreement in March 1956.

Less attention, however, has been given to what the Indonesian delegation to The Hague conference yielded to the Netherlands in economic matters. These concessions, that Cochran strongly supported the Netherlands in exacting, were extensive and with serious long-term consequences for the economic viability of the new Indonesian state after the Netherlands transferred sovereignty to the Republic of the United States of Indonesia (RUSI) at the end of December 1949.

From the outset of the Round Table Conference the Indonesian delegation was aware that a central Dutch strategy was to use the issue of debts "as a pretext to have an active say in, if not to decide on, the future financial and economic policy" of the new Indonesian state.[4] They were nevertheless willing to acquiesce in an initial corpus of economic concessions that, objectively perceived, were not out of line with most processes of decolonization where the ex-colonial power was in a relatively strong position, and which did not seem unreasonable to most of the Indonesian leadership. These provided for the restoration and protection of "the rights, concessions and licenses" that had been granted under the law of the Netherlands Indies and [were] still valid at the date of transfer of sovereignty, with the proviso that, in cases of expropriation, nationalization, or compulsory transfer of property rights, compensation would be paid within three years unless an arbitration board made up of representatives of the Indonesian and

Netherlands governments ruled otherwise. It was also stipulated that all regulations in the fields of labor relations, housing and other social welfare measures concerning labor were to be applied equally against Netherlands and Indonesian business enterprises in Indonesia. And in matters of trade the new Indonesian government agreed to grant "most favored nation" treatment to the Netherlands. Most of the Indonesian leadership had no great difficulty in accepting all these points. But when it came to the question of shouldering the enormous debt of the Netherlands East Indies there were strong differences and deep controversy dividing the two sides.

The Indonesian delegation held that the debt settlement should not hold up the Netherlands' transfer of sovereignty. They pointed out, as Alastair Taylor has observed, that "international law exempts the successor State from the obligation of assuming so-called odious debts," and argued that "these would include those amounts incurred for military purposes against the Indonesian independence movement."[5] And, as Taylor also observed, they pointed out that "the final debt settlements between India and the United Kingdom and the Philippines and the United States had been worked out following the transfers of sovereignty,"[6] noting also that the United States of America had gotten under way without shouldering any financial obligation to Britain.[7] The Netherlands, however, supported by Cochran, remained adamant that the debt question must be settled definitively *before* the conference ended in The Hague.[8]

The two sides remained far apart on the debt issue until Cochran threw his weight decisively on the Netherlands' side with what he termed his "compromise." And it was here that a deceptive element entered the dispute. For Cochran had succeeded in convincing Hatta and most of the Indonesian delegation that, unless they went along with his recommendations on this central financial issue, the United States could not be expected to follow through with the post-independence economic rehabilitation assistance that he would propose, nor could this assistance possibly materialize without his personal intervention with Washington on behalf of Indonesia. By this time he had managed to convince Indonesian leaders, Hatta in particular, that Washington's economic policies in support of their country would be no more than what he, Merle Cochran, recommended. Sumitro reported back from The Hague that in closing ranks with Cochran the Netherlands delegates "were making all efforts to impress upon us the fact that if we do not accept their terms, we would not have a good standing in terms of international credit and therefore, we certainly will not get American dollars as required for our first year, either from the Import–Export Bank or otherwise."[9]

In assessing the heavy pressure from the American representative, Merle Cochran, for the new Indonesian state to shoulder the large Netherlands East Indies debt, it must be understood that Cochran, like his superiors in Washington, attached greater importance to the economic health of the Netherlands than to that of Indonesia. The American government's priorities lay most heavily in Europe at this time. Its focus was primarily on rebuilding the war-weakened economies of Western Europe, certainly including the Netherlands, to resist the appeals of their Communist parties, while at the same time seeking to ensure the cooperation of their governments in building up a defensive alliance calculated to deter the potential of Soviet military power from moving towards Western Europe.

These Eurocentric preoccupations heavily outweighed concerns over the spread of communism in Southeast Asia or any military threat to that area from either Soviet Russia or Communist Chinese forces. Anyone aspiring to become the first American ambassador to Indonesia would have had to keep that obvious truth in mind. And certainly Cochran was astute enough to do so. Given this context, it was to be expected that he would want to be seen in Washington as a diplomat who accommodated the needs of the Netherlands sufficiently in its settlement with Indonesia to avoid an outcome that would seriously prejudice American economic and security priorities in Europe. And this he managed to do, albeit at a significant cost to what were Indonesia's best interests.

That calculation was clearly reflected in the debt settlement he prevailed upon the Indonesians to accept. The Netherlands was insisting that the now sovereign Indonesian state that emerged from The Hague Conference shoulder 6,100 million guilders of the Netherlands East Indies debt of 6,887 million guilders (approximately US$2,600 million) of which over a third (2,268 million guilders (approximately US$857 million)) was calculated to be owed to the Netherlands, 420 million guilders to third countries, and 3,328 million guilders (US$1,258 million) was reckoned as internal debt.[10]

In response, the Indonesian delegation submitted an aide mémoire, arguing that a hefty part of the debt that the Netherlands insisted it was their obligation to pay had actually been incurred by the Dutch army and navy in their military actions mounted to reestablish control over their former colony. The Indonesian delegation calculated that such Dutch military expenditures amounted to 3,024 million guilders, plus a further 539 million guilders for civilian support. After further calculations, they contended that a fair reading of the balance sheet would show that instead of Indonesia being responsible for shouldering the indebtedness of the Netherlands East Indies, it was actually the Dutch who owed the Indonesians over 500 million guilders.[11] Both Cochran and the Netherlands quickly brushed aside this Indonesian claim.

With Cochran closing ranks with the Netherlands on the issue, the new Indonesian government, the Republic of the United States of Indonesia, eventually felt obliged to accept a formula based on a "compromise" put forward by Cochran.[12] The Indonesian delegation agreed to take over debts totaling 4,559.5 million guilders (approximately US$1,723 million) which included the entire internal debt (of over 3,000 million guilders (US$1,134 million)) of the colonial government, plus 1,559.5 million guilders (US$589 million) of its external debt.[13]

Interest on the loans due the Netherlands was mostly pegged at 3 per cent and that on US loans to the Netherlands East Indies government ranged from 2 per cent to 2.5 per cent (respectively for a $62,550,412 line of credit for purchase of United States Surplus Property and the $15 million residuum of an Export Import Bank loan).[14]

This heavy albatross of debt (principal repayment and interest) to the Netherlands and other Western countries incurred by the outgoing Netherlands East Indies government seriously impeded the economic recovery of the new Indonesian state. It especially curtailed the new government's ability during its first five years to meet the heavy financial demands on it in its efforts to repair the enormous damage to infrastructure and economic enterprises inflicted by World War II, the Japanese occupation, and more than four years of fighting against the military forces of the British and Dutch. The new government continued to pay off this inherited indebtedness until 21 February 1956 when the cabinet led by the Masjumi Party's Burhanuddin Harahap, exasperated at least as much by the Netherlands' intransigent refusal to negotiate the status of West Irian as by the drain of debt payment, abrogated the entire economic and financial agreement reached in the Round Table Conference. By that time, however, the steady outflow of the Indonesian government's debt payments had left only $171 million of the debt outstanding.

Cochran's most powerful weapon for bringing the Republic's leaders to accept his terms in the Round Table Conference had been especially well suited to winning Hatta's compliance – the promise of substantial American financial assistance to the new government. As a well-trained economist who understood the seriousness of Indonesia's economic plight after the destruction wrought by World War II battles, the Japanese occupation and four years of revolution and its attendant fighting and scorched-earth policy, Hatta was acutely aware of his country's desperate need for financial assistance in getting its economy on its feet again. Thus, Cochran's repeated assurances – all unfortunately only oral – that abiding by his financial prescriptions in these negotiations at The Hague would ensure substantial subsequent American economic assistance was heavily persuasive with Hatta in yielding to Cochran on the crucial financial settlements as well as the disposition of West Irian (West New Guinea).

With respect to the financial concessions that Cochran and the Dutch were pressing on the Republic's negotiators, Sumitro Djojohadikusumo, the only Indonesian member other than Hatta on the Indonesian delegation with a solid training in economics, must be credited with playing a major role in mounting a significant rearguard action against them. That the success of this effort was only partial should not obscure its importance. Sumitro's regular messages back to the Indonesian representatives in Washington, copies of which were sent to me, made clear his solid grasp of the financial side of the debate and the implications for Indonesia of those major concessions it was being called on to accept. Although Sudarpo, Soedjatmoko and Palar tended to align themselves with Sumitro, Hatta, as the key member of the Indonesian delegation to the conference, and feeling the full weight of responsibility for Indonesia's success there, felt constrained to adopt a less confrontational attitude towards Cochran and the Dutch delegation Moreover, during the second half of the conference Hatta's health deteriorated, perhaps making him more susceptible to Cochran's pressure. Unable to operate at the height of his powers, by the end of the conference he was ultimately obliged to delegate more to subordinate members of the Indonesian delegation.[15]

So, fearful of losing Cochran's support for a speedy transfer of sovereignty, Hatta and several other key members of the Indonesian delegation reluctantly accepted the financial "compromise" upon which he insisted. But it is of central importance to appreciate that they did so in the expectation that he would deliver on his oral promises of major American financial assistance to the new Indonesian state that was to emerge from the conference. The subsequent bitterness of many of the Indonesian leaders is then understandable when all the United States ultimately provided their new state was merely $100 million in the form of a loan, which, of course, they were obliged to repay. So far as I am aware, this was the most ungenerous settling of accounts encountered by any major ex-colonial country.

And, as Indonesians now compared this American loan with the financial support the United States had so recently provided the Netherlands during the period it had been mounting its all-out effort to crush the Republic and overcome its struggle for independence, it is understandable that their feeling of betrayal increased. Here it is relevant to note a report published a year earlier on 22 December 1948, on the first page of the *New York Times* in the immediate aftermath of the launching of the Dutch attack on the Republic. Copies of the report were circulated widely among Indonesian leaders just as The Hague conference's final sessions were concluding.[16] The report observed that since the end of World War II American support to the Dutch had amounted to at least $979 million. This had consisted of $298 million in Marshall Plan aid for the Netherlands, another $61 million of Marshall aid earmarked for the Netherlands East Indies, $130 million for purchase of US war surplus supplies, $190 million for "civilian supplies as military relief" and Export–Import Bank credits of $300 million – that last figure alone being three times the amount of the Export–Import Bank loan the American government was now finally providing the newly independent United States of Indonesia.

Indonesian leaders could not help but dwell on the fact that the total of the several categories of post-World War II American economic assistance to the Netherlands over the period of its military effort to suppress Indonesian independence was then equal to more than nine times the amount of the long-awaited $100 million Export–Import Bank loan provided by the United States just after the transfer of sovereignty to help

Indonesia rebuild from a devastation largely inflicted by the weight of American-supported Dutch military power. Their bitter disappointment in Cochran – and the United States for which he claimed to speak – was understandable. Too rarely, however, have American officials recognized that Indonesian perception – finding comfort instead in the belief that the United States played the major role in emancipating Indonesia from colonial rule. It is difficult to understand how little appreciation contemporary American policy makers and their successors indicated of Indonesian feelings in this matter.

Initially euphoric with their now internationally recognized sovereignty, it took some time for many Indonesian leaders to appreciate the hard financial bargain they had felt obliged to accept and for their disappointment and disillusionment to grow into acute distrust of Cochran. That process was clearly abetted by Cochran's impatient inability to contain his own braggadocio in taking overly much credit for Indonesia's independence. This he sometimes untactfully expressed through an apparently quite unconsciously patronizing avuncular demeanor that increasingly nettled Indonesian leaders, finally including Sukarno as well as Hatta. And some Indonesian leaders and members of the Republic's delegation not unnaturally concluded that Cochran was well rewarded for shepherding through controversial agreements at the Round Table Conference – concessions that they felt seriously compromised Indonesia's best interests. Those who asserted this view cited his appointment as the first US ambassador to post-revolutionary Indonesia and his subsequent elevation to the highly prized position as one of the senior American representatives at the World Bank.

To the disappointment of the Republic's leaders, then, the promises of major American economic assistance, that Cochran had begun to make even before the Round Table Conference was under way, were not in fact backed by American policy, as he himself was in a position to know. Along with the treatment of Amir Sjarifuddin over the Renville Agreement, this misrepresentation was surely one of the great betrayals by American policy makers. It was to have powerful long-term as well as immediate adverse economic consequences for Indonesia. Sometimes in later years in talking with Hatta, I had the sense that he was privately both bitter and perhaps a bit ashamed at having been so badly misled by Cochran. He clearly preferred not to talk about him, and when he did he showed no glimmer of respect for him or appreciation of his role.

To simplify the equation of the conference's ultimate outcome, however, one can fairly conclude that, though the Netherlands came out ahead on two very important issues – Indonesia's shouldering of the Netherlands East Indies debt and the status of West Irian – the Indonesians were successful in securing the reasonably predictable transfer of sovereignty over the rest of Indonesia, as well as the much less assured denial to the Netherlands of its objective of using the issue of the debt as leverage for exerting continued influence on Indonesia's future financial and economic policy. The

Indonesians were also able to defeat the Dutch demand that as long as the Netherlands remained its biggest creditor the new Indonesian state would not "amend, modify or change existing financial and economic regulations without agreement of the Dutch," nor did the Indonesian government accept "the assignment of a certain percentage of proceeds in hard currency" of its exports for repayment of Dutch debts.[17]

5 McCarthy, Lattimore and Cochran

Soon after I returned from Indonesia and then again after the Round Table negotiations were under way, I had talks with Frank Graham of North Carolina and Owen Brewster of Maine, two of the most prominent Democratic and Republican senators critical of the Netherlands' role in Indonesia. To both of them I criticized strongly and in considerable detail the policies I understood Cochran was pursuing at the Round Table Conference. After conferring together, they jointly called on Senator Arthur Vandenberg of Michigan, the highly respected Republican Chairman of the Senate Foreign Affairs Committee, who had won a well-deserved reputation for bipartisan conduct of the work of his committee. He was sufficiently concerned with my criticisms of Cochran's policies as conveyed to him by the two senators that through them he invited me to prepare memoranda detailing my views. These I promptly submitted.[1] Graham later told me Vandenberg had read the memoranda and they had had some influence on American policy. Whether they did or not, they certainly had some effect on the next five years of my life.

I soon learned from friends of mine who occupied junior positions in the State Department that when he learned of my intervention Cochran was furious and vowed to keep me from returning to Indonesia; and he was influential enough to succeed in this by having my passport withdrawn for the next five years.

When Cochran first attempted this, the head of the Department's Passport Division, the powerful Ruth Shipley, admonished him that he could not simply order revocation of my passport but could only do so in accordance with reasons prescribed in the relevant departmental regulations. He was told that there were three circumstances under which a passport could be denied: (1) membership in a Communist party; (2) participation in the international Communist conspiracy; and (3) violation of the Logan Act (falsely representing oneself while abroad as a representative of the US government). My friends in the Department informed me that Cochran lost no time in throwing the entire book at me, charging that I had worked closely with the Indonesian Communist Party and its leaders and had represented myself as an agent of the American government – ironically the same charge the Indonesian Communists had made against me. (Apparently no one suggested to Cochran that there might be some incompatibility in these charges.)

Cochran's ability to support his accusations against me was initially enhanced by support from Arturo Campbell, the CIA agent with whom he had worked together in Indonesia and who was, I was told, still a friend of his. And so in supporting Cochran's charges Campbell, whom I had angered less than a year before because of my refusal to work with him when he visited Yogyakarta, was making good on the threats he had then made against me.

I had been quite unaware of Cochran's efforts to keep me from returning to Indonesia until the summer of 1950, soon after I had mailed my passport in for renewal with the object of returning for a brief follow-up visit there. On this visit I hoped to check further into several aspects of the revolutionary period upon which I felt I had not gathered sufficient information, and also to obtain data on developments that had taken place in the year since I had left. Such a visit seemed financially feasible because of an invitation from William Holland, head of the Institute of Pacific Relations, for me to give a paper on Indonesian nationalism at the Institute's annual conference soon to be held in Lucknow, India. With my airfare being taken care of that far, I thought I could afford the additional amount to get me on to Indonesia.

I well remember my utter shock and disbelief when I retrieved from the postbox a letter from the State Department's Passport Division stating that "in the best interests of the United States" it had been decided not to renew my passport. Feeling sure there had been some simple bureaucratic mistake, I promptly called the Passport Division where I was stonewalled completely until I finally reached a Mr Nicholas, one of Mrs Shipley's senior assistants. In a cold and unfriendly tone he informed me that he was not at liberty to discuss my case over the phone, but that I was free to come down to Washington to do so.

And so I did. When I got to the Passport Office Mrs Shipley had decided that she herself was to have the pleasure of telling me off. She entered the room, her eyes blazing, walked up to me and practically spat out: "Mr Kahin, the line between Communists and non-Communists is very clear, and you're on the wrong side of the line." Having evidently relished this broadside, she turned on her heel and strode off. And that was my personal introduction to the McCarthy period.

No one else then assembled in her office indicated any desire to talk to me, though a few had the grace to look embarrassed. I flew back home bewildered and very depressed. There was not yet in place an appeal process for those denied passports: that would not come for four more years. Though I wrote letter after letter to the Passport Division and various senior members of the State Department, I could get nothing but brush-offs. I had several good friends in the lower reaches of the Department who were warm in their solicitude, and confidentially told me of Campbell's intervention, but could suggest no remedy.

Letters of support on my behalf from Indonesian leaders, including a magnificent one from Sukarno, testifying to my being a good friend of Indonesia, expressing their surprise that I should be denied my passport to return and urging that I be permitted to, were dismissed by the Passport Division as irrelevant, as were letters from American academics and university administrators testifying to my non-Communist views and affiliations. None of these were given any weight by the Passport and Internal Security Division of the State Department, nor by the Eurocentric William Lacy, a friend and admirer of Cochran, who headed the Department's Office of Southeast Asia and Pacific Affairs – a position of pivotal importance in my case.

I soon discovered that my friends in the Indonesian representation in Washington had come to regard Lacy as generally supportive of the Netherlands in its dispute with the Republic of Indonesia, and as a major obstacle to their efforts to enlist backing from more senior State Department officials and members of Congress. Sudarpo, then the Republic's press officer in Washington, was further outraged when someone purporting to be an FBI agent telephoned his wife to inquire when I had lived in their house (which, of course, I had never done). Rightly or wrongly Sudarpo suspected Lacy of having been involved in what he regarded as a clumsy effort to undermine his support of me by implying that I was under FBI investigation – which, thanks to the Freedom of Information Act, I later learned had indeed been the case. Sudarpo was so angry that he stormed into Lacy's office, accused him of violating his diplomatic status, and, after threatening to make an issue of the affair, demanded an apology and got one.

The Indonesians in Washington – Sudarpo and Soedjatmoko especially – knew me and my record in Indonesia well enough to be outraged by Cochran's allegations against me and did their best to help me, but without success. One of their problems, as they came to recognize, was the quality of the legal counsel then attached to their new embassy, the loud-mouthed, self-assertive Joe Borkin (probably a holdover from the period when the notorious speculator Matthew Fox had contributed to the financing of the Republic's first diplomatic missions as quid pro quo for an expected, but never realized, share in its export profits). When it was evident to Sudarpo and Soedjatmoko that Borkin was not up to helping and that indeed his crude comportment was likely further to antagonize the Passport Division, they huddled together and emerged with an announcement puzzling to me: "We'd better call in C.C." That turned out to be Clark Clifford, the really big gun in their young embassy's arsenal. With this polished and very able friend of President Truman on my side, I might have had my case in really effective hands. But unfortunately he had to be briefed first by Borkin, and that process had barely gotten under way when Borkin's crudeness and abrasiveness so offended Clifford that he withdrew. The Republic's Washington office soon realized what a disaster Borkin was and disengaged his services, but it was too late to re-enlist Clifford, at least so far as my own case was concerned. And so my prospects seemed just as hopeless as before.

Of great assistance to Cochran at the very outset of his vendetta against me had been the backing he'd received from the CIA's Arturo Campbell, the now clearly vindictive agent whom I'd refused to help a year before in Yogyakarta. But to this advantage there had been added, beginning in the first few months of 1950, a new factor – quite extraneous to my experience in Indonesia – that Cochran could not have expected and which must have given him a very pleasant surprise. This development, several friends in the State Department told me, greatly increased Cochran's already considerable leverage against me and ensured that in his efforts he could count on the backing of Senator Joseph McCarthy's powerful ally in the Department of State, Scott McLeod, head of its Internal Security Division. This was the introduction of what was referred to as my "Lattimore connection" – a relationship of which I was myself proud but which I soon learned was a red flag to that senator and his associates.

It may be recalled that McCarthy in early 1950 loosed his preposterous charge that the Department of State was riddled with Communists. When pressed to prove this, at the urging of his major financial angel, Alfred Kohlberg, he selected as his main target Owen Lattimore, then known solely as a distinguished scholar of China and Inner Asia who had actually been only an occasional consultant to the Department, rather than an employee, but a man against whom Kohlberg had a long-standing grudge, that had festered into bitter animus. (Kohlberg was a millionaire, who had made his money from sweatshop labor in Shanghai that reportedly made lace for women's undergarments. Lattimore did not suffer fools or knaves gladly, and he had long placed Kohlberg in the latter category for what he regarded as his unconscionable exploitation of cheap labor.) When pressed to prove his case against the State Department, McCarthy had finally stated in March 1950 that his entire case would stand or fall on the vindication of his allegation of Lattimore's Communist connections, and specifically his charge that Lattimore was "the top Soviet espionage agent in the United States." Taking his cue from Kohlberg, McCarthy now insisted that the defeat of Chiang Kai-shek and the "loss of China" to the Communists were all to be attributed to Lattimore's treasonous conduct. (For those interested in these charges and the "loss of China" canard, I strongly recommend the magisterial and meticulously researched study by Robert P. Newman, *Owen Lattimore and the "Loss" of China*, published by the University of California Press in 1992.)

It was evident that McCarthy actually knew very little about Lattimore. I have always thought that he would never have dared to make the charges against him that he did if he had initially been aware of the fact, of which the press then also seemed quite oblivious, that President Roosevelt had secretly appointed Lattimore as his personal representative and political adviser to Chiang Kai-shek, the Chinese Communists' major adversary. (This appointment had been made in strict confidence, and I did not learn about it until later, but I've always respected Lattimore for not publicizing this role during his ordeal with McCarthy, even though it could have been an exculpatory argument of great weight against that senator's charges.)

I had come to know Lattimore and his ideas well, and I could immediately understand how blatantly false McCarthy's charges against him were. One could not have sat through three of Lattimore's graduate seminars – dealing with China, Sinkiang and Mongolia – as I did, and reached any other conclusion. Moreover, in September 1949, following my return from Indonesia I had been appointed as instructor on the tiny faculty of Johns Hopkins University's Walter Hines Page School of International Relations, of which Lattimore was director. And even as the most junior member of that faculty I had been privy to the administration of the school and his plans for building up its strength on Central Asia. (My teaching appointment was half-time, thus freeing me to spend the balance on writing my dissertation.)

One of the most glaring absurdities of McCarthy's attack against Lattimore, and largely ignored by the press, was the fact that, by dint of great effort, just before the Communist takeover of power in Mongolia Lattimore had rescued the country's Dilowa Hutukhtu, head of its extensive Buddhist establishment there, a position analogous to that of the Dalai Lama in Tibet. With the financial support of an American philanthropic foundation, Lattimore had managed to spirit the Dilowa, along with two of the country's most senior anti-Communist military officers, out of the country just ahead of the Communists' seizure of control. He brought them to Johns Hopkins, where they were to be the nucleus of a new Mongol Studies research program.

Two able young anthropologists from Yale, David Aberle and Harold Vreeland, were brought down to interview the three intensively over the course of a year, with the object of building up as much knowledge about Mongol society as possible. Harold and I shared an office, and I was able to get a feel for the nature of his work, which he much enjoyed and liked to discuss. So far as I could understand it, the methodology mostly followed among Yale anthropologists at that time was an inductive one wherein knowledge of a culture was built up from scratch bit by bit. They seemed to pride themselves that, by starting with a tabula rasa unclouded by previous secondary knowledge of a culture, they could remain more open-minded and keep previous findings from sullying their own objectivity. Though these two were unusually talented young scholars, this methodology proved initially to be quite a handicap.

I well remember walking into the office that Harold and I shared one morning, several months after he had begun his intensive interviewing of the Dilowa, to find him ashen-faced and totally despondent. Pointing to a box containing some ten inches of five-by-eight cards, he wailed: "What am I going to do? All those interviews; and they are going down the drain?" He then explained that, to his consternation, when the previous day he had sought to have the Dilowa elaborate on some of the data elicited from him in earlier interviews, this venerable old man had firmly corrected him, blandly observing that he had got it all wrong. To illustrate his point, and explain his frustration, Harold then began giving me some rather compelling examples. Some were pretty basic. For instance, as I recall, in one major complex of monasteries managed by the Dilowa Hutukhtu the center of the economy had been sheep, but in the later interviews the sheep culture had largely disappeared, and the raising of horses and cattle had become dominant.

When I suggested to Harold that he should promptly meet with the Dilowa and ask him to explain these disparities, some of which were extreme, he answered "Could you do that? He is likely to think that I'm either trivializing the information he has already been generous enough to give me or think I'm suggesting he was lying. I just can't do it." I could sympathize with his wanting to avoid such a confrontation, for the Dilowa was no ordinary person. Standing an erect six feet with lustrous gray eyes and seemingly centered upon some deep inner calm, he fairly exuded charisma (Figure 5.1). Though he was warm and genial, he was the last person in the world to whom one would want to even hint that he was

Figure 5.1 The Dilowa Hutukhtu

inconsistent in the accounts he had provided of religious organization and secular administration in his country.

Finally, after almost a week of anxiety and uncertainty as to what he should do, Harold got up enough courage to ask the Dilowa to relieve his puzzlement and make it possible for him to understand these many discrepancies between the data earlier given and those which he was now providing, especially as to his role in conducting the secular affairs of the extensive complex of monasteries for whose stewardship he was responsible. "Oh," said the Dilowa with a disarming smile, "I thought you were referring to an earlier incarnation." He then explained that the differing bodies of data related to the situations existing during two different reincarnations of his that were several centuries apart. Yes, there had indeed been some changes in the economy that supported his domain as between the two periods. Soon afterwards when I went into our office I found a much happier Harold Vreeland, and by his desk were several books from the university library on Buddhism – books that he had never read before.

Some comic relief in McCarthy's effort to make a case against Lattimore, and so far as I know never reported at the time, came when that dogged senator had one of his men steal the tape of a conversation in Mongol between Lattimore and the Dilowa. McCarthy seemed convinced that this would disclose something subversive about Lattimore that he could use, and quietly made every effort to get it translated into English. He sent it to the State Department, demanding that they translate it for him. It proved to be a difficult task, for there were many variants of the Mongol language, each spoken by a different banner (a sort of tribal subdivision). The foreign service officer in the Department who first received the tape didn't know that particular dialect and passed it on to an acquaintance who he thought might be familiar with it. This process was apparently repeated more than once, during which period the provenance of the original request was lost. Finally, the tape was sent on to a Mongol specialist who, though also not familiar with the dialect, said he knew someone who would be, and, without knowing the origin of the request, quite innocently sent it on to a friend who turned out to be Owen Lattimore! It was, of course, with great relish that Lattimore now obliged, and without comment solemnly presented to the State Department a translation of his conversation with the Dilowa that was transcribed on the tape.

I doubt that my actions in Indonesia disturbed McCarthy or that, initially at least, he even knew of them. His anger at me was, so far as I could learn, generated by two incidents relating to my support of Lattimore. The first was my perhaps rash visit to his Senate office soon after his opening attack against Lattimore in which he had ostensibly reproduced some of Lattimore's writings. It was clear to me, and certainly to Owen's wife, Eleanor, who had from the very start worked unstintingly for his defense, that McCarthy's rendering of these writings grossly distorted the original version. McCarthy's office personnel had clearly not anticipated being questioned about this and were

Figure 5.2   The Dilowa Hutukhtu with Owen Lattimore and Senator Millard
Tydings (D-Md)

Source: AP/Wide World Photos

surprisingly open and friendly when I asked to see the full text of what
McCarthy had said in his allegations of Lattimore's pro-Communist leanings.
It was immediately apparent not only that the statements of Lattimore to
which McCarthy referred had been taken out of context, but that widely separated parts of his writings had been cut out and pasted together. I was stunned
at the blatancy of this cut-and-paste operation, but, after taking extensive
notes, managed to hide my feelings and walk out of the office still on
outwardly friendly terms with its personnel. I then turned over my findings
about this dishonest procedure to Lattimore's lawyers, who made good use of
them, though without as much effect as I had hoped. Once they had given
publicity to this cut-and-paste procedure it could not have taken long for
McCarthy's office workers to have recalled my visit in quest of the texts he had
drawn on. Certainly when I returned to check out additional texts I found the
atmosphere in that office had radically changed. No one was prepared to help
me find the relevant material, and I was made to feel anything but welcome.

The second episode that aroused McCarthy's anger against me came
several months later, when I took the initiative in organizing graduate
students at Johns Hopkins in Lattimore's support. Some faculty members
there, though not as many as we had hoped, had already taken a common

stand to back him, and so it was not difficult for me to enlist a sizable number of graduate students in the social sciences and history. Our stand got only minor publicity, but we thought it was helpful. What I had not reckoned on was the strong, and outraged, opposition to my efforts by Professor Carl Brent Swisher, the chairman of my department – political science. He was furious at my having taken this initiative, particularly without his permission. He evidently did not relish what little publicity our statement elicited and clearly did not want to get on the wrong side of McCarthy. He ordered me to cease my efforts on behalf of Lattimore and demanded that all the political science graduate students who had signed a statement supporting him, which we had posted on the bulletin board, remove their names. "I don't want those names just crossed out," he said, "I want you all to take a razor or your pen knives and cut them out."

We were all jolted by our chairman's quite untypical behavior. I refused to remove my name, as did the majority of the graduate students. Professor Swisher was an expert in constitutional law who had published several well-received biographies of Supreme Court chief justices, and whose usual reserve and gentlemanly behavior contrasted sharply with his present state of wrath. He had seemed to be a lonesome, unhappy man whom we often saw standing in line during the day outside local cinemas, and previously we had felt friendly and sympathetic towards him despite his didactic and humorless style of teaching. We had noticed that the personal chemistry between him and the ebullient and sometimes unceremonious Lattimore was not warm, but we were surprised that, in view of his scholarly specialization, he had not joined those faculty members who had rallied to Lattimore's defense. Our disappointment was only partially relieved when Malcolm Moos, a senior and relatively liberal member of our faculty, explained to us that Swisher had become reticent about supporting beleaguered academics on the Left ever since he felt he had been unjustly attacked for having supported a politically radical friend several years before.

In any case, Swisher remained very angry with me for my continuing efforts to support Lattimore. He spelled out his disapproval and continuing anger first by refusing to back my efforts to reclaim my passport. And then, when in the fall of 1950, with my doctoral dissertation nearly finished, I began to scour the few possibilities for an academic job he called me into his office to advise me that as my department chairman he had an obligation to help me, but that he wished to advise me that he was prepared to write just one letter in my support and to no more than one institution. "So," he concluded, "when you ask me to write you'd better be sure it's to the university you really want to teach in." I knew he was angry with me, but I had not expected him to be so mean-spirited.

Lattimore was happy to write letters on my behalf, as was Rupert Emerson, the chairman of the Department of Government at Harvard whom I had been fortunate enough to interest in becoming outside examiner for my dissertation. Nevertheless, as I embarked on my job quest, I felt all too naked. For with Cochran's charges hanging over me, I felt it incumbent in every job interview to volunteer early on that my passport had been with-drawn, and mention the allegations of Communist affiliations that Cochran had leveled against me. Yet the person best suited to provide a sympathetic explanation of my situation, my department chairman, could hardly be counted on to provide this.

Indeed, I soon found that, so far as any backing from Swisher was concerned, the situation was much worse, for I had not calculated the extent of his vindictiveness. This soon became apparent when I applied for a position at Cornell University in November of 1950. It was then that Lauriston Sharp, a professor of anthropology, was seeking, with the backing of a grant from the Rockefeller Foundation, to build a program of Southeast Asian studies. He had been able to persuade Cornell's Department of Government on a strictly trial basis to add a position to its small five-man faculty for a specialist in Southeast Asian government and international relations for three years, with the salary for that period coming from the Rockefeller Foundation grant. If at the end of three years this new assistant professor's teaching had attracted a substantial number of students and his publication record was strong, the department would consider asking the university to take over funding of the position. The teaching responsibilities of such an individual would have to transcend such a "parochial focus" as Southeast Asia and cover Asia as a whole – both the comparative govern-ment and international relations dimensions. That meant the entire arc of countries from Pakistan, through India, Southeast Asia, China, Korea (then very much an American concern) and Japan. Today that might well seem a tall order. But in those days, with very few departments of political science offering anything on Asia, it was an unusual opportunity, and I jumped at the possibility of such a job at a major university.

The department soon began screening applications, and I was lucky enough to be invited to Ithaca for an interview. I took the train up to New Jersey, boarded the Lehigh Valley's sleeper at Hoboken and arrived the next morning in Ithaca. My discussion with Lauriston Sharp went well, for after all we had come to know each other pretty well on the three-week voyage from Southampton to Singapore and Batavia only two years before. My interviews with some of the members of the government department, however, seemed strained, and I felt that something was amiss. I took the train back to Baltimore feeling deflated and that I had not made the grade with the government department. Professor Sharp telephoned me to commiserate and told me he was utterly puzzled by the government depart-ment's attitude, but that in view of its stand there was no prospect of a job for me at Cornell. That was on 8 April 1951, long after most teaching posi-tions for the fall semester had been filled.

But then in quick succession two developments changed the situation. First, sentiment in Cornell's government department prevailed that, since the chairman of Harvard's government department, Rupert Emerson, had been outside examiner for my dissertation, his further opinion should be sought, especially since he was the only political scientist teaching at a major university in the country who was known to be a specialist on Indonesia. And second, it was finally concluded that it was foolish not to telephone my department chairman, Carl Swisher, directly and insist that he stop prevaricating and provide the reasons for his pejorative assessment of me. Only afterwards did I discover that not only had Swisher failed to send the letter on my behalf he had promised, but that when a member of Cornell's government department had then called him to get his oral assessment he had responded that two reasons for not supporting me were too delicate to put in writing or even discuss over the phone. (Here one should note that during the hysterical ambiance of the McCarthy period many people at Johns Hopkins who knew Lattimore thought that their phones were being tapped.)

Fortunately for me, offsetting Swisher were the letters from Lattimore and Harvard's Rupert Emerson. Emerson not only strongly supported me for the job but ranked me ahead of two Harvard candidates for it whose work he had been supervising. And he added his voice to those at Cornell who were insisting that Swisher be required to state his reasons for blackballing me. The letters from Lattimore and Emerson were then strong enough to induce several members of the government department to call Swisher back and demand that he provide some substantive explanation as to why he had blackballed me. His answer was that I was a "Quixotic liberal." When requested to explain why he so characterized me, he predictably referred to my support of Lattimore. And then when pressed for a further example told them they should know that I had helped the Japanese Nisei in the Seattle area when they were slated for removal to internment camps.

That did it. Swisher had not reckoned on the liberal instincts of Cornell's government department at the time. All four of its active members, including Robert Cushman, its distinguished professor of constitutional law, felt very much as I had about the disgraceful treatment of this minority of American citizens. And thus about a week later I was invited up to Cornell for a second interview, a much more thorough one than before. The atmosphere was markedly different from the previous occasion, and I enjoyed my discussions, even the intense two-hour grilling from Professor Mario Einaudi, the specialist in political theory who had been assigned the task of ascertaining whether I had any Communist proclivities.

And so I learned later that summer of 1951 that I was welcomed as an assistant professor in Cornell's Department of Government, and given the concurrent assignment of executive director of Lauriston Sharp's newly launched Southeast Asia Program.

The ugly pall of McCarthyism endured during the early 1950s, and a few friends of mine still at Johns Hopkins were the object of his investigations and others assumed they were. They advised me that I, too, should assume that he was out to get me if he could. That their speculation was well founded was brought home to me when I found that two students, funded by his financial agent Alfred Kohlberg, were regularly attending my lectures on US Far Eastern policy. I did not keep attendance records, and the classes were open to any who were interested. Because of the ongoing Korean war, which I undertook to cover, a sizable number of students who came to my lectures were not actually enrolled in my course, and I welcomed their attendance. I soon began to notice that two of them, who always sat together, were indefatigable note-takers, and I was naturally flattered at their rapt attention. It so happened that an editor of the student newspaper *The Cornell Sun* also noticed their deviant behavior. His interest piqued, and being of an appropriately inquisitive cast of mind, this young journalist took it upon himself to inquire into the reasons for their devoted attention to my wisdom. After a few beers, as he later recounted to me, the two devoted note-takers had no reluctance, and indeed evidenced some display of pride, in informing my young friend from the *Sun* of their mission on behalf of McCarthy, and paid for by Kohlberg, to check up on this suspect young professor. I must acknowledge that in learning this from this helpful editor I was sufficiently annoyed that I suspect my China lectures were even more critical of Chiang Kai-shek's stewardship than they had been before.

I wasted considerable time during my first four years at Cornell preparing myself, even as I was trying to get to sleep at night, for a confrontation in McCarthy's Congressional committee in Washington. Friends who were following McCarthy's antics felt it only logical that, because of my invasion of his office for the doctored records of Lattimore's writings and because of my organization of the Johns Hopkins students in his support, the senator would want to force me before his committee for a grilling. I was aware that through his agent Scott McLeod, head of the State Department's Internal Security Division, he would be provided with all of Cochran's and Campbell's allegations of my having Indonesian Communist connections, and I assumed that, in view of his past modus operandi in his committee's hearings, I could expect the senator would give me a rough time. And so I spent many hours during the early 1950s in readying myself for a confrontation, a process which was physically wearing and emotionally draining, but for which – naively perhaps – I was convinced I was so well prepared that I would relish the encounter. Evidently McCarthy felt he had more important avenues to exploit. And so, to my disappointment, I was never summoned to appear before his committee. But my sustained effort to keep at the peak of preparedness during his four years of ascendancy did require a considerable loss of time and energy that would have been much better invested in research and writing.

During all this period I spent even more time in trying to recover my passport. To that end I wrote many letters to leaders in Indonesia asking that they recount my actual role and conduct during my year there, and many to American friends asking if they could see their way clear to comment in writing as to the allegation that I had Communist leanings. I found this distasteful and humiliating, and I hated having to do it. But this is what Mrs Shipley and her assistants in the Passport Office insisted was expected, probably doing so to keep me busy and off their back.

I did manage to have an hour's talk with John Foster Dulles (then occupying the position of adviser to the State Department, presumably as an earnest of the Truman administration's devotion to a bipartisan foreign policy). But that audience was, I soon realized, a courtesy extended only because of my friendship with his son. Dulles evidenced no sympathy for my situation, and I was appalled at his lack of understanding of the force of nationalism in the Indonesian and Vietnamese revolutions and his conviction that if, following the independence of these countries, the administrators of their former colonial masters did not remain on to guide them, then the United States had an obligation to do so.

But though my efforts to regain my passport from the Department of State continued to run into stubborn resistance, my family, parents and friends continued to be supportive, and Cornell's president, Dean Malott, Knight Biggerstaff, chair of the Department of Far Eastern Studies, and members of its Government and Southeast Asia Program faculties continued to regard the charges against me as preposterous and gave me sustained moral support.

Some of my colleagues at Cornell were convinced that, with the appearance of my dissertation as a published book (*Nationalism and Revolution in Indonesia*) in 1952 my actual role in Indonesia would be so clear that the allegations of Campbell and Cochran would lose any weight they still might have. The book was fortunately well reviewed and helped induce Peter Odegard, the respected chair of the political science department at Berkeley, and departmental heads at a couple of other good universities to offer me tenure track positions, but it cut no ice with the Department of State. (I gave no encouragement to these offers, for I had been very well treated at Cornell and felt it would have been disloyal even to inform my department head that they had been made. I was later informed that to have reported this would have enhanced my prospects at Cornell, but I very much doubt it would have, for without any such nudging my successive chairmen, Herbert Briggs, Mario Einaudi and Clinton Rossiter, were all warmly supportive all the way to my receiving tenure in 1954 and a full professorship in 1959.)

And I enjoyed my teaching and the opportunity to help build up Cornell's newly launched Southeast Asia Program – an interdisciplinary effort dependent upon the existing departments, and itself offering only a minor to those pursuing PhDs in those disciplines. Cornell's new Southeast Asia Program attracted good graduate students, and I found it stimulating to work with them. It was undoubtedly the decision not to offer degrees that helped ensure our program would be able to work harmoniously with Cornell's discipline departments. Yale and Berkeley made the mistake of offering area studies degrees (though Yale only to the MA level, which was more acceptable to the discipline departments). Even at this early stage there was throughout the country a strong prejudice in most discipline departments, especially in the social sciences, against area studies. Often this reflected a narrow parochialism, but it was an attitude that prevailed though the 1950s and 1960s and after that grew even stronger and more intolerant. Those hapless students with degrees in area studies who sought jobs in the established disciplines found the gates heavily barred, frequently even in cases where their knowledge of the discipline was every bit as great as applicants in the more traditional mold who were blessed with actual degrees in the discipline.

But for more than four years the State Department remained adamant in its refusal to reinstate my passport, and I was thus still denied the possibility of returning to Indonesia, or for that matter traveling anywhere abroad. My colleagues in the government department and other friends advised me to hire a high-powered Washington lawyer, but the only one I had ever met, Clark Clifford, would, I knew, charge way beyond what a young assistant professor could afford. Finally, Robert Cushman, my department's most senior professor and an eminent specialist in constitutional law, volunteered to discuss my case with a well-known Washington civil rights activist, Eleanor Bontecue, who, he said, might know of some well-qualified pro-bono lawyer there who was more interested in principles than money. Cushman discussed my case with her and convinced her that I deserved some help. Fortunately she was able to interest in my case a first-rate lawyer, Walter S. Surrey, who had taken a number of civil rights cases on a pro-bono basis and was outraged at the recent spate of the State Department's arbitrary denials of passports. He was kind enough to listen carefully to the facts of my case and generous enough to agree to represent me for what amounted to no more than stenographic costs to his office.

As he looked into the matter, after questioning a number of people in the Passport Division and elsewhere in the Department, Surrey became almost as outraged as I had been. For a good half-year he kept battering away at them, making several of them uncomfortable, but without success until finally in mid-1954 Congressional action resulted in there being established the first appeal process for passport denials. True, the committee established to adjudicate appeals was made up exclusively of foreign service personnel, but it did have some autonomy, at least from Scott McLeod's Internal Security Division. Once this court of appeal had been set up, Surrey moved quickly to subpoena Merle Cochran to appear before it. Now comfortably ensconced in a highly remunerative position with the World Bank, the last thing Cochran wanted was the damaging publicity that could ensue from the grilling Surrey was sure to give him. Cochran promptly dropped all of the charges he had made against me, and very soon thereafter Surrey informed me that the Passport Division had decided to restore my passport.

6 Return to Indonesia

In early 1953 the Ford Foundation's Board of Directors concluded that the United States was embarrassingly deficient in the knowledge necessary to understand political, economic and social conditions in much of postwar Asia. It singled out Japan, India, Indonesia and Iran as areas where American scholarship was particularly deficient and where scholarly studies should be funded to help rectify this deficiency. In the course of their discussions an apparent majority of the foundation's board members concluded that special emphasis should be given to research on Communist movements in these countries, and this was envisaged as a major component of all of the studies.

The board vested Dr Paul Langer, a Japan specialist who had worked primarily on Japanese communism, with responsibility for exploring possibilities of developing foundation-funded research programs in several major American universities covering these four countries. Langer struck me as fair and decent but rather narrow-minded in carrying out his assignment. But fortunately the foundation's director of research to whom he reported, Cleon Swayzee, a former specialist in American labor history, had a broader vision and imagination.

During the course of 1953 and early 1954 Langer worked out arrangements at Yale with Professor Karl Pelzer to establish a research program on Indonesian agriculture and agrarian problems, and with an MIT economist, Benjamin Higgins, to develop a program focused on the Indonesian economy. It was this research program which developed a close working relationship with Harvard's Douglas Oliver and enlisted several able anthropologist protégés of his interested in Indonesia, including Clifford Geertz.

To meet his mandate for research on Indonesian communism Langer came to Cornell to discuss such a project with me. My recently published book, *Nationalism and Revolution in Indonesia*, being at that time the first postwar study of Indonesia, it was natural that he did so, for it was several years before any other such studies of Indonesia began to appear. And so I was fortunately in a strong bargaining position when, early in our discussions, he pressed for my directing a study exclusively focused on Indonesian communism and its potential for growth. But if substantial research funds were to be made available, it seemed to me irresponsible to restrict their use so narrowly. I told him so and that I was unwilling to direct a project that did not extend to other aspects of Indonesian society. With respect to the political dimension, I told him I thought it would have scant value if it focused only on communism, and that it should embrace the whole spectrum of Indonesia's politics, with the Islamic and social democratic components receiving equal attention. Langer himself had been chosen to conduct the foundation's Japan study and, having planned to focus it on Japanese communism, seemed to feel that the other country studies should follow suit. He made clear he didn't approve my wanting to broaden the scope of an Indonesian study, but was decent enough to promise to report my views to Cleon Swayzee, with whom I was then invited to go to New York to discuss them.

It was not without some trepidation that I called upon Swayzee, but I was soon put at ease by this gentlemanly old scholar. We quickly came to like and respect each other, and I found him to be almost as critical of the foundation's inordinate emphasis on communism as I was. He readily agreed that even those obsessed with the importance of Indonesian communism could understand it better within the context of the whole range of that country's political life.

I was extraordinarily fortunate in being able to deal with the Ford Foundation through such enlightened men as Swayzee and his assistant, and later successor, Clarence Thurber. They could not have treated me with greater understanding or kindness. It undoubtedly took some courage for them to recommend to Ford's Board of Trustees that Cornell be given a grant for Indonesian political studies with me as its director, when I was under McCarthy's cloud and when they were in full knowledge of Cochran's and Campbell's allegations against me, and knew that my passport had been withdrawn. Moreover, when in 1956, two years after I had regained my passport, I was recovering from a severe heart attack which had struck me while supervising the project's research in Indonesia, they successfully recommended to Ford's trustees that, to compensate for this, the project's life be extended and supporting funds be accordingly increased. In addition, and very importantly, they agreed to my request that the research project could incorporate Indonesian scholars as well as those from Cornell.

And they later, after initial reluctance, agreed that part of the Cornell grant could be used for something countenanced by the Foundation in no other such research project – establishing a journal devoted to scholarship pertaining to the project's area mandate. (It was this that made it possible to carry out Benedict Anderson's proposal for the Indonesia Project's publication of an interdisciplinary journal devoted to research on Indonesia, a highly successful biannual publication launched under his editorship in 1966 that emerged under the title of *Indonesia* and has now, over 35 years, run to 72 issues.)

Certainly if Cornell's Modern Indonesia Project can be deemed to have been a success much of the credit goes to Cleon Swayzee and Clarence Thurber.

The foundation's officers and trustees had also agreed that final delineation of the project's research program in Indonesia could await my discussions with Indonesian scholars and political leaders as to what they regarded as the highest priorities for research. And so for much of my first year as director of Cornell's newly established Modern Indonesia Project, from the fall of 1954 to mid-1955, I discussed the scope and emphases of its projected research with many knowledgeable people in Indonesia, including Sukarno, Hatta, Mohammad Natsir, Sutan Sjahrir, Muhammad Yamin and several professors I knew – including Djokosutono, dean of the law faculty, and Sumitro Djojojadikusumo, dean of the economics faculty at the University of Indonesia. It had seemed to me important to bring these people into the planning process, not only to benefit from their advice, but, I hoped, also to give them enough feeling of involvement – to make them supportive. This generally proved to be the case, and there is no doubt that over the course of the twenty years to which the project's research was finally stretched it considerably benefited from this. At the very least, the rapport established helped ensure that during most of this period all the Cornell graduate students bent on research in Indonesia were able to get visas.

The Modern Indonesia Project also benefited from backing by the Cornell administration, especially from the university's president, Deane W. Malott. He had been kind enough to write a letter on my behalf to the State Department when I first started the battle to recover my passport and early on took an interest in the research of the Indonesia Project. As an earnest of his support in 1958, early in the project's fifth year, he instructed the university administration to end the requirement that it pay rental for its office space on the campus, as most externally funded research projects were required to do. From then on the university shouldered the cost of maintaining the venerable old building at 102 West Avenue without requiring the project to pay rent.

The office space in question, along with a seminar room and small library room, was provided in a former, rather dilapidated, fraternity house on the edge of the campus, at 102 West Avenue, that had been condemned as living quarters but barely passed muster if used for office space. Despite its age, the building had a certain charm, and the graduate students, faculty members and visiting scholars who worked there over the remaining forty years of its life usually became deeply attached to it. And it clearly brought its denizens together in a sort of intellectual camaraderie that continued into the 1970s and 1980s when it absorbed not only those connected with the Indonesia Project but also scholars, young and old, working on other Southeast Asian countries as well. When that happened the Indonesian national motto in old Javanese painted over its front door seemed even more apt: "Bhinneka Tunggal Ika" (Unity in Diversity).

Despite Walter Surrey's success in getting my passport returned, and the endorsement and support by the Cornell administration and the Ford Foundation of the Modern Indonesia Project, its initial year was not smooth. For the State Department, especially its Passport Division and Internal Security Division, were very clearly strongly opposed to it. They were able to insist that my passport be valid for only a single probational year, and, having regretted acceding even to that, sought to have me intercepted and my passport recalled while I was in Japan and the Philippines, en route to Indonesia. Fortunately they had my travel schedule wrong, and I visited Tokyo and Manila before the American embassies there had been alerted to intercept me, pick up my passport and cancel its validity for Indonesia.[1]

Before finally returning my passport in September 1954, the heads of the State Department's Passport Division, Ruth Shipley, and Security Office, Scott McCleod, had insisted on my divulging to them all the details yet available as to my plans for the projected research project I had been asked to direct in Indonesia.

For those who did not live through the McCarthy period their attitude may well appear bizarre, if not incredible. Perhaps, however, the following frantic memorandum from the Passport Office's Ruth Shipley to Philip Bonsal, head of the Department's Office of Philippine and Southeast Asian Affairs, as routed through and approved by Scott McCleod, head of the Department's Security Division, should indicate the temper of the times and the extent of the opposition of these officials to me and Cornell's Modern Indonesia Project. I recovered this document many years later, thanks to the Freedom of Information Act, and reproduce it here (figure 6.1). It is dated 21 September 1954 and refers to my conversation with Mrs Shipley of 20 August, wherein at her request I explained the nature and purpose of the research Cornell and the Ford Foundation had asked me to conduct in Indonesia. (The first two blacked out censored words are undoubtedly the name "Owen Lattimore" and the last four are presumably the names of the several outstanding State Department China specialists that McCarthy had attacked and managed to oust.)

When I reached Jakarta the US ambassador, Hugh Cumming, who had succeeded Cochran and joined him in opposing the return of my passport, ordered me to appear at the embassy to admonish that if he found any evidence of my having contact with any Indonesian Communist he would confiscate my passport. He was cold and aloof and exploded with choleric anger when I suggested that I could not form a balanced picture of Indonesian politics without interviewing the leaders of its Communist Party, by then the country's fourth largest political party. I later found out from Cumming's successor as ambassador, John Allison, that Cumming had

Memorandum Dated August 20, 1954, of Conversation With George McTurnan Kahin

See ltr dated June 6, 1954 from Walter Sterling Surrey to PD!

It may not be within PD's province to anticipate the political consequences which may result from a project such as Mr. Kahin proposes to carry out in Indonesia. However, now that he has indicated, in some detail, the scope of the inquiries which he and others plan to make and the personnel to be employed, PD is apprehensive lest relations between Indonesia and the United States be seriously affected. Had PD been informed of the extent of his plans, it would have continued to hold up the issue of a passport to him.

You will note that Kahin, a protege and close associate of [redacted], was deliberately trained by the latter for work in Indonesia. (See tagged paper.) Giving Kahin the benefit of all doubt concerning his motives and purposes PD is of the opinion that he did not act as a reasonably prudent, loyal American should act when he was previously in Indonesia. Kahin has indicated that he was not in sympathy with United States policy respecting Indonesia and, from available information concerning his activities, it may fairly be assumed that he was intentionally engaged in a program designed to discredit the policy by impairing faith and confidence in our diplomatic mission in Indonesia. He now proposes to set up in Indonesia a staff numerically superior to the regular staff of the diplomatic mission to question Indonesians in all walks of life and of all political parties or factions about their political beliefs, in a study lasting four years. For what purpose? To write another book? Judging by his previous performance, there will be unrest, discord, and an association with revolutionary elements highly dangerous in a country as disturbed as Indonesia. Why do you risk this? There could develop competing missions in Indonesia, the official mission representing the government of the United States and an unofficial mission financed with funds provided by the Ford Foundation and purporting to represent Cornell University but having tie-ins with intellectuals in many other organizations.

If the national interest requires a total study of political and economical developments in Indonesia of the magnitude contemplated, it is believed that the Department of State, with the aid of the Department of Commerce, should make the study and that, instead of disassociating itself from the proposed project, the Department should control it. It is suggested that a project of the magnitude envisioned should receive very careful study in the Department at very high levels and that, bearing in mind that foreign experts and scholars and nationals of Indonesia are to be employed on the staff, the motives and purposes of the persons who intend to carry out the project should be carefully explored. It may be that the Department will wish to place a caveat against the undertaking. It would be far better to check it now, if checking is desirable, than to undertake remedial action next June, when Kahin's passport will expire.

You have the record of the [redacted], [redacted], [redacted], [redacted] and countless other Americans using American funds to betray China. Isn't the political situation in Indonesia too delicate and dangerous to tolerate the political interrogations and studies contemplated?

130 – Kahin, George McTurnan

Figure 6.1 Memo from Mrs Shipley to Mr Bonsal dated 21 September 1954

forbidden members of the Embassy to read my recently published book, *Nationalism and Revolution in Indonesia.*[2]

During the fall of 1954 and spring of 1955 while I was in Indonesia I was not totally absorbed in laying the foundations of Cornell's Modern Indonesia Project and managed to do some research of my own. Thanks to their perception of my role during the revolution I had prompt access to the country's principal political leaders. These included Mohammad Natsir, still prominent within the progressive wing of the Masjumi party, and a man whom I held in high respect. I thought his approach to Islam was important to understand and sought to do so, spending many hours discussing with him his political and religious concepts. There was a warm rapport between us, and we continued these sessions during my brief visit to Indonesia in mid-1956 that was unfortunately aborted by my sustaining a severe heart attack. When I returned in 1958–9, my hopes of completing these talks with him and a book based on them were dashed because he had left Jakarta for mid-Sumatra to join the PRRI rebellion. And when I returned again in 1961 he was in jail along with many other leaders of that regional rebellion.[3] So though I felt I had been able to develop a good understanding of Natsir's ideas, I never felt qualified to complete the book about them I had planned.

During the last week of April 1955 I turned briefly away from Indonesia's internal political life to attend the Asian–African conference in Bandung, sponsored by Burma, Ceylon (Sri Lanka), India, Indonesia and Pakistan, and attended by their representatives and those of twenty-four other countries in Asia and Africa. This was the conference by states of varying degrees of neutralist or other non-aligned postures that so upset the Eisenhower administration, particularly the Dulles brothers (John Foster Dulles was now secretary of state and his brother, Allen, head of the CIA). In fact the major preoccupation of the sponsoring states, and especially Nehru, Sukarno and U Nu, was to give the Chinese Communist government a more realistic understanding of its world environment, especially its Asian neighbors, while at the same time reducing tensions or potential tensions between them and China. From the standpoint of the five sponsors, even more immediate in precipitating the call for the conference was their alarm at the dangerously heightened tension in the Taiwan Straits between the United States and Mao Zedong's government, a situation which on the eve of the conference seemed explosive. By all well-informed accounts, Communist China's representative, Zhou Enlai, was unexpectedly successful in allaying fears of Chinese expansionism on the part of a number of the Asian states.

Though I was, of course, denied permission to attend any of the conference's closed sessions, at its conclusion members of its secretariat were kind enough to lend me for a twelve-hour period the full typewritten text of the proceedings, and I was able to make extensive notes on them. It was this, and visits during a month shortly after the conference to see government leaders and other officials in Cairo, Karachi and Rangoon – as well as

Jakarta – to ascertain their retrospective evaluations of the conference, that made it possible for me to write a very slim book about the conference and its achievements (The Asian–African Conference, Bandung, 1955).[4] Through two old friends I'd made in Yogyakarta during the Indonesian revolution, Thakin Tha-Kin and Mohamad Yunus, I enjoyed special access to Burmese and Indian leaders when in the month following the conference I briefly visited Rangoon and New Delhi to ascertain their retrospective evaluations of the conference.

In the long discussion I had in New Delhi with India's prime minister, Jawaharlal Nehru, I was taken aback by how narrow and dogmatic he was in his perception of the political side of Islam. In discussing Natsir's views with him, I found that he thought largely in terms of stereotypes stemming from his unconcealed dislike of the founder of Pakistan, Mohammed Ali Jinnah, and that he could not accept the possibility of an Islamic political leader espousing ideas as enlightened as those of Natsir. (And it was abundantly clear to me why Indonesian leaders were antagonized by his arrogant self-congratulatory demeanor.)

At Nehru's suggestion, the next day I met with Krishna Menon, the minister of foreign affairs, a man whom, I had been told, stood intellectually and politically very close to Nehru. Krishna Menon had agreed to receive me in his private suite in the imperial palace (once the abode of the British viceroy). A servant ushered me into his sitting room, where I found him propped up on a couch, his arms encircling a large bowl of grapes, which one after the other he was popping into his mouth. He offered me none of his grapes, but did pause sufficiently between mouthfuls to carry on a conversation.

I found his views very close to Nehru's with respect to Communist China. He was convinced that the Bandung Conference had been salutary in giving the Chinese a more realistic view of their international environment while at the same time giving the smaller states of Asia less fear of Chinese expansionism. But his perception of the political potential of Islam seemed every bit as narrow as Nehru's and informed by the same stereotype, as represented by Pakistan's Moh'd Ali Jinnah.

And it became abundantly clear to me also why Krishna Menon had antagonized Indonesian leaders so strongly. I was almost immediately aware of the overweening arrogance and self-congratulatory attitude of this undoubtedly very intelligent man. Indeed, I was so antagonized that I took a childish satisfaction when shortly after I had left his apartment I heard the sound of pounding feet behind me and turned to find a breathless and clearly embarrassed Krishna Menon, who blurted out, "I forgot to say that what I was telling you was all off the record!"

But personal impressions can have lasting effects, and it was later evident to me that the very negative view Sukarno and other Indonesian leaders had formed of Krishna Menon had a significant effect on their subsequent attitude with respect to the Portuguese colony of East Timor. It is my understanding that when in the early 1960s some members of Sukarno's entourage revived the idea of annexing that territory – a move that Sukarno and Hatta had previously resisted – a major factor in keeping Sukarno opposed was the fact that it had been Krishna Menon, then India's minister of defense, who had so recently – December 1961 – been the architect of India's invasion and annexation of the Portuguese colony of Goa. Sukarno was certainly not going to risk being regarded as following in the footsteps of Krishna Menon.

Following my talk with Krishna Menon, the tea that I took that afternoon with Indira Gandhi, Nehru's daughter, was a most pleasant contrast. When in later years she emerged as India's iron-strong prime minister I could not but marvel at the contrast with the apparently shy, sweet-tempered and self-effacing woman with whom I'd been able to relax over tea in 1955.

During the year 1954–5, and extending into visits in 1958–9, 1961 and 1963, I made a particular effort to understand Javanese political culture. The attempt was not very successful, and I never came close to the understanding developed by my colleague Benedict Anderson. To begin with, I would have had to be fluent in Javanese, were I to have made any real headway. But I had not even begun to learn Javanese, and even my grasp of Indonesian remained weak. But thanks to guidance from two close Indonesian friends, Selosoemardjan, secretary and adviser to Hamengku Buwono IX, Sultan of Yogyakarta, and Soedjatmoko Mangoendiningrat, a political essayist, publisher and historian, I was at least awakened to the importance of trying to understand a little of that distinctive political culture.

My growing consciousness of the importance of trying to understand it was precipitated in late 1954 by an experience I had in driving across Java and on to Bali with two Western-educated Javanese friends – Sumarman, a prewar graduate of the Dutch-run Jakarta law school and now secretary general of the Ministry of Internal Affairs, and his close friend, Roosdiono, a senior official in the same ministry and also one of the relatively few graduates of Dutch colonial advanced Western education. Sumarman was a talented workaholic widely regarded as the essential heart of the Ministry of Internal Affairs, and our trip was to be his first vacation in several years. I drove these two, together with their wives, in the well-used but surprisingly sturdy second-hand Dodge I'd purchased for the Modern Indonesia Project from the Cornell College of Agriculture and had equipped with reinforced springs suitable for the badly deteriorated roads we had to traverse to get across Java to Bali and back.

Sumarman had hoped to travel incognito, but almost everywhere we stopped he was besieged by people who learned his identity and who importuned the poor man with requests for all sorts of help. I remember that, shortly after we had taken the little ferry across the strait from Banyuwangi at the east tip of Java to Bali, the Rajah of Karangasem urgently requested a meeting with Sumarman on what he said was a matter of great importance.

The problem they discussed was indeed a serious one – certainly from the standpoint of the women of the rajahdom. The problem was that the rhinoceros skin that was regularly boiled to form an extract taken to relieve pain at childbirth had lost its potency after repeated boilings going back to before the Japanese occupation, and it was imperative to get a fresh one. I remember sitting discreetly well off to the side while Sumarman tried to explain to the old rajah that Indonesia's tiny residual population of these animals had dwindled to a handful living on the protected preserve in Kulon Progo at the extreme western end of Java, and that it was strictly against the law to kill any. Sumarman promised that when he next visited the preserve he would look carefully to ascertain whether any rhino had died or had broken a leg and could therefore be legally killed and skinned. That Sumarman was conscientious in trying to help was made clear to me when about two months later I happened to accompany him on a trip to the tip of West Java and witnessed him inquiring of village officials there as to whether anyone had heard of a sick or lame rhino. There were none, but he had clearly done his best for Karangasem. It struck us all that there was real irony in a situation where the appalling decrease in the rhino population was mainly attributable to the enormous sums Chinese traders would pay for rhino horns, prized by their countrymen for preparing a powder believed to ensure virility, and that the skin of the same animal was used by Balinese women who believed it held properties that could ease the pain from the consequences of that alleged virility.

On the return trip our route took us over the same road we had earlier traversed going east. Unbeknownst to me, but clearly understood by Sumarman and Roosdiono when we stayed overnight at the house of their close friend the *bupati* (regent) of Cirebon before driving on to Bandung, the military situation had changed radically since we had traversed the same road in the opposite direction a little over a week before. In the meantime, the troops of the anti-government Darul Islam had moved in to occupy much of the territory between the two cities. The Darul Islam had never forgiven the Republic's government for having yielded to the Renville Agreement of January 1948 and withdrawn its troops from the areas of West Java that they had wrested from the Dutch. Its strongly Muslim members had remained on to continue fighting the Dutch, had formed their own autonomous administration since then, and refused to lay down their arms or accept amalgamation of their forces into the post-independence Indonesian army. They had, in the early 1950s, maintained control over shifting areas of West Java and tied down the best battalions of independent Indonesia's army. And while we were in Bali they had surged into part of the area between Bandung and Cirebon, a development that Sumarman and Roosdiono learned about from their close friend the *bupati* of Cirebon soon after he welcomed us to his house.

My friends excused themselves immediately after our dinner with the *bupati* and closeted themselves with him for a good part of the night. And they were with him again the next morning while I breakfasted alone. A little later my friends indicated it was time to leave, and after I had thanked the *bupati* for his hospitality I got into the car with them and started on the drive of some ninety miles to Bandung. They seemed intensely preoccupied and very serious. For more than two hours they were absolutely silent and refused to respond to anything I said. I was convinced that I must have made some terrible insulting faux pas and soon gave up my lame efforts at humor. It was eerie. In the complete silence I could feel the tension that enveloped them. And as I began to congratulate myself on the absence of any military barricades to slow me down I noticed there were absolutely no peasants on the road – not a soul. The landscape for mile after mile was completely devoid of any visible human being.

Finally about ten miles short of Bandung we came to a military post manned by government soldiers. There was an audible sigh of relief from my four passengers, who now at once began to talk volubly and happily. They felt obliged to apologize for their silent behavior and tried to explain it to me. When we had arrived in Cirebon, they said, the *bupati* had warned them that Darul Islam forces had recently moved into a stretch of territory along the road connecting it to Bandung, and he had urged that we wait a few days before attempting to drive through. But Sumarman had also learned of what he regarded as very important problems that had arisen at his office in Jakarta and felt he could not wait longer to return. He, Roosdiono and the *bupati* were members of a small mystical group tied to a certain very powerful guru in Jakarta with whom they kept in close contact. Sumarman, Roosdiono and the *bupati* had been concentrating intensely together in Cirebon and while we were in the car afterwards in an effort to form a sort of mystical shield to ward off the threat from the Darul Islam, and that accounted for the tense silence they had maintained. Their intense mutual concentration, even with the many miles physically separating them from both the guru in Jakarta and the *bupati* in Cirebon, was then regarded as giving them protection against the threat of Darul Islam soldiers. Though I thought I knew these two Western-trained legal specialists well (in Jakarta I lived in Roosdiono's house which was next door to that of Sumarman, his closest friend), I would never have been aware of this important aspect of their personalities if it had not been for this fortuitously timed threat from the Darul Islam.

I'd hoped to spend the summer of 1956 in Indonesia working with the several Indonesians who were now involved with the research supported partly or wholly by Cornell's Modern Indonesia Project. I made what I thought was a promising start collaborating with Widjojo Nitisastro and Teuku Umar, two extremely able research assistants of Professor Sumitro Djojohadikusumo, dean of the University of Indonesia's faculty of economics, in drafting a research guide and questionnaires to be used in an extensive study of villages (twenty-three in Java and thirty in Sumatra) to be undertaken over a two-year period by students of their faculty. Most of these students were from middle-class families, and Sumitro and his two assistants held firmly to the maxim – one I enthusiastically applauded – that it was important for these urban-oriented students to "get their feet dirty" by being exposed to the realities of peasant life. And so, because of the importance of this project, it was provided the largest financial subvention of any of the research by Indonesians supported by Cornell's Modern Indonesia Project. This matched the funds made available by the Faculty of Economics and made it possible to double the number of students who carried out these village studies.

Getting this Village Project and several lesser studies under way had been exhausting for me, and one day when I was looking forward to a much-needed afternoon nap Widjojo dropped by with a friend to urge me to come and have tea with an elderly Dutch woman, a history teacher and friend of theirs, who was, they said, in a very depressed state. Since, they said, she shared some of my interests they thought it would cheer her up if I accompanied them to have tea with her. I at first demurred, for the heat in the very stuffy converted garage that was my room always left me limp in the afternoon, and I didn't feel up to socializing. But my two friends painted such a poignant picture of this little old lady that, most reluctantly, I agreed to go along. It was a big mistake for, as I then and later learned, in the tropics when you're exhausted and the heat and humidity are high you shouldn't push yourself and should take it easy if you can. My second, and most crucial mistake, was to do something else that no sensible person should do under such conditions – to keep myself going enough to meet this unexpected drain on my energy I took one of my carefully hoarded Benzedrine tablets – the first that I'd taken in Indonesia. As a result I got through the socializing at tea in fine fettle, but then in the middle of the night afterwards I awoke in my stifling little room with a very severe heart attack.

Early the next morning Roosdiono and his wife Luz, in whose house I was then living at Jalan Mendut 5, managed to contact the nearby hospital, and two orderlies soon appeared with a stretcher to carry me there. It wasn't clear how soon they would make it to the hospital for the stretcher was designed for the average Indonesian – a little over five feet tall. As the two orderlies sought to lift up the litter, the one responsible for elevating the end where my feet extended out well past the edge of the litter soon discovered that with my feet under his crotch he was in effect trying to elevate himself and me at the same time! After several attempts, which I am sure were more uncomfortable for him than for me, he finally solved the problem by a less orthodox method – standing to the side of the litter and reaching over it to the far handle. But they did manage to carry me across a rickety bridge over the gully behind the house and several blocks further to the public hospital where they deposited me on a cot in the huge room that constituted the main ward. I considered myself lucky, for my cot was in the middle of the room, a considerable distance from where were concentrated those poor wretches who were in the process of dying, with their all-too-audible moans and screams.

I was lucky in that there was soon brought in to occupy the cot next to me a bright young junior official from the Ministry of Foreign Affairs with whom it was a pleasure to talk. The Suez crisis was then in full swing, and when he discovered I was an American he was initially circumspect and reserved, but when he found I respected Nasser and sympathized with the plight of the Palestinians the barrier was broken and we both felt fortunate that we had someone to talk to who had shared interests and a roughly similar base of knowledge.

But his companionship, which lasted for less than a week, was the only mitigating circumstance. For though I was lucky enough to be attended by Jakarta's single Western-trained cardiologist, Dr Yap Tjong Bing, this doctor insisted on my following an unusually Draconian regimen. If I were to recover, he insisted that I would have to lie absolutely motionless in my cot for at least ten days. At first that did not appear to be too difficult an assignment. But as dusk fell, and mosquitoes commenced to sift through the many tears in the rotten fabric of the very old mosquito net that hung over my cot, the situation became very hard to bear, for I was not allowed to move my arms to slap the mosquitoes or otherwise ward them off. As a multitude of those little beasts dived in to feast on me I felt utterly helpless, but I remembered Dr Yap's stern admonition, and I did not want to return to the pain I had experienced before being admitted to the hospital. It took great determination, but I slapped not a single mosquito, while I enviously heard those on cots around me slapping happily away with understandable satisfaction.

Almost as hard to endure as the mosquitoes were the friendly ministrations of the husky male nurse assigned to me. Like most of the nurses in my ward he was an ex-guerrilla with very little of the training one assumes nurses to have. He was an innately kindly soul, but he seemed to feel that if he showed himself to be especially conscientious in his duties I would be more likely to reward him by giving him English lessons – for which he had an insatiable appetite. Unfortunately, the way he chose to impress me with his diligence as a nurse was in the daily sampling of my blood. He was supposed to jab one of my fingers with a needle and squeeze off a few drops of blood to be sent to the laboratory for testing. He seemed to take great pride in this part of the procedure, ceremoniously lighting a match to the needle to sterilize it – a process he called something like "cooking the dirty things." The needles, however clean, were very dull, and my fingers certainly felt them. Moreover, instead of jabbing just one, which I assumed, and later verified, was the standard procedure, in a display of his great diligence he proudly pricked all ten of my fingers, and I endured several days of this before I could get the attention of a doctor to intervene and end this nobly motivated carnage.

Strange as his methods have seemed to other cardiologists, Dr Yap's regimen worked, and after I'd spent ten days in the hospital he pronounced me strong enough to fly by stages back to the United States, where I received more orthodox care from cardiologists in Seattle and Ithaca. When I submitted my bill for my ten-day stay in the Jakarta hospital to New York Blue Cross their response was immediate, for given the prevailing rate of the US dollar to the Indonesian rupiah, it came to just $10.75.

My recovery after I returned to Ithaca went smoothly, thanks in large measure to the fact that in Daniel Lev I was fortunate enough to have a first-rate graduate student as teaching assistant in my lecture course, who was willing and able take over most of the course burden for the entire fall term. Dan was also unusual in that he was the only one of my graduate students who had a carpenter's license. Thanks to his efforts, the already condemned ex-fraternity house that provided the home for Cornell's Modern Indonesia Project lasted at least an extra decade after he expertly inserted steel posts and jacked up the building's dangerously sagging first floor.

It was through my friend Soedjatmoko Mangoendiningrat, or Koko as he was generally known, that I later experienced a further striking indication of the importance of Javanese mysticism and the extent to which it played a role in the lives of even some of the most Western-educated Indonesians. I had known Koko ever since meeting him together with Sjahrir in New York in 1948, and I had come to regard him as one of my closest friends. He was widely seen as Sutan Sjahrir's most brilliant follower, some believing him to be intellectually the stronger of the two. At the very least he was regarded as one of the most influential intellectuals in the country. And because of his broad knowledge of Western political and philosophical thought, as well as Javanese culture, he was seen by many as something of bridge between the two. His knowledge and political insight were shared not only with members of Sjahrir's Indonesian Socialist Party but were widely disseminated beyond it through his writings, and editorship successively of two very influential weeklies, *Het Inzicht* (Insight) – a response to Dutch publications during the period of British occupation in 1946–7 – and *Siasat* (Tactics), which was the major organ of Sjahrir's party, as well as his editorship in the 1950s of the influential daily newspaper *Pedoman*.

At Sjahrir's request Koko had gone to New York in 1947 to serve as a member of the Indonesian Republic's Observer Mission to the United Nations and then spent a year at Harvard's Littauer Center before moving to Washington in 1951 to serve as political counselor in Indonesia's recently established embassy there. Appalled by McCarthyism and disillusioned by Indonesia's post-revolutionary governments, he left the diplomatic service and towards the end of 1951 set out on a nine-month odyssey through Western and Eastern Europe in quest of political inspiration and securer political bearings. But he was soon keenly disappointed, perceiving striking disparities between ideologies and performance in all of the countries he visited – East and West European. It was only in talks with the maverick

Milovan Djilas in Yugoslavia that he encountered insights that seemed to him to have real relevance for Indonesia.

This European trip enhanced Koko's concern for Indonesian history – a subject which he saw his countrymen as having unconscionably neglected. And it was this deficiency among Indonesian intellectuals that kindled his concern lest Indonesian history be used for the political ends of those who would subordinate and distort it to the requirements of national myths and propaganda. That possibility we both saw, as did Sjahrir, as all too likely to be exploited by the Indonesian army and lead to a sort of neo-Fascism. Indeed, it was that potential as apparently embodied by some ambitious army officers that tempered Koko's and Sjahrir's criticism of Sukarno. For they realized that – like it or not – he was a major impediment to the ambitions of some army officers and was then, at the same time, also a barrier to expansion of the Indonesian Communist Party. Certainly during the 1950s and very early 1960s, Koko and Sjahrir, and most others in their Indonesian Socialist Party (PSI), saw the army as the greater of these two threats to the development of a plural political process in the country.

I became much intrigued by Koko's relationship with Sukarno. One could almost say that there was a "love–hate" relationship between the two. They appeared to respect each other – or more precisely different attributes in each other's persona. Sukarno respected Koko's intelligence, didn't like his closeness to Sjahrir but showed a sort of avuncular tolerance towards him. Koko, like Sjahrir in his later years, though critical and impatient of Sukarno, seemed to recognize increasingly during the late 1950s that in the face of growing army and PKI power, realism demanded trying to get along with him. They understood Sukarno's perceived need to balance off the army and the PKI against each other in order to stay at the top of the pyramid of power himself, and they preferred Sukarno at the apex to either of the others. It was only in the early 1960s after Sukarno banned their Socialist Party, together with the Masjumi, that their attitude began to change. Both Koko and Sjahrir worried that, as the army's power grew, the PKI's influence with the president would increase.

Along with Koko I was concerned at the lack of interest of most educated Indonesians in their own history and at the paucity of those who were seriously engaged in studying it. Following my return to Indonesia in mid-1958 for a year's stay, our common concern drew us together and we began to plan jointly the production of a book on Indonesian historiography that we hoped might help advance the flagging prospects for Indonesians developing a serious interest in their own history and in the methods that could help them study it. Koko had already done more than any other Indonesian I knew to grapple seriously with this problem, having broken the ice in a courageous and iconoclastic address to a National History Seminar at Gadjah Mada University in Yogyakarta in December 1957. His controversial statement there had a salubrious effect on the still anemic field that had continued to be overly reliant on earlier Dutch scholarship. Before an "Indonesian history of Indonesia" could be written, he argued, a great deal of new research would have to be carried out. He voiced his fear of an overly nationalistic reaction to the existing, often heavily Eurocentric, body of Indonesian history and urged keeping Indonesian history as free as possible from those who, in order to serve immediate political ends, would seek to subordinate it to national myths and propaganda. "I thought," he wrote me soon after the conference, "that I should concentrate on trying to protect the study of history from the impatient demands of nationalism." There would have to be great vigilance, he wrote, against "the danger that the need for a new national myth and the need for a more or less uniform way of looking at our past would induce, or seduce, people to adopt one particular viewpoint as the official version of Indonesian history – denying the legitimacy of others."

I was strongly drawn to these views of Koko's and joined him in an effort to produce a collection of historiographical essays that we saw as a first step in moving educated Indonesians towards more historical research and writing. We initially conceived of the project in 1957 but did not manage to complete it until 1965 when Cornell University Press brought out the 427-page volume *An Introduction to Indonesian Historiography*. This was predominantly Koko's work, he provided the intellectual drive behind it and most of the scholarly contacts that enabled us to incorporate the essays of twenty Indonesian and Western scholars besides his introduction and conclusion. My own part, though certainly time-consuming, was largely logistical. And the two other Indonesians listed as subordinate editors were included primarily to ensure broader acceptance of what we knew would be a controversial book. The process of editing was slowed because of the well-developed egos of some of the contributors and their insistence upon successive revisions of their chapters. But our effort was eased when in the fall of 1961 Koko was able to spend a semester at Cornell as a visiting professor and while giving an excellent seminar on modern Indonesian polit-ical developments had time – such as he didn't have in Indonesia – and facilities to help get us through the most difficult period of editing. The great pity was that copies of the book did not reach Indonesia until after Suharto's seizure of power and the intellectually stultifying and intimidating atmosphere that this ushered in.

Soon after I returned to Indonesia in mid-1963 Koko and I met. He was in an excited and exhilarated mood contrasting with his usual cool and sober mien. "We've done it!" he explained. "Suddenly there was a shaft of light and his *kris* came clattering to the floor." I knew that he and a few close friends had been meeting regularly for at least a couple of years in mystical seance with a man considered to be one of the most powerful gurus in Jakarta. Koko, full of excitement, went on to explain that their effort to obtain a special *kris* of Sukarno, their possession of which they were convinced would rob him of his power, had finally succeeded. A couple of years before he'd told me of this mystically bound group's efforts through sustained and intense concentration to wrest power from Sukarno, but I had paid scant attention, regarding this as simply one facet of Koko's complex inner personality. But this episode, and especially his graphic account of the "clattering" of Sukarno's *kris* on the marble floor was told in such vivid terms as to seem very real. I was stunned by the clarity and detail of his account and his own belief in its reality and significance. While I tended to conclude that he and his group had, through their intense concentration, somehow mesmerized themselves into believing that what they wanted to happen actually had occurred, I realized how important this was to them, and what a considerable psychological lift it had provided.

At any rate almost exactly a year later at the end of July 1964 when I received a very up-beat letter from Koko it seemed that maybe the locus of power was shifting. He wrote that Sukarno had informed him that he would like him to come to the palace for a talk and had at almost the same time announced he would appoint the Sultan of Yogyakarta as a member of his presidential cabinet in the potentially powerful position of coordinating minister.

It was then that Koko wrote me:

> I for one believe that this appointment signifies the beginning of the President's attempt to loosen his ties with the PKI [the Indonesian Communist Party] and to shift his international relations away from China. This in my view is bound to lead to increased friction with the PKI and will in turn even further precipitate a change in his foreign policy, leading most likely to an orientation in the direction of Europe (West and East) rather than the United States.

Developments in Indonesia did not follow Koko's expectations. Political polarization increased; the army's power grew; and the PKI's assertiveness and outspokenness became greater, with Sukarno appearing to lean on it for support even more. Probably his increased conviction that the United States' CIA was plotting against him significantly increased this disposition. At any rate Sukarno was sure that the CIA as an institution was continuing to plan his assassination.

His conviction stemmed from the nearly successful assassination attempt against him in November 1957 when he visited his children's Cikini school in Jakarta. An aide had saved his life by pushing him to the ground as the first of many hand grenades exploded, but eleven other people were killed and at least thirty seriously injured – most of them school children. At first Sukarno had been willing to accept the conventional wisdom that the principal suspect as the mastermind behind this assassination plot, Colonel Zulkifi Lubis – a former army intelligence chief and deputy chief of staff who had staged an aborted coup d'état a year before – was acting on behalf of an anti-Communist Muslim organization. But when a few months later it was definitely established that the CIA was supporting the Sumatra-based PRRI rebellion and that Lubis was its principal military strategist, Sukarno became convinced that the CIA must have also been behind Lubis in the Cikini assassination attempt. After that Sukarno found it easy to believe that the CIA was behind another nearly successful attempt to kill him when he visited Makassar in 1961. Sukarno's concern over assassination attempts were not all focused on the CIA, but they were no mere fantasy. According to Howard Jones, who served as American ambassador to Indonesia from 1958 to mid-1965, there were a total of seven "narrowly failed" assassination attempts against him,[5] three of them subsequent to the November 1957 attempt at Cikini.

When I last talked with Sukarno in August 1963, he was deeply worried that the CIA was still plotting against him. He said he was unsure who all its agents were in Indonesia, but that he had his strong suspicions. He, of course, believed, as almost all Americans in Jakarta suspected, that one of them was Bill Palmer, the rotund and affable man who ostensibly was in Indonesia over many years as representative for the American motion picture industry. Palmer, whose Cold War obsessions were all too obvious, was generally well liked by most of the American community in Jakarta, and even by some of those Indonesians who suspected he was an intelligence agent. Every Sunday he held a lavish open house in his villa high up in the cool Puncak Pass in the mountains about half way between Jakarta and Bandung. A handful of Indonesians and a larger number of Westerners, including lower-ranking Embassy personnel who could not afford to rent a bungalow in the Puncak, assembled at Palmer's villa on weekends where the political gossip was intense, even if not particularly well attuned to the realities of Jakarta politics. Palmer's popularity among those who could afford weekend retreats in the Puncak was assured by the fact that he did not join in the escalating payments of protection money to the local Darul Islam. He was admired because, instead of participating in this expensive operation, he avoided any molestation from these local insurgents by inviting them into his house for free movies every Sunday night after his Jakarta guests had left.

But Sukarno feared that some other Americans who regularly visited Indonesia were also tied to the CIA. One of his problems was that his own intelligence agency had confused the Asia Foundation, which at that time was widely regarded as CIA-funded, with the New York-based Asia Society, which I was confident had no such connection. I was pleased then and afterwards that I had been able to assure him that Claire Holt's close friend, Wendy Sorenson, wife of the architect who designed what was then Jakarta's only modern hotel, the Hotel Indonesia, was not involved with the CIA. But I later realized I may have been naive in telling him that I thought that another of his suspects, Guy Pauker of the Rand Corporation, had no such connection.

After I last saw him he clearly remained persuaded that the CIA was out to get him, and when White House aide Michael Forrestal visited Jakarta in

February 1965, Sukarno, in privately talking to him, charged that the CIA was "out of control" in Indonesia and that Ambassador Jones did not know what it was doing. When four months later Jones paid his farewell visit to Sukarno, the latter charged that the CIA was planning to assassinate him, together with Foreign Minister Subandrio and the chief of staff, General Yani.[6]

In view of the findings in 1975 of US Senator Frank Church's Select Committee on Intelligence, Sukarno had reason to believe that the CIA was one of the parties interested in arranging for his assassination. Unfortunately, under pressure from Henry Kissinger and the CIA's director William Colby, Church's committee backed away from its initial disposition to investigate allegations of CIA plans to assassinate Sukarno,[7] as well as several other heads of state. When the committee suddenly decided to drop its probe into this matter and cancel hearings at which I was scheduled to testify, its operations coordinator sought to justify this reversal by offering the lame – and revealing – excuse that it was difficult to discriminate "between the actual efforts of carrying out an assassination attempt and those involved in the effort [on the one hand] and the actual authorization for the effort as it involved American authority." Subsequent attempts of mine over the next more-than-twenty years to get transcripts of the committee's hearings with respect to both Sukarno and Cambodia's Norodom Sihanouk have been completely futile. The committee's staff in 1997 so fully stonewalled my efforts that I was unable even to get copies of the record of testimony I myself had given before the committee more than two decades earlier (in 1973).

It is relevant to note that when President Gerald Ford threw his weight behind Kissinger and Colby in their campaign to curb the Church committee's investigation into allegations of US assassination attempts against foreign heads of state, that effort came to a halt – and it was never resumed. The Senate Select Committee on Intelligence continues to this day, but its mandate to investigate these charges was not restored. Any possibility of Frank Church reviving these probes ended shortly afterwards when he was defeated for reelection to the senate from his home state of Idaho. With that state normally dominated by right-wing Republicans it had been almost miraculous that he had survived his opposition to the American role in the wars in Indochina, but now with the charge that his criticism of the CIA was "unpatriotic" his ability to win another election for the US Senate was further undercut and he lost.

7   Struggle over Malaysia

In evaluating the role of the CIA in Indonesia and ascertaining who its agents were, Indonesian intelligence was, on the basis of my own limited experience at least, no more deficient than the intelligence services of Britain, India, Malaya and the Philippines. Certainly that seemed to be the case in mid-1963 when these intelligence services concluded that I was "the top CIA agent in Southeast Asia." No one could have relished this irony more than my friend Howard Jones, the US ambassador to Jakarta, who shared my negative evaluation of the CIA's role in Indonesia and had for several years known of the efforts by its agents there to have him replaced by undermining his reputation on charges of his being too soft on communism and too indulgent towards Sukarno.

My exalted reputation as a top CIA agent in Southeast Asia was apparently accorded me by British intelligence for a brief period in 1963. Since their intelligence services often out-performed the CIA in the area, however, it would not be fair to infer that assigning me this status was typical of the quality of their other evaluations.

This apparent aberration must be understood against the background of the plan by Britain and Malaya to establish a new federated state of Malaysia out of Britain's recently emancipated colonies of Malaya, Sabah (North Borneo), and Sarawak – plus, initially, Singapore, with its huge naval and air bases, as well as the oil rich Sultanate of Brunei, technically a British protectorate, not a colony.

Part of the context for the emergence of the Malaysia concept was Britain's pressing need to reduce her existing heavy defense expenditures "East of Suez," a prospect unwelcome to Washington, Canberra and Wellington, particularly at a time when the growing military power of Communist China appeared to them as increasingly minatory. Though the basis for this assumption was in fact highly questionable, the presumed threat was given greater credence by the existence of large overseas Chinese communities in Malaya, Singapore, and also in the northern Borneo territories. There was a widespread, though quite untested, conventional wisdom in Britain, Australia and the United States that these overseas Chinese communities were more likely to be loyal to China than to the countries in

Southeast Asia to which they had emigrated. And it must be emphasized that this view was shared in moderation by the leadership of the Philippines and very strongly by Indonesia's army and some of its political leaders and parties.

For the British, undoubtedly the most important, and certainly the most immediate, precipitating factor in moving toward the establishment of Malaysia was the increasingly radical leftist temper of politics in Singapore that developed during the early 1960s. Unspoken publicly, but very important, was the realization that such a merger would do much to smother radical political dissent in that important trading center, for it would mean that the well-developed internal security system built up by the British in Malaya would subsume that of Singapore. In an enlarged arena of control, political radicalism in Singapore could be more easily contained. It was also argued that if Singapore and Malaya could be merged, both would benefit economically. Thus, Singapore's inclusion in the federation would mean that Britain's major naval and air base east of Suez could be better protected, while her sizable economic stake in Malaya would not suffer. Whatever the full range of Britain's motivations, there is no doubt that what seemed to be an increasingly unstable and perilous political condition in Singapore by early 1962 was the most immediate precipitating factor in London's decision to move ahead rapidly with the establishment of a Malaysian federation embracing Malaya and Singapore.[1]

But the incorporation of the Borneo territories in the proposed federation was more controversial. The British had initially favored separate political evolution for these British territories, a policy which seemed likely to eventuate in an independent Borneo federation, possibly including the tiny British protectorate of Brunei as well as Sarawak and North Borneo. The tremendous gap in economic, political and educational development between Malaya and Singapore, on the one hand, and the Borneo states, on the other, was generally acknowledged to be a major impediment to common constitutional evolution.

The Malayan prime minister, Tunku Abdul Rahman, however, was extremely apprehensive over the domestic political consequences of merging his country with Singapore, and he remained opposed to the idea until persuaded that a political formula existed to ensure that the Chinese would remain in a minority position, not merely in terms of population but also in political representation and power. This could be achieved if not only Singapore but also the territories in Borneo were federated with Malaya. Thereby, the proportion of Chinese in the federation would drop (if only Malaya and Singapore were merged, Chinese would have outnumbered Malays by 44 per cent to 42 per cent), and within such an expanded framework it would be possible to ensure that political power would remain primarily in the hands of Malays.[2] He thus publicly expressed his interest in the prospect of a Greater Malaysia embracing Malaya, Singapore, and the Borneo territories.[3]

If the politically turbulent and unpredictable situation in Singapore can be said to have precipitated Britain's decision to establish Malaysia, then it was the rebellion that broke out on 8 December 1962 in the Sultanate of Brunei – slated at the time to be a component of the Malaysian federation – that precipitated the opposition of the Philippines and the Republic of Indonesia to it. Prior to the Brunei rebellion there was no clear indication that Indonesia or the Philippines would oppose Britain's evolving plan for the creation of Malaysia, even if that federation incorporated the northern Borneo territories. But the Brunei uprising and its quick suppression by British troops flown in from Singapore and Malaya were clearly critical in sparking the open opposition of both Indonesia and the Philippines.

With a land area of only 2,228 square miles (only slightly larger than the state of Delaware) and a population of a little over 150,000, Brunei was appropriately known as the "Shellfare State,"[4] for the oil field which it sat astride was one of the richest in Southeast Asia. It produced enough profits to keep the Shell Oil Company, the British government and most of Brunei's population reasonably content – even though the disparity in income between the sultan and his entourage and the bulk of the population was very wide.

Brunei was an important component in Britain's plan for the enlarged Malaysia federation, and its incorporation was strongly applauded by Malaya which envisaged that small state's oil wealth benefiting the proposed new federation and contributing greatly to its economic viability, and in a way that would assist all the other participants, including, of course, Malaya itself. But though he was initially drawn to the idea of his country's entering the projected new federation, the Sultan of Brunei became progressively more cautious, and then clearly ambivalent about the prospect. He found Tunku Abdul Rahman, Malaya's prime minister, condescending and arrogant and he saw little advantage in lining up with the other Malayan heads of state to await his turn at being the relatively powerless king of the envisaged federation. By joining Malaysia he foresaw Brunei losing its own sovereignty and very probably control over the revenue from its oil and natural gas.

The sultan faced a difficult dilemma, for though by resisting pressures to join Malaysia he could rally the formative nationalist and proto-nationalist support from a significant portion of his usually apolitical population, he would thereby have to oppose the British, who held final authority as the protectorate power and found it to their interest to have Brunei join the proposed federation. The sultan's throne rested to a critical degree on British military support, particularly on two British-officered Gurkha battalions, but, in addition, on a British-officered police force, and also, of great importance, British-controlled intelligence and counter-intelligence units. Offsetting this British leverage to some extent the sultan had some leverage of his own: the threat that he might cease banking his own oil revenues with the Bank of England, and thereby remove a major prop to Britain's sterling currency. All this, and the increasing popular discontent of the Brunei people with the privileged position of the sultan's aristocratic entourage that wielded often autocratic power in some important sectors of the state's administration, was poignantly appreciated by the sultanate's senior British civil administrators, as well as being generally sensed by Malayan, Philippine and Indonesian intelligence.

Very few historians have given much attention to the condition of Brunei at this time,[5] but it is worth noting that in the first elections held there in August 1962, which were monitored by the British, A.M. Azahari and his radical People's Party (Partai Ra'ayat) won in a landslide (54 out of 55 seats) on a platform that opposed Brunei's entering the projected Malaysian federation, and instead advocated establishing a state of north Borneo, incorporating Sarawak and Sabah (North Borneo) together with Brunei.[6] This, the British would not countenance and they refused to allow the Legislative Council, which would have resulted from the elections, to convene.

With their political success denied, Azahari and his followers staged an uprising on 8 December 1962, which became known as the "Brunei Revolt" directed against British policies particularly with respect to the projected Malaysian federation. British Gurkha forces soon quelled the uprising and a state of emergency was proclaimed under which Azahari's party was banned. Both Indonesia and the Philippines gave a measure of encouragement to Azahari,[7] and there were certainly those in Sukarno's military and civilian entourage who contemplated the possibility of an Indonesian invasion of Brunei. But Indonesia's meddling was almost completely restricted to supplying Azahari with arms,[8] and Philippine support was even less concrete.

Although in the aftermath of the revolt it would have seemed that joining Malaysia would provide the Brunei sultan with some protection against his hostile Indonesian and Philippine neighbors, negotiations between him and Kuala Lumpur foundered in July 1963, and he ultimately decided to opt out of the new federation. This was in part because the Malayan government refused to promise he would be its first king (actually putting him at the bottom of the list of the Malay sultans), and to at least an equal degree because he feared Brunei would lose control over its oil revenues. He was also very conscious that the revolt represented widespread popular opposition within his sultanate to Brunei's joining the federation. Most important in reassuring the sultan in his desire to retain his independence was the fact that the British government did ultimately agree to leave in Brunei the two battalions of British-officered Gurkha troops that were the indispensable supporters of his rule.[9] In return for this, he undertook to keep all of his enormous oil income from Brunei's Shell oilfields in sterling rather than any other currency. In a sense, then, the sinking British pound was to an important extent kept afloat on the back of Brunei's spectacular oil production.[10]

After the suppression of the Brunei revolt, the Indonesian government on 20 January 1963 announced a policy of "Confrontation" against Malaysia, and a few days later President Diosdado Macapagal of the Philippines also denounced the proposed federation. Initially the Indonesian "confrontation" consisted mostly of verbal attacks and occasional small-scale operations across the borders between Indonesian Kalimantan and the still-British-controlled north Borneo territories. In an effort to calm the mounting tension, President Macapagal convened a meeting with the leaders of Malaya and Indonesia in Manila in early June (7–11) 1963 where President Sukarno, Tunku Abdul Rahman and Macapagal discussed the possibility of coming together in a proposed confederation "of nations of Malay origin," tentatively named Maphilindo, which would incorporate the Malaysian federation together with the other two states.

In mid-1963 I sought to study the problem of relations between Indonesia and the projected Malaysia federation, in the process making visits to Malaya, Sarawak, North Borneo (Sabah), Brunei, Indonesia, and the Philippines, where I concluded this research in Manila during the Maphilindo Conference held in late July 1963 by the Philippine, Malayan and Indonesian governments in an effort to reconcile their differences over Malaysia's creation.

During June and early July, I visited all three of the north Borneo territories, interviewing both British officials and political leaders in Sarawak and Sabah. In Brunei I had some informative discussions with the sultan, the British chief of police, an official who showed some empathy and understanding of Azahari and his followers, and with the United Nations economic advisor to the sultan's government, an American economist whom I found livid with outrage at the way in which the British had disregarded Azahari's electoral victory. I also benefited from the understanding at the time and retrospectively of my old friend Tom Harrisson, who from his office in Kuching and during occasional trips to Brunei worked with British intelligence during this period.

When I went on to Indonesia I had extensive interviews concerning the emerging Malaysia problem with leaders of the major Indonesian political parties, with former vice-president Hatta and with several senior army officers, including chief-of-staff General Abdul Haris Nasution. Among them there was a uniformly powerful opposition to the formation of Malaysia, though not always for the same reasons. Hatta and Nasution were most strongly opposed because of their expectation that the large Chinese population in the territories of the putative new state, and their economic power relative to the Malays, would ensure that they dominated it politically as well as economically. And, somewhat unrealistically, I thought, they saw most of these local Chinese as currently or potentially closely tied to the Communist government of China.[11] President Sukarno was much less inclined to distrust overseas Chinese, at least those in his own country, and had quietly done much to protect them from Indonesia's military. Together with the army and the Indonesian Communist Party (PKI), he did, however, see the threat of neocolonialism in a continuing British military role in Singapore and other military bases in the new state. Here, it should be noted that the perception of both the Indonesian military and Sukarno that Malaysia posed a military threat was powerfully nurtured by their recollection of Britain's and Malaya's recent support from these bases of the PRRI and Permesta rebels from 1958 through 1961. (Not until after the surrender of Sjafruddin Prawiranegara and Burhanuddin Harahap on 28 August 1961 did the American embassy in Jakarta report to Washington that the PRRI rebellion had collapsed, with only one top Permesta leader, Ventje Sumual, still active.)[12]

On 20 July 1963 I drove up to Bogor for the appointment with Sukarno I'd requested shortly after arriving in Indonesia from his chef de cabinet, Mohamad Ichsan. The old Dutch governor general's palace there, surrounded by its beautiful deer park, was a much more congenial place for an interview than the other governmental palace in the center of Jakarta. Sukarno, relaxed and expansive, started off by asking why the United States supported the idea of Malaysia and why Americans seemed to have so little understanding of the situation in Malaya and northern Borneo. He commented:

> I am against Malaysia unless the people there have a chance to make their own choice. There must be a referendum, a plebiscite – I don't know which; but the people there must have a chance to express their views. What the British have done is merely to ask some of the chieftains whether they want Malaysia. Of course, because of their relationship with the British they naturally say "yes." It's just like the Dutch did at Malino – exactly like in South Celebes where they brought together the feudal leaders and asked them whether they didn't want a state separate from the Republic.

I knew from Howard Jones that Sukarno was then still trying to make up his mind as to whether he would accept President Macapagal's invitation to attend a conference in Manila, that would include the leaders of Malaya, the Philippines, and Indonesia (Maphilindo) and would discuss the question of Malaysia. I was brash enough to ask him whether, as a writer of Indonesian history and given the brief time I could extend my stay in Southeast Asia, it would be more important for me to try and understand the very tense and complex political situation that had developed in East Java or cover Macapagal's still putative Maphilindo conference in Manila. Sukarno chuckled and said he'd still not made up his mind as to whether he would go but that if he did it would be more important for me to go to Manila – "not only for the history of Indonesia, but for all Southeast Asia." He would know in the course of the next week, he said, whether he would make the trip to Manila, and it would depend on the attitude of the Tunku. Then giving me a broad grin, he said: "If I go then you can come along with me; I will make the arrangements for that; I'll get in touch with you."

Bogor is about half way to the Puncak pass where US ambassador Howard Jones, like many members of the diplomatic community, had a weekend retreat in its cool and bracing climate. Jones had rented a medium-sized bungalow there still bearing the name "Mirasole," given it by its prewar Italian architect. It had a swimming pool in which the water was unbearably cold in the morning, but just pleasantly cool by late afternoon. Its small staff of servants included an excellent cook. Jones had earlier invited me to spend that weekend there, and I was looking forward to my stay there with him and his warm and friendly wife, Mary Lou.

Jones was delighted when I told him of the possibility of my accompanying Sukarno to Manila and thought that there was at least a fifty–fifty chance that the president would follow through with an invitation. As for himself, though he was keenly interested in the conference, the wrong signals as to American policy would be sent, he said, if he were to be seen in Manila while it was in session. Yet he wanted to be "in the wings" as it were, so that he could be kept abreast of developments and in a position to offer his advice when possible. Jones knew that my views on the mooted Maphilindo confederation, which would embrace the three participating countries, were close to his, that I had only recently visited Malaya and the Borneo territories that were to make up the projected Malaysian federation and that the likely members of the Indonesian delegation either knew me or realized that Sukarno trusted me. Consequently, he thought I would be able to understand what was going on at the Manila Conference and be in a position, if I were willing, to serve as a sort of link between him and the Indonesian delegation. The problem would be how to maintain contact with each other during the conference in some way that would keep his presence under cover. Being a friend of Ambassador Stevenson, the US envoy to Manila, he was confident he could arrange for social invitations that would permit me to meet him at the embassy on a few occasions. But that would not be sufficient, and after some thought Jones came up with a formula that provided for more regular contact, and was far more discreet. During the conference, every evening at about 5 p.m. he would show up at the back door of the USO (United Service Organization) – the civilian-manned social organization that was an adjunct of almost every major US military base around the world – and expect to meet me there. As Jones described this scenario, he appeared to become more and more convinced that Sukarno would actually invite me along to Manila in his entourage. And to my surprise he did.

I had heard nothing for about a week after my 20 July meeting with Sukarno, when very early one morning there was a phone call from the palace, informing me that I was invited to accompany him and his delegation to Manila and asking me to take my luggage down to the palace within three hours. I did so, and late that same morning found myself settled in a comfortable seat aboard the Constellation Sukarno had rented for the trip. We flew north over Borneo and Palawan down into Manila's airport. During the flight Mohamad Ichsan, Sukarno's chef de cabinet, explained the logistics to us – there were about twenty-five people in the delegation, he said, and we would all be put up at the venerable Manila Hotel, and all of us would be provided our own transportation. When we landed we should look for a car with special new license plates that would bear the number of our position on the delegation.

Then Ichsan's assistant began handing out to each passenger copies of a paper listing the names of the members of the delegation, each prefixed by a number. I'd not expected to receive a copy, for I was not aware that I was to be considered a delegate. But to my astonishment there, thirteenth on the list, stood my name. I'd assumed that if I were to appear there it would be in some separate category, such as "observer" or "writer," but I was mixed with the actual delegates on the list headed by Sukarno, with Foreign Minister Subandrio as second. Very much puzzled I went over to sit next to Ichsan, who good humoredly listened to my concern. Sukarno had just wanted me to come along with the group, he said, and had not suggested that I was to fit any special category. "We're all glad to have you along," Ichsan said, "and you don't need to worry about any special duties." I was free to do whatever I wished at the conference and talk to whomever I wanted. But undoubtedly some members of the delegation, including Subandrio, would welcome discussing matters with me from time to time. That, of course, suited me splendidly. Pointing out to Ichsan that I might want to write about the conference and didn't want to appear beholden to anyone, I did finally manage to get him to agree, quite reluctantly, to my paying my own hotel bill, but he refused to consider my paying for the car and driver that would be put at my disposal, arguing, quite reasonably, that this would involve him in too much unwelcome bookkeeping.

Our plane put down in Manila on schedule and taxied over beyond the terminal to a place where a cluster of cars were drawn up. As I walked down the steps I spotted one with the license plate No. 13 – a venerable Packard, well polished, but at least thirty years old, with a gracious and attentive driver of about the same vintage. I liked him well enough, but did from time to time dismiss him so that I could take a less recognizable taxi.

The next morning, 30 July, I was driven in No. 13 to the conference hall. There a group of pretty girls from the University of the Philippines had been assigned the task of ushers, and had, I was told, been given lessons in protocol the previous day. My arrival caused some quite discernible conster-nation among them, for I did not fit any of the categories that they had been taught. After an intense huddle and audible whispering among the group, one of them detached herself and approached me to guide me to the seat that the group had apparently decided would be most appropriate to my station. I was then escorted up the middle aisle of the conference hall to a section occupied on the right-hand side by a group of ambassadors, and was seated next to the Indian ambassador. As I returned after the first intermis-sion, I saw a man who turned out to be the British chargé d'affaires standing next to the Indian ambassador, who then relinquished his seat to him. And so from then on I found myself sitting next to a very curious British diplomat. He was intrigued that I had come to the conference in Sukarno's entourage and he clearly could not believe that my presence there was simply because of my friendship with Sukarno. It was evidently from this baffled British diplomat that the story emanated that I was some sort of high-level CIA official.

That idea, I soon found, had resonance among the Philippine and Malayan representatives attending the conference. It may well have been reinforced when I attended a dinner given by William Stevenson, the American ambassador to the Philippines, a large affair to which many local Americans had been invited. It had been more convenient for me to go there in a taxi rather than in diplomatic car No. 13. As my cab came abreast of the Philippine constabulary guard post at the entrance of the ambassador's residence, the constabulary officer there attempted to draw me into conversation as to who was this mysterious American that had accompanied Sukarno. Was he important? Was he a big shot? To which I could not restrain myself from answering: "Yes, he is very important."

The conference opened with unexpected éclat on the morning of 30 July, with President Diosdado Macapagal of the Philippines making the opening speech. Commencing rhetorically, he asked: "Will this conference be a success?" No sooner had he completed that first sentence than the power failed, the lights went out and the air-conditioning went off.

Just across the central aisle of the conference room from where I had been seated with the group of ambassadors was a section reserved for senior members of the Philippine government. Among those that took the initiative of presenting themselves to me during the first intermission were Salvador Lopez, the minister of foreign affairs, and Ferdinand Marcos, president of the Senate. Both treated me with great deference, and in the short time before the conference resumed open session asked questions designed to assess my role in the American foreign policy establishment. Both said that they hoped to talk with me further after the session.

As the first day of the open session of the conference broke up late that afternoon, I walked along with the others from my section down to where I knew my No. 13 should be waiting. Suddenly my arm was gripped from behind by Salvador Lopez, who walked me briskly along with the others to where the chauffeur-driven cars awaited. As we walked towards what I assumed to be Lopez's car, the door opened from one parked just behind it and out jumped Ferdinand Marcos muttering that his wife awaited us at home. Lopez had been outmaneuvered. He looked both startled and angry as he loosened his grip on my arm and permitted Marcos to draw me into his car while saying as calmly as he could that he would telephone me later. I was startled by this quite unexpected little episode – feeling a bit like the prettiest girl at the senior prom being fought over by the school's two star football players.

We drove along in silence, for it was clear that Marcos realized that I saw myself as having been more dragooned than invited into accompanying him.

I had no idea at that point that I was being regarded as the senior CIA official in Southeast Asia, but it was clear that he thought I was important in the American foreign policy establishment. Since I did then know a good bit about US policy in the area and that of most of the Southeast Asian states, my questions to him and answers to his, though often guarded, were such as to reinforce his belief. When we reached his house – a substantial one – his wife Imelda was not there and he apologized, saying that shopping always made her late. When she finally arrived and he had introduced us, he politely suggested she could retire since we had a particular matter to discuss that would not interest her. She obediently withdrew and we settled down to a long and circumspect fencing that was at least useful to me in learning what one of Macapagal's principal political rivals apparently thought about the concept of Malaysia and the appropriate role of the Philippines in the international arena.

I sensed he was frustrated in being unable to establish my role in the American foreign policy establishment, but it was easy for me to keep him in the dark, since I had no such role. More than two decades later when I again saw Marcos, I was surprised to find that he still remembered the frustrating lack of meaningful discourse that we had experienced that morning. (Though he no longer regarded me as CIA – and laughed over his mistake in 1963 – he had on this later occasion erroneously concluded that I was a useful channel to the Pentagon.)

Lopez seemed to take no umbrage at what he referred to as my "kidnapping" by Marcos. He did call me, and on 5 August we had a long discussion about the conference. It was evident, however, that in speaking to me he felt unsure as to whether through me he was ultimately addressing an American or an Indonesian audience.

For both audiences he wanted it understood that the idea of Maphilindo had originated with Macapagal in June 1962. (According to Jones, the idea was indeed originally Macapagal's and to Subandrio's surprise had been quickly supported by Sukarno.) Lopez gave no indication that the Maphilindo concept was regarded as a helpful context for advancing the Philippine claim to North Borneo (via the Sultan of Sulu) – very likely because he didn't share Macapagal's need to keep this issue alive for the sake of advantage in Philippine domestic politics. He emphasized that Maphilindo would not mean that the Philippines had altered its attitude towards SEATO, for it regarded that organization not as an "arm of a great power," but as an organization of "common interest" to its members. "Heretofore we have been regarded as agents of a foreign power," he said – evidently referring to Malaya as well as the Philippines. "But this time we are doing it on our own – according to our own lights, we three peoples, deciding for themselves without guidance of others and their interests." If the differing foreign postures of Maphilindo's three component states made it seem incongruous, then one should look for a parallel with the Nordic Council where, he said, two of its states were members of NATO, Sweden was neutral and Finland "was obliged to play ball with the Soviet Union." (I'd not previously heard of the Nordic Council and am not sure the concept ever assumed much reality, but he insisted it was the most apt model of what the Philippines hoped Maphilindo would become.)

The remainder of Lopez's exposition of the rationale for Maphilindo, with its emphasis on the threat from Malaya's and Singapore's Chinese, was, I think, quite genuine and strikingly like that of Indonesian leaders, especially Mohammad Hatta and General Nasution. This was a factor, it should be noted – as has rarely been the case – that was not prominent in Sukarno's opposition to the formation of Malaysia. (As I noted before, those concerned with the welfare of Indonesia's Chinese minority have for the most part failed to appreciate the extent to which Sukarno blocked actions of elements of the Indonesian army bent on persecuting them.)

Lopez emphasized that Macapagal's concept of Maphilindo had been inspired "precisely by this problem of the Chinese," and the desire to control them within Malaya, Singapore and the Borneo territories. He cautioned:

> Singapore is exploding and the power relationship between the Chinese and Malays in the projected area of Malaysia is changing. With the very narrow margin they have now – even with the addition of predominantly non-Chinese Borneo populations – how can the Malays long maintain political superiority, given the greater political sophistication and wealth, not to mention the increasing numbers, of the Chinese? Using Maphilindo to control the Chinese – especially the Singapore Chinese – is like dissolving a lump of sugar in a cup of coffee. [Maphilindo would provide a bigger cup than Malaysia] "but to make the sugar dissolve Maphilindo will have to be much strengthened."

During the course of the conference I was able to keep in fairly regular contact with Jones. Relying on the scenario we had sketched out before the conference, I met him twice in Stevenson's house and a couple of times at the rear of the USO, where he appeared a bit disheveled and convincingly like some middle-aged GI recovering from a hard night on the town. Thanks to seeing Ichsan or Subandrio daily, I was able to keep Jones well posted beyond what he could learn from Stevenson, and he reciprocated with information, especially from the British side, that helped me fill out the picture.

On 31 July, just a day after Macapagal, Sukarno and Tunku Abdul Rahman had begun their private discussions, it looked as if they had reached an impasse. Macapagal and Sukarno still held that there had to be testing of public opinion in the British Borneo territories before they were incorporated into the projected federation of Malaysia. The Tunku, all the while keeping in touch with the British, initially resisted this idea. But Sukarno insisted that when he and the Tunku had met together privately in Tokyo they had agreed on such an ascertainment and that, furthermore, the Tunku had then stated that, should a controversy arise over this, the date for the formation of Malaysia could be extended. Without apparently having gotten clearance from the British, who were reportedly furious at these concessions, the Tunku on the next day, 1 August, concurred in Sukarno's recollection of their meeting in Tokyo and confirmed that they had agreed there that, in case controversy arose, the date for the establishment of Malaysia was extendible.[13] The British insisted that no further ascertainment of opinion was necessary in their Borneo territories, since in the local elections they had recently conducted there the indigenous inhabitants who had been elected were largely in favor of their area joining the Malaysian federation.

There was reason to feel sympathy for the Tunku, caught between British pressure, on the one hand, especially as brought to bear by commonwealth relations minister Duncan Sandys, and his own self-respect, and the expectations of the nationalist Malay community, on the other. But in agreeing with Sukarno's recollection of what had transpired between the two in Tokyo, the Tunku had in effect joined in a common front with Macapagal and Sukarno and shown his willingness to give a United Nations ascertainment of opinion in the Borneo territories and the Maphilindo idea a try.

That cleared the way for the solution Subandrio and his team, supported by Sukarno and Macapagal, had been so intensely working on. This focused on an ascertainment of local opinion in Britain's Borneo territories with a UN cachet that would make it difficult for Britain to oppose. Formulating this proposal had required close consultation with UN Secretary General U Thant, who would be charged with organizing the process, and had involved considerable cable traffic between Subandrio and Indonesia's representative in the United Nations, Lambertus Palar.

Early on the morning of 2 August, Subandrio called to invite me to have breakfast with him to announce his success in this effort. As I entered his suite in the Manila Hotel he and his staff were exuberant. "We've done it," they said, confident that their last cable from Palar meant that U Thant had agreed to carry out an ascertainment of opinion in the British Borneo states. Subandrio and I had a long discussion, and though he did not specifically ask me to do so, it was clear that he expected I would be able to relay it on to Washington – whether through Jones or Ambassador Stevenson. He, of course, knew I had no CIA connection. (Until 1996 when I discovered a copy of the relevant cable from Stevenson to the State Department dispatched later that day I had no way of knowing how accurately my talk with Subandrio had been reflected. However, recently upon comparing it with the notes I wrote up after meeting with him, it is clear that his rendition was remarkably accurate.)[14]

The most important points made to me by Subandrio were that he had just received a message from Palar that morning that U Thant had told him a UN-sponsored referendum would take about six weeks and that it would require at least one or two weeks of preparation before the referendum could be commenced. Subandrio perceived a plebiscite as giving the people of North Borneo and Sarawak a wider choice than mere adherence to Malaysia. For instance, they should have a chance to vote on whether they wished to join a separate North Borneo state or whether they wished to be part of the British Commonwealth. And the plebiscite in North Borneo (Sabah) should take into account the Philippine claim, with Sabah having the additional option of joining with the Philippines. In answer to my question, Subandrio stated that, in any referendum or plebiscite, "We will not ask that they [the peoples of Sarawak and Sabah] should have the option of joining Indonesia." Subandrio thought that the results of an ascertainment by the United Nations would be about what the Tunku and Tun Razak (Malaya's deputy prime minister) anticipated – that is that the people of Sarawak and North Borneo would vote to join Malaysia. "This we will accept," he said, "and when I get back to Indonesia I will have to work hard to sell it to our people."

He said that the threat of Chinese subversion could not be met adequately by Malaysia, but that maybe Maphilindo could be worked out to contribute to a solution of the Chinese subversion problem. He said that Sukarno was still suspicious of British influence in Malaya and feared that they were propping up feudal elements there.

Later that same day, 2 August, I had a talk with Ambassador Zaidin, Malaya's ambassador to Manila, and a key member of the Malay delegation to the Maphilindo conference. He had evidently seen Subandrio and then checked with the British earlier that day. He told me that the British would not permit any plebiscite "or any testing of opinion" before 31 August, but that they would probably permit a UN Commission of Enquiry to begin an investigation before then – something that Malaya could agree to. The maximum concession by Malaya, he said, would be to postpone the formation of Malaysia for a short time if the testing of opinion by the UN secretary general was some process "other than a referendum or plebiscite." The position of Malaya was that any referendum would have to come *after* Malaysia was formed.

Mid-morning the next day I met with Howard Jones who had now himself had a chance to talk with Subandrio. Subandrio had told him that although the Malayan delegation was willing to go along with the Indonesians regarding a UN ascertainment in the British Borneo territories, and to this end was prepared to postpone the date for the establishment of Malaysia for a brief period if the UN found it necessary, he doubted the Malayans would be able to stand up sufficiently to the British on this matter, since the British remained adamant for an 31 August date. Subandrio, Jones said, was confident Indonesia would accept the establishment of Malaysia, so long as a genuine testing of opinion was made, but he had emphasized that "it must not be a farce." He had asked Jones if the US could probe the British to induce them to defer the date for Malaysia's establishment. He had added that the only two major sources of opposition to Maphilindo were Britain and Communist China.

That evening, at Macapagal's reception at Malacanang palace, Subandrio sought me out to tell me, as Zaidin had indicated, that though Malaya was agreeable to a UN ascertainment prior to 31 August, the British were still balking and would permit no UN intervention in the British Borneo territories prior to that date. As it was now evident he could reach Ambassador Jones through me, he made a proposal that the Indonesian side thought might break the deadlock, and that he hoped Washington would support. This was that, in the period before holding a plebiscite under UN authority in the British Borneo territories, they should be administered by "a temporary UN Commission" along the lines that had recently been used in West Irian before the UN ascertainment there.[15] If the British still objected, Indonesia would agree to let Malaya be the trustee authority prior to the holding of a UN-administered plebiscite. I dutifully passed this compromise proposal on to Jones, but have no idea as to how it was received in Washington. In any case, it was well designed to make the Indonesian position look more reasonable there, and thereby perhaps increase the pressure that the Department of State through Roger Hilsman, the assistant secretary for Far Eastern affairs, and presumably Averell Harriman, the under secretary of state, were applying through the British foreign office – which appeared to be significantly more open-minded with respect to the Malaysian problem than Britain's Ministry for Commonwealth Affairs under Duncan Sandys.

In any case, by 5 August the Indonesian, Malayan and Philippine delegations had managed to hammer out a compromise formula whereby Indonesia and the Philippines would welcome the establishment of Malaysia if "the support of the people of the Borneo territories" was verified through an ascertainment by an "independent and impartial authority," the United Nations secretary general or his representative. Even though anathema to Duncan Sandys, this was acceptable to the British foreign office. It eschewed any reference to a plebiscite or referendum – that the British would clearly not countenance – and instead provided for a UN ascertainment of local opinion through consultation with local leaders, particularly those who had been chosen in the recent elections in North Borneo (Sabah) of December 1962 and Sarawak of June 1963. Since, in both of these elections – however representative they actually were – mostly only leaders who had supported their British mentors' plan for Malaysia won, the outcome of a UN survey that gave major weight to their opinions could be easily foreseen. But the process was such that Sukarno and Macapagal would be able to tell their people that not only had they been consulted in the process of Malaysia's establishment, but that – and this was the essential ingredient – the establishment of Malaysia came only *after* it had been ascertained that the peoples of North Borneo and Sarawak had been consulted and had agreed to this. The Philippine and Indonesian presidents were further protected from nationalist criticism at home by virtue of it being agreed that the UN teams in these two Borneo territories would be accompanied by several observers from both Indonesia and the Philippines – a concession fought bitterly by Duncan Sandys, but which in fact involved too few people under too great constraints of time to make much difference.

That was the core of the formula essential to induce Sukarno and Macapagal to "welcome" the formation of Malaysia. Also important to them and their domestic audiences was the agreement that foreign military bases in Malaya, the Philippines, and Indonesia were to be regarded as "temporary" and not to be used "directly or indirectly to subvert the national independence of any of the three countries," and that each would "abstain from the use of collective defense to serve the particular interests of any of the big powers."[16] And the British could save face since they had sustained their central point that their authority in territories over which they exercised sovereignty could not be challenged by externally conducted plebiscites or referenda.

Finally, it had been agreed among Indonesia, Malaya and the Philippines in their conference in Manila – and this too was incorporated in the statement they announced at its conclusion on 5 August – that the three conference members would maintain the originally ad hoc confederation of Maphilindo as an ongoing consultative body designed to work out any differences that might arise among them, with a secretariat of its own to help sustain this function. As Jones later observed, "Duncan Sandys, Minister for Commonwealth Relations, was outraged ... But the three Southeast Asian heads of state had presented the British with a diplomatic fait accompli and the British, albeit with ill grace, bowed to it."[17]

Actually the group most outraged at the speed and superficiality of the UN ascertainment of the opinion of these Borneo peoples was a substantial part of the British colonial civil service that had been governing them. A good many of these officials had developed warmly protective attitudes towards their colonial wards and felt that, in view of the dependency of most local leaders on the colonial power structure, few of them could be expected to register opposition to the formation of Malaysia if this was what Britain pressed for.[18]

Despite the conference's inauspicious beginning, Sukarno and Macapagal left it feeling vindicated, Sukarno telling me on the flight back to Jakarta that he was pleased with its outcome and that he considered it had been "a success." Not so the British, especially Duncan Sandys, their minister for commonwealth relations.

Very soon the waters that the Manila conference had seemed to calm began to roil violently. First, Duncan Sandys seriously impeded the smooth functioning of the UN ascertainment teams by refusing to accept the presence of some members assigned by Indonesia, on the specious grounds that they were intelligence experts – something to be expected of practically all such personnel, regardless from which of the three countries they came. He made transportation arrangements difficult for many of the observers and went so far as to insist that accommodations were so limited that junior observer personnel would have to sleep in tents. As a consequence of obstacles created by Sandys, Indonesian and Philippine observers were unable to be present for three of the six days that the UN ascertainment was carried out in North Borneo.[19] Roger Hilsman, then US assistant secretary of state for Far Eastern affairs, observed that U Thant later reported:

> It is a matter of regret that this understanding [on observers] could not have been reached earlier, so that all observers could have been present in the territories for the entire period of the enquiries and that questions of detail pertaining to the status of the observers were unnecessarily delayed even further after their arrival. A more congenial atmosphere would have been achieved if the necessary facilities could have been granted more promptly by the Administering Authority [i.e. Sandys and the colonial officials answerable to him].

As Hilsman notes: "In one fell swoop, Sandys had handed the Indonesians what the in-between world would regard as a provocation, a 'neocolonialist' violation of the Manila accords with which to beat the British and Malayans, and a plausible excuse to deny the Secretary General's findings if they favored Malaysia."[20]

If this were not sufficient to scuttle the Manila accords and ensure Indonesia's resumption of its "confrontation" policy, Sandys managed to achieve such an outcome soon afterwards.[21] Under what Hilsman describes as "apparently heavy pressure from Sandys," the Tunku made a broadcast on 29 August, two days before the originally scheduled date for the establishment of Malaysia. He then not only proclaimed 16 September as the new date for its establishment to give U Thant sufficient time to complete his ascertainment process, but then gratuitously added the provocative assertion: "The position that Malaya has all along taken is that the ascertainment of the Secretary-General is not a condition which will determine whether Malaysia should be formed or not." Sandys himself then made a roughly similar announcement.

With regard to the Tunku's announcement, U Thant later wrote in his final report that it "led to misunderstanding and confusion and even resentment among other parties to the Manila agreement, which could have been avoided if the date could have been fixed after my conclusions had been reached and made known." And Hilsman commented, "I did not see how such a blatant insult could be ignored by the Indonesians and Filipinos."[22] As Howard Jones, then the diplomat in closest touch with Sukarno, correctly observed: "Whether or not Sukarno thought the survey would show support for Malaysia, on balance it appeared that prior to the August 29th announcement [by the Tunku and Sandys] he was willing to accept the UN verdict." On the basis of my talks with him and with Subandrio and other members of the Indonesian delegation returning from the Manila conference, I can attest to this having indeed been the case.

Against the background of the reckless statements of the Tunku and Duncan Sandys, U Thant's final report, which was made public on 14

September, was something of an anti-climax. On the basis of the findings of the ascertainment mission he had sent to British Borneo, the UN Secretary General concluded that

> the majority of the peoples of Sabah (North Borneo) and of Sarawak have given serious and thoughtful consideration to their future, and to the implications for them of participation in a Federation of Malaysia. I believe that the majority of them have concluded that they wish ... to engage, with the peoples of the Federation of Malaya and Singapore, in an enlarged Federation of Malaysia.

Predictably, after the provocative Sandys–Tunku announcement, Indonesia and the Philippines rejected U Thant's findings, both then refusing to accord recognition to the new Malaysian state. Sukarno and Subandrio held that the UN's survey had not been conducted in accordance with the Manila agreements. Unrealistically, they called for a second UN survey before Indonesia would recognize the new state. Without, then, the approbation of its two Maphilindo partners, but with the full support of London and Washington, the Malayan government, amidst considerable fanfare in Kuala Lumpur, announced the establishment of the new Federation of Malaysia on 16 September. Indonesian crowds stoned the Malaysian and British embassies in Jakarta, and a Malaysian crowd, denouncing the Indonesian Communist Party and calling Sukarno a "tool of [PKI head] Aidit," stoned the Indonesian embassy in Kuala Lumpur, removing the Garuda shield from the front of the embassy and taking it to the Tunku.[23] On 17 September Malaysia broke diplomatic relations with Indonesia, and the next day an Indonesian mob attacked the British embassy in Jakarta, and burned it to the ground, while the police stood by without interfering.

The strong opposition from the governments of Indonesia and the Philippines towards the Malaysian Federation was, then, not so much at the substance of the project as at the unnecessarily abrasive and provocative *procedure* in attaining it. It was especially what they regarded as Britain's unnecessarily precipitate, cavalier and self-righteous modus operandi, and particularly its lack of consultation with them over the establishment of this new state on their very borders, one that Jakarta and Manila saw as manipulated by Britain, that outraged President Macapagal of the Philippines, Sukarno and the Indonesian army. That was the way the US ambassador Howard Jones saw it when he initially reported on the matter to Washington. He was later overruled, and the Johnson administration finally took a stand squarely behind Malaya and Britain, primarily, I believe, to ensure continuing British backing to the American effort in Vietnam.

Guerrilla activity launched across the border from Indonesian Borneo into Sarawak and Sabah, that had subsided during the Maphilindo conference and the period of UN ascertainment, soon increased to a considerably higher level. And in October 1964 the Indonesians recklessly escalated their military operation when they began paratroop drops of armed military personnel on to Malaya itself. As Frederick Bunnell has observed, this generated adverse repercussions internationally.

> The mere fact of Indonesia's extending her armed subversion to the territory of Malaya proper hurt her cause, for even Djakarta formerly recognized Malaya as a sovereign state ... In short, the logic of Indonesia's case against the inclusion of the Borneo territories in the Federation of Malaysia could not be convincingly stretched to justify attacks on Malaya proper.[24]

If the Indonesians had not been so foolish as to begin parachuting these soldiers into Malaya they would probably have kept Ambassador Jones's reporting to Washington in their favor, but that stupid and quite fruitless undertaking, with most of these hapless Indonesians either quickly shot or captured, made it much easier for supporters of London and Kuala Lumpur to get their way in Washington, and resulted in a further loss of sympathy for the Indonesian position in the dispute in many other capitals as well. (Most of these ill-trained parachutists were airforce troops and not army commandos, the top army command being unwilling to sacrifice its own elite troops on such a fruitless and dangerous exercise.)

Despite Indonesia's refusal to recognize the new state, and the Philippines' initial unwillingness to do so, Malaysia soon gained widespread international recognition – to the chagrin of Sukarno – even from numerous Third World countries. And it was able to purchase arms from the United States as well as other Western states. For Sukarno, probably the bitterest pill was the successful effort of Britain and the United States at the end of 1964 to engineer a seat on the UN Security Council for Malaysia. In January 1965 Sukarno was foolish enough to denounce the United Nations as an imperialist-dominated organ and proclaim Indonesia's withdrawal from that organization and the establishment of a rival, competing body – the Conference of the New Emerging Forces, headquartered in Jakarta. This injudicious exercise in pique lost Sukarno support at home as well as in additional capitals around the world. But despite mounting reservations among many in Indonesia's officer corps, its militarized confrontation policy against Malaysia continued.

By early 1965, as Hilsman observes, the United States "had abandoned its efforts to steer the new nationalism of Indonesia into constructive channels, and moved to a hard line in support of the British effort to isolate Indonesia politically and contain it militarily."[25] But for Britain the continuance of Indonesia's confrontation policy developed into an enormous financial and military burden. Even with the entry of Australian combat troops to augment British forces in the area, London was obliged to draw deeply into its military reserves, even to the point of transferring some units from her Army of the Rhine to the defense of Malaysia. But most serious of all for Britain was the financial hemorrhaging necessary to support her air, naval and ground forces in Malaysia.

In the meantime the federation had lost two of its critical components. As noted earlier, the Sultan of Brunei, despite much cajoling from Kuala Lumpur had, after a period of indecision, decided to keep Brunei out of Malaysia. And although an election had resulted in Singapore's decision to join the federation, frictions between the Tunku and Lee Kuan Yew led to its expulsion from Malaysia in August 1965. From 1965, then, the Federation of Malaysia consisted merely of Malaya and the north Borneo states of Sabah and Sarawak.

The principal factors in precipitating Indonesia's and the Philippines' contestation of the formation of a federation of Malaysia were, then, first, the forcible suppression by Britain and the Sultan of Brunei of the local political party opposing the formation of Malaysia, just after it had won by an overwhelming margin Brunei's first open election; and second, the subsequent provocative announcement of the British and Malayan governments that Malaysia would be established on 16 September 1963, regardless of the findings of a scheduled United Nations mission charged with ascertaining the views of Britain's Borneo territories as to whether they wished to join the putative new state. That gauche move was perceived by both presidents Macapagal and Sukarno, as well as by the US assistant secretary of state for Far Eastern affairs, Roger Hilsman, and the American ambassador to Indonesia, Howard Jones, as a flagrantly provocative violation of the agreement arrived at in Manila only some three weeks before.[26] As Roger Hilsman remarked to one of his British friends regarding London's attitude throughout the negotiations: "I knew that some of the people I would have to deal with in this job were going to be emotional. But I never dreamed that among the most emotional of all would be some Anglo-Saxons."[27]

The process was especially galling to the Indonesians because they maintained that early in the course of the Maphilindo conference Tunku Abdul Rahman had confirmed to Sukarno the agreement reached in their May meeting in Tokyo, namely, that in case of a controversy arising over the formation of Malaysia he would be prepared to extend the date for its establishment.[28] British actions throughout this period brought Sukarno to liken their policy in the formation of Malaysia to the policy of divide and rule promoted by the Netherlands as a federal solution in 1948–9 to prevent Indonesia's achievement of complete independence.[29] Sukarno, then, believed that Malaysia was taking on the quality of a "feudal anachronism" – something he already saw the congeries of sultanates of Malaya proper as constituting.

8   Cornell and the coup

During September 1965 my attention was focused almost exclusively on the Philippines and on Vietnam (where my opposition to the American involvement in the war was already bringing me to accept invitations to as many speaking engagements as I could manage). In that month I was sent by the Rockefeller Foundation to assess their programs at the University of the Philippines, and my trip to Manila made it possible for me to stop over in Paris in mid-September on the way home. There I met with my friend Philippe Devillers and with Tran Van Huu (once Bao Dai's prime minister) and a few other Vietnamese political refugees to discuss the current Vietnamese situation before returning to Ithaca.[1]

Awaiting me on my return was an invitation to address an ecumenical religious gathering in Boston at the end of the month that was to be devoted to a discussion of the Vietnam War. Since Philip Berrigan, a Jesuit priest for whom I had great respect, was going to speak, I didn't see why they needed me. But they then informed me that the State Department was sending one of their junior members to argue the administration's case, and, while they believed that Fr. Berrigan could be counted on to handle well the moral and ethical dimension, they felt that I might be able to offset the State Department representative's expected emphasis on the political side. I accepted their invitation, flew to Boston and engaged in a spirited debate with this official who, along with many others in the foreign service, had been dragooned into carrying out such roles all across the country.

A man from one of the Boston radio stations asked me if after the meeting I would come to his station for an interview. I accepted, and it was then that from my absorption with the Vietnam war I was abruptly pulled back into the orbit of Indonesia, which I'd left once Johnson escalated to his savage bombing campaign. To my complete surprise the radio official informed me that shortly before he'd left the station for the Vietnam conference a report had come in that there had been a military coup in Indonesia and he would like our interview to focus on that as well as Vietnam. I had not been closely following events in Indonesia, but, even if I had, I would have been utterly surprised at this turn of events in a country that I thought I knew reasonably well. So I disappointed this station official by telling him I really didn't have a clue as to the nature of this development.

Back at Cornell I found my very able graduate students there who specialized on Indonesia – Ben Anderson and Fred Bunnell, together with Ruth McVey who had received her doctorate in 1961 and was now a research fellow at Cornell's Center for International Studies – equally astonished at what had happened. And so too was my friend and former graduate student Daniel Lev, then teaching at Berkeley. The three at Cornell soon launched into a collective effort to learn all they could about the still mysterious coup, scouring all the national and provincial Indonesian newspapers in Cornell's library – the major Indonesian collection in the country – and listening to radio broadcasts from Indonesia. This effort culminated on 10 January 1966 with their production of a very tentative 161-page analysis, appropriately entitled "A Preliminary Analysis of the October 1, 1965 Coup in Indonesia." It was in the best sense of the word a tour de force, an impressive analysis, especially given the limited data they had to work with.

In the opening paragraph of the synopsis of the paper the authors summarized its tentative conclusions:

> The weight of the evidence so far assembled and the (admittedly always fragile) logic of probabilities indicate that the coup of October 1, 1965, was neither the work of the PKI nor of Soekarno himself. Though both were deeply involved, it was after the coup plans were well under way. They were more the victims than the initiators of events. The PKI was entangled before it knew what was happening: Soekarno mistakenly attempted to take advantage of the situation created by the deaths of six of his top Generals. The actual originators of the coup are to be found not in Djakarta, but in Central Java, among middle-level Army officers in Semarang, at the Headquarters of the Seventh (Diponegoro) Territorial Division.

In addition to the analysis leading to this conclusion, the paper presented some alternative possibilities and gave translations of some of the most important documents appearing in the critical days and weeks following the coup. Twenty copies of the paper in its entirety were mimeographed and circulated for comments and criticisms to various scholars and officials, both inside and outside Cornell, who were asked to treat it confidentially. This was largely because some of the controversial conclusions reached there could have endangered former students and colleagues in Indonesia who we all felt could possibly be held accountable for the views expressed in the paper. In view of the large-scale massacres then taking place in Indonesia, this appeared to be a real danger. Unfortunately, at least one of the copies of the analysis was reproduced and circulated widely, rapidly acquiring notoriety as the so-called "Cornell Paper."

The various conclusions in the analysis were certainly different from the official analyses of the Suharto regime, both the one proffered at the time, and the several official versions that appeared over the next two decades. And it differed considerably from both initial and subsequent US government versions, including the most extensive of these, the one produced by the CIA in December 1968, *Indonesia – 1965: The Coup that Backfired.* Publication and dissemination of that study is the only instance known to me where the CIA took the initiative in declassifying one of its own studies and sending it without solicitation to a few select members of the public – in this case a handful of American Indonesia specialists, of whom I was one, who had seriously questioned the State Department-supported official Suharto regime version of the events surrounding the coup and the subsequent massacres it perpetrated. (There were at least two other CIA studies released to a few people, but they were much briefer and less substantial.)

On 27 January 1966 I went down to Washington at the invitation of Congressman Clement J. Zablocki, chairman of the Subcommittee on the Far East and the Pacific of the US House of Representatives Committee on Foreign Affairs for hearings on "United States Policy Toward Asia." As did others invited to testify, most of whom were academics, I prepared a memorandum for the committee, which at least a couple of its members, including Zablocki, appeared to have read. After summarizing this in just over two pages of oral presentation, which focused mostly on Vietnam but also embraced critical accounts of American interventions in Burma and Indonesia, I answered a series of questions, many of which dealt with Indonesia. There I took strong issue with the committee members' evident persuasion that the coup leaders in Indonesia had "a close allegiance to the Communist Party in China" and that the Chinese Communist government had backed the coup. Rather than there being evidence of outside support of the coup, I said that it "was an internal army affair," and that it released "tensions that had been building up for many years between the [Indonesian] Communist Party and the army leadership." I noted that "although the coup was not predictable, it had been assumed that the army – if given the opportunity – would attempt to crush the Communist Party." These remarks were consistent with the views of Anderson, Bunnell and McVey, and, of course, deviated sharply from the official line then being assiduously propagated by Suharto and his adherents.

When I was next in Indonesia, in June 1967, I had a long meeting with Colonel Taher, the intelligence officer who headed the Indonesian government's office charged with interrogating political prisoners and ostensibly responsible for coming up with a standard government account of the coup. The so-called "Cornell Paper" was now well known in Jakarta, and he questioned me about it. I informed him of its character and told him that if we were to produce a fuller and more scholarly account of the coup and its context, we needed to get hold of much more pertinent documentation. He and the six lieutenant colonels who flanked him in their interrogation room promised to get me some of the documents we had specifically identified that were pertinent to understanding the coup. I made similar requests to the judge advocate general, Kabul Arifin, and Nugroho Notosusanto, who headed the historical section of the Ministry of Defense, who also promised to send the materials.

Nothing of course eventuated, but when I was again in Indonesia in early 1971 I again sought these documents, this time from General I.J. Kanter, who was now the army's judge advocate general. I told him that because the so-called "Cornell Paper" had so frequently been misquoted, doctored and misrepresented, we wished to set the record straight and would soon be publishing it in its original form. I invited him to have an official Indonesian government account prepared, which we could publish in the same volume with this earlier analysis. He initially seemed enthusiastic at the idea, but there was no follow-up and presumably he was overruled by a higher authority. Nor did any of the documents I had requested ever arrive. Thus, in late 1971 the Cornell Modern Indonesia Project published *A Preliminary Analysis of the October 1, 1965 Coup in Indonesia* by itself in exactly its original form, but with a brief introduction by Ben Anderson.

In October 1975, the Indonesian government informed us that a group headed by Lt General Ali Murtopo, deputy chief of the State Intelligence Coordinating Body (BAKIN), President Suharto's private intelligence service, and Major General Benny Murdani, head of intelligence in the Department of Defense and Security, wished to come to Cornell to give us a full briefing on the 1965 coup and its background. The group of about a dozen military men and government intellectuals arrived on 24 October, and agreed to participate in an informal seminar with our most knowledgeable graduate students, followed by several hours of private discussion with Ben Anderson, Fred Bunnell, Ruth McVey and myself. While these talks were very cordial – though sometimes animated – the key questions remained unanswered. General Murdani promised that as soon as he returned to Jakarta he would arrange for the documents we had requested over the previous eight years to be sent to us.

A few months later, in the early spring of 1976, I requested permission to enter Indonesia to visit my wife who was carrying out dissertation research there. I was informed that I was on the "black list" but would be permitted on "compassionate grounds" to join her for two weeks in Jakarta, and later for a further two weeks in Padang. They asked, however, that while I was in Indonesia I should visit CSIS (the Center for Strategic and International Studies), the government "think tank" whose honorary chairman was General Ali Murtopo. I was taken to General Murtopo's house, where he started a conversation about the Indonesian revolution. He said how good it would be to have further studies of the period, and that he could furnish a lot of material. After our talk I was taken back to CSIS where two other members of its board (Harry Tjan and Jusuf Wanandi [Lim Bian Kie]) proposed an affiliation between the Cornell Modern Indonesia Project and

CSIS, and offered to set up a well-funded project on the nationalist movement and the revolution, of which I would be co-chairman along with an unnamed prestigious Indonesian scholar. As politely as I could, I declined, saying that at Cornell we never went in for affiliations, and had indeed turned down a request from Kyoto University for a similar relationship.

Later that year, I was informed by Benny Murdani that he and General Murtopo were sending a delegation to Cornell bearing pertinent documents and were prepared to engage in a two-day private seminar during which they would answer all our questions. Accordingly on 27 November 1976, there arrived at Cornell a group of three generals, a colonel and a major, all members of General Murdani's staff and headed by Brigadier General Datuk Mulia. They brought with them for deposit in Cornell Library's John M. Echols Collection on Southeast Asia more than 200 pounds of documents, nicely bound records of trials of those allegedly involved in the coup – but, alas none of the documents we had requested.

There the matter rested. My name remained on the black list, now together with my wife's, and for fifteen years neither of us was able to visit Indonesia officially, until finally the ban was lifted in 1991.[2]

9   Opposition to the Vietnam War

I had begun to oppose American military involvement in Vietnam during France's post-World War II effort to reassert control over the country, when the Truman administration had backed her with crucially important financial support, arms and the sea-borne transport of her troops. My opposition had grown as direct American involvement escalated under Presidents Eisenhower and Kennedy, and it became more intense as President Lyndon Johnson in 1965 sent in US combat troops and resorted to heavy bombing. But until March of that year my criticism was limited to my classes and seminars at Cornell and to encouraging graduate students critical of the US role in Vietnam. I didn't think I had the qualifications to do more.

Soon after I began teaching at Cornell in 1951, I did, however, manage to arrange for outsiders knowledgeable of Vietnam to contribute to my seminar on "Governments and Politics of Southeast Asia," and ultimately in the early 1960s to a seminar devoted exclusively to the Vietnam War. In addition to several American scholars, these visitors included Ngo Dinh Diem in 1953 and soon thereafter the State Department's dissident Vietnam specialist Paul Kattenburg, and Bernard Fall, whom Cornell's Southeast Asia Program thought highly enough of to support for a year in Ithaca while he finished his doctoral dissertation for nearby Syracuse University. During that year he also prepared a monograph, *The Vietminh Regime*, which we published in our Data Paper series.

Though our Southeast Asia Program made a considerable effort to bring in scholars from outside to lecture and lead semester seminars on Vietnam, the stark paucity of qualified American specialists on that country was discouraging, and we often had to look abroad for qualified people. Lauriston Sharp, the Program's first director, induced Tatsuro Yamamoto, the eminent Japanese Vietnam scholar from Tokyo University, to teach a semester seminar, but though he was excellent, his interests were confined to precolonial Vietnam. When I was Program director (for a decade beginning in 1961) I invited for the fall semester of 1964 P.J. (Paddy) Honey of London University's School of Oriental and African Studies (SOAS) to give a seminar on modern Vietnam. He was a complete disaster – absolutely rigid in his Cold War perception of Vietnam, and so unwilling to accept differences of opinion among the students as to drive even those most supportive of the US role into rebellion. He boasted to them over the fact that the Pentagon asked him frequently to Washington for consultation. (When it came to Vietnam or Cambodia, most American foreign policy officials steadfastly took the position that the US could manage things there much better than France had done and that there was nothing to be learned from French specialists.)

To help atone for my mistake in inviting Paddy Honey, I was fortunate enough to induce the highly respected, and much more knowledgeable, French Vietnam scholar, Philippe Devillers, to give the special seminar on Vietnam that our Program mounted at Cornell in the summer of 1965 for faculty members from other universities in the Eastern United States. (I learned much from him and subsequently saw him whenever I was in Paris, where over the years I met with members of the Quai D'Orsay and various French journalists concerned with Vietnam as well as with Vietnamese exiles.) Another British Vietnam (and Cambodia) specialist, Donald Lancaster, also gave a semester's seminar that helped offset what Paddy Honey had wrought.

There were a good many others with special knowledge of Vietnam whom over the course of the next decade we were able to invite to Cornell to help our students understand conditions in Vietnam and aspects of the war there that were not readily available through normal channels. Among these, in addition to several American academics who wrote on the country, were several US army officers, including the maverick and unusually outspoken Colonel John Paul Vann, and three controversial generals of the South Vietnamese army – Ton That Dinh, Tran Van Don and the unusually candid Nguyen Khanh – all of whom spent an afternoon or two with my seminar.

Probably the most valuable contributions by any of these visitors was made by Britain's former prime minister, Anthony Eden, who had served as co-chairman of the crucial 1954 Geneva Conference on Vietnam. During his visit to Cornell, 11–12 March 1969, he clarified some of the more controversial features of that conference. Most important was his adamant insistence that it was understood there that the demarcation line separating Vietnam at the 17th parallel was "expected to be provisional" and should "not in any way be interpreted as constituting a political or territorial boundary." It was never, he emphasized, expected to become "a lasting political boundary." Equally important, but never acknowledged by American policy makers, he went on to affirm that Ho Chi Minh and the Vietminh would never have agreed to the armistice with the French achieved in the Geneva Agreements if it had not been firmly stipulated in them that within two years internationally supervised elections would be held throughout Vietnam. (Tran Van Do, who at the time of Geneva was foreign minister of Bao Dai's government, fully endorsed Eden's view when I discussed the matter with him in Saigon nearly a year later.)[1] If the Eisenhower administration had not so blatantly violated that provision, what needless losses in life and physical destruction could have been avoided! There is no doubt, as US intelligence then testified, that the adherents of Ho Chi Minh would have won a fair election;[2] and a temporarily severed Vietnam would have been united almost two decades before it actually was. And what would American policy makers have lost other than some of their own over-heated hubris? But that hubris was sufficiently enduring to ensure that the administration, and its successors, would, on the basis of this violation of the Geneva Agreements, assert the right to build a separate, artificial, American protégé-state in the southern half of what was nevertheless one country infused by a single nationalism, and sustain it – despite the cost in Vietnamese and American lives – for more than two decades.

It was not until January 1961 that I made my first visit to Vietnam, a very short one and just to Saigon, primarily to see three of my graduate students there – Gene Gregory, Ngo Thon Dat and Nguyen Thai. I stayed with my old friends, Lloyd Musolf, then a senior AID official on leave from Michigan State University, and his wife Berdyne, and, in addition to talking with a few of the small number of foreign correspondents then there, had a long talk with Ngo Dinh Diem (who I understand never released anyone from his monological embrace in less than three hours).

So although I'd managed to read much of what was available in English and French about modern Vietnam, my knowledge of the country was very limited. But despite this, to my surprise, during the course of 1965 I found myself being regarded as knowledgeable about modern Vietnam and Vietnamese–American relations. This was primarily because there were so very few even pseudo-specialists on Vietnam in the United States, with most of them in the government and, whatever their views, usually, because of their junior positions, unable or unwilling to criticize the administration. (Paul Kattenburg was an isolated exception.) And, with most of Congress and the American public supportive of the administration's Vietnam policy until mid-1967, it was all the more difficult for even so senior a government official as George Ball to be an effective critic. (As I remember, for example, it was not until at least about late 1966 or early 1967 that one could discern that anything near a majority of the students at Cornell opposed the war.)

Moreover, with respect to such an unfamiliar and exotic area as Southeast Asia there was a tendency among Americans to assume that, if a scholar was regarded as a specialist on one country in the area, he or she must have special knowledge of the others as well. Since I had published on Indonesia, ergo I must be able to speak with authority about Southeast Asia as a whole. (This expectation, I found, also attached to China specialists.) And since I was director of the major program of Southeast Asian studies in the country and had edited a book on the governments and politics of the area, including Vietnam, there was all the more reason to suppose that I was knowledgeable about that country.

It was apparently on the basis of this slender reed of expertise, that, to my surprise, I was invited to Washington on 5 March 1965 to participate in a discussion of Vietnam policy by an organization of politically concerned scientists, the Council for a Livable World. It was a small but impressive group assembled there, and they ensured a lively discussion by asking good questions. (I remember being especially impressed by Professor Bernard Feld and a young Harvard professor of biochemistry, Matthew Meselson.) Among about thirty of us sitting around a long table I was one of a few non-scientists who had been invited. By far the most prominent of the outsiders, and appropriately seated at the head of the table, was the legendary General Edward Lansdale, the ex-CIA agent credited with having ensconced Magsaysay in power in the Philippines and then asked by John Foster Dulles in 1955 to repeat that success with Ngo Dinh Diem in South Vietnam. He launched our discussion with an account of recent Vietnamese history and the American involvement. I was astonished at the number of misleading statements and clear errors in his glib exegesis. Nor had I realized the extent to which careful preparation of my class lectures at Cornell had equipped me to confront these shortcomings, and though I had little experience in debate I found myself occupying the center stage with the venerable-looking general. He was essentially coasting on the basis of his reputation and was glaringly misleading on a number of important points. This was especially marked with respect to the terms of the 1954 Geneva Agreements that ended the Franco–Vietnamese conflict, provisions that I had studied very carefully, together with how the US had departed from them in establishing Diem in power.

Apparently these scientists thought I had been effective in criticizing the official rationale for American involvement in Vietnam. Several congratulated me and a group of physicists invited me to prepare a critique of US Vietnam policy for the upcoming June issue of their organization's publication *Bulletin of the Atomic Scientists*, an issue that was to have a major focus on the Vietnam War. I promptly set about doing so, inviting my Cornell colleague John W. Lewis to collaborate with me by incorporating material on the way China figured in the equation of US–Vietnamese relations, an aspect I felt poorly qualified to deal with. Our article was widely reprinted and, I was told, found many readers outside, as well as inside, their usual circle.

It was, I believe, to a large extent because of an initiative by members of the Council for a Livable World, that at the beginning of May 1965 I was invited through Harry Benda and Mary Wright, two friends of mine at Yale, to represent academic critics of US Vietnam policy in a debate against McGeorge Bundy, Johnson's national security adviser. Under the auspices of the just-formed National Teach-In committee, organized by Marshal Sahlins and colleagues of his at the University of Michigan, a two day anti-Vietnam War "Teach-In" was to be held in Washington two weeks hence on 16 May 1965.[3] Rather naively, I sent Bundy a copy of the article John Lewis and I had just completed for the *Bulletin of the Atomic Scientists*, so that he would know where I stood. He promptly responded with a rather patronizing note saying that he looked forward to the debate and believed my intentions were honorable. With the help of Ben Anderson and several of my best graduate students I began working very hard to prepare what I hoped would be a strong opening statement for the debate.

When I got to Washington I found that President Johnson had just ordered McGeorge Bundy to the Dominican Republic where the domestic scene and American interests were in disarray, and that Bundy had asked Professor Robert Scalapino, an East Asia specialist at the University of California at Berkeley, and a strong supporter of the administration's Vietnam policy, to replace him.[4] My contribution to the debate was, I think, rather colorless – I remember that Max Frankel wrote in the *New York Times* that I "spoke without fire" (I was simply too tired to do otherwise), but the Teach-In, incorporating statements by numerous other academics as well as the debate, was broadcast by radio and television throughout the country to several hundred colleges and universities which had been hooked up especially for the event. Although there had been nothing stellar about my debating style, my substantial opening statement was generally well received, and I found it reproduced in several antiwar pamphlets as well as in a few books afterwards, and I soon began to receive invitations to speak from several campuses.

Also important in establishing me as an antiwar critic was my appearance on a televised performance in Washington, 3 August 1965, on a major program of WETA devoted to public issues with Peter Lisagor, Washington Bureau Chief of the *Chicago Daily News*, as moderator. Senator George McGovern had liked my statement at the National Teach-In and asked me to join him on this program in debating William Bundy, the assistant secretary of state for Far Eastern affairs, and Senator Gale McGee, a well-known hawk on the Vietnam war. Bundy was considerably more articulate and knowledgeable than Lansdale, and McGovern was a good deal better informed and effective than McGee. I found myself primarily debating Bundy and doing better than I thought I would.

It was my performance in that debate that apparently convinced Bill Bundy that I was a war critic worth trying to co-opt, and led to his inviting me a few months later to membership on his powerless, but from the government's view politically respectable, East Asia Advisory Committee. I was advised by those who knew Washington better than I did, that this committee, made up of about a dozen academics under Bundy's chairmanship, was largely window-dressing and part of a public relations effort to demonstrate that the Johnson administration's policies in East Asia, particularly in Vietnam, enjoyed the support of American scholars specializing on current developments in Asia.

Friends told me that I was correct in seeing the invitation as an effort at co-optation, but pointed out that Bundy wouldn't have invited me unless he expected I would pass a security check, and that with such clearance I would be able to see documents relating to Vietnam that I would never otherwise have access to. But even more important, they pointed out that as a member of this committee I could hardly be denied permission to enter South Vietnam and travel around the country. Antiwar congressional staff members with whom I talked were in accord in urging me to accept the position in order to get to Vietnam and thereby be able to speak with greater authority. This was for me a compelling reason to accept. The appointment involved no pay, only reimbursement for occasional trips to Washington, and was compatible with my teaching obligations. I was skeptical, however, that I could pass the security check needed for access to the classified materials which the committee was supposed to discuss. Bill Bundy promptly relieved me of any concern over that matter, saying he was fully aware of my earlier dispute with Senator Joseph McCarthy, that it was of no consequence but rather, was something to be proud of, pointing out – correctly – that he himself had been the target of a vicious attack by that senator.

So I agreed to become a member of Bundy's committee in the State Department, and, as he had predicted, the process for gaining clearance for viewing some classified materials was, with his backing, very brief.[5] So in the fall of 1966 I attended my first meeting of this council, and found myself to be the only outspoken "dove" on the war and facing others, including Robert Scalapino, who were in various degrees "hawkish." Bundy was a fair and effective chairman and treated me in a consistently gentlemanly fashion, and I think I was reasonably restrained, except on occasions when George Carver, the CIA's Vietnam specialist, talked to us and I took strong exception to some of his seriously misleading statements.

The classified materials circulated among us were meager and of no real importance, but, thanks to my membership on this committee, I was now in a position to plan for a visit to South Vietnam.

Two circumstances combined to make my visit to South Vietnam, of 22 December 1966 to 19 January 1967, a successful one. The first was, as I've mentioned, my membership on Bill Bundy's East Asia Advisory Committee, which both enabled me to get permission to enter the country – not easy for those known to be opponents of the American military involvement there who lacked press credentials – and gave me access to US military transportation facilities to move around inside it. The second was the unusual entrée to and trust of the politically engaged Buddhists of the Vien Hoa Dao, usually referred to as the "Buddhist Institute,"[6] that I was fortunate enough to obtain – something that US embassy and CIA personnel in Vietnam lacked.

Had it not been for the help of these anti-South Vietnamese government Buddhists and their underground organization I would never have been able to accomplish half as much as I did. Most important, I had access to their top and middle-range leaders and held their trust sufficiently for them to talk to me much more openly than they would to US government officials, most of whom they had good reason to regard as their enemies. These Buddhists put me in touch not only with progressive Catholic leaders, whom the Saigon government regarded as beyond the pale, but also with some lower-level NLF cadre, and even Bao Dai's former minister of justice, Trinh Dinh Thao, to whom they introduced me shortly before he actually joined the National Liberation Front (NLF). (He emerged a little over a year later as one of its top leaders and president of its non-Communist adjunct, Alliance of National, Democratic and Peace Forces.)[7]

My access to the leaders of the politically engaged Buddhists – both those of the Vien Hoa Dao who worked openly, albeit under close government surveillance and frequent arrests, and those tied to them who operated underground, was quite fortuitous. This good fortune I attribute almost entirely to Thich Nhat Hanh, a remarkable Buddhist monk, who, despite his relative youth among the militant Buddhist leadership, was already widely revered in Vietnam as a philosopher and poet, as well as a founder of the Buddhists' Van Hanh University and School of Youth for Social Service. When Nhat Hanh applied for a visa to visit the United States the US Saigon embassy suspected, correctly, that his main purpose was to speak out against American military intervention in his country and denied his request. But because of his standing at home the embassy thought it imprudent to deny him a visa outright and told him he would need an invitation from a reputable American organization before his request could be considered. He had been unable to get such sponsorship when I heard about his plight. Fortunately, I was able to obtain an official invitation for him from Cornell University to lecture on Vietnamese history and Buddhism, and on the strength of that he was able to obtain a month's visa. Once in the United States, he was, of course, able to do more than talk about these subjects, and because of his excellent English and impressive personality he was persuasive in arguing against the war. At the end of the month he had, not unexpectedly, been warned that jail or worse awaited him if he returned to Vietnam, and accordingly secured visas for France and several other European countries, where he lectured, before later being able to obtain another American visa in October 1967.

Nhat Hanh was deeply grateful for my help in getting him the visa and, after having ascertained my views on the war and found that I hoped to visit Vietnam at the end of the year, he offered to help ensure that I would be accepted by the Buddhist Institute leaders there and their underground. To that end he sent messages to his colleagues in Saigon and told me how to get in touch with them once I was there. To make unobtrusive contact I was to go soon after my arrival in Saigon to a particular pharmacy and ask for a special prescription. I would find that I was expected, and someone in the pharmacy would take me in hand and start me out on a round of meetings.

A few days after I arrived in Saigon I went to the pharmacy, and the scene unfolded exactly as Nhat Hanh had told me it would. I soon found myself being whisked through the traffic of Saigon and its smaller sister-city of Cholon, holding on precariously – and often, I acknowledge, a bit fearfully – to the back of the Lambretta expertly piloted by one or the other of two young Vietnamese women who worked in the Buddhist underground: Do Thi

Nga, whom I met at the pharmacy, and Cao Ngoc Phuong, Nhat Hanh's closest associate, a Buddhist nun whom he ultimately married. Both were courageous, dedicated both to social service among the poor and to ending the war. My presence on the back of their motor scooter was a new test of their courage, for especially in the narrower streets and alleys it was hard for most of the urban population to distinguish these two very attractive young women from the numerous high-class prostitutes who cruised the streets to pick up Americans on the look out for them. I was apparently the first American passenger these two women had transported, and they and I could see the disapproving looks and sense the hostility of the clearly anti-American populace. It became especially tense when we were stopped in traffic or had to make our way slowly up some rutted alley. I felt guiltily responsible for the scornful taunts that were often hurled at them. But I could not have had better guides and entrée to the people I wanted to meet, for both women were highly respected in progressive Catholic as well as Buddhist circles.

One of the least understood, and certainly least chronicled, aspects of the American involvement in Vietnam was the part played by politically engaged Vietnamese Buddhists. Although in earlier centuries Buddhists had played important political roles, this was a new phenomenon in recent Vietnamese history. Constituting about 80 per cent of the population of South Vietnam, as against the 10 per cent that was Catholic, the Buddhists had begun to coalesce as a political movement during 1963 in the face of repression by Ngo Dinh Diem's Catholic-dominated government. Their political awakening was then welcomed by the Kennedy administration (and especially its pro-consul in Vietnam, Ambassador Henry Cabot Lodge) once it had decided to embark on a course aimed at ousting Diem. But though their enhanced political activity was momentarily acceptable to the Kennedy administration during that delicate period, once Diem was dead the Buddhists, and the antiwar popular backing they commanded, ran directly counter to American plans for Vietnam. Their views could by no means be fitted into the rigid polarized Cold War framework that leading officials of the new Johnson administration sought to impose upon South Vietnam.

Nor is there any reason to suppose that things would have been any different had Kennedy not been killed, for he was every bit as rigid a Cold Warrior as Johnson, and Johnson – more's the pity – inherited the same set of senior advisers that had already encouraged Kennedy to intervene militarily in Vietnam. For these presidential advisers, American power and their own hubris were so intertwined in their stewardship that both their own self-esteem and the security of their jobs would not brook acknowledgment that the Vietnam policies they had recommended to Kennedy had been mistaken. For them, particularly the most powerful – McGeorge Bundy, Cabot Lodge, Robert McNamara, Walt Rostow, Dean Rusk and General Maxwell Taylor – that meant adamant opposition to any consideration of a negotiated settlement with the NLF or Hanoi involving either the Saigon government or the

United States. Any hint of negotiations, they insisted to President Johnson, would destroy the morale and resolve of the military junta that constituted the Saigon government, bring about its swift collapse, and with that the position of the United States in Vietnam and its prestige in the world beyond. The only basis they would countenance for an end to the fighting was one where, in effect, the NLF would "throw in the towel" and Hanoi agree that Vietnam remain divided into two "nations," with the southern half maintained as a separate political entity controlled by an anticommunist regime.

One can perhaps better appreciate the narrow tenaciousness of Johnson's senior advisers if one realizes that early in his presidency, during the fall of 1964, they not only refused to offer him the possibility of a negotiating scenario, despite his request for all US options in Vietnam, but kept from him both a well-reasoned memorandum from Under Secretary of State George Ball urging a negotiated settlement between Saigon and the NLF, and a proposal from U Thant, secretary general of the United Nations, who had been able to obtain Ho Chi Minh's approval for direct talks between the US and North Vietnam. In the latter case, they kept even William Bundy, assistant secretary of state for the Far East, in the dark until early 1965.

With the succession of short-lived Saigon governments that succeeded Diem all significantly dependent upon Buddhist support for their survival, these senior American officials looked at the politically engaged Buddhists with an increasingly jaundiced eye. This was especially the case for Henry Cabot Lodge after his return to Vietnam as ambassador in 1965 (after a brief absence in the United States where he had run unsuccessfully for the presidency on the Republican ticket). For it became disturbingly evident to the administration that as a price for their support, the Buddhist leadership demanded that the Saigon government keep open the possibility of a negotiated settlement with the NLF and their shared goal of a neutralized South Vietnam. Top priority for the Buddhist leaders was an end to the fighting, a stand that was largely responsible for their wide popular appeal, and they were confident that they shared sufficient common ground with the NLF to make possible a compromise solution.

The unwillingness of the Buddhist leaders to fit into the Johnson administration's polarized Cold War view of Vietnam was not only unacceptable but acutely frustrating for the president's top advisers. The parochialism of these officials was simply too great for them to understand Vietnam's politically engaged Buddhists. Their limitations are reflected in their plan to bring Tibet's Dalai Lama to Vietnam to teach the local Buddhist leaders "lessons in citizenship," and McGeorge Bundy's charge to his staff to find a "Buddhist psychologist" who might bring a better understanding of what was for him the Vietnamese Buddhists' irrational minds. Neither of these efforts was successful. In their impatience and frustration with the Buddhist leaders, Ambassador Lodge and the head of his embassy's political section, Philip Habib, tended to be dismissive, contemptuous and increasingly hostile towards them. This view was not only reflected in their reporting to

Washington, but was regularly conveyed in briefings to visiting American congressmen and newly arrived journalists.

Though during this period the CIA was better informed about South Vietnamese politics than Lodge's embassy, it too had difficulty in understanding the position of the Buddhist leaders. In a memorandum of 25 February 1965 assessing domestic political groups, its bafflement was clear when it sought to characterize the views of Thich Tri Quang, paramount leader of the Vien Hao Dao (Buddhist Institute):

> Thich Tri Quang's views and aims are basically unknown; his possible Viet Cong (NLF) ties have been examined at length but never established ... This group [that led by Thich Tri Quang and his close associate Thich Thien Minh] appears to be moving toward an openly espoused neutralism but still veils its goals in obscure language.

Within the Johnson Administration there was during 1965–6 ongoing alarm at the possibility that the Buddhist leaders could channel the mounting tide of antiwar sentiment in South Vietnam into the creation of a government that would demand a ceasefire, a negotiated settlement with the NLF, and ultimately the departure of all American troops from the country. Such a prospect was, of course, anathema to US policy makers. For however difficult it was to request the American public's backing of an escalating military intervention to maintain a hawkish, anticommunist military junta in power in Saigon, having done so, it would be patently absurd to demand the public's support for a peace-oriented, neutralist government that insisted the United States leave Vietnam. Indeed, it had been concern over this prospect that lay behind American support of the coups that removed Diem's successors – first, General Duong Van Minh and then General Nguyen Khanh.

The clash with the Buddhists came to a head in the spring of 1966 when the Buddhist activists entered into a marriage of convenience with General Nguyen Chanh Thi, the popular and effective commander of the I Corps area, whom the current heads of Saigon's military government, Marshall Nguyen Cao Ky and General Nguyen Van Thieu, were endeavoring to oust. Led by Tri Quang and many other prominent monks, the Buddhists attracted an impressive amount of popular support, not only in the five northern provinces of South Vietnam (the I Corps area) but in Saigon and other parts of the south as well. The precipitating act came when Ky, with American backing, attempted to dismiss General Thi from his command. News of his dismissal sparked widespread protest demonstrations in Hué and Danang that became known as the Buddhist Struggle Movement. The Buddhist leaders were able to assert control over the protest, "seeking to turn it from one simply demanding Thi's reinstatement into one calling for national elections to replace the military junta with a civilian government." They were sufficiently strong to exact two important promises from Premier Ky: first, that free elections would be held for a Constituent Assembly which would in effect be a bridge to representative civilian government; and second, that no political reprisals would be visited upon the Buddhists or on the non-Buddhists who supported them.

It was only, the Buddhist leaders insisted, because they had firm assurances from Ambassador Lodge that the United States would see to it that Ky carried out these promises, that Tri Quang and his lieutenants were willing to call off the Struggle Movement and agree to give up the de facto political autonomy they had secured in the I Corps area and cooperate with Ky's government. On the basis of these promises, Tri Quang and Thich Don Hau – probably the most respected and influential monk in Hué – and other Buddhist leaders called off antigovernment agitation and restored order in the five northern provinces. They held back from insisting that Ky and Thieu step down before elections because they appreciated this was not politically realistic and would risk a major confrontation with American power. Tri Quang went to Hué and appealed to its residents to "stop all activities causing disturbances" and, over considerable opposition, prevailed in his argument that "the present government may remain in power until a constitutional assembly is set up."

Thus the movement, led by Thich Tri Quang and other prominent Buddhist monks, and supported by the South Vietnamese army's locally posted 1st division in Thua Tien Province, and its 25th division in Quang Nam, was very close to toppling South Vietnam's military government and replacing it with an antiwar regime prepared to negotiate with the NLF and Hanoi. Though senior American officials – civilian or military – refused publicly to acknowledge it, this Buddhist-led movement might well have succeeded in displacing the Saigon regime, at least in Vietnam's five northern provinces, had the Americans not intervened heavily and militarily on the side of Ky and Thieu.

The challenge mounted by the movement precipitated within the administration in Washington an "abortive re-look at policy," which ended in their agreeing with Ambassador Lodge and General Westmoreland that US forces should help Ky to crush the Buddhists and their supporters. The administration followed a two-pronged strategy. On the one hand, it gained the temporary support of both Buddhist and non-Buddhist proponents of civilian government by its promise to hold elections within four to six months. But, at the same time, it initiated efforts to divide the Buddhist leadership, took strong measures against further Buddhist and student demonstrations in Saigon, and laid plans for a military expedition against Danang. Having accepted American assurances that their military forces would not intervene, the Buddhists found they had been deceived. US planes ferried Saigon's troops and new US heavy tanks from Saigon first to American-protected bases in Danang, and once the movement had been crushed there, on up to the US-protected airbase near Hué. Thereby Premier Ky was permitted to airlift in his elite troops from Saigon to air bases outside Danang and Hué where he was able to build up overwhelming forces.

General Westmoreland then ordered a reluctant General Lewis Walt to deploy his Danang-based US marines to block pro-Buddhist South Vietnamese troops stationed in southern Quang Tri from crossing over the only bridge leading into Danang and coming to support the Buddhist leaders. Marines also blocked efforts of the major contingent of pro-Buddhist 25th division troops already in Danang from firing on Ky's troops once they had landed in their American-protected enclave abutting the US Danang airbase. Supporters among General Thi's I Corps troops were thus kept out of Danang and out of the air bases at Danang and Hué by a ring of American armed forces. Meanwhile, Ky's troops were soon ordered to move against the Vietnamese troops supporting the Buddhists and against the Buddhists themselves. They smashed the Buddhists' political organization and arrested many of their key leaders.

These American actions, together with Ambassador Henry Cabot Lodge's rank duplicity in promising that there would be no retribution against supporters of the Struggle Movement, and that the national elections it had called for would be held if Tri Quang called off the revolt, outraged and deeply antagonized the local population throughout the entire I Corps area.[8]

Having succeeded in Danang and Hué, Ky and the junta felt strong enough to clamp down on what remained of Buddhist power in Saigon. One of the top three Buddhist leaders, Thich Thien Minh was seriously wounded in a grenade attack and a few days later government troops blockaded the compound of the Buddhist Institute (Vien Hoa Dao), ultimately storming the building and ousting its occupants.

Many Buddhists found it difficult to understand why US behavior in 1966 contrasted so sharply with the support they had received from the Americans three years earlier against Diem. But certainly their two top leaders, Thich Thien Minh and Thich Tri Quang, understood clearly that the principal reason for US support against the Saigon government in 1963 was that President Diem and his government had been insufficiently cooperative and effective as instruments for securing American objectives. In contrast, the year 1966 saw a Saigon government in power that was equally opposed to Buddhist aims, but one that was judged to be fully supportive of US objectives and sufficiently amenable to American direction. For Washington policy makers, these qualities substantially outweighed whatever criticism the American public might register of US cooperation with Ky's government to crush the politically active Buddhists. By 1966 American officials had come to regard the Buddhist-led Struggle Movement as committed to negotiating a compromise political settlement with the NLF and ending America's military and political roles in Vietnam. By then the Struggle Movement marshaled so much popular backing that unless US military power supported Ky and Thieu against it the Buddhists' immediate political demands would have had to be met.

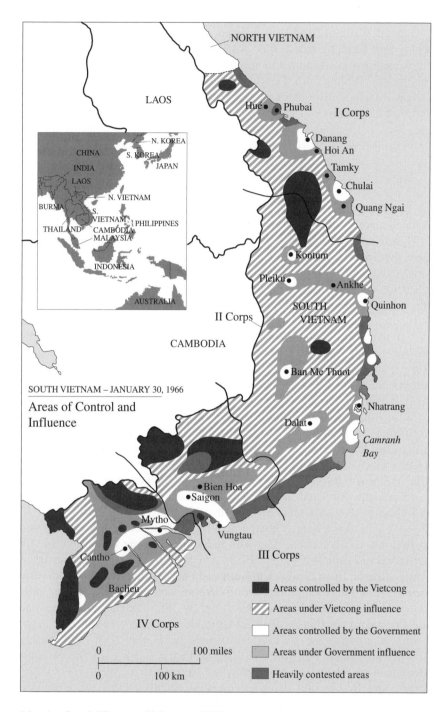

Map 4   South Vietnam, 30 January 1966

Source: George Kahin, *Intervention*, p. 402

10 Casualties and pacification, 1966/7

On 17 December 1966 I flew to Hong Kong where I stayed two nights and had good talks with several journalists, including my old friend Bernard Kalb, who was at the time a CBS television correspondent whose mandate covered Vietnam. Upon my arrival at Saigon's Tonsonhut airport on the morning of 19 December, I was met by John Negroponte, a bright, well-informed, but cautious and reserved embassy political officer whom Bill Bundy had asked to meet me, reserve a hotel room and arrange transportation for me inside the country.[1] With his assistance I was able to clear the various South Vietnamese bureaucratic impediments at the airport and proceed into the city. He introduced me to a couple of other US government people, clearly in intelligence. Negroponte had a good command of the Vietnamese language and was kind enough to accompany me and translate a few hours of the proceedings of a couple of meetings of the largely docile Constituent Assembly – most of whose members had been thoroughly intimidated by the ruling junta led by the head of the airforce, Nguyen Cao Ky (as prime minister) and General Nguyen Van Thieu (as president). But he left me alone and did not interfere with my own agenda, as I developed it.

I made my own contacts with American and other journalists, getting off to a good start with my old friend Bernard Fall over dinner on 23 December,[2] and the next evening with Ward Just, the able *Washington Post* correspondent. I was armed with an apparently flattering letter from the still influential General Nguyen Chanh Thi (the former pro-Buddhist commander of I Corps who had been fired by Ky and, under considerable pressure from General William Westmoreland, had gone into enforced exile in the United States).[3] I had gotten to know Thi in Washington, where he was ensconced at US government expense in a large apartment across Connecticut Ave from the Washington Hilton. His letter of introduction enabled me to make contact with Colonel Pham Van Lieu, who had been Thi's top political adviser and head of the national police until ousted half a year before by Ky and Thieu. Colonel Pham Van Lieu still had wide contacts in the army and enthusiastically put me in touch with a half dozen other dissident army officers. For the most part, he accomplished this through a series of lavish lunches or dinners, marred only by an apparently irresistible impulse to remind his guests that it was at such a dinner that agents of Ky had tried to poison him.

But, of course, it was also necessary for me to get some measure of the top government leadership, and when I'd last been in Washington I was advised by one of Bill Bundy's staff to be sure to talk to the top political adviser, General Pham Xuan Chieu, who was referred to as "the political brains" behind Ky and Thieu. I asked Negroponte if he could arrange an appointment for me with this general, whose formal position was as secretary-general of the Military Directorate, the select group of officers that worked with and advised Ky and Thieu. He was delighted to do so, observing that Chieu was highly intelligent, politically sophisticated and would be able to provide a good insight into the thinking of Ky and Thieu. With no apparent difficulty he promptly made arrangements for an interview on the morning of 1 January 1967. I had assumed we would have about an hour together, but Chieu warmed to his role and we were together a full two hours.

I was surprised at General Chieu's candor and stunned by what he had to say – especially in view of how highly American officials had touted his "political sophistication." His message was so glaringly deviant from what the Johnson administration had been telling Congress and the American public that there could have hardly been a more dramatic illustration of how far it was misleading them. After discussing the lack of consensus within society and the need for the military's continuing to play a strong governmental role, he went on to say:

> To defeat the Communists we must win against them both politically and militarily. First militarily.
>
> But we are very weak politically and without the strong political support of the population that the NLF have. Thus now even if we defeat them militarily, they can come to power because of their greater political strength.
>
> After defeating them militarily, we will have to be able to destroy their political organization and political infrastructure among the people.
>
> Thus we now only have – with the support of our Allies (the US, Korea, etc.) – a strong military instrument, but we are without a political instrument that can compete with the Communists in the South. Such a political instrument we must now begin to create, a process that will take a generation or at least ten years. The first step is to build a consensus among ourselves ... We must maintain a military struggle while we build up our political strength. When the military struggle ends, we must have reached a stage of political superiority. It is unrealistic to speak of a ceasefire until after we have built up our political strength to a point where we can compete with the Communists successfully – a decade from now at least. Thus, Johnson's statement at Manila

that US troops would begin withdrawal within six months of a settlement makes no sense. We must have military victory plus political superiority first.

Moving on to discuss military prospects, General Chieu said that the Ky–Thieu government was convinced that military victory would ultimately require carrying the ground war into North Vietnam, and acknowledged that this might require a million American troops and would probably bring China into the war. If larger US and Korean forces were insufficient to defeat the Vietcong (NLF) and Hanoi, then contingents of Chiang Kai-shek's forces and other anticommunist Asian troops, including the Japanese, should be used. He continued by asserting that it was a charade to talk of a Sino–Soviet split; the Communist countries were still a bloc, and it might be necessary to "move on to World War III in order to remove the Communist menace in Vietnam." In comparison to the macabre exegesis of this "wise man" of the Ky/Thieu government, the hawkish harangues of Colonel Pham Van Lieu and his dissident friends seemed refreshingly rational.

Shortly before I left the States a debate had developed in the media as to whether US planes were causing significant civilian casualties in Vietnam by their aerial delivery of napalm – ignited jellied gasoline that burned deep into a person's flesh, often causing death and in most cases at least severe maiming. First authorized for use in Vietnam by President Kennedy, by 1965 it constituted between 8 and 9 per cent of yearly bombing tonnage there, with a total of 338,000 tons dropped in the course of the war. The official position of the American military was that extreme care was used in employing napalm and that there were very few civilian casualties. There was, however, enough skepticism of this claim by American correspondents in Vietnam that to fend it off the administration enlisted the help of an eminent medical specialist, Dr Howard Rusk, sending him to Vietnam to report on the situation. After visiting several hospitals he reported that there were, as the administration insisted, very few cases of civilians being exposed to napalm and that most of those so designated were simply the victims of burns from exploding kerosene stoves, not US napalm.

I asked my two young Buddhist escorts about this question, for I had found that they had done volunteer work in Saigon's hospitals and had good connections there. They knew a good deal about Dr Rusk's visit and told me that, though they were confident he was an honest man, he had been badly misled. To begin with, they said, most napalm casualties occurred in rural areas distant from hospitals, and many victims were not lucky enough to make it to a hospital before they died. In the Saigon–Cholon metropolitan area victims who were able to get to the hospitals were dispersed so that the normal visitor would be unable to spot any concentration of them. And Dr Rusk had been calculatedly misled – in effect "led down the garden path."

During his visits, they said, patients had been moved around within the hospital wards to ensure he would at most encounter no more than a very few of the napalm cases that were actually there. They said that if I inquired, I would be given the official line that there were no napalm casualties, and that if I persevered and was given permission to examine the wards of the local civilian hospitals I could expect the same sleight-of-hand that Rusk had encountered. It was the day before Christmas and Do Thi Nga, apparently not wishing to trespass on my religious sentiments, hesitatingly asked if by any chance I might be free on Christmas morning. When I assured her that I would be just as free as any other day, she seemed much relieved, and said she thought she could arrange for private visits to the central hospital and the Nhidong children's hospital. She explained that the administrators of the hospitals were Catholics and could be expected to be absent on Christmas day, leaving their running to Buddhist subordinates and interns, several of whom she knew.

And so on Christmas morning of 1966, Do Thi Nga picked me up and escorted me to these two hospitals, first the large central hospital. There I was taken in hand by a couple of bright young Buddhist interns who substantiated what she and Phoung had told me about dispersion of napalm patients, both among and within hospitals, and the chicanery that had confronted Dr Rusk. They thought him incredibly gullible and were indignant at his proposition that most alleged napalm cases were actually the result of exploding kerosene stoves, explaining to me in more detail than I could absorb the clearly evident differences in their effects. And they could not contain their outrage at American protestations that napalm only hit military targets, with little harm to civilians. Then they led me back into a few wards where thirty-five serious napalm cases, about half of them children, were being treated. Most poignant of all, and still deeply etched in my memory, was a poor little boy whose head and face had been hit by napalm and melted into one large, tear-drop shaped blob of ruddy flesh with a single cyclopean eye staring out. Severely shaken by this, I afterwards went on to the children's hospital and saw more child victims of napalm. Altogether Christmas was a macabre experience, and in fact for over a year afterwards I sometimes had nightmares about what I had seen in these wards.

A Visit to The First Corps Area: January 1967

Hué

On 4 January 1967 I flew up to Hué, the old imperial city and now capital of Thua Tien, one of the five provinces in the I Corps area. Some six months before, together with Quang Nam, the province to its south, it had been the main center of the Buddhist Struggle Movement against the US-supported regime headed by the two military officers, Nguyen Cao Ky and

Nguyen Van Thieu, respectively prime minister and president of the Saigon government.

I readily discovered that American actions in support of Ky and Thieu and the Lodge–Westmoreland alliance in this affair had not only antagonized much of the local population in I Corps area, but had also angered the American consul and his staff in Hué as well as numerous other American civilian and military officials I met there. They told me that General Walt, as commander of the 40,000 marines in I Corps area, had prided himself on having developed relatively good relations with the Buddhists and the local South Vietnamese military. And thus he had keenly resented having to follow the orders of General Westmoreland and Lodge obliging him to intervene and block efforts of the local military in support of the Buddhists' Struggle Movement.

As for the Hué area itself, these Americans had found particularly despicable the actions of US military advisers attached to the pro-Buddhist 1st division who, they assumed, acted on Westmoreland's orders. These US military advisers, they said, had lured large numbers of the division's troops away to Quang Tri province to the north, so that when Ky's forces were airlifted in to the American-protected haven at the US Phu Bai airbase close to Hué, the city could not be effectively defended. Tri Quang was taken prisoner and flown to Saigon, and many of the other monks were arrested, together with numerous student leaders from the University of Hué. Most of them were still in jail nine years later when the Saigon regime fell. And many of the university and high school students who evaded arrest had fled to the mountains to join the NLF.

Understandably when I arrived half a year after these events, I found the mood of much of the local population downcast and sullen, and the students whom I met who still remained at the university were bitterly anti-American and proud of having torched the US consulate and USIS office in what they referred to as an "act of retribution." I was struck by the fact that though the US consular staff was not happy about the destruction of their offices, they nevertheless had respect and some sympathy for the students. They were also incensed at the credence given by some Americans to a clandestine local radio, acting for Ky's Saigon government, that purported to be Buddhist and which undertook to discredit the Buddhists' Struggle Movement by making wild and excessive statements.

As a consequence of the drastic suppression of the Buddhist Struggle Movement Ky's government had become suspicious of most of the administrative apparatus in these two I Corps provinces to the point of paranoia because of their support – active or passive – of the movement, and had fired or shifted much of its personnel. American civilian officials and marine officers with whom I spoke were unanimous in their opinion that this rooting out of so much of the local non-Communist administration, and the purging of the two army divisions that had supported the Struggle Movement, were the major causes of the near collapse of what they referred to as the "pacification program" in the two provinces of Thua Thien and Quang Nam. And this had resulted in a much greater extension of the areas administered by the NLF (Vietcong).

Against this background, it was not surprising that I found the population of Hué the most depressed of any city or town I visited in Vietnam, and certainly with the most outspoken bitterness against the United States. The American vice-consul told me that in the six-month period since the Buddhists had been smashed, the Vietcong (NLF) had moved into many areas of the city that had previously been under Saigon's control and that the city's central police station had been mortared three times from distances of less than a mile. A doctor from the hospital informed me that only a week earlier he had witnessed an NLF attack on the South Vietnamese army barracks just beyond the edge of the city. On the road between Hué and the US marine base eleven miles away, at night and even during the day vehicles traveled in twos for safety. It was unsafe even during the day to visit the royal tombs situated less than two miles to the south of Hué, and even one of the city's major suburbs was unsafe at night for supporters of the Saigon government because of the degree of the NLF's (Vietcong) penetration. Indeed, a few of the students whom I'd met at the university took me into that suburb after dark to meet with colleagues who, after the suppression of the Struggle Movement, had joined the NLF.

As one of my concerns was civilian casualties, while in Hué I visited the city hospital to get a rough idea of the major causes for their injuries. Only a partial picture could be derived by visiting hospitals, I had been advised, since in much of Vietnam, as here, a large number of civilian casualties from the fighting who survived were unable to reach any of the country's few, and widely dispersed, civilian hospitals. Here in talking with the hospital staff, and random sampling of the records attached to the bottom of each patient's bed, I was able to test the accuracy of a report compiled by the staff at the end of November which had indicated that nearly 90 per cent of the war casualties were caused by American and South Vietnamese aerial bombardment or artillery – by far the highest rate tabulated by any of the hospitals I visited in Vietnam.

Danang and Hoi An

Then on 6 January 1967, I flew to Danang, capital of Quang Nam, the province directly to the south of Thua Tien. There I first spent several hours in its surgical hospital, one serving those Vietnamese wounded civilians throughout the I Corps area fortunate enough to be transported to it. I was told that two years before the hospital had approximately 300 patients and now, even though only the most serious casualties were admitted, the number had grown to about 700. Of these, 95 per cent were war casualties, with about fifteen to twenty admissions per day. The staff estimated that most of the casualties were victims of small arms and mortar fire. They didn't seem keen to discuss the relation of American bombing to the casualties. In this hospital I was not able to inspect patients' records (usually found attached to the bottoms of beds) and had the impression that the staff were discouraged from discussing the impact of the bombing on civilians. But I could not conclude it had been insignificant, given what I had been told by hospital staff in Hué and the fact that in Quang Nam province, apart from the refugees who had moved to its capital of Danang, the Saigon government's refugee office had calculated as of 30 November 1966, that the total number of refugees from the war was 88,511. The staff did, however, respond to my question about civilians who were victims of US air-delivered napalm attacks. "About a dozen or so" cases had been admitted during the previous two months, much less, they said, than the earlier rate.

Later that day I had one of those uniquely rewarding experiences wherein I was convinced I'd accomplished something useful. Sunday was the next day, and the marine colonel with whom I was talking was at his wit's end as to what to do with those marines stationed in Danang who were off duty on that day. He said he had just two options for them: a swim at nearby China Beach or a visit to the US television station in Danang. The first was always popular, but the beach couldn't accommodate everyone who wanted to swim, and a single visit to the television station was enough for most of these marines, some of whom found it boring to begin with. I told him I thought there might be a third option, assuming it was still extant, namely the Cham Museum, for which I knew Danang had long been famous (Figures 10.1, 10.2). He had not heard of it or the Chams, so I explained that, several decades earlier, the French had established in Danang (then called Tourane) an excellent museum housing some of the best examples of Cham sculpture. His interest was immediately aroused when I explained that the Kingdom of Champa some seven to twelve centuries ago had one of its main centers in the Danang area, that the Chams had fought, often successfully, against both the Vietnamese and the Cambodians, and that only in the seventeenth century had the Vietnamese in their push to the south overrun the last districts of the then much-shrunken Cham kingdom.

We searched for and soon discovered the museum. Its beleaguered curator we found trembling with rage at the fact that a unit of the South Vietnamese army stationed close by was using part of one wing of the museum as a urinal, and he was helpless to stop them. (Here one must note that most Vietnamese look down on Cham culture as having been distinctly inferior to their own.) The colonel and I were initially incredulous. We accompanied the curator through the main rooms of the museum, both of us admiring the excellent collection, which, despite the pilfering of a few of the smaller stone images, was still in good shape. (The statuary reminded me of figures from about the same period in central Java.) The colonel whistled in admiration as we walked though several rooms of exhibits until we arrived at the infamous lavatory. We immediately shared the curator's indignation, and the

Figure 10.1   Cham Museum in Danang, 1994

Figure 10.2   Cham Museum in Danang, 1994

colonel swore that the marines would see to it that the South Vietnamese troops were kept from so desecrating the museum again.

He warmly thanked me for having alerted him to something far superior to the TV station for off-duty Danang-based marines to visit on Sundays. And I volunteered to ask my Cornell colleague and eminent Southeast Asian historian, Oliver Wolters, for his help in producing a one-page description of the Chams' history and culture to be reproduced and given to the marines who visited the museum.

The next day I had an experience which provided a particularly enlightening insight into the situation facing most American troops in Vietnam, including the 60,000 US marines in the I Corps area. Among the five provinces this embraced was Quang Nam, together with its recently autonomous city of Danang (South Vietnam's second largest, with a population, recently more than doubled by refugees, of about 500,000). According to a group of marine military advisers with whom I then spoke, the total population of Quang Nam province (excluding its capital of Danang) as of 31 December 1966 stood at 568,288, of whom approximately 150,000 were refugees.

The breakdown of population control of the province (minus the capital) provided me by these officers was sobering when contrasted to the generally upbeat press briefings then being provided by the US military spokesmen in Saigon. Of this total just 19,967 were living in eighteen hamlets regarded as "secure"; 171,241 lived in 246 hamlets regarded as controlled by the NLF (Vietcong); and 377,080 lived in 295 "contested" hamlets, where in just over half most hamlet officials refused to reside at night (several hamlets constituted a village).

I mentioned to these marine officers that I soon hoped to visit the port of Hoi An, the province's second largest town, which lay some twenty miles to the south. (Centuries before, bearing the name of Faifo, it had won fame as the funnel for Japanese trade into Vietnam.) Knowing that I was interested in the situation in refugee camps, they told me I would find a large one, holding about 25,000 people, on the outskirts of Hoi An. They cautioned me that, although an American artillery unit was just outside the town, the marine TAOR (Tactical Area of Responsibility) extended only about two-thirds of the way to it, and that the last eight miles of the road were unsafe after dusk. The area the marines patrolled, of course, went much farther, and extended all the way to Hoi An and beyond.

The next morning, on very short notice, I was invited to attend what the marines called a "County Fair." Since Al Francis, the knowledgeable political adviser to the III Marines Amphibious Force headquarters in Danang, knew that I'd wanted to go to Hoi An anyway, he informed me that it would be possible to combine the trip with a brief excursion a short distance off the road south to include a "Fair" that had gotten under way earlier that morning. These were fairly standard marine sweeps into areas embracing a few villages that were believed to harbor some Vietcong (NLF) soldiers.

These operations were conducted suddenly, with all possible secrecy, and centered on casting a broad net over the area, which was then drawn in to assemble the local population under guard. Interrogations were then conducted to distinguish those suspected of being Vietcong, and then those so identified were carted away to jail or concentration camp. I was glad to go along, and we departed almost immediately.

This particular County Fair was being conducted well within the marines' TAOR, a little over seven miles south of Danang near the junction of the Hoi An road with a much smaller one leading off to a coal mine to the west. As we approached a scene of considerable activity, we were waved through by marines at the periphery and directed to the command post on a very small hillock not far from the highway. There I met Lt Colonel Donabidien, commander of the battalion that was carrying out this exercise. He was a robust, heavy-set, cigar-chewing man who appeared to have the respect and warm feelings of his troops.

It was obvious that the colonel didn't think much of County Fairs and was carrying this one out as matter of routine on orders from above. He said that in the actual fighting over a three-month period his battalion had suffered almost 150 casualties (six of them the day before) and that these losses were about average for marine battalions in the I Corps area. A higher casualty rate was being encountered in the guerrilla-type warfare that was now displacing the earlier large-scale engagements. A great many men were now being lost to sniper fire.

When I asked Donabidien what his major problem was, he seemed to jump at the chance to explain, as if the problem had been bottled up and had long needed release.

> We have to operate blind; that's the worst problem. There's not a single marine in my battalion who can speak or understand Vietnamese, and that's the case with nearly all of our units. They've assigned my battalion a Vietnamese city slicker from Saigon as interpreter; he's got his own little ax to grind, and I absolutely don't trust him.

The colonel then invited me to walk over to where an interrogation was going on about a quarter of a mile away, where, he said, I'd get a clearer idea of the problem he faced. There I found huddled together a group of well-guarded Vietnamese men from the area, encircled, who, since they were most of the remaining few young men in the villages, were suspected of being Vietcong. They were awaiting their turn to be interviewed by a young corporal from South Carolina accompanied by the "city slicker" from Saigon.

I immediately understood Donabidien's concern. The questions being asked by the corporal in English, and then presumably being translated accurately by the Saigonese interpreter, were very simple, and it seemed unlikely that they could uncover any significant information. But then it was impossible to know how both questions and answers were being relayed through the smartly dressed interpreter. "Are you Vietcong? Do you know any Vietcong? Do they come to your village at night? Have you ever seen any Vietcong?" That was the level and almost the extent of the questions. Of course, the young kid from South Carolina couldn't be expected to do much better, and even if he had, with the process filtered through the "city slicker," whatever that man's own private agenda, one could hardly rely on any information elicited as being reliable.

In the midst of these interrogations I suddenly heard a great commotion about 100 yards away where the rest of the village populations had been assembled. When I'd first seen them they had looked both puzzled and bored while supposedly being entertained by some young woman singing to them over Saigon Radio. But that had now changed, and as I walked over to see what was happening I found at the edge of the crowd about a dozen people clasping bottles of blue liquid, from which it turned out they had just drunk, and were violently retching. The bottles turned out to be a then popular American mouthwash known as Micrin. They hadn't been properly briefed as to what the pretty blue liquid was and assumed it was to be drunk, not just swished around in their mouths to overcome bad breath. As I approached the group a very flustered and rather stout American in civilian dress ran up to me and sputtered: "Damn, they were supposed to send me soap and toothpaste, and all I got was this damned Micrin." Embarrassedly and self-mockingly, he volunteered, "I'm the 'hearts and minds' man." I don't know whether he was from AID or CIA, but he was certainly unhappy. And so were the astonished Vietnamese peasants, now dubiously clutching their Micrin bottles and unsure what they were supposed to do with them. Needless to say, old Mr Hearts and Minds didn't know enough, if any, of the Vietnamese language to enlighten them. All he could do was to take a swig and then spit it out, which to them clearly seemed a useless procedure.

After a couple of hours talking to a number of GIs and officers, I took leave of Colonel Donabidien and proceeded uneventfully with Al Francis on to Hoi An. That ancient town, nestled on the northern bank of a good-sized river, with its rows of handsome centuries-old Japanese and Chinese merchant houses, seemed peaceful except for the intermittent blasts of marine artillery from a battery at the edge of the town. When I asked what they were shooting at I was told that this was simply an ongoing Harassment and Interdiction (H and I) fire directed across into areas deep on the other side of the river to ensure that the Vietcong would be unable to concentrate forces there for a possible attack on Hoi An. With the artillery barrages, complemented by periodic air strikes, this area, referred to more straightforwardly by some of the officers as a "free-firing zone," had been transformed into a sort of southern buffer which it was expected would protect Hoi An against the Vietcong. I asked what had happened to the people living in the area being bombarded and was told that more than half from the villages there had left to seek the shelter of a refugee camp just outside Hoi An run by the South Vietnamese army. There I found more than 25,000 sullen refugees crowded into tents or a few shabby, dilapidated buildings that were crammed into a muddy, barbed-wire-enclosed piece of land – it could more accurately be called a concentration camp than a camp for refugees. Indeed, those who were permitted to go out of the camp required a special pass. Having seen the grim conditions under which these peasants had to live I could appreciate how pleased they must have been when Vietcong forces overran much of the town and freed those in the camp later that year on 15 July and again on 27 August.[4]

Quang Ngai

Late that afternoon I returned to Danang, and early the next morning, 8 January, flew the short distance south to the next province, Quang Ngai, and its capital of the same name. There I met with Dr Bui Hoang, the province chief, and several American military and civilian officials. I was informed that out of Quang Ngai's presently estimated population of around 700,000 about 32 per cent lived in "secured" towns or hamlets under control of the South Vietnamese government (GVN), and the remainder were either under Vietcong control or were "contested." In the province there were about 80,000 refugees from the fighting, of whom 16,724 were now in refugee camps.

When I sought more focused information on the province's important district of Son Tinh, I was told that out of its population of 108,200 a total of 37,514 lived in secure areas (controlled by the GVN) and 43,600 were estimated to live in Vietcong-controlled areas. There were eleven hamlets with a population of 13,525 classified as "undergoing security" (which meant that the hamlet chief and his staff were willing to sleep there overnight), and another 11,560 living in twelve hamlets designated as "undergoing clearing" by ARVN (Army of South Vietnam) or "Free World" forces, mostly Korean. Out of the district's total population, 26,587 were classified as refugees, of whom about 8,700 were in refugee camps.

In a briefing from US military officers, I was told that 31 per cent of the population of the province was under control of the Saigon government, 38 per cent was controlled by the Vietcong and the remainder was contested. But in terms of area, about 90 per cent was Vietcong controlled. There was a reinforced marine regiment based on Chulai in the province to the north, some of which was deployed in northern Quang Ngai and there was one brigade of Korean marines and one regiment of ARVN operating in Quang Ngai as well as 9,400 South Vietnamese government militia ("Regional" and "Popular" forces). There were two regiments of Vietcong operating regularly in the province and two others coming in from time to time from outside to augment them.

It would take, these US briefers said, at the very least an additional regiment of US or Korean troops to provide sufficient security for a successful pacification effort. The South Vietnamese government (ARVN) troops in the province were not effective and had "a long way to go" to become so. They had major problems of leadership, were underfed, and needed their US battalion advisers for longer-term assignments than the six months that was standard. And as for the twelve-month tours of duty of US army forces, and thirteen months for US marines, this was not adequate. The norm should be for eighteen months, they said, because it took "at least three months to get adjusted and six months to get in stride."

What stands out most vividly from my visit to Quang Ngai are the talks I had with Jim May, a civilian from the Agency for International Development (AID) who was senior adviser for the US pacification program for this province. Jonathan Schell, who met him some eight months later, had a remarkably similar experience that he describes in his excellent book, *The Military Half*. I spent the evening and overnight in May's large, heavily sandbagged house – ample time for him to explain his views. Schell later found him attired as I did. Atop a none too spare six-foot frame rested a Mexican sombrero; he had a large black mustache and wore cowboy boots. Rarely have I encountered a man more seriously bent on looking "macho."

On one point May was adamant: the refugees in the Quang Ngai camps, like those in the one I had seen outside of Hoi An, were the lucky ones. They had food and shelter, but there were larger numbers who couldn't be accommodated in the camps and had to fend for themselves after they left their villages to seek safety from further bombing and artillery shells by camping along the main highway or the outskirts of the provincial capital. And then, sounding like a sort of unpolished precursor of Samuel Huntington, he opined that for those in the camps enjoying leak-proof corrugated sheet steel roofs and a reliable supply of food and safe drinking water, it was a "modernizing experience." When I asked him why so many refugees had been "generated" (that being the official jargon), he acknowledged that it was primarily the consequence of US and South Korean artillery and American bombing. He then became aggressively defensive in justifying this. Didn't I realize that the villagers themselves bore responsibility if they didn't oust any Vietcong who visited or lived in the village? In a war, he gravely pronounced, civilians had that responsibility.

When I ventured to suggest that many, if not most, of these Vietcong had grown up in the village and regarded it as their home, he was impatiently dismissive and reiterated that, if the rest of the village didn't want to be regarded as Vietcong and treated as such, they had the obligation of ousting anyone who was Vietcong or supported them. If any village provided food or any other supplies to the Vietcong "we have the right to regard them as pro-Vietcong and the whole village must take the consequences." And anyway, he said, the bombing by American aircraft or shelling by artillery was done as humanely as possible, since in almost every case the village was warned by leaflet or otherwise that the inhabitants should leave because in a stipulated period it was going to be targeted. By displacing and controlling these village populations the Vietcong could be deprived of food and labor. Sensing my disapproval of the way the US was "generating" refugees, May chuckled, "If you don't approve of the way we get people to leave villages, maybe you'd prefer the way the Korean regiment in Quang Ngai does it. The way they warn villagers against contact with the Vietcong is to skin one and tack the skin up on some tree near the village." Whether or not his story was apocryphal, there is no doubt that Korean troops operating in Vietnam had already acquired a reputation for great cruelty.

I later found it surprising how little notice the American press gave to the presence of Korean troops fighting on the US side in Vietnam or the astronomical remuneration Korea was provided for making them available. At 50,000 they were by far the most numerous provided by any US ally in Vietnam, indeed, more than twice as many soldiers as all the others fighting on the American side and much more heavily subsidized than their Thai and Philippine counterparts. (Of all foreign troops fighting on the American side only the Australian–New Zealand battalion was not supported by the American taxpayer.) The presence of these foreign auxiliaries in what the Johnson administration referred to as its "Many Flags" presence in Vietnam was useful in its public relations with the American public in building the notion that it had significant support in Vietnam from "our Free World allies," but it was very expensive.

Not only did the Philippine, Thai and especially the Korean governments reap heavy rewards, but in addition their soldiers were paid enormous extra allowances, the Korean private being paid a bonus from the US treasury equal to twenty times his regular pay.[5]

Ward Just, the able correspondent of the *Washington Post* had visited Quang Ngai some two weeks before and, basing his account on US army sources, had written in its 24 December 1966 issue that civilian casualties were running at about 1,000 per month and exceeded the number of US and Vietcong casualties combined. With that report as a point of reference, I spent my last hours in Quang Ngai visiting the provincial hospital. The staff, both American and Vietnamese, were very helpful, but the American director clearly resented my visit (perhaps because of my mention of Just's story). From the staff I learned that 75 per cent of those admitted came from within a radius of just 15 miles, that 85 per cent of the cases were war casualties and that 30 per cent of the total were children under the age of thirteen. The staff had ascertained that approximately 70 per cent of the war casualties admitted were "Free World" inflicted and that about 30 per cent were Vietcong inflicted, almost all of them from land mines.

Just before I started out on my little survey of the hospital the director had asked me if I would like to see all the wards, and I had naturally said that I would. He told me I was free to walk through them unattended, which I did. When I'd completed my rounds he asked me if I'd noticed anything of interest, and I mentioned that my curiosity had been aroused by one ward where all the patients seemed to be heavily perspiring. "Ah, yes," he said with unconcealed satisfaction, "that was the bubonic plague ward." I didn't think that the inoculation I'd had against the plague nineteen years before in Indonesia could possibly still be effective, and I showed my concern. "Don't worry," he said, "I'll tell you what the symptoms are, so you'll know whether you'll need medical attention." The key symptom, he explained, was a painful swelling under each arm. I felt that he'd deliberately set me up, and I departed without thanking him for this helpful information. But I did remember it.

About a week after returning to Saigon I had an opportunity briefly to examine another area of military activity – in Long An, the second province immediately south of Saigon, located on the northern fringe of the Mekong Delta. I was fortunate in having two especially knowledgeable guides – Colonels Sam Wilson and John Paul Vann. Both were recognized as experienced and effective military officers who were sensitive to the political context of military operations.

Early on the morning of 15 January 1967 I drove south to Tan An, capital of Long An province about twenty miles from Saigon, with David Brown, a modest Vietnamese language officer from the US embassy. There we met Colonel Wilson and were later joined by Colonel Vann. Wilson was to leave in five months to direct a special army school at Fort Bragg concerned with insurgency and pacification. In the meantime he had been put in charge of an operation, now in its second month, designed to ascertain whether it would be feasible – politically as well as militarily – for US troops to operate in the Mekong Delta area, with its swampy terrain and high concentration of rural population. Long An Province, with its capital of Tan An two feet above sea level and its highest point only twenty feet above sea level, had been chosen as the trial area. Wilson was in charge of both military and political aspects of the operation. He told me that he had just concluded, on the basis of his experience in the province, that it was feasible to introduce US troops in the delta, but that military success did not ensure political success. This was from the outset difficult, he explained, because it had to be recognized that the Saigon government lacked popular support and the ARVN (Army of South Vietnam) was of such uneven quality, being especially poor in Long An. But apart from that there was a sort of operational equation that meant, especially in heavily populated areas such as this province, that if military success was accompanied by too large a number of civilian casualties the operation could easily backfire as far as any hope of political success was concerned. To have an operation successful in a political sense meant reducing military effectiveness because of the necessity of avoiding civilian casualties. For instance, Wilson explained that, instead of securing a helicopter landing area in the normal way, by "neutralizing" the area with an artillery barrage, which inevitably killed civilians, in Long An American helicopters had been required to land without benefit of artillery preparation of the terrain, and this had been more costly in terms of US lives.

I noticed that while we were talking, just across the bridge north of Tan An 155 howitzers had opened up firing rounds of support for ARVN troops seeking to advance towards a district capital four to five miles to the north-west that had been attacked by a full NLF (Vietcong) battalion the night before. As this was an ARVN operation clearly no such calculus regarding civilian casualties attended its operation. The ARVN regiment and auxiliary units from the division stationed in the province were hopeless, Wilson said. That ARVN division, standing at 70 per cent of authorized strength, had a desertion rate that averaged 1,000 men per month and was one of the two worst in the entire South Vietnamese army. It had been strengthened with the addition of the two US battalions, under Wilson's command, but he felt it would take another three US battalions to develop real momentum in the current pacification effort.

Despite the fact that this rich province of some 400,000 people was so close to Saigon, of its approximately 600 villages only 90 were effectively controlled by the government ("effectively controlled," he said, meant that village officials were willing to remain there at night). The NLF (Vietcong) regularly operated two full battalions plus two heavy companies within the province – about 3,500 armed men, as against slightly more than 7,000 ARVN plus the two US battalions.

According to Wilson and Vann, the normal pattern for the US pacification effort in Long An, as elsewhere, was for US forces to go after NLF concentrations and break them up into units sufficiently small so that ARVN forces could deal with them successfully. In the area to be pacified the ARVN troops would then form a protective encircling shield against the Vietcong; and inside it the RF (regional provincial forces – a sort of militia) and lesser-trained PF (local popular forces) would protect the particular village. Since the RF and especially the PF were locally recruited they would be close to the local population and be expected to have a real interest – because of family and community ties – in protecting it.

The weakest link in this arrangement, however, was the ARVN itself which was simply not suited to the task of developing rapport with the local population. Unfortunately the usual relationship was one of harsh, heavy-handed treatment, with no empathy for the villagers. "Stealing the peasants' chickens and pigs is the norm and violation of their women frequent." The usual picture, Wilson said, was one of ARVN soldiers driving a heavy army truck down a village street at 45 miles an hour in a huge cloud of dust – unmindful of the danger to pedestrians and animals, thus antagonizing the peasantry. The ARVN was "not suited to the job of pacification, but it wasn't suited for combat either. It is poorly led and avoids combat as much as possible, bypassing the enemy, rather than confronting it. And most of its officers are corrupt." Wilson was confident of the ability of US forces to defeat all major Vietcong concentrations: "The main military problem we can handle, but the political side is a different matter – to defeat the Vietcong politically."

After John Paul Vann joined us we flew in his helicopter some fifteen to twenty miles to a beleaguered district capital to the east and slightly north of Tan An to inspect an immediately adjacent village that was now in the final stages of a two-month pacification effort. An area of about 2 sq km, incorporating this village and the district capital, was held by an ARVN battalion and a special forty-six-man pacification team made up of men recruited exclusively from Tan An and nearby. The area could only be reached safely by helicopter and just over a kilometer from the center of the town the Vietcong controlled the area at night.

Our helicopter put down at the town's central square and we walked over to the abutting adjacent village that had been the object of the pacification program. Despite its proximity to the garrison town it had been held by the Vietcong only two months earlier before the pacification program here had begun. Accompanied by the local pacification chief from the town, and with David Brown as interpreter, we began going from house to house asking questions of some of the peasants living there concerning the security situation.

According to the pacification chief, two Vietcong mines had recently gone off in the village, killing three PF (popular force militia) soldiers. He said he intended to arm twenty peasants from the village and that with the ten PF militiamen already assigned to it that should be sufficient to defend it from the Vietcong. He had a telephone line to the advance post of ARVN at the edge of the town which he could call upon in case of emergency. He said he had identified four families in the village as Vietcong and was keeping a close watch on them. And there were four others whom he regarded as sympathizers. A further four families, he said, had earlier been "seized" by the Vietcong and were still with them. When I asked how the inhabitants made a livelihood, he said that, in addition to those who worked the land, a number of them worked in the fish-paste factory that I could discern at a bend in the river a little over a mile from the village. Though they had to walk through an area controlled by the Vietcong it did not molest them and indeed encouraged them and some of the townspeople to work there, since the factory paid taxes to it and not the Saigon government.

I then asked a question which had apparently not been asked before, namely, how many of the sixty-one families who farmed the land in the village owned the land they worked. The pacification chief had no idea, and apparently it was not a question that either Wilson or Vann was wont to ask. So we began to inquire at several of the houses, and the answer was the same – just three out of the sixty-one families owned the land they worked. And where were the landlords who controlled the rest of the land? It turned out that they were all absentee landlords, most of whom lived in the nearby garrison-protected town, with a few others in a nearby village or in Saigon. I was astonished to learn from Wilson and Vann that questions regarding land tenure were not asked, though rather embarrassedly they acknowledged that such information could indeed be relevant in assessing prospects for pacification and understanding the political attraction of the NLF (Vietcong). And, of course, as was well known to Wilson and Vann, once the NLF was in firm control of an area it could ensure peasant support by dividing among the landless peasantry the lands of absentee landlords, who were especially numerous in the Mekong Delta.

I returned to the US on 23 January, and just under two weeks later I was flying en route to a four-day conference at the University of Chicago on China's relations with the other states of Asia, when I first noticed a painful swelling in both armpits. I recalled the warning the hospital director at Quang Ngai had given me and after arriving in Chicago, I sought out the conference chairman and explained that I thought I might possibly have bubonic plague and didn't want to inflict myself on the others attending the conference. He promptly telephoned the university hospital and arranged for an immediate examination. I must have been regarded as a real emergency, for one doctor was waiting to go over me and was soon joined by two others. I had the most thorough medical examination I've ever experienced, and was, of course, much relieved when the doctors finally concluded I definitely did not have the plague. They told me that my symptoms were probably simply a consequence of the unusually intense schedule I'd maintained in Vietnam, and that this had led to an exhaustion such as was often manifested by the swelling of glands in the armpit.

Much relieved, I went to the conference room where some twenty people sat around a long table. News of my possibly bearing the plague had preceded me, and though the chairman cheerily announced that it had been definitely determined that I did not have that scourge after all, some apparently felt it best to play it safe. And so as I sat down in an empty chair, people squeezed together and parted from me on both sides, leaving me sitting in lonely isolation.

From the Chicago conference I flew straight to Washington, DC, where William Bundy had me to lunch to talk over my Vietnam impressions. He was cordial and interested, even though it was soon evident that I had not been converted by my experiences there to any greater support of administration views and had in fact emerged with my criticism considerably reinforced. At his request, I spent several hours talking with two of his senior subordinates, Leonard Unger and Robert Miller. Then two days later – after seeing Senator Clifford Case about Vietnam and a few Indonesian friends – I visited General Thi (still ensconced in the luxurious digs provided at US government expense), who was keenly interested in what had been going on in his old bailiwick, the I Corps area. I went back to Cornell for a week, returning to Washington on 23 and 24 February for discussions on Vietnam, first with Senator Robert Kennedy and then William Fulbright, whom Case and Kennedy had apparently alerted to my Vietnam trip.

On 17 March, at the request of Senator Lee Metcalf and William Fulbright, I returned to Washington for a long talk with Metcalf, and then something totally surprising – a special luncheon arranged by Fulbright for twenty senators drawn from both political parties. I'd thought I'd be having lunch with him alone, but he'd been interested in the information I'd given him when we'd talked two weeks before and thought it important enough to have brought together this group. While they ate I talked about what I considered my most important findings in my trip to Vietnam and then they asked questions. I managed to cover a good deal in my talk – the failure of the US pacification program, the role and political orientation of the South Vietnamese army, civilian casualties, refugees, the Constituent Assembly, and the Buddhist opposition and its objectives. The reception was very positive and several of the senators tarried afterwards to express their appreciation. Fulbright appeared delighted and later told me that I'd been instrumental in "turning around" one influential Republican in the group. He asked me to write up what I had said as quickly as possible so that it could be more widely disseminated. It was the beginning of a warm and trusting relationship with Fulbright that I much valued.

11 Possibilities for peace, 1971

Audrey Kahin[1]

George's involvement with Vietnam occupied nearly all of his attention in the late 1960s. In addition to his regular teaching and writing duties, he spent much of his time speaking against the war on college campuses throughout the United States. In Washington he worked with Senators McGovern and Fulbright and other representatives in the Senate and Congress who were opposed to the administration's Vietnam policy, preparing for them historical and political analyses of the background to the war, the balance of political forces in Vietnam and in the other countries of Indochina, and the negotiating positions of the various sides. After the Johnson administration began talks in Paris with representatives of the Hanoi government and the PRG (Provisional Revolutionary Government of South Vietnam), he made several trips there to discuss with all sides their different perspectives on the possibilities of reaching a negotiated end to the war.[2]

In the course of a trip to Southeast Asia in 1970–1, after spending several months of research in Indonesia, George's focus shifted back to the situation in Indochina. We visited Saigon for two weeks in July 1971 (we had paid a brief visit there at the end of 1969 and early 1970), as well as spending brief periods in Laos and Burma. Most of our time in South Vietnam was spent in Saigon, interviewing a vast range of people, not only Vietnamese – both military and civilian, students and government officials, Buddhists and Catholics – but also American officials, military officers and journalists. We also had long talks with a few of George's graduate students, notably David Elliott, accompanied by his wife Mai, and Gareth Porter, who were conducting field research for their doctoral dissertations. David made it possible for us to visit My Tho province in the upper Mekong Delta on 24 July, and, while Mai and I remained in My Tho, George and David went off to the village of Vinh Kim in Samgiang district to assess the situation there. They were wanting to check up on a report by Peter Jay which had appeared in the *Washington Post* three weeks earlier about unrest in the region and the unpopularity of the current district chief.[3] In his notes of the trip George wrote:

On the way down to the village just off Highway 4 at 11 in the morning we encountered a large-scale government operation that had been launched into a line of trees which looked to be about three-quarters of a mile north of Highway 4. There was a large assemblage of tanks and armored vehicles with four huge-tired wheels that could obviously go through quite swampy places. A number of helicopters flew overhead persistently throughout the day.

We had a long talk with the chairman of the village council, supported from time to time by the hamlet chief and several others living in the district. The chairman was son of one of the largest landowners in the district, his father having an unusually attractive house, and he himself having received a letter from the NLF indicating he had been marked for assassination, "a death warrant," he said. The chairman observed that the Government of Vietnam [GVN] was something like the traditional dragon, with a head, the national level in Saigon, and a tail, village government, with nothing in between. Later this was brought up again in conversation and the chairman corrected himself, saying: "There is something in between and it is a snake – the military-staffed provincial and district levels of government." There was general agreement on this proposition.

He told us that approximately half of the district was an H-and-I [Harassment and Interdiction] area, into which the government pumps artillery and some air strikes daily, and he estimated that since 1965 approximately one-tenth of the district's civilian population of 40,000 have been casualties, with about 40 per cent of the total, about 1,600, being killed. This is apart from the military casualties of outside GVN troops.

While we were talking an ambulance backed up to a landing on the river and three bodies were taken aboard – government "Popular Forces" soldiers who had been killed the previous night 2 km to the west across the river. Every few days people are killed, he said, but during the last three years every couple of days three to four soldiers on an average are killed in the district. The worst year, with the largest number of casualties was 1968 and the heaviest period of H & I fire was after the American 9th division took up headquarters in a nearby base (occupied by it from February 1967 to late 1969 and early summer of 1970 – two US regiments were withdrawn respectively in late 1969 and mid-1970).

Every house that I saw outside of the very center of the village had bullet or shrapnel holes in it. About half of the district is regarded as insecure. About two-thirds of the district's rice area is now in production. (One could see that just outside the village a great many people had been regrouped in and around it, away from any rice fields, and their livelihood was seemingly dependent on fruit orchards.) ...

During the day, throughout the course of several conversations with local notables the theme was emphasized that only the US can end the war, and that the first step to be taken was to withdraw all American troops. The chairman had a slight amendment that this should wait until the end of the elections. However, the head of the PRA, cousin of one of Vietnam's leading musicologists, urged that not only should there be an immediate withdrawal of all American troops, but that this should be accompanied by stopping all American military supplies to the GVN. That, he said, would stop the fighting and oblige the GVN to think realistically about a peaceful settlement. I pointed out that Nixon often argued that withdrawal of American troops would precipitate a blood bath in Vietnam, instigated by the NLF. This man and the Chairman both pointed out that in fact the blood bath was going on right now. People were continuously being killed. (The willingness of this notable to take chances on an immediate withdrawal of all Americans and an accommodation with the NLF is all the more significant given the fact that the Vietcong in 1969 slit the throat of his neighbor who protested when they were taking him away.)

The house of this notable, like the grander house of the father of the chairman, whom we visited, located about a mile and a half away, were both pocked by holes from bullets and shrapnel. While we were talking, at precisely 5 p.m. howitzers in the district compound opened up in what appeared to be wide-ranging H & I fire. The chairman's father, one of the largest landowners in the district, showed us correspondence he had had with the American 9th division in 1969 asking for compensation for destruction of much of his house by shelling. He had completed all the forms and gotten them in on time but never received a cent. If a man as influential as this could get no compensation, what of others?

... David observes that the people we had been seeing during the day represented some of the ablest of those unwilling to join the NLF and the most promising for the government to build on if its policies were attuned to that endeavor; but the government is alienating even these people, including the largest landholders and even a village chairman who has received a NLF death warrant.

It was in the context of the discussion of the government's alienation of people in the district that I asked the chairman whether many people during the last few years were joining the NLF. He said approximately 20 per cent of the youths of military age had joined the NLF each year during the last few years.

During July, preparations were under way in South Vietnam for the first presidential elections to take place since 1967. There was some hope that, despite the amount of repression and intimidation that prevailed, the election might ultimately be a reasonably fair one. If that were the case, Duong Van Minh, who had been the nemesis of the US for a long time, seemed likely to win against Thieu and Ky.[4] Minh had spent several years in exile in Bangkok, but on his return had attracted a lot of support, particularly from the Buddhists and some of the progressive Catholics and other antiwar elements, who encouraged him to run in the forthcoming elections. When we spoke with Minh he was very circumspect, but it was generally expected that if he won the elections he would move toward a negotiated settlement.

So while we were in Saigon many of our interviews focused on the possibility of the elections providing the US with a face-saving way out of Vietnam. Several Buddhists and Catholics expressed the view that if the US was really interested in negotiating a settlement, it could remove support from Thieu and indicate its approbation of Minh so that he could be elected. They felt that with Minh, there was at least some chance of moving toward compromise and settlement with the NLF. Expressing lukewarm support for Minh, they described him as "a tool of the Americans, but one that will be used if the Americans are wanting to move towards peace."[5] The conversations George had in the delta had reflected a similar hope:

> The general theme ... concerning elections was that things were absolutely hopeless under Thieu and that almost any change would be an improvement. They wanted any person who could bring peace, and several inferences suggested that, of the candidates they were likely to get, Minh was clearly preferable (he comes from My Tho province). As one of them said, our situation is like men crossing the desert under a blazing sun; anything that looks like an oasis with water we will desperately make towards.

Before coming to Saigon we had spent a couple of weeks in Laos, and while in Vientiane George interviewed the Hanoi government's top representative there. In addition to discussing the Laotian situation, they talked about the Vietnamese negotiations and possibilities for peace and the plan that had just been floated by Clark Clifford (who had succeeded Robert McNamara as secretary of defense in 1968). George later noted:

> The Hanoi representative asked me what I thought of it, and I could see some problems with it. He was quite interested in my views and said: "You should really go and talk to our people." At the time, we were planning to fly to Burma, so he suggested I meet with people in their embassy in Rangoon. We did so, and though the Hanoi representative in Burma could not give us a visa, he said that if we returned to Laos, we might well be able to get one there. So, when we got back to Vientiane [after our visit to Saigon], their chargé d'affaires had received permission from Hanoi to give us visas. Together with my wife, I flew to Hanoi with the announced purpose of learning what their negotiating position actually was.

At the beginning of July the PRG had come out with a new "seven-point" negotiating program which was supported, of course, by Hanoi. They did so probably in the hopes of encouraging the possibility, opened up by the forth-coming elections in South Vietnam that, if Thieu were replaced by Minh, some steps could be taken toward a compromise settlement. Both Hanoi and the PRG clearly thought that a moderation in their negotiating position, as represented in the "seven points," could encourage elements associated with Minh, and make feasible an accommodation that would serve the inter-ests of both North and South Vietnam.

The extent to which the PRG had been publicizing its "seven points" in the countryside of South Vietnam was reflected in George's notes, taken when he had visited the Vinh Kim district in the Mekong Delta in late July, where he wrote:

> It is unsafe to go on the other side of the river for more than a short distance, and indeed on 20 July [1971], anniversary of the Geneva Accords (what Saigon refers to as "the Day of Shame") the NLF distributed pamphlets 1,500 yards on the west side of the river (presumably at night) containing Mme Binh's [the NLF's prime nego-tiator] new seven-point proposal. On the northwest side of the village there is a road that is regarded as safe for only about 400 yards. We stopped about 300 yards down the road, half way between two military posts where the NLF had on 20 July put up a huge NLF banner during the night.

The Thieu government was sufficiently worried about the attraction of the "seven points" to the war-weary South Vietnamese as to arrest student leaders for holding a meeting on 16 July to discuss them.[6]

So the primary aim of our visit to Hanoi was to discuss this seven-point proposal of 1 July. But George was also interested in finding out more about Hanoi's policies towards the ethnic minorities in North Vietnam, meeting with Vietnamese intellectuals and exploring the possibilities of an exchange of scholarly materials between Cornell's Southeast Asia collection and the Historical Institute in Hanoi. We were both also interested in seeing the countryside outside of Hanoi and the effects of the war on the country and people.

We left Vientiane on the Soviet flight, with clouds preventing us from seeing the landscape below for most of the way, until not far from Hanoi they cleared, and hills became visible as we passed over the huge Red River on our approach to the town, which itself looked quite small. We were met at the airport by members of the Vietnam Committee for Solidarity with the American People, and both of us were presented with bunches of flowers. As we drove into the city, I was impressed with the number of bicycles and the crowds of children who peered at us, curious but friendly and smiling. Hanoi was a complete contrast to Saigon, its tree-lined boulevards appearing very green, compared with the stunted stumps that were all that remained along the Saigon streets, and no sign here of the armed defense posts that were dotted throughout Saigon. But one could see the manholes, where the population had taken refuge during the earlier air raids, many of them now half-filled with water and lacking their covers. But also in contrast to the graceful South Vietnamese women in their lovely *ao dai*, here there was little color and the girls and women all wore short tunics over black trousers. Most of the men wore pith helmets, and these, together with the yellow colonial buildings and tree-lined streets, were a reminder that it was less than twenty years since this had been the capital of a French colony. Our hotel called Peace (Hoa Binh) was also old colonial – appearing considerably older than the Majestic, where we had stayed in Saigon.

In requesting a visa George had emphasized that he was "an independent scholar without governmental connection" and that his primary interest was "in securing a clearer idea of their negotiating position, and in particular a further elucidation of the 7-Points." So on our second day in Hanoi, we had a long four-hour session with Hanoi's former representative to the Paris talks, Ambassador Ha Van Lau, whom Prime Minister Pham Van Dong had assigned to explain the negotiating position of the DRV government. Two days later we met with Nguyen Phu Soai, the deputy chief of the PRG's Special Representation in Hanoi. I took down all the interviews verbatim, and we sent a copy of the one with Ha Van Lau over for him to check.

In addition to a series of interviews, we visited the Museum of the Revolution, the Temple of Literature and the major tourist sites in Hanoi, then on 11–12 August made a trip south to Thanh Hoa. As we drove through the southern suburbs of Hanoi into the countryside, the heavy destruction from the three-and-a half years of bombing was still very much in evidence. Bomb craters littered the highway and along the adjacent railroad tracks there was still the bombed and twisted wreckage of freight cars and engines. Every bridge along the whole route had been bombed and partly reconstructed, with our car having to ford some rivers where the bridges had not yet been rebuilt. Two cities, Phu Ly and Ninh Binh, had been virtually leveled, as also had Thanh Hoa, where, like the others, most of the town was now made up of buildings with bamboo wattle walls and thatched roofs. We spent the night in one of the few buildings that had not been destroyed – a former secondary school that had been made over into a lodging house for visitors.

Shortly after our arrival in Thanh Hoa, we visited a workshop (part of a dispersed factory) built in 1966 which made spare parts for cars, agricultural equipment and trucks. It was now operating in a cave cut out of solid rock in a small mesa-like mountain about 100 feet tall that thrusts right up out of the fringe of Thanh Hoa city. Bomb craters marked the approaches to the cave that was dark and rather damp, but pleasantly cool. During the worst of the bombing people had lived as well as worked there. When we arrived the men and women stopped work to sit at the table with us to drink, talk and sing. They entertained us with revolutionary songs – one on Thanh Hoa province and its tradition of resistance and another about the cave in the northern part of Vietnam where Ho Chi Minh lived between 1941 and 1943. Then one of the girls recited a poem about standing at the river at the 17th parallel looking to the south, and they ended with a chorus: "We will liberate the South."

While in Thanh Hoa we were taken to the famous bridge over the river Ma a few miles to the north of the town, which had been under intense American air attack between 1965 and 1968. It is called the dragon's jaw bridge because the hills leading up to one side resemble the body and head of a dragon; a single hill on the other side is called the pearl, which the dragon is supposedly stretching out to grasp. The bridge was scarred and pock-holed from the blast of numerous bombs but according to our guides it had sustained no direct hit and they claimed to have shot down ninety-nine planes before the bombing ceased in April 1968.

We then went to a beach about eleven miles from Thanh Hoa where, in rest houses and one large hotel, cooperatives apparently organized holidays for their workers – a number of girls from an embroidery cooperative were there while we were. Single-masted fishing boats were anchored off shore and lots of people were swimming. Most of our group (including George) joined them in the water.

On our way back to Hanoi we drove about fourteen miles east from the main highway to visit Phat Diem, the capital of Kom Son district of Ninh Binh province, one of the predominantly Catholic provinces of North Vietnam. Throughout the district were scattered a large number of substantial stone churches, some of them quite large. A majority of these had been damaged by bombs, some very badly; a few had only the tower standing and one had completely disappeared except for the entrance. One sizable church in the center of Phat Diem was presumably back in operation because it had a new roof. The whole area had been subjected to intense bombing and much of the town and surrounding countryside evidenced widespread destruction.

The concentration of so many well-built and clearly expensive church buildings struck one as very impressive and likely to have absorbed a considerable part of the region's wealth. We were unable to get much solid information on the condition of the Catholic population. Despite the exodus of so many of the Catholics from here in 1954, we were told that half of the province's population of about 90,000 was still Catholic. When George asked how many priests were left in the district he was told simply that there were a sufficient number to minister to the people and officiate at all the celebrations. We were told that about 1,000 Catholics had gone south, mostly younger men, who left their wives and older folk in Phat Diem with the idea that when elections were held and the country reunified in 1956 those left behind could join them. "Thus, we who remained were left with many dependents to look after."

In our few remaining days in Hanoi we met with North Vietnam's prime

Figure 11.1   With Prime Minister Pham Van Dong, Hanoi, 13 August 1971

minister, Pham Van Dong (Figure 11.1), representatives of the minority areas, and had another long session with Ha Van Lau, in which he answered our further questions and expanded on the parts of the earlier interview that had been less than clear.

As soon as we got back to Bangkok, George prepared a long memorandum for Senator Fulbright, writing to him in an accompanying letter on 20 August:

> During my stay in Hanoi [Prime Minister] Pham Van Dong, with whom I had one meeting, assigned Ha Van Lau to spend as much time with me as I deemed necessary to secure a clearer perception of the negotiating position of the DRV government, and I had two long meetings with him, one running to four hours. In addition, I had a long and useful talk with Mr. Nguyen Phu Suoi, the Deputy Chief of the Special Representation of the PRG in Hanoi ...
>
> As a consequence of these discussions (and briefer talks with several other officials) I have returned with data which provide, I believe, a significant elucidation of important parts of the 7-Point July 1st proposal ... My wife, who takes shorthand, took verbatim notes in these interviews. Ha Van Lau went over the notes on our four-hour interview with great care to ensure that they were correct, making corrections where he felt they were called for ...
>
> I feel confident that in reading this memorandum you will conclude, as I have, that the 7-Point Proposal does in fact provide a great deal of real substance for discussion – if the Administration

should develop a genuine interest in exploring the possibilities for a negotiated settlement.

Overall, I received the impression that the relatively moderate character of this new proposal (including the clear willingness to go a long way towards meeting the American position on US prisoners), reflected the Communists' belief that it would be attractive enough to induce the Administration to exert sufficient influence in South Vietnam to ensure that the October Presidential election would bring to power someone other than Thieu – a new Saigon administration which would be serious about commencing negotiations with the PRG.

Senator Fulbright tried to use this as leverage on the State Department but to no avail. It was clear that Washington was not interested at that stage in finding a compromise solution that could allow the possibility of withdrawing American troops from Vietnam. As George later wrote, "The interesting thing was that the administration was so anxious *not* to give the impression that there was a possibility for a reasonable, negotiated settlement that it leaked the memorandum to a columnist named Joseph Kraft, who came out with a column on September 30 which badly distorted the substance of my report. He said that even this fellow with dovish inclinations, Professor Kahin, had come to conclude that the negotiating position [of the NLF and Hanoi] was just too tough to make any settlement possible."

The elections in South Vietnam went ahead on Thieu's terms and he was re-elected. Because we had little access to American newspapers while we were in Asia we didn't see Kraft's column until much later. George's response did not appear in the *International Herald Tribune* until 12 November, when he concluded:

> Mr Kraft's column will undoubtedly be welcomed by an administration which is trying to convince Americans that the Vietnamese Communists are the main obstacle to fruitful negotiations. But dispassionate scrutiny of the evidence will show that it is President Nixon who has been primarily responsible for the impasse at Paris. Indeed, he has turned his back on important opportunities to negotiate an end to the war which were advanced in the PRG's July proposal.[7]

12 North Vietnam, 1972

When my wife and I had talked with North Vietnam's prime minister, Pham Van Dong, in Hanoi in August of 1971, I had gently chided him for having invited to visit his country only those Americans known for their outspoken opposition to the war. He had immediately accepted my argument that it was important to supplement their visits with those by more influential Americans – both those who had taken a public position against the US role in the war, but could speak with greater authority if they had actually visited North Vietnam, and those who were still on the fence but would be more likely to join the critics once they could actually see conditions in North Vietnam for themselves, rather than being dependent on the picture prepared for them by the Nixon administration. While Pham Van Dong had readily agreed with my assessment, presumably not novel to him, he said he didn't know how to go about selecting such a group. I acknowledged this difficulty but suggested that as a first effort a group of university presidents might be appropriate. He liked the choice and said he would get in touch with me when arrangements could be worked out.

I'd almost forgotten about this prospect when out of the blue there arrived just over a year later a cable from Hanoi authorizing me to bring over four such presidents for a week's visit, with a reasonable leeway provided as to the dates selected. I realized that even with as much as a month's latitude for picking the date for the trip some of those whom I invited would not be free, but I was confident that, if I cast the net widely enough, some would be eager to take advantage of this unusual opportunity. I assumed that presidents of major universities ought to be able to raise the airfare to Hanoi (there would be no expenses once they got there) and that prominent educators would value the opportunity to see as much for themselves as was possible with respect to an issue that engaged their student populations so heavily. And with the tide of opinion in the country now beginning to run against continuing the war, I thought that at least some of these men would have the courage to brook the criticism that would still inevitably come from the now diminished numbers of hawkish members of their communities. At least, I thought, that would be the case for presidents of privately endowed universities who were not beholden to state legislatures for their funding.

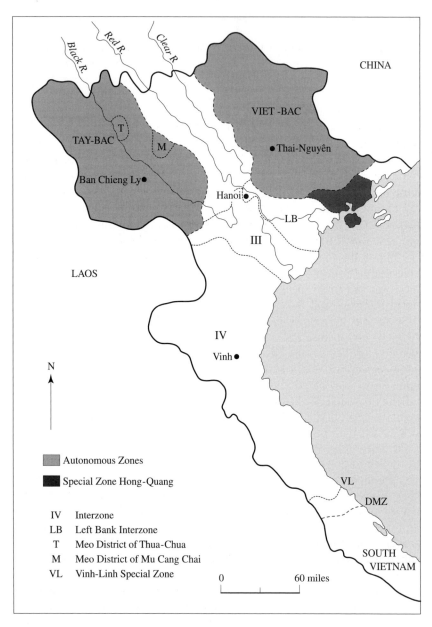

CHINA

Black R.

Red R.

Clear R.

VIET-BAC

TAY-BAC

T

M

•Thai-Nguyên

Ban Chieng Ly•

Hanoi•

LB

III

LAOS

IV

Vinh •

N

Autonomous Zones

Special Zone Hong-Quang

IV	Interzone
LB	Left Bank Interzone
T	Meo District of Thua-Chua
M	Meo District of Mu Cang Chai
VL	Vinh-Linh Special Zone

VL

DMZ

SOUTH
VIETNAM

0   60 miles

Map 5   North Vietnam's territorial divisions, 1963

Source: Fall 1963: 150[1]

Although I realized that few of these men would have ever heard of me (though in fact a couple did volunteer that they liked the book I had co-authored, *The United States in Vietnam*), I knew that Dale Corson, the highly respected president of Cornell, stood behind me and was prepared to speak favorably about me to any of the presidents I contacted. (He himself had a number of engagements that prevented him from making the trip.) And I understood that several of them did call him. But it was the same pattern with almost all of these presidents, whether Harvard, Yale, Princeton, Chicago, Columbia, Duke, Michigan, MIT, North Carolina, Stanford or Vanderbilt. It seemed to start off hopefully and with real interest in participating in the trip. "I can see that this is a good idea and that it's important for people like us to get over there and see what's actually going on." In every case they wanted a little time to think the matter over, and in some cases to consult with senior colleagues or members of their boards of trustees, before getting back to me. The most significant departure from this norm was Jerome Weisner, president of MIT, who I understood was against the war. He told me he would first have to check out the matter with his friend Henry Kissinger and get his approval, or at least his assurance that they would not attack him publicly if he took the trip. I didn't expect that he could get any such assurance, and he did not call me back.

As for the others, the responses, usually a day or two later, were pretty much the same. "Really sorry I won't be able to make it; but my schedule is such that I just can't manage it." And either explicitly or implicitly almost all expressed the point made by Robin Fleming, president of Michigan, a liberal reported to be against the war: "I'm really two people – myself and president of the university; it's a fine line, but I can't speak out as an individual without being regarded as a spokesman for the university." I was especially disappointed with the negative response from the president of Stanford, Richard Lyman, who I knew had considerable flexibility with his schedule since he was enjoying a year's sabbatical leave. But I appreciated his honesty when he explained that he was afraid of the use his right-wing critics would make of his going on such a trip. I am sure that was a consideration of many of the others, though they refrained from saying so. Harvard's Derek Bok also disappointed me, for I knew his wife, Gunnar Myrdal's daughter, to be strongly opposed to the American role in Vietnam. (Half a year later I embarrassed and angered him at a small luncheon he gave celebrating Alex Woodside's promotion to tenure at which I assured Bok that, though the Vietnamese prime minister had been disappointed at his inability to accept an invitation to visit Vietnam in the fall of 1972, the invitation still stood open.) And from my admittedly limited perspective I did find it a bit incongruous that he should have entitled his magnum opus, published a decade later, *Beyond the Ivory Tower: Social Responsibility of the Modern University*.

It finally dawned on me that I had been naive and had greatly underestimated the caution of even prominent educational leaders against risking actions exposing them to the possibility of public criticism. But as the last departure deadline approached I was fortunate enough to get a positive response from the only other non-president whom I'd approached, Professor Robert Dahl of Yale, a recent head of the American Political Science Association, and a man for whom I had great respect, and whom Hanoi had been willing to add to the four putative presidential visitors.

Dahl and I flew independently to Paris where we met on 20 September before going to the North Vietnamese embassy the next morning to get our visas. I knew that he was deeply concerned over the health of his son, and I could sense his agitation when it became clear that neither Air France nor Aeroflot (the only two airlines flying in to Hanoi) could guarantee schedules for the return flight from Hanoi back to Paris. When we got back to the hotel he put through a call to New Haven to see how his son was faring. The news was sufficiently discouraging for him to conclude it would be irresponsible to continue on to Hanoi, and so he then returned to the United States. I understood how he felt and sympathized with his decision, but was nevertheless much disappointed, for not only did I like his company but I also knew that he had more stature than I among American academics, and that his reporting would have carried greater weight than mine.

And so after the long Air France flight via Moscow, Tashkent and Bombay, I arrived in Hanoi at 11 a.m. on 23 September (Figure 12.1). I'd assumed that the people in the North Vietnamese Paris embassy would have alerted their colleagues in Hanoi that only I, and not a delegation of American university presidents plus Robert Dahl, would be arriving. But they had never gotten around to doing so. And thus as I descended the plane's stairs a bevy of excited young girls came running up bearing bouquets of flowers to be bestowed on the expected American educators. I was deeply embarrassed and chagrined by the expectations I had been responsible for arousing and my incapacity to deliver a single university president. I must acknowledge that I was impressed by and grateful for the understanding shown by Mr Tran Trong Quat, the senior official sent to meet me and my phantom colleagues, as we walked across the tarmac, with me rather ridiculously clutching my bouquet.

Despite my failure, government officials, especially the minister of education, Nguyen Van Huyen and Tran Trong Quat could not have been more cooperative in helping me develop the schedule I requested. Remembering that the main purpose of my 1971 visit had been to determine Hanoi's actual negotiating position, they volunteered interviews which I was happy to accept with the foreign minister, Nguyen Duy Trinh, and with Ha Van Lau, the prime minister's specialist on negotiations, with whom my wife and I'd had such fruitful talks the year before. (I had no intention of asking for an interview with Pham Van Dong, for after my failure to deliver even a single university president that would have been much too embarrassing.)

They also recalled that the year before I had expressed interest in their minority peoples and said that, if I wished, they could arrange for me to spend a few days in the Viet Bac, the large administrative area south of the

Figure 12.1 Arriving alone at Hanoi Airport, 23 September 1972

China border inhabited by the most important of these non-Vietnamese groups. I was indeed still interested, and I also realized that such a trip north could be very important in getting some idea of the extent to which overland traffic from China might be compensating for the recent blockade of Haiphong and lesser North Vietnamese ports that Nixon and Kissinger gloated had strangled the flow of arms, munitions and food from outside Vietnam. So we planned for such a visit. And they said they would try to arrange a meeting with General Chu Van Tan, a member of the Nung minority, who was the present administrative head of the Viet Bac, and who had been one of Ho Chi Minh's closest friends and served as the first minister of defense in his Vietminh government.

When I'd left the US there had begun to emerge a dispute as to whether Nixon and Kissinger were telling the truth in their repeated assurances to the public that their recently launched bombing campaign had spared the city of Hanoi. I wanted to try and check into this, and I found the Vietnamese officials more than willing to let me see for myself. Finally, to my great good fortune I was assigned a superb interpreter, Vu Quang Chuyen, a most intelligent, cooperative, and low-key instructor in literature who taught Dickens and Mark Twain at Hanoi University, and would have accompanied the whole group of presidents had they arrived. He never sought to take the reins and happily adjusted to what I wanted to do.

On only one occasion did Chuyen take the initiative, and I was most grateful that he did. Most of the day after my arrival I spent looking at bomb damage, but as we set out on our tour, we passed by the large Catholic cathedral, and I, being curious as to the extent of religious freedom and it being Sunday, suggested we stop by for a look at the 6 a.m. mass. (So as to avoid times that were favored by US bomber pilots this was the second mass, the first having been held at 5:30 a.m.) I was surprised at how full the cathedral was, and especially at the large portion of the congregation who were young. There was good organ music and a choir.

Not realizing that the question of religious freedom in North Vietnam was at issue in the United States, Chuyen was mystified at my interest in the cathedral and also my desire to visit several Buddhist temples, to which he also dutifully accompanied me. Finally he asked me: "Aren't you interested in *our* national religion?" Now it was my turn to be mystified, and I indicated I was. He said he would show me, and took me to the beautiful small Lake of the Redeemed Sword not far from the center of the city where a lovely little arched wooden bridge led to a minute island upon which stood the large one-storey Ngoc Son temple.

Side by side within the temple were three good-sized altars. The first, as one entered, was devoted to the god of earth and water and the third to Buddha. It was the central altar to which the major part of the crowd that came over the bridge paid their respects. Rising over its rear was a larger than life mail-clad warrior, Tran Hung Dao, the Vietnamese general who had defeated the invading Chinese-Mongol army in the thirteenth century. He was flanked by the lesser statues of two of his generals – Da Tuong, head of his elephant corps, and another general whose men swam under the invaders' boats in the river. This was, I learned, one of seven shrines in Hanoi dedicated to Vietnamese heroes or heroines who over the centuries had fought against Chinese invaders. Others were dedicated to the Truong Sisters, Quang Trung and General Le Thung Khiet. There could not have been a more compelling example of the engrained anti-Chinese thrust of Vietnamese nationalism. It was all the more striking, I thought, that large numbers visited these shrines even while the country was heavily dependent upon military supplies and food from China.

In the little old French colonial vintage Thong Nhat (Solidarity) hotel where I'd been put up I'd talked my first night with members of the International Control Commission (ICC – a vestige from the 1954 Geneva Agreement) who were quartered there. These lonesome chaps were eager to talk to any fresh face and had already been kind enough to warn me to choose the Vietnamese food rather than the potato-dominated "European" fare that the hotel also offered. They were a frustrated lot – one Canadian, one Pole, with an Indian serving as chairman – because on really important matters their reporting had to be based on unanimity. There was by now such a polarization in the positions of the Canadian and Polish members – mirroring the Cold War cleavage – as to preclude meaningful reporting, which in any case was supposed to go through the co-chairmen of the 1954 Geneva Conference, Britain and the Soviet Union, neither of which seemed any longer to be interested in their conclusions. But that did not mean that they, as individuals, especially the ICC's Indian chairman, were not disposed to discuss their findings with individuals such as me.

The ICC's chairman was happy to talk to me at length about the bombing of Hanoi, proud of the fact that he had taped recordings of many of the air attacks, including an especially heavy one of 16 August, which he played for me. The heavy thuds and rumblings recorded in this same little hotel room seemed ominous, but he assured me that the very center of this city, where the hotel was located, had never yet been hit. But well inside the city's boundaries many bombs had recently been dropped, and he told me some of the places to visit.

The next day after morning appointments with Nguyen Van Huyen, the minister of education, and Colonel Ha Van Lau, I set out together with Chuyen to see some of the bombed sites that the ICC had mentioned to me. (I used my own camera and film so that there could be no question as to the authenticity of the pictures I took.) I was quite surprised at the extent of the damage I saw – all well inside the city. So this was "precision bombing confined to military targets"! A large four-storey secondary school which I estimated to be one-and-a-half to two miles from the city's center lay in ruins, one side collapsed from the bombs which I learned had been dropped on 4 July 1972, the day of a particularly heavy raid of thirty-four sorties against Hanoi. In that same raid a four-storey block of workers' quarters had also been badly smashed. (I was told that fortunately most of the workers were at their jobs and that only four people had been killed and fifteen wounded in the attack.) I saw another somewhat smaller block of badly damaged workers' flats (I've lost my note of its date, but it had also been recent).

There were numerous other smashed buildings whose location I had learned that we could have visited, but in the limited time at our disposal (some of the afternoon being spent visiting the cathedral and the several other religious shrines), I elected that we go to the central Bach Mai Hospital (known as Rene Robin Hospital during the French period), which the ICC had told me had been bombed. It was located about 5 km from the very center of Hanoi, but several kilometers inside the city's outer edge. I was told it had been hit in a raid on 27 June and was surprised at the size of the huge crater that I estimated to be 35–40 feet across that had been carved out by a large bomb immediately alongside one of the hospital's wings. Dr Do Doan Dai, the director of this 900-bed hospital, told me that they had been very lucky and had been able to evacuate the patients to bomb shelters in time and lost only one doctor and one hospital worker. He had been surprised that a bomb should have been dropped on the hospital, since it was a large, easily identified building with open space around it. All that bomb damage inside the city seemed incongruous on that quiet, sunny Sunday, but my perspective was to change during the last three days of my visit when I spent considerable time in bomb shelters.

That evening I was invited to attend a performance of Vietnamese dancing put on in honor of a group of antiwar American activists who had successfully negotiated the release of two captured US pilots, Norris Charles and Markham Gartley, and were due to leave the next morning. Led by Cora Weiss, the group included William Sloane Coffin, Dave Dellinger and Richard Falk, as well as Charles's wife and Gartley's mother. Because we had to be attentive to the performance there was less opportunity to talk with them than I would have liked. But I learned they were being given permission to take out mail from some of the POWs that remained, something that Cora Weiss had managed on a previous trip, and I made a mental note to myself that I would try to do the same before my own departure.

The next morning I got up very early to view more sites of bomb destruction and have talks with the NLF delegation to Hanoi, and I was pleased to be informed that arrangements had been made for a trip north, for which I should be ready to leave that night at 7:30 p.m.

I learned a great deal from that trip and it is still vividly etched in my memory, but rather than try again to reconstruct an account from my notes it makes more sense, I think, simply to adopt here the account of it I wrote some three weeks afterwards, when my memory was still fresh, and which appeared in the *Washington Star* of 22 October 1972.

Some 50 miles to the north and northwest of Hanoi and the flood plains of the Red River lies a vast arc of tumbled hills, mountains and narrow, fertile valleys stretching all the way to the China border. This is the Viet Bac, North Vietnam's West Autonomous Region.

Covering about one-fifth of the country's territory, its ragged terrain supports less than 2 million of its 21 million people. Most of its population are members of more than 20 non-Vietnamese minority ethnic groups, and over this area are scattered more than half of North Vietnam's 3 million minority peoples.

It was apparently because Hanoi's Minister of Education and other officials knew from my writing and a previous visit that I had a serious interest in these minorities that I was the first Westerner permitted to travel north of Hanoi since President Nixon launched his all-out bombing campaign in April.

On the night of September 25 I left Hanoi on the drive north. We left after dark, for traffic along the road that leads to North Vietnam's fourth largest city, Thai Nguyen, and beyond to the China border has been a major magnet of US air attack. It is more prudent to travel at night because bombing is much less frequent and because vehicles are then harder to spot from the air.

Also, once it is dark the heavy truck traffic to and from the China border moves at slower and safer speeds. Whenever I was obliged to travel in the region during the day I was less unnerved by the threat of sudden air strikes against the road than by the breakneck rush of the drivers gunning their trucks at top speed as they crossed open stretches of a mile or two between those welcome havens of tree-lined roads.

The four hours spent the first night – traveling some 70 miles to a cave north of the city of Thai Nguyen that was to be my bomb-proof base – were largely free of strain. The only real exception was when we were caught for 10 endless minutes in bright moonlight on a bridge over a sizable river because a truck ahead of us suddenly broke down and came to a standstill. My feeling of helplessness was increased on being told that in case of an attack I should not jump off into the water because the concussion of nearby bombs would drown me.

That night being bright with a large clear moon, I could see a great deal during the 50-mile drive between Hanoi and Thai Nguyen – capital of the Viet Bac and before the bombing North Vietnam's only center of steel production.

Road-building

The immense flow of heavily laden truck traffic coming down from China drove home the point that Nixon's mining of the coastal waters has simply altered the course of the supply-flow from the Soviet Union and China. And the building of all pipelines from China has meant that few trucks need be encumbered with loads of gasoline.

It was not only the flow of truck traffic that impressed me. I was quite unprepared for the tremendous amount of heavy road-building equipment parked intermittently along the road, some poised to be put into instant use at first light and some even then taking advantage of the bright moonlight to work at night.

At many points I could see gleaming in the moonlight the crushed lime-stone surfaces of recently constructed auxiliary roads often running roughly parallel to the main highway – alternate routes and countless bypasses to be used in case bombs temporarily cut stretches of the highway.

The North Vietnamese have carried out what must be one of the greatest crash programs of road-building in history – and they lack neither the manpower nor modern road-building equipment to maintain it. Ships may no longer be able to unload heavy Soviet and Chinese equipment, but over the spider-web of roads reaching down from the China border, huge six-wheel trailer trucks, along with a host of smaller ones and occasional ox carts and two-wheel, man-powered pushcarts, keep the supplies moving.

Even if the heavy and incessant US bombing of the main highways were many times more accurate it would not significantly reduce this traffic. Insurance against this are the numerous alternate roads, spurs and bypasses as well as the ingenuity and wide range of resourcefulness already demonstrated by the Vietnamese in their capacity to repair bomb-damaged roads and small, fixed bridges quickly and to replace longer bridges by temporary spans rapidly assembled from large but well-dispersed stockpiles of pontoons and girders.

However, American bombing has not been accurate. This had already been brought home to me when, on the day before my trip, I had seen the 40-foot crater a bomb had recently left near the center of Hanoi's main hospital and the extensive damage to worker's quarters and schools which were well inside the city's inner limits.

But it became even clearer from the extent of damage to the peasant hamlets along the road I traveled to the north. At no place was the road obstructed by bomb damage. In general, our planes seemed to have been a great deal more successful in hitting the numerous hamlets lining the road than the road itself.

The damage was particularly evident very early the next morning when, after a few hours sleep at the cave, I was again driven over part of that same road. Repeatedly along a stretch some 10 to 15 miles long I saw pairs of fresh bomb craters, bracketing the road usually 200 to 300 feet from it. In one section of a little over a mile and a half were four such sets of craters, three of them leaving smashed peasant hamlets, but none of them hitting the road.

The next day, while I was sitting out an air raid in the cave, a heavy bomb was dropped on that same stretch of road. Towards sunset when it was safe again to travel I saw the new crater that had been added since I had passed by early in the morning. It was only about 150 feet from the road but the roadbed was still intact and the trucks were still barreling along it. I remember hoping as we raced by that the peasants who a day before would have called the wrecked structure near the crater their home had been away in the fields when it happened.

Death trap

Further along we passed through the outskirts of Thai Nguyen. This was the city which, being near to coking coal and iron ore, was to have been the key to the industrialization that the Democratic Republic of Vietnam had launched in its first five-year plan.

I could see only part of the city, for it is regarded as something of a death trap, having been hit hard eight times since April 16, most recently only a week before.

What is left of it is an area that drivers simply want to get through as soon as they can. Traffic may slow down as it approaches an American city, but quite the opposite here.

The blast furnaces had been destroyed once more. The large power plant, repaired after the Johnson period of bombing, had been hit again and sat like a broken steamship among lesser debris.

In one quarter of the city one of the largest complexes of building spared by the Johnson bombing now lay in shambles. What had it been, I asked. "Our national veterinary clinic and water-buffalo breeding and upgrading center," I was told. Reluctantly our driver stopped long enough for me to make out what had been stalls and the masses of twisted iron stanchions.

Like other Vietnamese cities and towns, Thai Nguyen has decentralized and dispersed as much of its facilities, industry and administration as possible. This could not be done, of course, with blast furnaces and a central power station.

But light industries, as well as schools, colleges, hospitals, clinics, city and provincial offices, and markets could be. And thus much of what once was clustered in this city of over 100,000 is now spread out through an area of probably a thousand square miles. A large part of these dispersed facilities are housed in caves, some natural, and others cut into the face of the abundant limestone escarpments and mountains that rise to the west and north of Thai Nguyen.

Schools and colleges too large to be accommodated in caves have been spread out over wide areas, often merging with peasant villages. The Pedagogical School of the Viet Bac Autonomous Region is a good example. Initially dispersed from Thai Nguyen after it was first bombed in September 1965, it has been dispersed again since the Nixon bombing began, with six units spread over the five provinces of the Viet Bac.

One evening I visited a component that trains teachers for grades five to seven. There, far even from any secondary road, more than 700 students and their teachers live in a peasant village on the edge of a forest.

The classrooms, small dormitories and dining rooms and kitchens look like peasant houses, with thatched roofs and walls of bamboo matting. They have not infringed on the peasants' lands, and have cleared a few vegetable plots for themselves.

I was told that the rapport which was evident between the peasants and the students stemmed from the fact that most of the students come from peasant families. But perhaps equally important, the local peasants benefit from the services of the school's metal-working shop in repairing and sometimes manufacturing agricultural implements for the villagers. The students take turns in preparing their own food, in cleaning classrooms and in digging and keeping in shape the deep trenches and other kinds of air raid shelters.

I was told that preparing such protection against bombs is not an academic exercise, for even isolated villages (and that is what this school looks like) have frequently been bombed.

Isolated village

Concerning this statement I later expressed some skepticism to the Vietnamese who were accompanying me, and late that night after we had returned to our base I asked them whether it would be possible to be shown some such village.

They said there were several that could be reached from the cave, and being very tired I asked to be taken to one that was not too distant. The next morning, after driving north for about half an hour, we turned off onto a single-track dirt road that soon led through a small village, and then became an even narrower track.

After another mile along this fading road where we passed only bullock carts and bicycles, we turned due west, fording a sizable stream and then for another mile followed a dirt track which was almost impassable for our Soviet Jeep and where the tracks of our tires were the first that had registered. This meandering path brought us into a beautiful valley, green with rice fields, nestled among low hills.

Finally, not far from the fringe of a hamlet strung out along the edge of the little valley floor our Jeep could go no further and we had to walk the rest of the distance. Even before we reached the first peasant house I could see that large areas of the rich fields were marred by large brown holes, encircled by fresh dirt blasted out from the holes.

I was just beginning to count these bomb craters, having come to 19, when we walked up to the first house in the hamlet, one badly damaged by a nearby bomb hit, as was the case with most of the houses I saw. I had stopped counting bomb craters at 34; but the villagers urged me to accompany them further up the narrow track, where I could see more smashed houses, bordering more bomb-splotched rice fields.

They told me there were a total of 116 bomb craters in an area 1.5 kilometers long and averaging about 500 meters wide. I have no reason to doubt that figure.

I walked at will through the area looking at one smashed house after another, talking freely to the inhabitants through my interpreter, Vu Quang Chuyen, a superb and sensitive linguist, who had once taught English Literature, specializing in Dickens, at Hanoi University. These people were nearly all members of minority groups – mostly Nung or the usually much rarer Cao Lan.

Whether we talked to the narrow-visaged Nung or the incredibly broad-faced Cao Lan, a look of sheer incredulity came over their faces as they recounted the sudden sweep of planes, which they estimated at between 15 and 20, over their village [Figure 12.2] at about 10:30 a.m. on Sept. 12. Altogether 116 bombs, small but devastating – each leaving craters 12–15 feet across – had been dropped.

Thirteen of their people were killed, they said, and five seriously injured. They had never seen planes before, not in the French period, not in the Johnson period, and never before in the Nixon period. The only building in that little valley not made of thatch and bamboo-matting was the hamlet's small brick cooperative grain storehouse, located near the entrance of the valley. It was one of the few buildings that had not been hit. I don't know whether it was the Air Force or the Navy that hit this little hamlet, but I would like to ask them why.

Having seen this remote village, I was not surprised when one evening I visited the emergency surgical section of Thai Nguyen's central

Figure 12.2   Dong Giong hamlet, 27 September 1972

Figure 12.3   Thai Nguyen hospital

Figure 12.4   Patients in Thai Nguyen hospital

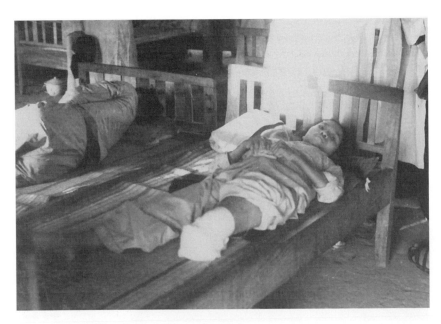

Figure 12.5   Patients in Thai Nguyen hospital

hospital [Figures 12.3, 12.4 and 12.5] and heard the stories of some of the recently injured patients. I was told that all 11 of those whose recent or impending operations earned them the right to lie temporarily in the safety of this cave were peasants from villages 10 to 15 kilometers from Thai Nguyen. Two were from one of the hamlets I had just seen crushed by bombs close to the highway north of the city.

From Doan Ket village in Dong Hy district was a boy of eight who had lost both legs in a bombing attack of Sept. 9. His 16-year-old sister, who was at his bedside to look after him, said that his mother, older brother and younger sister had been killed in the raid.

Opposite him lay Dinh Thi Thuc, a pretty girl of 17 from the Hoa minority, whose village of Dong Tien in the same district had been bombed on Sept. 13. She began in a low, controlled voice to recount how she and two young friends had been out gathering firewood at the edge of a clearing when a plane suddenly swooped in and bombed. Her two companions were instantly killed, she said, and her leg was badly hurt.

She looked from me down to the amputated stump and lost her composure. Her eyes blazed and then welled with tears as she spoke with great bitterness, and broke off sobbing. The only word I could make out was "Nick-son." I turned to my interpreter. He was visibly upset and seemed reluctant to proceed with the translation, but when I pressed him he continued. "She says, I cast not even a small stone at America, and no one in my village did. Why do you come here to bomb us? Why does your Nixon want to kill us?"

Cave hospital

Most of the other patients seemed stunned and subdued or just too weak to talk. But another exception was Vuong Xuan Ba, a father who shared a bed with his two little sons. The hamlet of this 38-year-old peasant had been bombed only five days before on Sept. 22. Dr Koan Quy, director of the hospital's surgical unit, explained that the injury to this man's throat and to the cheekbones of his 4-year-old boy were being successfully treated, but that he was still worried about the 6-year-old boy, whose severe skull damage impinged on his brain.

Initially in slow measured tones the father told of a lunchtime air raid that killed 39 people in his hamlet, leaving only 14 alive. As he talked he became angry, but when he came to recount how his wife, eldest boy and younger daughter were killed he began to cry and looked away.

North Vietnam's Viet Bac is a fascinating mosaic of ethnic minorities that would surely delight any anthropologist.

Here are about half a million Tay and over 300,000 Nung, both of whom speak a language related to that of the Thai and Lao. They live alongside about a quarter of a million Meo and a slightly smaller number of Yao, together with a congeries of other ethnic minorities whose numbers are much smaller.

To anyone who has followed the course of the Vietnamese revolution, this area is of particular interest, for it was here that Ho Chi Minh's Vietminh established its first bases for struggle against the forces of the Japanese occupation and later against the French. If Ho and his largely Vietnamese following were to achieve success they could do so only by developing a reasonably harmonious and cooperative relationship with the non-Vietnamese ethnic minorities who lived in these mountains and upland valley areas.

That they were successful is attested to by the military historians of their revolutionary war. Whether or not their policies stemmed from simple political expediency, they stand in marked contrast to the hostile and oppressive relationship that exists between the Saigon government and the Montagnard minorities of the south.

Throughout my visit, nearly all of the local officials I encountered appeared to be from the minority groups, and it is a fact that there are a number of senior officials in the central government who have been recruited from several of the country's major minorities. Possibly the best measure of the mutual confidence between the Vietnamese and these groups is to be found in the number of high-ranking army officers recruited from them.

Undoubtedly the most illustrious leader from among the minorities is Chu Van Tan, a member of the Nung minority, who holds the rank of lieutenant general in the army and is secretary general of the Lao Dong Party for the Viet Bac. He is also vice chairman of the standing committee of North Vietnam's National Assembly, a member of its National Defense Council, and commander of the armed forces of the Viet Bac Autonomous Region.

Chu Van Tan, 62, was a close friend of Ho Chi Minh and is one of the senior leaders of the revolution. In the early 1940s he played a major role in establishing anti-Japanese guerrilla bases in northern Vietnam and later became the first minister of defense in the Vietminh government.

I had a relaxed and informal talk with him in the cave where I was based [Figure 12.6].

He appeared especially to enjoy answering my questions concerning early contact with the American OSS (Office of Strategic Services) and his assignment in 1945 to provide military protection to some of their members who were operating out of Kunming in southern China.

Toward the end of our talk, only a short time after the nearby explosion of a heavy bomb, General Tan put his finger to his lips and asked me to listen carefully. "Can you hear the trucks?" he asked. Indeed I could. Despite the bombing attack one could still hear the sound of truck traffic a few miles away, moving along again in broad daylight, and in numbers that were apparently no less than before.

Figure 12.6   With General Chu Van Tan outside cave near Thai Nguyen, September
     1972

There were a couple of interesting details that I believe I neglected to incorporate in the article. One was the fact that because of persistent American
bombing close to the mouth of the cave where General Chu Van Tan
rendezvoused with me he was stuck for longer than he expected and, poor
fellow, was subjected to a three-hour interview before it was safe for him to
leave the cave, get into his well-camouflaged command car, and depart. It
had been Chu Van Tan whom, during the last year of World War II, Ho Chi
Minh had assigned to work together with and protect the American OSS
agents against the Japanese.[2] Among other things, he said, his unit
responded successfully to the OSS request to attack the Japanese-held town
of Tam Dao to liberate the French held there. It protected and provided
horses to the OSS, but its most dangerous mission was to rescue downed
American pilots and get them to Allied headquarters in China. (In appreciation the OSS, he said, provided enough carbines and pistols to equip a full
company of his men.) I could not help being struck by the irony that this
man who had rescued American pilots nearly three decades before was now
being bombed by a later generation of American pilots.

  Another incident on the trip north was the appearance of a mystery plane
only some 25 miles north of Hanoi on the night we were driving back from
that cave. There weren't supposed to be any planes out, and the security
agent then traveling with us was embarrassed at its sudden appearance, but

prudent enough to order us to tumble out of the car into a deep adjacent ditch. The plane swooped low, making several passes before proceeding on into the night. We didn't have the feeling the security agent really knew what he was talking about, but accepted his final verdict that it had been one of their own MIGs.

The day after my return to Hanoi the outskirts of the city were subjected to a series of bombing attacks. During the morning attack I spent a bizarre hour in a section of the hotel's basement air-raid shelter with two Pathet Lao diplomats – their ambassadors to Beijing and Moscow – who could speak neither French nor English. We passed the time jovially drawing pictures of our families for each other's scrutiny. I went out afterwards to shop at the government's store and barely made it back to the hotel as the air-raid sirens started again. Fortunately there were no attacks in the early afternoon as I spent a very fruitful two hours with Nguyen Duy Trinh, the foreign minister. But just as I returned to the hotel, the bombing started again with two to three bomb thuds per minute. The next morning it resumed at 7:58 and culminated with a very heavy bomb that badly shook the hotel, but did no damage to it, apparently landing on the outskirts of the city. But shortly afterwards there was commotion outside the hotel as people gathered to watch a new and strange sight. Floating high over Hanoi was a large yellow parachute being wafted by the wind out towards the coast. I learned that two of the attacking bombers had been shot down and that the pilot of one had safely ejected and using this apparently larger than usual parachute was being blown out over the Gulf of Tonkin, where it was believed he was rescued by some US ship. Presumably, I was told, the other pilot was killed in the crash of his plane.

Against that morning's background, it seemed ironic that I should learn early in the afternoon that my request to take out letters from some of the incarcerated US POW pilots was acceded to and that if I wished I could meet at 4 p.m. with the seven whose letters I was free to carry back to the States. Although mindful that this might well be a public relations gambit and that there was no basis for assuming that the condition of these seven POWs would be anything like a representative sample, I readily agreed to do so, for it would at least provide me with a basis for enlightening their particular families as to their physical condition. With a Vietnamese official present, some were understandably morose and not very talkative. But a couple were outspokenly angry and indignant at having learned – I know not how – that Nixon had justified the current bombing as a means of speeding their release. Their letters home had, of course, been carefully inspected to ensure that they contained no sensitive information useful to the US military, including the location of their jail. But these pilots were nevertheless clearly happy that their letters would actually reach their wives, girls and parents; and I was able to pledge to them that I would see to this as well as report on their physical appearance – which outwardly at least indicated they were in reasonably good health. I asked that photos of them be taken as I was meeting them so that I could send these along with the letters when I got back.

The day before there had arrived at my hotel a seasoned and well-informed CBS television correspondent, John Hart, apparently the first such person to have been admitted, at least in recent years. He and I had a couple of meals (Vietnamese food) together and got along very well. His major concern was Nixon's blockade and how effective it was. To that end he had been able to go to Haiphong but had been unable to get permission to go north, as I had. He was most envious of my having been able to make that trip and keenly interested in what I had learned – especially the way in which roads, rapid road repair, and the railroad and gasoline pipeline were compensating for the blockade of Haiphong and smaller ports, indicating what he himself had suspected – that the Nixon–Kissinger claim of having interdicted the flow of supplies into North Vietnam was flagrantly fraudulent. He was also interested in my reporting that the bombing in the areas I had traveled was so highly inaccurate as to result in many civilian casualties. He asked me whether I would be willing to broadcast my findings over CBS when I got back to the States, and I readily agreed. Before I left he had a positive response and said that as soon as I got back to New York they wanted me to get in touch with them so that they could promptly arrange for the broadcast.

The night before my departure Ha Van Lau, Nguen Van Huyen and Tran Trong Quat gave a private dinner for me where the discussion was devoted to likely terms of a negotiated settlement which they believed was now imminent. They were au courant with the state of the negotiations between Kissinger and Le Duc Tho, and, while they did not have the authority to provide me with the details, were clearly intent upon giving me hints of some salient points. The most important were the concessions agreed to by Kissinger with respect to US acquiescence to the right of North Vietnamese troops to remain in South Vietnam and recognition of the status of the PRG (NLF) authority in the South. These would permit the North Vietnamese to withdraw what had been one of their cardinal conditions: namely that Nguyen Van Thieu, the head of the South Vietnamese government, would have to be replaced before any meaningful agreement could be reached. (They were sufficiently vague on this central point that I was unclear whether this interdependence was potential or had actually just been agreed upon.) Less ambiguous were their terms for a bilateral armistice with the US whereby there would be a concomitant withdrawal of residual American troops and the releases of American POWs – both processes to be begun and completed on the same date. The PRG (NLF) and Saigon would have to work out their own separate armistice and prisoner exchange, without any American involvement, a provision which, I later learned, left the PRG (NLF) feeling that some of its central interests had been given short shrift by Hanoi.

They, of course, had no way of knowing that Kissinger, after having agreed to initial a draft agreement with Hanoi and then assured the American public on 31 October, on the eve of the presidential election, that "Peace is at Hand," would acquiesce to Nixon's then reneging on the agreement, and insisting on additional concessions by Hanoi and the PRG (NLF). Or that he would then sign on to Nixon's ruthlessly brutal twelve-day "Christmas Bombing" campaign in the vain effort to get them to comply.

The next day, 30 September, my departure was delayed by more bombing, the heaviest yet, with the incoming Aeroflot plane obliged to turn back to Vientiane. The last bomb fell at 11:16, the Aeroflot plane returned and landed in mid-afternoon, departing at about 4 p.m. So I began the long thirty-six-hour flight to Paris, changing to Air France after a five-hour layover in Moscow. Having discovered that a first-class ticket on Aeroflot cost only 10 per cent more than the standard fare I settled happily into a seat in the snug first-class section in the tail of the plane, where the other five seats were occupied by Soviet citizens, apparently diplomatic and technical personnel. The large and muscular stewardess soon appeared with a tray of glasses filled with vodka. She seemed distressed that I alone among the six declined a glass, the first of many that she offered. (I was dead tired from the frenetic pace I'd been keeping and just wanted to sleep.) She seemed genuinely concerned at my abstinence. Her compassion took over and with a warm maternal smile she proudly presented me with a bottle of chilled Georgian champagne. It was for me alone, and since she had already uncorked it, I had to accept it. If there had been any doubt about my ability to get to sleep, this bottle overcame it. It dawned on me that in every Aeroflot plane in which I'd ever flown the stewardesses were formidably large and brawny, and I began to appreciate why one never heard of their planes being hijacked. It would take a brave hijacker to challenge one of these women!

During the five-hour wait in Moscow Airport for my Air France flight to Paris I compensated for my vodka-free flight from Hanoi by indulging in the incredibly inexpensive premium caviar and vodka served there. After flying to Paris and overnighting at an airport hotel, I flew on to New York, arriving there on the evening of 2 October and checking in to the old Abbey-Victoria hotel.

Following John Hart's instructions, at 9 a.m. the next morning I called CBS where I was told that John Hart had cabled them of the importance of what I'd observed, that they had been expecting my call, and would now make arrangements for my broadcast. I was to sit tight in my hotel room while they did so, and they would be back to me soon as to exactly when I was scheduled in their studio. And so I waited, and waited. They finally called me early the next morning sounding embarrassed and rather sheepish. They wouldn't be able to put me on television after all, they said. They were terribly sorry, but couldn't explain their decision to me over the phone. If I were agreeable they wanted to have Bernie Kalb, who they understood was a good friend of mine, fly up from Washington to explain their decision to me over lunch. Mystified and keenly disappointed, I agreed.

Bernie took me to a very nice French restaurant, but neither one of us had much appetite. He was clearly ill at ease – a most unnatural state for this normally warm and outgoing man. And so very soberly he carried out his mandate. There were, he said, two principal reasons why CBS had reversed itself and decided against putting me on. To begin with, my reporting on the bombing of Hanoi and other areas and the civilian casualties caused by it would not be welcome, in view of the fact that CBS officials believed the American public had had a bellyful of reports of these casualties and other atrocities and could be expected to turn their television sets off if subjected to more such unpleasant reports. But by far the most important consideration was that my findings on the failure of Nixon's interdiction policy was not only contrary to what the generals and pilots were reporting, but that it directly contradicted what Nixon and Kissinger had been boasting to the public. He explained that for CBS to be the source of such a report at this particular time risked so antagonizing Nixon as to bring failure of its current effort to obtain the re-licensing of its affiliates from the Federal Communication Commission, a body which Nixon had pretty much packed with his own choices.

Before returning to Ithaca that night I spent the time telephoning families and friends of the seven POW pilots whose letters I was carrying. They all seemed pleased to learn that their pilot was alive and looked well, with a letter and a picture to be mailed to them the next day. But a couple seemed suspicious and fearful that by receiving the letters they might be doing something unpatriotic. I guessed that the uncertainty and worry they had experienced had contributed to their state.

Before traveling to Washington I spent eleven days in Ithaca trying to make up for the lectures and seminars I had missed, holding phone conversations about Hanoi's and the PRG's negotiating positions with William Sullivan, the deputy assistant secretary of state, upon whom William Rogers, the secretary, especially relied for Vietnam matters (Kissinger did his best to cut Rogers out of them), with a General Odum at the Pentagon about the condition of the seven POWs, and with members of Senators Fulbright and McGovern's staffs.

Having been invited by Martin Agronsky to appear on his popular television program I flew down to Washington on the afternoon of 16 October. When I got to his studio he rather apologetically informed me that I would have to share the program with a State Department spokesman – "We have to have balance on our programs," he explained. This appeared to be the case only where someone was critical of Nixon, I discovered. Fortunately the State Department's choice was a clumsy proponent of Nixon's Vietnam policy and antagonized Agronsky (as well as presumably the television audience) by carrying in a copy of his recently published book and partly using the occasion to advertise it. But I ran into the "balance" problem again the very next day when I discussed writing a long piece for the *Washington Star* with one of its editors. (Thanks to a former student, recently White House correspondent of the *Los Angeles Times*, Stuart Loory, this Washington newspaper had invited me to write about my trip to Vietnam – the account that I reproduced earlier.) This editor informed me that as a matter of "balance" the page upon which my article appeared would have to be shared by one from a priest who was a White House speech writer for Nixon named John McLaughlin (later, after leaving the Jesuit Order, he became famous for chairing NBC's program, "The McLaughlin Group"). Predictably, his article was a vigorous defense of Nixon's bombing.

After talking informally with several journalists at the National Press Club, a broadcast over National Public Radio and long interviews with George Wilson, military affairs specialist on the *Washington Post*, and Richard Dudman of the *St Louis Post-Dispatch*, I returned to Ithaca on the night of 18 October to try and do justice to my lecture course and seminar, write an op-ed piece for the *New York Times* and work on a long article on negotiating positions that the venerable editor of the *New Republic*, Gilbert Harrison, had asked me to write. He was holding space for me in the upcoming issue with an imminent publication deadline and urged me to hand-carry my uncompleted draft down to Washington so that I could complete it there in time.

Somehow Clark Clifford (Johnson's last secretary of defense) and Paul Warnke (a former assistant secretary of defense, and clearly the most enlightened of any senior Johnson administration official with respect to Vietnam) had learned that Kissinger was in Vietnam in connection with what they believed to be the final stage of negotiations. Kissinger had flown to Saigon on 19 October to induce Nguyen Van Thieu, head of the South Vietnamese government, to support the agreement which he expected to initial together with the Hanoi government and PRG (NLF) on the 22nd. Clifford and Warnke were keenly anxious to know more regarding the positions of Hanoi and the PRG and thought that I might be able to enlighten them. So they had a car and driver awaiting me on my arrival at National Airport which took me to their office. In discussing this with them, I think that, as in the article I was preparing for Gilbert Harrison, I was overly cautious and scrupulous in describing what I'd learned over dinner that last night in Hanoi.

But matters were moving too fast for this to really matter. For earlier on 24 October, even before I left Ithaca for Washington, Thieu publicly denounced, without revealing the content, the agreement that Kissinger and Le Duc Tho had just arrived at in their Paris talks. With Thieu intransigent, Kissinger first postponed and then canceled the initialing of the agreement originally scheduled to take place in Hanoi on 22 October. Feeling betrayed, the Hanoi government four days later, 26 October, publicly released the full text and history of the negotiations. Kissinger then scrambled to regain his footing before a suspicious American audience and called a major press conference, where he indicated there were no significant differences remaining to be bridged, and announced that an agreement was now in sight and that "Peace is at hand."

There was understandably great confusion as to where matters really stood. At this point Kissinger in his negotiations could no longer count on the backing of a Nixon who was supremely confident that on 7 November he would win by a landslide against Senator George McGovern. Nixon now felt free to turn his back on the negotiations, for the time being at least, and move closer to Thieu's position. And Kissinger, if he wanted to keep his job, would have to abandon the agreement he had produced and once again conform to Nixon's unpredictability.

With the collapse of the agreement implicit in Thieu's denunciation of it and with Hanoi's then going public as to its content, two friends (Richard Barnet and Cora Weiss) and I flew to Paris on the morning of 27 October to talk with the deputy North Vietnamese representative in the Paris negotiations, Nguyen Minh Vy, at their headquarters in Choisy Le Roi to try to ascertain how all this had affected their negotiating position. We found him understandably outraged at what he felt had been Kissinger's betrayal and quite unwilling to retreat from the position Hanoi had taken in the draft previously agreed upon. He pointed out that they had gone into the final, crucial round of talks that began on 8 October with the clear understanding that Kissinger spoke for Thieu and had his assent with respect to the US position. It had been understood, he said, that the agreement negotiated should be signed by Hanoi and Washington with the "concurrence of their respective allies," that is, the PRG and Saigon. He saw Nixon's sudden insistence that any accord between the US and Hanoi first have the concurrence of Thieu as a "pretext" for putting off signing the agreement that Le Duc Tho and Kissinger had finally hammered out. The US, he said, had now postponed the schedule for ending the bombing and signing the agreement three times without setting a further date.

Nguyen Minh Vy was especially concerned at what he regarded as a major change in the understanding arrived at concerning prisoner release. This, he said, had called for the release of *all* prisoners held by both sides without reservation. "But now," he said, "the US doesn't want to return political prisoners [of which Saigon's jail were full], saying this is the competence of Saigon." The US now assumed no responsibility for any of the prisoners – even those it had turned over to Saigon authorities. This meant, he said, that Kissinger had in the October draft shifted his position and reneged on the understanding that prisoner exchange meant *all* prisoners, including civilian political prisoners held by Saigon. (Thus Hanoi would be expected to release American POWs, but the US would not reciprocate by bringing Thieu's government to release civilian political prisoners, who were, of course, almost all adherents of the PRG (NLF).)[3] He was clearly furious that Kissinger should now refer to this difference as simply "a linguistic difficulty."

Appreciating how important the question of political prisoners must be for the PRG (NLF), I detached myself and got a taxi to the headquarters of the PRG mission in the Paris suburb of Verrières le Buisson. There I talked with the head of their delegation, Madame Nguyen Thi Binh, whom I'd met there two years earlier. I found her extremely depressed by the abandonment of her many people in jails and concentration camps, and it was clear that her bitterness extended not only to Kissinger, but to Hanoi's negotiators as well. I sensed she felt that during the course of the negotiations Hanoi's representatives had not been sufficiently concerned over the fate of political prisoners held by the Saigon government and had been lax in insisting on the explicit language needed to protect them.

After a full afternoon of discussions the three of us flew back that evening, dead tired, to New York to find that someone had arranged a press conference for us at the air terminal – hardly what we needed at that point. I flew on to Washington that night, and the next day talked with Senator McGovern's staff, Richard Dudman, Murray Marder and Paul Warnke. A two-minute interview with Marvin Kalb over CBS television taught me how difficult it is to discuss anything so complicated as negotiating postures in simple terms within so little time. I felt that I had done poorly and reproached myself for not having been better prepared.

When I returned to Ithaca, in addition to trying to catch up on my course work, I also returned to the dismal task of finding university presidents willing to go to Vietnam. Having struck out completely in my earlier effort, I had realized that one important impediment might well have been the timing of the invitations, and concluded that if they could be made for the inter-session period that began in December it might be easier for them to make the trip. Accordingly, after I had arrived in Hanoi alone on 23 September, I discussed my initial failure with the appropriate officials. They seemed at least partially to understand this problem of scheduling and indicated it would be worth trying to make a second effort later, one wherein I could assure interested university or college presidents that they would be given every bit as much access as I was now being promised. Approximately a month later, on 27 October, when I made the hectic one-day visit to Paris with a small group to discuss negotiation postures with the Hanoi and PRG (NLF) embassies, the North Vietnamese ambassador took me aside to tell me that Hanoi had given a green light for receiving a group of four academic presidents for November or early December. He asked me to keep in touch with him since he had direct communication with Hanoi.

And so, soon after my return to Cornell I began to repeat my efforts of September, returning to those who had seemed most sincerely interested then (including Robert Goheen and Andrew Cordier, respectively, recently retired presidents of Princeton and Columbia) and added a good many more candidate institutions where Cornell's President Dale Corson or others indicated to me prospects might be relatively good – among them Amherst, Earlham, Haverford, Indiana, Johns Hopkins, University of California at

Santa Cruz, Mt Holyoke, Notre Dame, Pennsylvania and Washington University (Saint Louis). I think that Andrew Cordier, the recently retired president of Columbia, who, I knew, had been ill earlier would have responded positively this time around had his physician not overruled him. At Notre Dame I was unable to get beyond Theodore Hesburgh's secretary who admonished that he was already planning to make a trip to Latin America, could not possibly make two trips, and that it would be up to his conscience as to which he made. (If she actually told him of the Vietnam option, he clearly decided against it.) As for the others, it was pretty much the same depressing pattern as in the first round. Undoubtedly during this second round the likelihood of acceptance on the part of all of those invited was even further diminished by Senator Edward Kennedy's unsuccessful effort to get clearance from the Nixon administration for his effort to send four doctors to North Vietnam. And so, there were no takers, except for the doughty ex-President of Columbia, Andrew Cordier, and a friend of mine, John Whitmore, a former Cornell graduate with a good command of the Vietnamese language and now an assistant professor of history at Michigan who had agreed to accompany him. Unfortunately after many messages and confirmation from Hanoi via Paris, Cordier ran into opposition from his physician and so he, along with Whitmore, was obliged to cancel the trip, though Whitmore was later able to go there alone.

Having won by an overwhelming majority in the presidential election of 7 November 1972, Nixon appeared to have no reservations in completely undoing the progress made in the Paris negotiations. Taking over all the more-than-sixty changes – some minor, but some of fundamental importance – that Thieu had asked for, he now charged the ever-obedient Kissinger to double cross himself as well as Hanoi and confront the Vietnamese with these new demands. Kissinger complied. Hanoi and the PRG were furious and countered with new demands of their own. Nixon then, apparently following Kissinger's advocacy,[4] decided to escalate heavily the ongoing bombing campaign against North Vietnam, seemingly confident this would break its will and bring it into compliance with his new set of demands. On 18 December he authorized bombing attacks by some 200 B-52s focused on Hanoi and its port of Haiphong, the two largest urban areas in the North. Extending over twelve days, this unprecedentedly heavy "Christmas Bombing" caused enormous destruction and loss of civilian lives. The loss of American planes and pilots was also extensive, the US Strategic Air Command indicating its concern over the large numbers of its B-52s shot down – from its point of view, planes intended for use against the Soviet Union in the event of hostilities, and not to be squandered in Vietnam.[5]

Nixon and Kissinger badly misjudged the reactions of both the American public and Hanoi. The brutality of the Christmas bombing outraged many Americans and members of Congress. Only two months after his massive majority in the presidential election, Nixon now found his approval rating in the polls had dropped to 39 per cent and numerous congressmen who had previously given him at least tacit support on Vietnam policy now joined with those who opposed it, with the probability that when Congress reassembled after the Christmas recess it would introduce legislation likely to cripple his efforts to further shore up Thieu's government.

As for the North Vietnamese, they refused to yield in the face of the punishing bombardment to which Nixon and Kissinger subjected them. When Nixon offered to stop the bombing if negotiations could resume they accepted, but when discussions again got under way in Paris in early January 1973, they refused to accept any change of substance and insisted on adherence to all the main points that had been agreed upon in October, limiting Kissinger's efforts to save face to only a few inconsequential cosmetic changes – balanced by a few of their own.[6] And in a specious effort to ensure Hanoi's implementation of the agreement that was finally signed on 27 January, Nixon felt obliged to send Prime Minister Pham Van Dong a secret letter on 1 February, indicating that the United States would fulfill Article 21 of the agreement calling for the US to "contribute to healing the wounds of war and to postwar reconstruction" with a grant of aid over five years of $3.25 billion with the possible addition of $1–1.5 billion in food and commodity assistance.[7] He presumably calculated that this rather vaguely worded promise would ensure that the boat would not be rocked during the sixty-day period during which Hanoi was required to release all American POW's. It is remarkable that after all their dealings with Nixon, Hanoi's officials would have been naive enough to believe that Nixon would actually deliver on this undertaking.

It must, I think, be observed that not only could Nixon have gotten the same terms in October 1972 that he secured in the Paris Agreement of 27 January 1973, but that he could have done so at the beginning of his administration in 1969 – without the loss of additional thousands of American and scores of thousands of Vietnamese lives. Others, of course, have reached the same conclusion. Based upon a careful study of the negotiating positions of Hanoi and the PRG (NLF) during the Nixon administrations and before, involving unusual access to the views of Hanoi and the PRG (NLF), I feel justified in strongly endorsing this conclusion.

13 Cambodian neutrality and the United States

Of all the countries of Southeast Asia, it seems to me Cambodia stands out as the one where the involvement of the United States has been most obscured from the American public. But that involvement has been extensive, critical to the shaping of its political history, and has had a deep effect on its present character. No doubt the obscuring of this deplorable record has in part been a consequence of its having been so heavily overshadowed by the attention deservedly focused on the glaring brutality of the Pol Pot regime. But the record of American involvement must be laid bare if one is to understand events in Cambodia leading up to and following its invasion by American troops on 30 April 1970.

As he launched his invasion, Nixon assured the American public that "American policy since the 1954 Geneva Agreements" had been "to scrupulously respect the neutrality of Cambodia." Nearly a decade later Kissinger brazenly asserted in his autobiography that with respect to the coup that removed Sihanouk from power, and thereby opened the way for the invasion, "We neither encouraged Sihanouk's overthrow nor knew about it in advance."[1] Neither statement can be realistically assessed without knowledge of the background of US involvement in Cambodia.

Son Ngoc Thanh and the Khmer Serei

Most accounts of American–Cambodian relations have either ignored or greatly underrated the importance of two Cambodian names. These names, "Son Ngoc Thanh" and "Khmer Serei," I first encountered on a brief trip to Cambodia at the end of January 1961, but I didn't become aware of their importance until a later visit to the country in August 1967. At that time much of Cambodia seemed like an oasis of calm compared with the battles that were then raging in neighboring Vietnam. On 9 August 1967 I had the opportunity to make a trip from Phnom Penh, where we were staying, to a Cambodian–Vietnamese border area (Figure 13.1), in the company of Paul B. Johnson of the American Friends Service Committee, to inspect the sites of two very recent cross-border incursions by armed units from South Vietnam that had penetrated a few kilometers into Cambodia's Svay Rieng province.

Map 6   Cambodia in Indochina

Source: (Smith, *Cambodia's Foreign Policy* (1965), Ithaca NY: Cornell University Press, frontispiece)

Figure 13.1   On Cambodian–Vietnamese border, 9 August 1967

There was clearly evident some physical destruction (houses and a temple) with casualties reported on both sides. Assuming that both attacks had been made by troops of the South Vietnamese army, I was surprised to hear, through our interpreter, that the Cambodian soldiers who were accompanying us were discussing whether one of the attacking units might have been the Khmer Serei. This kindled my interest in this organization, and upon my return to Phnom Penh I devoted most of my time to learning more about it from various foreign embassies, from the UN's De Ribbing Mission (mandated by the United Nations to help resolve border disputes between Cambodia and Thailand and restore diplomatic relations between them),[2] and from members of the International Control Commission (ICC) for Cambodia.[3]

There was a striking common denominator of agreement among these sources. They all saw the Khmer Serei as an instrument of American policy, working in harmony with Thailand and South Vietnam, either to unseat Sihanouk or at least push him away from his neutralist course and align his international posture to conform more closely with that of the United States. They all saw this policy as running counter to a substantial tide of Cambodian nationalism with which, in the public eye, Sihanouk had become closely identified. In short, this external pressure on Sihanouk, most clearly manifest to the public in the destructive cross-border incursions of the Khmer Serei, was counterproductive to the objectives of the United

States and its two Southeast Asian allies. Within Cambodia there was widespread outrage at the suffering inflicted by the Khmer Serei's depredations that resulted in further legitimizing Sihanouk's leadership and strengthening his domestic political position.

Thus, much of the international community, including the ICC and Western embassies, were then opposed to the drift of US policy in supporting this anti-Sihanouk force under its leader, Son Ngoc Thanh. In view of the fact that the Australian embassy had been charged with representing American interests following the break in Cambodian–American diplomatic relations two years earlier, some of the views expressed by the Australian ambassador, Noel Deschamps, are particularly significant.[4] He vouchsafed that most of the Khmer Serei had been recruited from the Khmer Krom in southern Vietnam "ostensibly" to fight against the Vietcong, but had then been transported by air or ship to Thailand where they became the major components of the Khmer Serei, with a considerably smaller number having been recruited from the Cambodian minority in eastern Thailand (Surin Province). In view of US allegations that Sihanouk had been unwilling to effectively contest alleged Vietnamese Communist penetration of Cambodia's eastern frontier, the ambassador was keenly incensed that of the Cambodian army's 17,500 actual combat troops (out of an overall total of at the most 35,000 men in the entire army) half were deployed along the Thai border in an attempt to block Khmer Serei incursions there. He asserted that the cross-border activities of Son Ngoc Thanh's Khmer Serei had over the previous two years considerably surpassed the earlier penetrations from South Vietnam.[5]

When M.K.L. Bindra, head of the ICC, invited me to look at the map in his "incident room" upon which each cross-border penetration of a military unit into Cambodia was indicated by a pin, I was astonished by the size of the cluster of bees depicted by the pins inside Cambodia's frontier with Thailand. There appeared to be at least three times as many as inside the frontier with South Vietnam. Both the ICC and the De Ribbing mission had concluded that, however extensive the role of the CIA in backing the Khmer Serei, it was now the US military that was playing the major role in supporting Khmer Serei actions across the frontier with South Vietnam. According to the ICC, these recent crossings from South Vietnam had been "undertaken on the responsibility of junior [American] officers below the rank of colonel," while the De Ribbing mission was explicit in charging that "the US army in Saigon supports these Khmer Serei operations into Cambodia," and endorsed reports that they were encadred by US special forces.[6]

After that first encounter I began to look more deeply into the history of the Khmer Serei which by 1967 had become such an instrument of US policy, and over the years I have had the opportunity to burrow in relevant American and British archives for further material. In the following pages, I have done my best to trace the roles of Son Ngoc Thanh and his Khmer

Serei in US policy towards Cambodia in the period from the Eisenhower administration through that of Nixon, and especially in the coup that removed Prince Norodom Sihanouk from power in early 1970 and paved the way for Nixon's reckless invasion of Cambodia at the end of April of that year, and its catastrophic consequences.

For approximately eight years after the end of World War II Son Ngoc Thanh was Cambodia's most popular nationalist leader, a fame that Cambodia's young king, Norodom Sihanouk, did not suffer gladly. Their rivalry became a major theme in Cambodia's internal politics, one that was encouraged and manipulated by the US with varying degrees of salience until Pol Pot and the Khmer Rouge seized Phnom Penh in 1975.

Born in 1908, Son Ngoc Thanh was a Khmer Krom (southern, or down-river, Khmer) from Tra-Vinh province in Vietnam's Mekong Delta, where there then lived close to a million ethnic Cambodians whose origin went back to the period when this area was part of the Cambodian kingdom. Thanks to his wealthy ethnically Cambodian father and Sino-Vietnamese mother, he acquired a French education, culminating with law school in Paris. Returning to Indochina in 1933, he worked for an initial year in the secretariat of the French colonial administration of Cochin China and tried unsuccessfully to enter the colonial civil service. While in Saigon he is reported to have become friendly with a small group of young liberally inclined minor French officials who helped him find employment in the National Library in Phnom Penh. There he worked closely with the strongly nationalistic Buddhist Institute of Cambodia, in the process becoming influential with the Buddhist clergy and emerging as secretary of the institute in 1935. He helped found, and claims to have become director of what, with a circulation of 5,000, was probably the most influential Cambodian nationalist weekly, the journal *Nagaravattaj*.

His initially cautious but increasingly assertive anti-French nationalism apparently found considerable support among the clergy and numerous civil servants. His close ties to an influential, strongly nationalist Buddhist monk whose incarceration sparked a large anti-French "monks' demonstration" on 20 July 1942, resulted in a French directive for Son Ngoc Thanh's arrest. Before this could be put into effect, he fled Phnom Penh and ultimately found refuge with Japanese officials in Bangkok, who agreed to send him to Japan, where he remained for almost three years.[7]

Several months before Son Ngoc Thanh's escape, the French administration in Cambodia had chosen a successor to the recently deceased Cambodian king, Sisowath Monivong. In doing so, they passed over more senior and experienced eligible members of the royal families and selected Norodom Sihanouk, whom they thought to be an unassertive and tractable 18-year-old boy from the Norodom, rather than Sisowath royal branch. Here it must be remembered that France in annexing Cambodia had maintained its monarchy, an institution they left shorn of all real power, but for decades manipulated as a legitimizing symbol, behind which, until Japan's World War II occupation of the country, French authority was near absolute.

Until the final months of World War II the pro-Vichy French colonial administration in Indochina collaborated with Japan. Japanese troops were permitted to transit Cambodia into Thailand on their way to Malaya and Burma, but only a small number were actually stationed in Cambodia, beginning in late May 1941. The exercise of Japanese authority remained limited and generally yielded place to that of the French colonial administration until March 1945, when, in a sudden coup, simultaneously executed in Laos and Vietnam, the Japanese ousted French officials and took over full control.

Son Ngoc Thanh remained in Japan until after its government ended its entente with the French in March 1945 and ordered King Sihanouk to declare Cambodia's independence. In returning Son Ngoc Thanh to Cambodia in May, the Japanese were clearly hoping to take advantage of his anti-French nationalism. They initially had Sihanouk, who apparently himself also perceived Thanh as useful in securing support from the Buddhist clergy, appoint him foreign minister in the new Cambodian government that they sponsored, and ultimately prime minister on 13 August, in the final days of their control.

Apart from its anti-French stance, Son Ngoc Thanh's program at the time was apparently not radical and, according to David Chandler, "involved supporting the king, the royal family, and the [Buddhist] monastic order."[8] From the standpoint of the anti-Vichy pro-Gaullist French who arrived two months after the end of the war, Son Ngoc Thanh's major error was probably to seek diplomatic recognition not only from Thailand (which during the war, with Japan's support, had annexed most of Cambodia's north-western provinces of Battambang and Siem Reap) but also Ho Chi Minh's newly established Vietminh government. On 15 October 1945, France's General Leclerc, backed by a contingent of British/Indian troops from General Douglas Gracey's recently installed command in Saigon, flew to Phnom Penh, seized Prime Minister Son Ngoc Thanh and deposited him in a Saigon jail.

Many of Thanh's followers then joined the major anti-French maquis, the Khmer Issarak (Independent Cambodia) movement. Among that Thai-supported and somewhat splintered group probably the most important commander was Dap Chhuon, a man of some charisma who was reported to lead more than a thousand troops. Dap Chhuon's major base was in Cambodia's Siem Reap province, which Thailand returned, together with Battambang, to French-controlled Cambodia in 1946.

Though they sentenced Son Ngoc Thanh to twenty years in prison, the French soon discovered that he was such a redoubtable nationalist symbol that in 1947 they found it wise to get him out of Indochina and sent him into exile in France under the rubric of "administrative detention."[9] Four years later, in late October 1951, just a month after Cambodian elections in which the strongly pro-Son Ngoc Thanh Democratic Party had again emerged as by far the strongest party, the French, at Sihanouk's urging, permitted Thanh to return to Phnom Penh to a popular welcome so tumultuous that the French dared not interfere. Sihanouk, who had urged the French to permit Thanh to return, may have expected that this gesture would, as Michael Leifer believes, "conciliate opponents of the throne."[10] Or, as David Chandler suggests, he may have expected that Thanh's popularity could be exploited "to lever concessions from the French," and that his presence would split what had emerged as the country's largest political organization, the strongly nationalist Democratic Party,[11] or at least moderate its increasingly anti-royalist orientation.

Whatever his calculations, both he and the French soon realized their error, for Song Ngoc Thanh, buoyed by the strength of his evident popular support, almost immediately manifested as strong an anti-French nationalism as he had shown before his arrest and exile. He publicly called for full independence, asserting that this was not possible with the continuing presence of French troops, and in January 1952 he established a newspaper that was forthright in hewing to this line. His position clearly contrasted with the relatively weak gradualist and accommodationist nationalist goals pursued by Sihanouk in dealing with French authority. By early March 1952 Son Ngoc Thanh's clearly successful efforts to arouse public opinion had exceeded the limits of French tolerance. They shut down his paper, and he fled Phnom Penh with a small group of supporters to join a group of Khmer Issarak operating in Siem Reap province near the Thai frontier. There he broadcast by radio that he was leading the resistance against French rule, and his call now had a pro-republican and moderately anti-royalist character.

As Michael Leifer has observed, Thanh's flight "increased the differences between the King and all those who desired genuine independence." It had made Sihanouk "uncomfortably aware that the people had come to view his gradualist approach to the question of independence as a sacrifice of national rights."[12] Sihanouk now moved rapidly to align himself with the strong current of anti-French nationalism. His hand was considerably strengthened by the over-extension of French troops in Cambodia, who were assigned not primarily to fight the Khmer Issarak but to contain the operations of augmented numbers of Vietminh troops there. (Indeed, it had been the calculated strategy of General Giap to challenge French forces in Cambodia in order to draw them away from Vietnam.) By mid-1952 the French realized that if they were to have much chance of prevailing in Vietnam, a far more important place for them than the other two Indochina states, they would have to draw back most of the troops that had become tied down in the much less crucial Cambodian operation. Sihanouk was astute enough to realize that, with their forces already well-overextended in fighting the Vietminh in both Vietnam and Laos, the French could ill afford to keep sufficient troops in his country to maintain control if he were to rally Cambodian royalist nationalists to join the Khmer Issarak in a common effort against the French occupation. And thus, to insure a more friendly Cambodia on their western flank in Vietnam, the French were increasingly obliged to appease Sihanouk in his newly charged nationalist aspirations.

Holding this strong card and now more fully awakened to the power of Cambodian nationalism, Sihanouk soon took an increasingly confrontational position with the French. But initially he enlisted their help in what Chandler terms "a pincer movement against the Democrats,"[13] the dominant strongly pro-Son Ngoc Thanh political party some of whose leaders had a year earlier formed the cabinet. The speedy dispatch of substantial French troop reinforcements to Phnom Penh enabled Sihanouk to defy parliament and stage a coup ending its power and that of its cabinet. With French troops surrounding the parliament building, he was able to take over as prime minister and appoint a non-Democrat cabinet. Chandler suggests that "The French probably thought that after they had helped him sweep the Democrats aside, he would abide by their glacial timetable for relinquishing control."[14] But no sooner had he seized power than he broadcast a message committing himself to the achievement of independence within three years. However skeptical the French may have been, he meant to fulfill this commitment, and he was to succeed.

Seven months later, in February of 1953, Sihanouk embarked on what he later termed his "Royal Crusade" to attain this goal of independence. He was helped by the increasingly desperate straits in which France found herself in Vietnam, but as he later bitterly recalled, he received no encouragement from the United States. American policy was still firmly behind the French in Indochina, and sought to do what it could to ensure that the Vietminh would not overcome them. When Sihanouk arrived in Washington in April, Secretary of State John Foster Dulles disappointed and antagonized him by insisting that the defeat of the Vietminh took precedence over Cambodian independence. Only after "the menace of Communism is dispelled in your country," Dulles advised him, would the United States undertake "to induce France to recognize your complete and total independence and sovereignty." Differences with France, Dulles lectured, would "only serve the cause of our common enemy."[15] Altogether Sihanouk's 1953 visit to the United States was not a happy one, and Chandler observes that during it his "dislike of the Americans hardened into a conviction that the United States and its policies were inimical to him."[16]

Despite the lack of support from foreign states, including Thailand, Sihanouk steadfastly persevered with his crusade and, benefiting from the Vietminh's mounting successes against France, finally, beginning in August 1953, secured a series of concessions from the war-weary French, culminating in full independence that November.

In the spring of 1954 Sihanouk's alienation from the United States was reinforced when Washington turned down his request for military assistance to halt the invasion of several regular Vietminh battalions into northeastern Cambodia. They appeared to signal a dangerous augmentation of the Vietminh-supported and encadred anti-French maquis operating from bases in the Cardoman mountains to the west of Phnom Penh. Probably this brief invasion, which began in early April, was a tactical move by the Vietminh to divert the possibility that French reinforcements from Cambodia would attempt to relieve the siege of the French garrison at Dienbienphu, now in its final stage. But its purpose might also have been, as Michael Leifer suggests, to widen the territorial base of pro-Vietminh guerrillas in Cambodia so as to strengthen their case in the upcoming Indochina sessions of the Geneva Conference which were to begin in May 1954.[17]

Sihanouk, however, had little reason to be critical of the agreements arrived at when that conference concluded on 20 July. Not only did it ratify his country's full independence and sovereign control over the whole of its territory, but, consistent with this, all foreign troops in Cambodia (Vietminh – of which there were two divisions – as well as French) were obliged to leave the country within ninety days, and they all did so. Moreover, the Vietnamese "volunteers" that had joined the Vietnamese-supported Khmer People's Revolutionary Party were subject to the same deadline for departure, and that group had been permitted no standing in the conference and had no voice there. The departure of the Vietnamese left the Cambodian majority of that Communist-oriented maquis considerably weaker, with further defections occurring following the achievement of full independence. That goal now attained, there were also massive defections from the considerably larger Khmer Issarak. Additionally at Geneva, Cambodia – in contrast to Laos and Vietnam – was granted the right to enter into alliances with other states and secure the foreign military supplies necessary to maintain her security.

But there was one part of the Geneva Accords that Sihanouk was not anxious to implement. This was the stipulation – roughly similar to the Geneva provisions for Vietnam and Laos – that *all* Cambodian citizens, including those who had been in insurgency against French rule, would be guaranteed the right to rejoin the national community and participate as voters or candidates in elections scheduled for 1955.[18] Leifer observes that for Sihanouk,

> the prospect of elections, in which Issaraks and their allies in the Democratic Party could participate without restraint, foreshadowed a return to the earlier situation [where in the elections of 1947 and 1951 the Democratic Party had won more than two-thirds of the seats in the National Assembly], but with the likely differences that the Assembly would prove more vigorous and that the throne would rule less and reign more. The King's attitude to Son Ngoc Thanh [still highly regarded by most members of the Democratic Party] indicated his

apprehension, [and he] was absolutely determined not to permit Thanh or his close supporters any role in Cambodian politics.

He refused his old rival's efforts to meet with him, and he had Thanh publicly denounced as a traitor and "one who had sought to obstruct the efforts to achieve independence."[19] Once again Son Ngoc Thanh was forced into exile, returning now to one of the few remaining Khmer Issarak bases in northwest Cambodia's Siem Reap province.

Even in Thanh's absence the Democratic Party, with its solid nationalist credentials – won for its early calls for opposition to French rule and full independence – long preceding Sihanouk's espousal of those goals, was by far the most widely supported party and was expected to win easily the national elections in 1955 prescribed in the Geneva accords. But Sihanouk, with the parties he had sponsored having done so poorly in the 1951 election, was determined not to let this happen. To free himself of existing restraints, constitutional and otherwise, he suddenly abdicated as king in March 1955, turning over the crown to his supportive and tractable father. And now as Prince Sihanouk, he prepared for a no-holds-barred contest with the Democrats and smaller opposition parties. Still heading the executive arm of government, he ordered a repression of these groups that was sometimes very brutal and in most cases thoroughly intimidating.

Chandler notes that independent newspapers were closed down, their editors imprisoned and "[d]uring the campaign, security forces intimidated candidates, beat up campaign workers, tore down posters, broke up meetings, and threatened Democrats and their supporters," with "nearly all the Democratic candidates, fearing for their lives," and taking refuge in Phnom Penh. As if that were not sufficient to assure victory in the election, Sihanouk had the most effective campaigner of the Democratic Party kidnapped and held in prison until after the election was over.[20] In view of all this, plus the destruction of a number of ballot boxes, it was only surprising that Sihanouk's party won no more than 83 per cent of the vote, capturing every seat in the National Assembly. "Having thus eliminated the Democratic opposition," Lancaster observed, "Norodom Sihanouk himself assumed the office of Prime Minister on 26 September."[21]

In view of these events, it was understandable that some of Sihanouk's opponents, whom he was now unable or unwilling to co-opt into his newly elected government, would flee to the old Khmer Issarak base in northwest Cambodia to which Son Ngoc Thanh had repaired. Whereas the raison d'être of the Khmer Issarak had been opposition to French rule, with only a relatively modest anti-royalist attitude on the part of a minority of its members, the inclination of those who now gravitated to Son Ngoc Thanh's leadership was not only strongly anti-Sihanouk but, for most, anti-royalist in general. Badly beleaguered militarily, they needed outside support, and it was natural that they should seek and receive it from Thailand – just across the border from their major redoubts in northwest Cambodia and the country that had provided some backing to the Khmer Issarak during its struggle against the French.

Given the realities of the international context in which Cambodia was obliged to live in 1955, it seems likely that if Son Ngoc Thanh had then headed Cambodia's government he might well have espoused much the same neutralist nonaligned foreign policy that Sihanouk was soon realistic enough to embrace. But whatever his inclination might have been, in the precarious existence he and his followers now faced, their dependence for military and other supplies on Thailand, an anti-neutralist state that had aligned itself firmly with the United States, made such a stance unlikely.

Launched in 1958, the Khmer Serei (Free Cambodians), headed by Son Ngoc Thanh, was an armed Cambodian political movement recruited primarily from the Cambodian minorities in South Vietnam's Mekong Delta and Thailand's Surin province. With its objective the overthrow of Sihanouk or, failing that, pressuring him from his neutralist stance and into alignment with American policy in Southeast Asia, it was covertly supported by South Vietnam, Thailand, the CIA, and ultimately the US Department of Defense as well. Though American efforts were initially largely counterproductive, they played a crucial role in the coup that ousted Sihanouk in 1970 and contributed significantly to shoring up the disastrous successor US-supported Lon Nol regime until it was overthrown five years later.

Sihanouk and the Eisenhower administration

When Cambodia first gained its independence, Sihanouk, fearing the potential of Chinese power (and secondarily that of Hanoi), was initially disposed to look to the United States for protection, despite its earlier lack of support. But against the backdrop of the delicate and often precarious negotiations of the mid-1954 Geneva Conference that finally concluded the eight year Franco–Vietminh war, any direct American commitment of support to Cambodia's protection was hardly realistic, and his hopes were disappointed. And during the latter stages of the Geneva Conference when the US-sponsored, fundamentally anti-Communist, collective defense treaty that was soon to emerge as the Southeast Asia Treaty Organization (SEATO) was in gestation, Sihanouk was realistic enough to understand – at least after admonitions from Anthony Eden (co-chairman) and Bedell Smith (the US representative) – that if Cambodia were to become a member of SEATO it would be difficult to expect Beijing to support his country's fundamental objectives at the conference (the right to enter into alliances that conformed with the UN Charter, obtain the foreign aid necessary for her security, and evacuation from Cambodia of all Vietminh troops). Thus, he was satisfied to have Cambodia remain outside official membership of SEATO, while being given a measure of protection against Communist aggression, by accepting coverage of the treaty's protocol. This passive protocol status, designed by Secretary of State John Foster Dulles, for

Cambodia (along with Laos and that part of Vietnam south of the 17th parallel) did not require actual membership in SEATO, with the obligations involved. It was seemingly at least a more moderate stance which, as was hoped, did not appear to upset the Chinese unduly.[22]

Sihanouk, and other Cambodians, could hardly miss the fact that the central reason for SEATO's establishment was to protect the separate anti-Communist state that the United States was endeavoring to build up in the southern half of Vietnam as French military forces evacuated it. With Vietnam his country's traditional enemy and the part of it that bordered on his own country being shaped into a bastion of American power, it is understandable that Sihanouk would soon conclude that Cambodia's security depended on its getting along not only with North Vietnam, but even more importantly with both the United States and China. And that meant refraining from a close dependency on either of these major powers. That realization was the genesis of his opting for the neutralist, nonaligned foreign policy that soon became the hallmark of his stewardship.

For that orientation to become firm, however, it was necessary for Sihanouk's initially acute fear of Chinese power to be significantly diminished. And that was achieved at the Bandung (Asian–African) Conference held during the second half of April 1955. There, China's astute prime minister, Zhou Enlai, succeeded in allaying much of Sihanouk's concern.[23] A year before, during the Geneva Conference, Zhou had made clear his adamant opposition to any possibility of the United States establishing bases in Cambodia, and presumably he still was worried about this prospect. In any case, at Bandung he made a special effort to reassure Sihanouk of China's peaceful intentions. (This was clearly evident in the restricted, unpublished verbatim record of the conference which I was permitted to read overnight at its close.) The amount of time and effort Zhou devoted to Sihanouk relative to delegates from other small countries was striking. At Nehru's urging, and with him as witness, Zhou joined in a private meeting with the delegates of Cambodia, Laos and North Vietnam, where he and North Vietnam's prime minister, Pham Van Dong, assured Cambodia and Laos of noninterference in their affairs. And in the plenary session the next day, in positing China's adherence to the principle of noninterference or nonintervention in the internal affairs of other states, Zhou cited as examples Cambodia and Laos. He stated that, with respect to these two countries, he wished to repeat the assurances he had given to Nehru and Burma's U Nu between the sessions of the Geneva Conference.

Undoubtedly even more important to Sihanouk was the special luncheon at which he was Zhou's sole guest. The presumption at the conference was that at this luncheon Zhou and Sihanouk reassured each other as to their countries' intentions. Afterwards Sihanouk stated, citing India's Five Principles of Co-Existence (among which were "nonaggression and noninterference in each other's internal affairs"): "He personally assured me that

China will always faithfully adhere to the Five Principles in its relations with Cambodia and have a friendly feeling toward my country."

Although Sihanouk's firm espousal of a neutralist, nonaligned foreign policy was agreeable to the People's Republic of China (PRC), it clearly was not to the Eisenhower administration. Washington's distrust of Sihanouk grew after his visit to Manila in early February 1956 where he rebuffed what was presumed to be an American-backed effort by the Philippines to persuade Cambodia to join SEATO. This was followed ten days later by a public statement in Beijing in which Sihanouk rejected the protection extended to his country under that treaty's protocol, and then accepted a $22.4 million aid grant from China, which from his neutralist perspective could be regarded as a token offset to the more substantial American assistance Cambodia was already receiving.[24]

The reaction of the United States' two allies, Thailand and South Vietnam, was almost immediate, and Sihanouk returned from China at the end of February to find that these two neighboring states had closed their frontier with Cambodia. This lasted for seven weeks, during which Cambodia's only avenues of trade with the rest of the world were cut off. (This was before the port of Sihanoukville had been established and was undoubtedly a spur to its rapid completion.) Additionally, Sihanouk alleged that Son Ngoc Thanh was mounting armed raids from Thailand into Cambodia. Whether these measures were calculated to coerce Cambodia to join SEATO, as Sihanouk alleged, or were meant simply to weaken his government, they did not dissuade him from adhering to a nonaligned, neutralist international stance. A few months later he visited and established diplomatic relations with the Soviet Union, Poland and Czechoslovakia, with all three countries extending Cambodia modest amounts of economic assistance.[25]

Here one must recall the Eisenhower administration's adamant opposition to neutralism. In the Manichaean Cold War view of its leaders, any state's adoption of such a posture could only weaken the international position of the United States, to the certain benefit of the Communist powers. As David Chandler observes: "One effect of Sihanouk's choice of neutralism was to encourage U.S. special services, including the Central Intelligence Agency (CIA), to support any anti-Communist Khmers they could find."[26]

By far the most important of such groups was the Khmer Serei (Free Cambodians), established in 1958 under the leadership of Son Ngoc Thanh. Essentially an outgrowth of the old Khmer Issarak, and with much of its original membership having served in that organization, the Khmer Serei was from the outset avowedly anti-Sihanouk and dedicated to the displacement of his government.[27] This being so, and with the Khmer Serei significantly dependent on support from Washington's firmly aligned and strongly anti-Communist ally, Thailand, it was probably inevitable that the Eisenhower administration would wish to support it and its principal leader,

Son Ngoc Thanh. It is not clear when American agents first made contact with them, but from the outset support could easily be supplied through Thailand and Ngo Dinh Diem's newly emerged South Vietnamese state. Both of their governments fully shared Washington's antipathy towards Sihanouk and his neutralist policy and on their own were already disposed to support the Khmer Serei. Increasingly Sihanouk came to regard these two American-aligned states as acting not only in accord with, but on behalf of, American opposition to his regime – especially South Vietnam, which from the outset he recognized as absolutely dependent upon American power.

Sihanouk's perception of South Vietnamese–American solidarity could only have been enhanced when in June 1958 a battalion of South Vietnam's army crossed the frontier, briefly occupied a village, and before retiring moved border markers several kilometers deeper inside Cambodia.[28] His appeal to Washington for intervention on Cambodia's behalf elicited only its counsel for moderation and the admonition by its ambassador, Carl Strom, that US military aid might be suspended if the Cambodian army used US-supplied equipment to engage a friendly power (i.e. South Vietnamese forces).[29] In view of the fact that more than a quarter of Cambodia's budget was dependent upon American financial assistance, with this covering roughly five-eighths of military expenditures,[30] this was a serious threat.

Strom's response and the hostility of South Vietnam and Thailand led Sihanouk "to conclude that Cambodia required the concrete support of other powers," and within less than a month, on 13 July 1958, he initiated diplomatic relations with China.[31] That move surprised and further antagonized Washington and resulted in Strom's recall for consultation. There he was reported to have learned that "a threat of aid suspension was being considered as a first step towards removing Sihanouk from power." Strom, however, "was said to have argued convincingly that this tactic, which had recently been employed successfully against Premier Souvanna Phouma [another leader wed to a neutralist policy] in Laos, would fail in Cambodia."[32]

Britain and the United States had strikingly different attitudes towards neutralism in the area. In the British view, a neutralist foreign policy seemed entirely appropriate for Cambodia, as well as for Laos. Nor did London manifest the rancor towards Cambodia that senior Eisenhower administration officials nourished. Thus, the very first paragraph of the "Annual Review of Events for 1958" prepared by the British ambassador in Phnom Penh for the foreign secretary read: "The two lessons drawn from the year seemed to be, first, that if Cambodia were to enjoy internal stability Prince Sihanouk would have to remain permanently in power and, second, that as long as he did so, the course of foreign policy, though occasionally erratic, would be maintained in the general direction of independence and neutrality."[33]

Washington's perception was rather different, and as Chandler observes, Cambodia's establishment of diplomatic relations with China "encouraged U.S. intelligence services to seek alternatives to the prince."[34] This effort was evidently reflected in early 1959 with the Dap Chhuon Affair, an event that appears to have fully crystallized Sihanouk's conviction that the United States was bent on ousting him.

Siem Reap province in northwest Cambodia fronted on Thailand's Surin province, the part of that country with the largest ethnic Cambodian minority. In 1958–9, probably a majority of the Khmer Serei were based in the northern frontier areas of Siem Reap, close enough to the border to have access to some logistical support from Thailand, and to find sanctuary there if hard-pressed by Sihanouk's forces. At this time the governor and military commander of Siem Reap was Dap Chhuon, once a major Khmer Issarak commander but a man Sihanouk thought he could trust. Though Dap Chhuon's troops had been formally integrated into Cambodia's national army he maintained full control over them, and in the words of a contemporary official of the US embassy in Phnom Penh, ruled Siem Reap "as a more or less private fief."[35] Presumably unknown to Sihanouk, Dap Chhuon had maintained cordial relations with Thai authorities, and, according to Chandler, "his outspoken anticommunism had also drawn favorable comment from Saigon, where Ngo Dinh Diem suggested to an American visitor [in August 1958] that it might be feasible to conduct joint operations against Communist insurgents along the border using Chhuon's forces." The State Department regarded Chhuon as representing a "pro-U.S., anti-Communist element" but backed away from the proposal.[36]

Whether or not President Eisenhower himself was interested in Sihanouk's removal, on 2 January 1959, he was given an intelligence summary signed by his son, John S.D. Eisenhower, which read: "Dap Chuon, a powerful anti-Communist warlord, is seeking U.S. support to overthrow Sihanouk. His plan would involve support from Thailand and South Vietnam. Like other conservative Cambodians, Chuon is alarmed by growing Communust influence."[37] By this time, according to Chandler, "Chhuon's plans to remove Siem Reap from Cambodia ... were well advanced," with his "long -term goal being to destabilize Sihanouk's regime."[38]

Against the backdrop of the US intervention on behalf of anti-Sukarno regional rebellions in Indonesia that was at this time winding down, John Prados notes that in 1958–9

> the Americans attempted to forge a direct relationship with a Cambodian army regional commander named Dap Chhuon. It was hoped that, in a reincarnation of the strategy that had failed in Indonesia, the Cambodian general would mount a coup to overthrow Sihanouk, or, failing that, form a separatist regime, which the United States could recognize and assist.[39]

On the basis of what Secretary of State Dulles' confidant and appointee during these years as liaison between State and the CIA, Hugh S. Cumming, later told me, it seem possible that Prados's assessment was correct. For in discussions I had with him in the mid-1970s, Cumming informed me that the Eisenhower administration had regarded the formula it applied to Indonesia in 1957–8 as applicable elsewhere in Southeast Asia as well.[40] He did not stipulate which these other Southeast Asian country or countries were, but the neutralist nonaligned stance of Sukarno that so infuriated the Eisenhower administration was most closely approximated by Sihanouk in Cambodia and Souvanna Phouma in Laos. Although the administration's heavy-handed intervention in Laos and resultant displacement of Souvanna Phouma are reasonably well known,[41] the more indirect effort mounted by South Vietnam and Thailand – against Sihanouk has been much better veiled.

Because of the apparent general parallel in the Eisenhower administration's approach to Indonesia and Cambodia at this time, it should be helpful in understanding the Cambodian case to note briefly the nature of the Indonesian experience. Informing the approach of Eisenhower and John Foster Dulles to Indonesia was their reading of the causes for the failure of American policy towards China in the late 1940s. A major reason for the "loss" of China to the Communists, they believed, was the Truman administration's over-emphasis on trying to maintain China's full territorial integrity in the face of what they believed was only temporarily superior Chinese Communist power. It would have been more realistic, they argued, to have had Chiang Kai-shek give up the most vulnerable areas of the country temporarily, while husbanding his military strength in more easily defended territory pending a rollback once the Communists had, as they believed was inevitable, alienated the populations in the areas they had occupied. Eisenhower and Dulles were determined to avoid this mistake in their approach to Southeast Asia, and they made clear to Cumming that they were prepared to see countries break up temporarily into "racial and geographic units" which could afterwards provide bases for moving against Communist power in other parts of their territory.

Whatever the merits of this assessment, it constituted an essential part of the marching orders both Eisenhower and Dulles conveyed to Hugh S. Cumming as he was about to leave for his assignment as ambassador to Indonesia, a posting that ran from 1953 until early 1957. This approach continued to guide Cumming after he returned to Washington to become Dulles's principal aide in fashioning policy towards Indonesia during the American intervention of 1957–8.[42] It was an assessment that clearly fitted with the administration's roughly concurrent approach to Cambodia at the time of the Dap Chhuon affair.

With respect to Dap Chhuon, Chandler's recent (1991) history of Cambodia has done much to lift the veil of secrecy which long hid the event, as have recently declassified British Foreign Office documents. But many relevant US State Department documents, as well as those of the CIA, have remained, at least up to my visit to the US National Archives on 20 May

1996, classified and unavailable. (Even for documents from the State Department Central Files there is an enormous gap in the coverage of what has been released – covering the critical period leading up to the Dap Chhuon Affair of 25 September 1958 to 10 January 1959.)[43]

From the outset Ngo Dinh Diem's government, and especially Diem's powerful brother Ngo Dinh Nhu, were heavily involved in Dap Chhuon's plot against Sihanouk. On 7 February 1959 an Air Vietnam plane from Saigon landed at Siem Reap's airport carrying seven cases of wireless equipment and two South Vietnamese wireless operators who were seen through Cambodian customs by Dap Chhuon himself. From the South Vietnamese government Chhuon also received, either directly by plane to Siem Reap's airfield or via the head of the South Vietnamese diplomatic mission in Phnom Penh, 270 kg of gold to pay his forces.[44] Flights, probably carrying arms and ammunition, also came in from Thailand, with whose government Dap Chhuon's ties had for long been especially strong.[45]

It is not clear how early the United States was involved in Dap Chhuon's plot. But Richard Bissell, newly appointed by Allen Dulles as head of the CIA's directorate of clandestine operations (deputy director of plans), ordered Charles Whitehurst, head of the agency's Cambodia desk to "send a radio operator with the coup planners," because he wanted to be kept promptly informed as to the coup's progress.[46] To achieve this objective a CIA operative in the US Phnom Penh embassy, Victor Matsui (an American of Japanese parentage), turned over a high-powered transmitter to Dap Chhuon so that he could keep in touch with the American embassies in Phnom Penh and Saigon (and possibly CIA headquarters in Washington), and made at least one trip to Siem Reap to confer with Chhuon's brother.[47]

Before Dap Chhuon's plans could be executed, the Chinese, Soviet and French embassies and members of the French business community had learned of at least their broad outline and had all alerted Sihanouk. The fact that no such warning came from the American embassy made Sihanouk suspicious that the United States was involved in the planned coup even before he learned of Matsui's role. Before Dap Chhuon had marshaled troops from the two provinces under his command, Sihanouk on 21 February sent the chief of staff of his army, General Lon Nol, backed by two loyal battalions, to Siem Reap where an apparently much surprised Dap Chhuon was caught and promptly executed.[48] The reality of the plot was confirmed for the Phnom Penh diplomatic community when, on 26 February, Sihanouk invited its members to Siem Reap to show them the radio transmitters, gold, and "captured code books and file copies of telegrams sent and received which clearly established [the] connection with Saigon" and contained "fairly obvious references" to the head of South Vietnam's diplomatic mission in Phnom Penh.[49]

The State Department categorically denied any American role in the plot against Sihanouk but acknowledged privately to the British that the Thais and South Vietnamese were "deeply involved."[50] The French ambassador in

Saigon informed his British counterpart that though it was "non-diplomatic" US personnel who had participated in the plot, nevertheless "Americans were in it up to the neck."[51] While the British foreign office was initially skeptical of French reports of American involvement, by 11 February the British ambassador to Phnom Penh no longer was. Reporting to London, he noted that the usual visits of the Americans to the French embassy had "suddenly ceased just before the conspiracy blew up" and that this "coupled with the rather sudden visits to Singapore and Bangkok by the American Ambassador [to Phnom Penh] and his Counselor, certainly gave the French the strong impression that the Americans were up to something and were playing a lone hand." Then, evidently referring to the role of non-diplomatic Americans (and probably to his own career), he observed that "those who have served in South America have had [the] experience of different American organizations pursuing different policies in one and the same country." He concluded with the observation that "My own personal view, for what it is worth, is that some American organization was to some extent mixed up in some of the intrigues connected with the conspiracy and that the State Department representatives, if not directly involved, were not unaware that something was going on."[52]

By 20 April it was clear that senior British foreign office officials had come to share the interpretation and concerns of their Phnom Penh embassy and that they were worried over the wider repercussions. This was clear in their comments on the evaluation they had then just received from R.H. Scott, the British commissioner general for Southeast Asia. The marginal handwritten note on the report by one foreign office official read: "We too have been unable to convince ourselves that there was absolutely no involvement in the Dap Chhuon plot on the part of American Officials." His more senior colleague noted:

> The truth of the matter is the explanation which suggests itself naturally: some official Americans had links with Sam Sary [another opponent of Sihanouk pledged to his downfall] and Dap Chhuon and these links did in fact have the effect of supporting and encouraging them, although they were not meant to – or rather, would only have been meant to if the plot had been successful. I suspect that Mr. Parsons [the recently appointed US assistant secretary of state for Far Eastern affairs] has more "considerable shocks" in store for him if this has been one.[53]

Evidently one of the "considerable shocks" alluded to was Graham Parsons' reaction when the British foreign office's D.F. MacDermott informed him of the rumor that Dag Hammerskjold, secretary general of the United Nations, had told India's Prime Minister Nehru that he thought "the Americans had been connected with the recent incidents in Cambodia."[54] Just over a week later the foreign office had confirmation, and further details. The Australian chargé d'affaires in Saigon (presumably relaying what he had learned from the Australian ambassador to New Delhi) reported that Hammerskjold "spoke with considerable heat and emphasis in Delhi, and announced his intention of seeing President Eisenhower immediately on his return to the United States and warning him that this kind of activity simply could not continue." He added that "Hammerskjold did not apparently accuse either the State Department or CIA: other American agencies were responsible. This, as you know, [has] been the French line throughout."[55] The secretary general of the United Nations must, then, have been referring to the US military, and most likely the Defense Intelligence Agency (DIA).

Within six months of the abortive Dap Chhuon coup the Cambodian government alleged a revival of extensive Khmer Serei activity within the country. Their armed bands were reportedly being infiltrated into Cambodia from South Vietnam, and Son Ngoc Thanh was accused of preparing a sabotage and guerrilla movement for action from the Thai frontier. The British embassy in Phnom Penh was unsure of the veracity of these reports,[56] but, according to an official CIA source, by 1960 Khmer Serei were evidently being given military training inside South Vietnam.[57] Their activities within Cambodia, however, appear to have remained at a low level until the fall of 1963 when a continuing series of vicious anti-Sihanouk broadcasts were launched from South Vietnam and ultimately Thailand. As with the Khmer Serei's armed incursions into Cambodia from these two countries, Sihanouk – with good reason – thought these broadcasts were being supported by the CIA. That conviction, together with his outrage at the Ngo Dinh Diem government's brutal repression of South Vietnam's Buddhists, and the depredations of South Vietnamese troops who crossed into Cambodia allegedly, or actually, in pursuit of the forces of Vietnam's National Liberation Front (NLF), brought Sihanouk to break off diplomatic relations with South Vietnam in late August 1963. His belief that the United States was at least witting of, if not complicit in, the broadcasts and border transgressions of both Khmer Serei and the South Vietnamese army and airforce gave special poignancy to his stunned reaction to the coup in early November that resulted in the deaths of Diem and his brother Ngo Dinh Nhu. Although Sihanouk was relieved to see them out of power, he was convinced – correctly – that the coup had been dependent upon American backing. He now became haunted by the fear that the United States would similarly arrange for his deposition.[58]

The defamatory radio broadcasts from South Vietnam and Thailand did not cease and, convinced that the United States could easily end both the broadcasts and the Khmer Serei and South Vietnamese military's incursions, Sihanouk threatened to cut off all US economic, military and cultural assistance if these activities continued. They did, and on 20 November 1963 he made good his threat. He did so following a special meeting of Cambodia's National Congress to which he presented two thoroughly intimidated recently captured members of the Khmer Serei, who obligingly stated that the CIA provided ammunition and funds to their organization.[59]

Chandler writes that President Kennedy had not been aware of the Khmer Serei until presented with this crisis of 20 November, at which time Assistant Secretary of State Roger Hilsman "told him that the United States had indeed 'played footsie' with the Khmer Serei in the Eisenhower period and that 'there was money involved'." The president had apparently wanted to defuse the situation but he died two days later before any action could be taken.[60]

14 Cambodia and the Vietnam war

During 1964, as US military intelligence became increasingly convinced that Vietnamese Communist forces were finding sanctuary on the Cambodian side of the border with South Vietnam, Cambodian relations with the United States and South Vietnam reached what the British embassy in Phnom Penh characterized as "an all time low." In its annual review for 1964 for the British Foreign Office it went on to state that "A series of deplorable frontier incidents served to reinforce traditional Cambodian hatred and distrust of the Viet-Namese," with "the most inglorious, but not least typical of these episodes" being "the combined infantry and air attack by South Viet-Namese forces in the pursuit of alleged Viet Cong guerrillas on the 19th of March against the defenceless Cambodian village of Chantréa (Seventeen peasants were killed and 14 wounded)."[1] In explaining the American version of the attack, Secretary of State Rusk acknowledged that an American adviser had accompanied the South Vietnamese ground forces into Cambodian Chantréa and that following the bombing attack four Americans had briefly landed there with South Vietnamese officers. But Rusk said that when it became clear that an error had been made they all promptly withdrew. None of the American personnel, he stated, was engaged in any firing or had directly engaged in the military action during this incident.[2]

Cross-border incidents, especially bombing by the South Vietnamese airforce continued spasmodically throughout the year and beyond, the rationale being allegedly increased Vietnamese Communist activity from Cambodian border bases into Vietnam. Border clashes became especially heavy in September and October, with US and South Vietnamese spokesman in Saigon stating on 28 October that increased Vietnamese Communist activity from Cambodian bases was responsible for five US–South Vietnamese air sorties against targets in Cambodia the previous week.[3]

The pressure on Sihanouk's regime was applied primarily by the US-financed and armed Khmer Serei. It is not clear whether Lyndon Johnson became aware of the CIA's support of this group, who were sometimes trained, encadred and led by US Special Forces (Green Berets). These specialists in counterinsurgency warfare had been introduced into South Vietnam in 1962 at which time they were on loan to the CIA.

About two years later, when the mission became too big and too expensive for the CIA to hide, it was turned over entirely to the Special Forces and run openly under Army financing ... In their heyday, the Special Forces in South Vietnam numbered about 2,700 men and commanded a 45,000 man mercenary army of hill tribesmen and ethnic Cambodians, Chinese and Vietnamese. At the height of their operations they ran more than 60 remote posts, primarily along the rugged border with Laos and Cambodia.[4]

The Special Forces and CIA strengthened the Khmer Serei by recruiting additional mercenaries from the indigenous ethnically Cambodian (Khmer Krom) population of South Vietnam's Mekong Delta. The new recruits were trained by US Special Forces in South Vietnam,[5] and along with some of the existing Khmer Serei were incorporated into American-led Special Forces units based along the South Vietnamese side of the border with Cambodia. Son Ngoc Thanh, the principal recruiter, worked closely with the CIA and US Special Forces and a US helicopter ferried him among these border bases.

According to William Shawcross, some of the Khmer Serei were brought into another branch of the Special Forces, the Studies and Operations Group, which was "responsible for clandestine reconnaissance and sabotage missions into Cambodia and Laos" and which during the 1960s "secretly slipped across the Vietnamese border in search of Communist trails, hospitals, bases, villages." In 1967, he states, "without the knowledge of Congress, these operations were institutionalized under the name Salem House (later changed to Daniel Boone)," with these teams "allowed to delve up to 30 kilometers inside Cambodia" and "authorized to place 'sanitized self-destruct antipersonnel' land mines as they went."[6] A retrospective account published by the *New York Times* some three years after the event reported that a Green Beret officer, whose unit of five Americans and eleven Khmer Serei had been involved in these cross-border operations, had been convicted by a US military court of killing one of the Cambodians under his command. Noting that, according to testimony at the trial, the United States used the Khmer Serei, an organization "dedicated to the overthrow of the legitimate government of Cambodia on covert missions into that country in 1967," it reported that they were paid by "the Special Forces and American intelligence groups."[7]

It is not certain whether by 1965 MACV (Military Assistance Command Vietnam) had taken over the financing of these elements wholly or partly from the CIA, but by then control over them would appear to have been vested primarily with MACV.[8] The memorandum prepared for President Johnson's national security adviser, McGeorge Bundy, by his principal assistant for Southeast Asian affairs, Chester Cooper, noted that during 1965 a "pincer movement by MACV ... in [South] Vietnam to the east [of Cambodia] and the Thai/Viet supported [and Thailand-based] Khmer Serei

on the west" had left Cambodia's fate "gravely threatened." (In general in
the Indochina states, by this time, the division of authority and responsibility between the CIA and Department of Defense appears to have often
been unclear.)[9]

UN Secretary General Dag Hammerskjold's previously cited reference to
"other American agencies" is especially pertinent for the decade preceding
Nixon's 1970 invasion of Cambodia. For, with the growing American military support to Ngo Dinh Diem's US-dependent regime, the Pentagon and
especially the US army and its intelligence arm, DIA, became deeply
concerned with developments in South Vietnam's immediate neighbor and
soon emerged as a third player in American policy towards Cambodia,
along with the State Department and CIA. The Pentagon's actions were
often just as covert as those of the CIA, and ultimately it emerged as the
most important of the three American players. This process was already well
under way by 1965, as is indicated by a knowledgeable and prescient memorandum of 6 January 1966 to McGeorge Bundy, then Johnson's national
security adviser, from his chief lieutenant for Asian affairs, Chester Cooper.

> One problem in '65 is the fate of Cambodia – now more gravely threat-
> ened (as we have indicated) by pincer movement of MACV (the US
> Military Assistance Command in Vietnam) to the east and the Thai/Viet
> supported Khmer Serei on the west. Through deft handling of the
> present proposal for strengthening the ICC [the International Control
> Commission deriving from the 1954 Geneva Conference] or a new
> Cambodia conference, we might just retrieve Sihanouk – who remains
> one of the only popular charismatic leaders of the region and well
> worth retrieving. Unfortunately, we lack both a strong advocate sending
> cables out of Phnom Penh and a strong Cambodia lobby at State – so
> the views of Bangkok, Saigon and DOD [Department of Defense] are
> seldom effectively counterbalanced.[10]

Clearly by the time of the major escalation of US military intervention in
Vietnam in the second half of 1965 there was nothing monolithic about
American Cambodian policy. The Pentagon, and especially its army headquarters in Saigon (MACV), was out in front in shaping policy in
Cambodia. In contrast, the State Department appeared to be moving
towards a more moderate position towards Sihanouk's government,
including an effort beginning in December to stand down Khmer Serei
attacks by suspending South Vietnamese financial and arms aid to Son
Ngoc Thanh,[11] and then during the next two years moving gradually
towards a resumption of diplomatic relations.

Nor should one assume that the CIA itself was monolithic. Although
there is no indication that CIA activists in the field were not fully cooperating with the now strongly interventionist Cambodia policies of the
Pentagon, at least as early as September 1964 an assessment by the CIA's

Directorate of Intelligence showed a grasp of Cambodian realities that was hardly compatible with the covert actions of its operatives in Cambodia. The following extract makes this very clear.

> There is no evidence of Khmer Serei forces in Cambodia or of important Khmer Serei sympathy among the Cambodian people. There are, however, numerous armed Khmer Serei in South Vietnam and Thailand. Although the Khmer Serei Movement is probably not capable of deposing Sihanouk [phrase sanitized] any increase in its activity will add to Sihanouk's sense of isolation and strengthen his belief that only a closer alignment with Peiping will protect Cambodian security ... Sihanouk hopes that a closer accommodation with Communist China will not only deter an immediate threat from South Vietnam, but constitute a long range hedge against what he views as the somewhat more distant but equally dangerous threat of a unified Vietnam under Hanoi's hegemony.[12]

This had not, however, hindered Khmer Serei operations. In late December 1964 the US embassy in Phnom Penh reported that a recent Khmer Serei military attack from Thailand into Cambodia's Siem Reap province was "the most serious incident reported for many months" in that border area. On 5 March 1965 the embassy reported "Khmer Serei broadcasts past two weeks have increased in belligerency, accusing Prince [Sihanouk] of poisoning water" in three northwestern Cambodian provinces, "of mental illness and general incompetence, and of being a pawn of Communist China." These broadcasts also claimed "successful military operations along [the] Thai border during period February 9 to 21" and announced "determination to launch attack to 'liberate Cambodia and the Cambodian people'."[13] Similar reports emanated from the British embassy during the early months of 1965, with the Foreign Office concluding: "Khmer Serei activity mounted from Thailand and South Vietnam is continuing along the well established lines."[14]

However heavy the pressure the State Department may have applied for support to Khmer Serei forces to be suspended in late 1965, it too was clearly ineffective. The Khmer Serei attacks continued. On 22 April 1966, the British embassy in Phnom Penh reported that the Khmer Serei "are mounting regular (if still small scale) armed incursions from Thailand," and observed that "The Khmer Serei movement is not a genuine part of the Cambodian political life. It is an external organization covertly supported by the Thai and South Vietnamese governments with the object of overthrowing the Sihanouk regime. Its chief methods are subversion and terrorism."[15]

With American intelligence having concluded in the fall of 1964 that Vietnamese Communist forces were beginning to infiltrate into South Vietnam from bases in eastern Cambodia just inside the frontier, the US rationale for supporting the Khmer Serei was no longer confined to under-mining Sihanouk's regime. Consequently, beginning in 1965, a second, but seemingly fully compatible, objective was added: to collect intelligence on and, insofar as feasible, disrupt and impede these Vietnamese Communist penetrations. Sihanouk's little army of under 32,000,[16] spread over an area as large as South Vietnam, and ironically primarily tied down in fighting the US-supported Khmer Serei, was in no position to seriously contest the passage of these Vietnamese Communist forces. Nor could his army stop the sporadic incursions of South Vietnamese army units into the frontier areas, nor the increasing bombings in these areas by US aircraft of what a woefully inept American military intelligence insisted, mostly erroneously, were sanc-tuaries harboring Vietnamese Communist forces – operations which found few of them, but killed many Cambodian peasants.

Sihanouk's long-festering anger at the pressure against his beleaguered government by what he had come to regard, correctly, as American-financed and armed Khmer Serei incursions launched from the soil of two US allies, together with his outrage at these US bombings and sporadic cross-border incursions by South Vietnamese army units (occasionally with US advisers), were primarily responsible for his decision in May 1965 to break off diplo-matic relations with the United States.[17] During the next year pressure on Sihanouk by these American-supported mercenaries increased, with the Cambodian government reporting 130 violations of its territory launched by armed forces from Thailand alone.[18]

An escalation in US cross-border activities was portended when at the end of November 1965 it was reported that American field commanders in South Vietnam had been authorized "to engage enemy forces on Cambodian territory in certain circumstances." The British were seriously alarmed by this, their embassy in Phnom Penh foreseeing that it raised "the great danger ... that Cambodia will be somehow sucked into the Viet-Namese war."[19] Indeed, the British Foreign Office was sufficiently worried lest "as a result of pressure from [American] military circles" the idea of bombing Cambodian territory become a reality that on 7 December it instructed its ambassador in Washington to bring up the matter and point out that any such move against Cambodia "even if operationally justified, which is arguable, would be bound to have serious political consequences" and, among other things, "render it more difficult for us to maintain our present degree of public support for United States policies in and over Vietnam." The Foreign Office was clearly dissatisfied with the explanation then proffered by President Johnson's national security adviser, McGeorge Bundy. It advised its ambassador to Washington:

> We find Bundy's argument rather disturbing, if it is to be understood as implying that American forces would be prepared to bomb Cambodian territory simply on the assumption that Viet Cong forces with whom contact had been lost had crossed the border and were hiding somewhere

in the area. This would not be compatible with any conception of "hot pursuit" or "self defence" known to international law and we should have great difficulty in defending such American action.[20]

Concern over the danger inherent in this more aggressive American posture brought Britain's ambassador to Washington to meet again with Bundy three weeks later. But this discussion was even more worrying than the first. Bundy could not give assurances that instructions to American military commanders "would be obeyed to the letter because that was not humanly possible" but averred that he had no doubt that US military authorities "could be trusted to ensure that there were no significant breaches of the orders." Though he himself was inclined to agree that there was not much substantial organized aid going to the Viet Cong across the border, he held that the frontier was undoubtedly to some extent a safe refuge and that "it was very hard to expect a military force to cease fire when their opponents had reached a certain point on the map."[21] The Foreign Office then noted that, despite the efforts of its ambassador in Washington, the American government had issued a statement

> which implicitly confirms that American commanders in Vietnam have authority to pursue the Viet Cong into Cambodian territory and, for this purpose, to employ artillery fire and close air-support against Cambodian territory. Although the U.S. Government have assured us that the implementation of this policy will be strictly controlled ... the wording of the announcement ... appears to give American military commanders considerable latitude.[22]

This expectation was to be amply fulfilled.

During 1966 there was a substantial increase in the incidence of both US bombings of and overland penetrations into areas inside Cambodia's eastern frontier, aimed primarily at limiting use of this area by Vietnamese Communist troops. As Don Noel, one of the few knowledgeable American correspondents to spend a significant amount of time in Cambodia during this period, discovered, there was a sharp increase in Cambodian civilian casualties from these cross-border violations. In August 1966 US planes bombed and strafed the Cambodian village of Thlok Trach at the very time that damage from a US air attack of two days earlier was being inspected there by members of the International Control Commission (ICC) for Cambodia and military attachés from several Phnom Penh embassies.[23] Apparently none of the foreigners was hurt, but Sihanouk's government reported that three Cambodians were killed and nine wounded.

The reservedly apologetic reaction to this episode by a spokesman of the US Saigon embassy and his insistence that the village was in South Vietnam and not Cambodia incensed not only Noel but much of the Phnom Penh diplomatic community. The nature of this American response was such as to rub salt into the wound of the attack itself, and Sihanouk's anger could have been predicted. He responded by announcing on 13 August that, as a result of the US position on the attack, he would cancel his scheduled September meeting with US ambassador-at-large, Averell Harriman, to discuss Cambodian–US diplomatic relations, presumably with the object of restoring them. Not until three days after Sihanouk's announcement did the State Department, after still insisting that its maps showed that Thlok Trach was on the Vietnamese side of the border, concede that the visit of the ICC to the village on 2 August had clearly indicated that the area was under the jurisdiction of the Cambodian government. In view of the evidently increasing divergence between the relatively reconciliatory approach of the State Department towards Cambodia, especially as embodied in the aborted Harriman visit, and the increasingly harder line of the South Vietnam-based US military, it is plausible to assume that the latter was pleased with the political consequences of the Thlok Trach bombing, even if it had not actually planned that outcome.

The US military's much increased interest in Cambodia, especially following the enormous build up of the American presence in South Vietnam during 1965–6, was by that time no longer primarily attributable to the Vietnamese NLF's spasmodic occupation (generally shifting from one locale to another) of small and difficult to detect border enclaves located short distances inside Cambodia's frontier with Vietnam. Beginning in 1966–7, a second important factor had been added – the growing conviction of the US military in South Vietnam that military supplies from Communist countries, especially China, were being transported to Cambodia's eastern frontier and on to Vietnamese Communist units operating in South Vietnam's Mekong Delta.

But there was considerable controversy among both American policy makers and the foreign embassies in Phnom Penh as to whether this conviction was true, or if true whether a significant amount of supplies were involved. Certainly the existence of any such influx of military supplies through Cambodia was difficult to detect. The major reason for this, as only later became clear, was the deep and essential involvement of the Cambodian army in this operation, and the fact that its transport of the supplies from the port of Sihanoukville to Communist Vietnamese forces just across the South Vietnamese frontier was effected in two discrete stages. First, at the port of Sihanoukville the Cambodian army's trucks picked up shipments of French weapons which were actually earmarked for the Cambodian army's use, together with much larger quantities of arms from mostly Chinese vessels destined for Vietnamese Communist forces in South Vietnam. The trucks carried these weapons to Cambodian army warehouses in Phnom Penh. The military attachés of Western embassies in Phnom Penh carefully scrutinized this stage of the transport, and they were initially led to conclude that arms flowing through Sihanoukville were going not to Vietnam but, quite appropriately, to the Cambodian army and were being stored in its own warehouses. What was not then appreciated was that Lon Nol and some of his officers had arranged for the arms destined for Vietnamese Communist forces to be later sent in these same Cambodian army trucks at night to the frontier. In the process, Lon Nol, as head of the Cambodian army, and favored members of his officer corps received very handsome remuneration.

There was double irony in the situation: Lon Nol and some of his senior officers who participated so heavily in this corruption were generally regarded by US intelligence as "pro-American" (and were hoping that the US economic aid, upon which their salaries had been substantially dependent before Sihanouk had cut it off in 1963, would be resumed); and the major stretch of road (Sihanoukville to Phnom Penh) traversed by the Cambodian army trucks in transporting these military supplies was the US-financed "Friendship Highway."

This pattern was first adumbrated for me during my 1967 visit to Cambodia, when in talks with Australian Ambassador Deschamps he stated that he and his armed services attaché had been able to trace all the arms coming in from Sihanoukville to the Cambodian arms depots. He volunteered that, of course, "they could not be sure what happened to them afterwards," but they were satisfied that "no appreciable amount could be diverted from there to Vietnam, even though it was possible that corruption could lead to small amounts finding their way across the border."[24]

By this time some American officials were also alleging that Sihanouk was permitting the northeastern corner of Cambodia to be used as a conduit for military supplies being sent to NLF forces operating in the northwestern sector of South Vietnam. Bindra's ICC staff and Deschamps' service attaché told me that they had recently explored this jungle-clad area sufficiently to establish that it was so devoid of roads that any supplies would have to be transported by human porters and therefore could be no more than a trickle. Moreover, they and others argued that logic dictated that supplies so transported from North Vietnam could more easily be carried into this part of South Vietnam by way of southeastern Laos.

Having been told that the Indonesian ambassador to Phnom Penh and his military attaché had very recently reconnoitered northeastern Cambodia near the Vietnamese frontier, I also discussed this matter with them and found that they agreed with Bindra's and Deschamps's assessment. Ambassador Budiardjo volunteered that, in checking into reports of military activities in the area, he and his military attaché had discovered that what was involved were military units of the anti-Saigon Vietnamese Montagnard elements operating (on both sides of the Cambodian–South Vietnamese border) under the banner of FULRO (*Front Unifié pour la Lutte des Races Opprimées*), and supported (clandestinely) by both the Sihanouk government and in some cases by the US Army's Special Forces. [25]

The last year of the Johnson administration, 1968, was marked by an increasing bifurcation in the Cambodia policies pursued by the State

Department and the Pentagon. The State's initiative in trying to restore US diplomatic relations with Cambodia was welcomed by Sihanouk. He had been under mounting pressure from his army and right-wing political factions in Phnom Penh to restore these relations, for they expected such moves would lead to a resumption of Washington's financial subventions. And Sihanouk could no longer rely upon countervailing support from China, which was then reaching the height of its Cultural Revolution. (Perhaps also then affecting Sihanouk's calculations was the possibility that he was aware that the still militarily weak Cambodian Communist Party (Khmer Rouge) was moving towards open insurrection, a posture which it formally espoused in January 1968.) The State Department's mission to Phnom Penh during the first week of January 1968, led by Chester Bowles, US ambassador to India, successfully prepared the way for the reestablishment of diplomatic relations, with the final steps taken in June 1969. Chandler believes that the Bowles visit "forestalled U.S. military plans put together in 1967–8 to invade Vietnamese sanctuaries in Cambodia."[26]

In meeting with Bowles, Sihanouk acknowledged the presence of Vietnamese Communist sanctuaries inside Cambodia's eastern borders and urged the strengthening of the ICC's inspection teams in the expectation that this "would reduce U.S.–South Vietnamese incursions and bombing raids." The US supported this proposal "because it felt that the teams could confirm and publicize the presence of Vietnamese bases on Cambodian soil." It was in these same discussions that Sihanouk indicated that "he would not object if the U.S. engaged in 'hot pursuit' in unpopulated areas" of the Cambodian frontier, and that if American forces "pursued VC forces into remote areas where the population would be unaffected he would 'shut his eyes'."[27] Although the term "hot pursuit" can legitimately be applied to on-the-ground infantry operations (and has long been applied to naval operations), it has no relevance to a bombing campaign. Yet it was the attribution to Sihanouk of this statement that later brought Kissinger and Nixon to use it in their self-righteous and utterly specious attempt to justify the secret sustained carpet-bombing of Cambodian frontier areas by B-52s that they directed within two months of Nixon's coming to office.

This highly secret bombing campaign, known as "Menu," was begun on 18 March 1969[28] in response to a request from the commander of US forces in Vietnam, General Creighton Abrams. It focused on suspected Communist bases inside the Cambodian frontier, one of which, COSVN (Central Office for South Vietnam), was the supposed headquarters of Vietnamese Communist forces operating in South Vietnam. Utilizing high-flying and notoriously inaccurate B-52s, making a total of 3,630 raids, the campaign continued over the next fourteen months into areas of varying concentrations of civilians as well as suspected concentrations of Vietnamese Communist troops. The US Joint Chiefs of Staff, Shawcross writes, warned that there was danger to Cambodian civilians but the White House ignored this reservation. "In response to Nixon's demands for total and unassailable secrecy, the military devised an ingenious system that the Joint Chiefs liked to describe as 'dual reporting' ... The bombing was not merely concealed; the official *secret* records showed that it never happened." Both the secretary of the airforce and its chief of staff were kept in ignorance, and the Senate's Foreign Relations Committee "did not find out about the unauthorized and illegal extension of the war into a neutral country until 1973." Shawcross concludes: "Peasants were killed – no one knows how many – and Communist logistics were somewhat disrupted. To avoid the attacks, the North Vietnamese and Viet Cong pushed their sanctuaries and supply bases deeper into the country, and the area that the B-52s bombarded expanded as the year passed. The war spread."[29]

15 Coup against Sihanouk

Beginning in 1966–7 and becoming much more discernible by 1969, the balance of forces within Cambodia had been shifting in ways much more difficult for Sihanouk to manage. The socioeconomic foundations of his state had been strained and weakened. The government's major role in managing much of the economy, which had considerably increased in 1964 following the ending of American economic aid, had become clumsy and increasingly ineffective. A steady expansion of secondary and tertiary levels of education had for several years far outrun the capacity of the private economy and bureaucracy to absorb the young graduates, leaving an ever-increasing number of discontented urban unemployed.[1] Sihanouk's abrupt ending of American economic assistance in 1963 had been only very partially offset by other sources of foreign economic assistance. Discontent had risen within the bloated bureaucracy and especially among army officers, a significant proportion of whose salaries had been dependent upon American financial aid and who saw their income shrink soon after it was ended in 1963. US military assistance had covered slightly over 25 per cent of expenditures for defense in 1963, and its absence appears to have been primarily responsible for a subsequent increase in the overall budget deficit by almost the same percentage. (The continuing growth of deficit financing was such as to bring the governor of the National Bank to warn in 1966 that it would inevitably lead to "social discontent as a result of the decrease in the purchasing power of the currency.")[2]

Laura Summers has observed that during the late 1960s "The official political economy that was supposed to favor rural cultivators was clearly breaking down leaving approximately 20–50% of all peasants in increasingly desperate straits."[3] The government's dependency on foreign currency earned by the country's rice exports increased its efforts to force peasants to sell their rice crop to it at officially set prices, causing widespread peasant resentment. Sihanouk's prime minister, General Lon Nol, was so heavy handed and abusive in enforcing this requirement in the Samlaut area of the rich province of Battambang as to help fan resentment into a brief and largely spontaneous rebellion, for which the still very small Cambodian Communist Party (Khmer Rouge) was happy to take largely unearned credit. Sihanouk, though apparently himself muddled as to the causes of the rebellion, removed Lon Nol from office.[4] But a major cause for the government's pressure on the peasantry remained. This was the leakage across the frontier into South Vietnam of a major portion of the rice crop (and hence of the country's ability to earn foreign exchange) which was smuggled through local Chinese merchants and/or Lon Nol's army officers as intermediaries into the hands of Vietnamese Communists or Chinese merchants based in South Vietnam, all of whom were ready to pay much higher prices than the Cambodian government.[5] As a consequence, legally channeled export earnings from rice dropped in 1969 to approximately a quarter of what they had been in 1967 and 1968.[6]

There seems to be little evidence that this situation resulted in Sihanouk himself losing favor among the peasantry, whose regard he had long assiduously cultivated. But it was very clear that the state of the economy, and especially the loss of American economic assistance, had resulted in a mounting disaffection among the upper and intermediate levels of urban society, most of whose standard of living significantly declined during the second half of the 1960s. It was the increasing discontent of this element that nourished what Sihanouk referred to as the "Right Wing" in Cambodian politics. Its strength grew as Sihanouk moved against urban high school students and graduates radicalized, in part at least, by the paucity of employment prospects, thereby, along with other factors, weakening a sufficiently countervailing force on the left to permit him to balance the extremes in the political spectrum.

Despite General Lon Nol's gauche handling of peasant unrest in the Samlaut affair, Sihanouk retained confidence in him, keeping him in charge of internal security and appointing him deputy prime minister soon afterwards. The "Right Wing" or conservative faction, including its most influential leader, the successful businessman Prince Sirik Matak, shared Sihanouk's confidence in Lon Nol. Sihanouk won domestic acclaim when the United States recognized Cambodia's frontiers (despite opposition to this from the Saigon government), thus paving the way for a resumption of Cambodian–US diplomatic ties in June 1969. But to the chagrin of Sihanouk and keen disappointment of the conservatives and many other urban dwellers, the renewed diplomatic ties were not accompanied by a resumption of either American economic or military assistance. Meanwhile the government's fiscal hemorrhaging had continued apace as a consequence of rice smuggling across the frontier.

Under pressure from the growing financial crisis, the unrelenting Vietnamese Communist and American pressures against the eastern frontier, and the conservatives' increased influence, Sihanouk in August 1969 convened a special national conference to deal especially with the economic situation. Its members elected Lon Nol to replace the ailing Penn Nouth as prime minister – a selection agreeable to Sihanouk, but they gave the second largest vote and position of deputy prime minister to Prince Sirik Matak,

Sihanouk's most influential critic. Only four of the sixteen-member cabinet appointed by the new prime minister could be regarded as Sihanoukists. But the prince's faith in Lon Nol's loyalty continued, even after a visit to Hanoi in early September for Ho Chi Minh's funeral when, according to Chandler, the Vietnamese prime minister, Pham Van Dong, complained to him that "Lon Nol had recently accepted a substantial payment in dollars from the Chinese for Cambodian rice and medicine to be shipped to the NLF but had never handed over the rice."[7]

The new Lon Nol–Sirik Matak leadership pressed for a reversal of Sihanouk's semi-socialist economic policies, including an end to state banking and other poorly functioning monopolies, many plagued by bureaucratic corruption, and opening scope for greater private investment. When in October Lon Nol sustained serious injuries in an auto accident and was obliged to fly to France for a long period of medical treatment (from which he apparently did not return to Cambodia until early 1970), Sirik Matak emerged as acting prime minister and carried this effort forward with great energy. After a back-and-forth struggle with Sihanouk, who apparently approved of only minor changes, Sirik Matak and his supporters had by January 1970 emerged ascendant in the shaping of government economic policy, with the four Sihanouk loyalists resigning in protest. During the second half of 1969 it had become clear that Sihanouk's power within Cambodia was ebbing.

There is certainly truth in T.D. Allman's conclusion that "By choosing to rule indirectly through a premier and cabinet Sihanouk also allowed the army and bureaucracy to fall under his enemies' control."[8] But, of course, other factors also contributed to his weakened grip. Among them was his apparent loss of confidence in how to address his country's financial crisis, and the diversion of much of his attention into his often consuming hobby of film making (films that were generally regarded as disasters).[9] But undoubtedly most important was his preoccupation with the Vietnamese Communist enclaves inside his eastern borders – both the continuing presence of the NLF and North Vietnamese troops there and the profligate bombing of these areas by American planes. Also demanding was the sustained pressure by the Nixon administration for him to take measures to eliminate or contain these Vietnamese enclaves – which Cambodia's small and under-armed military forces were powerless to carry out – and cut the supply line from the port of Sihanoukville that presumably nourished Vietnamese Communist forces in the enclaves as well as those across the border in South Vietnam. In this last step – a very important one – Sihanouk was ultimately moderately successful, despite the collusion of Lon Nol's army officers in these smuggling operations. The US embassy in Phnom Penh was clearly pleased with his actions in reducing the flow of supplies during the second half of 1969. It noted that it was in August that the last ship was permitted to unload arms and munitions at Sihanoukville, and that some 5,000 tons of munitions and other supplies already in the pipeline to the Vietnamese Communists were then held up by the Cambodian government in its depots.[10]

But these efforts, however significant for some in the State Department, did not satisfy Nixon and Kissinger, and even less the Pentagon's US army proconsuls in South Vietnam. As Seymour Hersh has noted,

> Sihanouk's harshest critics were in the American military, and they did more than complain. His immediate overthrow had been for years a high priority of the Green Berets reconnaissance units operating inside Cambodia since the late 1960s. There is also incontrovertible evidence that Lon Nol was approached by agents of American military intelligence in 1969 and asked to overthrow the Sihanouk government.[11]

The *Washington Post* retrospectively reported that "as early as July 1969 senior U.S. advisers in Vietnamese provinces bordering Cambodia were crossing over to confer with Khmer [Cambodian government] officers."[12]

Well before a physically exhausted Sihanouk left Phnom Penh on 6 January 1970 for his scheduled annual medical check up in France, American intelligence agents were, as David Chandler puts it, "renewing ties established in the early 1960s with sympathetic Cambodian officials, including Sirik Matak."[13] According to Daniel Roy, a confidante of Sihanouk highly knowledgeable about Cambodian politics, in 1966 Chau Seng, then an influential minister of Sihanouk's cabinet,[14] learned "with certainty" that those on the "extreme right" in Cambodian politics (among whom Sirik Matak was probably the most prominent) "emboldened by General Suharto's coup in Indonesia had chosen the initially reticent General Lon Nol to be the instrument of an analogous operation" in Cambodia. When Chau Seng conveyed his suspicions to Sihanouk, Lon Nol demanded he be ousted from the cabinet. Sihanouk complied but nevertheless reappointed Chau Seng to an important cabinet position a few months later.[15]

Chau Seng's suspicions were well founded. According to Indonesia's then ambassador to Cambodia, airforce Lt General Budiardjo, the Indonesian military understood that their Cambodian counterparts "looked to Indonesia as an example for army removal of a head of state" and that "as early as 1967 Lon Nol was in touch with Indonesian army officers, and contact continued with the Indonesian army thereafter. They, the Cambodians, frequently came to see me in the embassy." General Dharsono, Indonesia's ambassador to Bangkok, also played a major role in fostering this relationship, making frequent trips to Phnom Penh.[16] According to William Shawcross, the CIA too made use of Indonesia's Phnom Penh embassy: "This was a two-way street. The Indonesians were giving tactical advice to Lon Nol and reporting to the Agency his plans and other diplomatic intelligence from Phnom Penh."[17]

In December 1969 and January 1970 a team of Cambodian officers secretly visited Indonesia to study how the Indonesian army had managed to overthrow Sukarno.[18] But well before then the US military was deeply involved. One indication of this was its covert operation beginning at least as early as September or October 1969 to train Cambodians in Indonesian military facilities, ostensibly for "civic action" duties, but actually for combat operations. The American ambassador to Indonesia, Francis Galbraith, was aware that a civic action program was under way at a base of Indonesia's Siliwangi division in the mountainous area around Lembang in West Java, involving as usual a few US officers in the training (as was widespread in the Indonesian army). But he was astonished and outraged to find Cambodians were being trained there by US Special Forces officers sent down from South Vietnam. This supposedly secret operation came to light in December 1969 when the proud American officers of these Cambodian "civil action" trainees on their graduation day exuberantly mounted a parade through the city of Bandung, during which the accompanying American officers proudly put on their Green Berets, thereby making clear not only that the US was involved in the training of Cambodians in Indonesia, but that the purpose was for a rather more lethal objective than mere civic action.[19]

Henry Kissinger denied any American role in the overthrow of Sihanouk. In his memoirs he brazenly states: "We neither encouraged Sihanouk's overthrow nor knew about it in advance. My own ignorance of what was going on is reflected in two memoranda to Nixon."[20] Commenting on this, Seymour Hersh aptly writes: "It was the only point in his 1,500-page memoir when Kissinger took any credit for ignorance."[21] The evidence against Kissinger's statement became so strong (in part because of data in William Shawcross's criticisms, soon published in his *Sideshow* in the same year) that Kissinger is reported to have recalled his manuscript for amendments before its publication in 1979.[22] It should be noted that while any American role in the coup against Sihanouk has usually been attributed to the CIA – and there is no doubt that it was in close contact with, monitored, and at least initially encouraged the Cambodians who carried out such action – it was the US military that in the end played the crucial American role.[23]

The most detailed published account of the Nixon administration's planning for the removal of Sihanouk is probably that of Samuel Thornton, a highly esteemed yeoman first-class intelligence specialist in the US navy, who was attached to its Saigon command from mid-May 1968 to mid-May 1969.[24] Several well-qualified writers have taken serious note of his account.[25] Like them, he took strong exception to Kissinger's disclaimer of American complicity in the coup that removed Sihanouk from power. According to Seymour Hersh, Thornton presented his account in 1976 to the Senate Intelligence Committee (whose Select Sub-Committee to Study Governmental Operations with Respect to Intelligence Activities, headed by Senator Frank Church, was then investigating alleged assassination attempts against foreign leaders) but that to his knowledge nothing came of this.[26]

I can well understand the committee's apparent lack of response to his information. For after testifying before the committee on 9 October 1975 with respect to assassination attempts against Indonesia's President Sukarno, I discovered that the committee was under tremendous pressure from Kissinger and CIA head William Colby to lay off, and had yielded to the extent of putting the recent CIA station chief on Taiwan, Harold Ford, in charge of its investigations concerning Sihanouk as well as Sukarno. The chairman of the committee, Senator Church, had learned of testimony I had given to another sub-committee of the Senate Foreign Relations Committee earlier that year on the coup against Sihanouk,[27] and requested that in a second meeting with his committee staff regarding Indonesia, we should extend the scope of our discussions to Cambodia as well. As noted earlier, however,[28] shortly before I was scheduled to testify again, the committee's operations coordinator informed me that the committee had elected not to continue its pursuit of information regarding assassination attempts against Sukarno. It was soon evident that under increased pressure from President Ford, as well as Kissinger and Colby, the committee had agreed to drop both Sukarno and Sihanouk from its investigations and drastically limit these to alleged US involvement in assassination attempts in just five countries – Cuba, Congo (Zaire), the Dominican Republic, Chile and South Vietnam.

Kissinger's denial of any American involvement in the coup that ousted Sihanouk in his letter published in 1979 in the British journal *The Economist* – in response to criticisms of his role in Cambodia in a review of William Shawcross's just-published *Sideshow* – rekindled Thornton's desire to make public his understanding of developments leading up to the coup. In a letter to *The Economist*'s editor of 11 October 1979, Thornton focused especially on Kissinger's allegation that "the United States government was in no way involved" in the overthrow of Sihanouk, a proposition which he stated was, based on his own knowledge, mistaken. Presumably in deference to Kissinger, the cautious editor of the journal, Andrew Knight, felt constrained to carry out an exhaustive check on Thornton's account, pursuing this with a panel that was anything but neutral and objective – including Kissinger himself, the CIA's Richard Helms, and two US admirals. When members of this panel did not corroborate Thornton's statements, Knight wrote him that it would be "irresponsible" for *The Economist* to publish his account. Remarking on this decision, Seymour Hersh appropriately commented: "If all journalists used Knight's method of asking those at the very top about their possible misdeeds, none of the major investigative stories of the past two decades would have become public."[29] Given the US government's continuing refusal to release pertinent documents and the tendency for many decisions concerning covert actions to be limited to oral communication, it is difficult to check on all of Thornton's account, but enough can be corroborated to suggest that those points that cannot be verified at least merit careful scrutiny.

Thornton states[30] that in late 1968 a Vietnamese US intelligence agent relayed a request from "a high official" in the Cambodian government via that agent's US intelligence case officer, who spoke to Thornton after debriefing the agent. The request "was for an indication of possible U.S. reaction to a call for military assistance by leaders of a coup against Prince Sihanouk in which General Lon Nol was to be the principal." After this request had been validated "a special intelligence operations proposal was developed to support the coup." This proposal called for "a request for authorization to insert a U.S.-trained assassination team disguised as Viet Cong insurgents into Phnom Penh to kill Prince Sihanouk as a pretext for revolution," together with "a request for use of Khmer Krom mercenaries, then undergoing U.S. Special Forces training ... to infiltrate key Cambodian Army units stationed in Phnom Penh in order to support the first stages of the coup." Then,

> after assassination of Sihanouk, General Nol was to declare a state of national emergency and issue a public request for U.S. military intervention to preserve order in the country, a task which would necessarily include assaults in force against suspected NVA/VC sanctuaries inside the Cambodian border.

Thornton states that he "was present at the discussions which resulted in this plan, helped prepare the proposal to use Khmer Krom elements, and personally delivered this portion of the proposal to the action officer on the MACV [US Army's Military Assistance Command, Vietnam] intelligence staff."

In late February or early March 1969, Thornton continues, the National Security Council had reviewed and given "blanket approval" to implement the plan, with the message of authorization stating that "exceptional interest" in it had been expressed by what was referred to as "the highest level of government."

Thornton states that Lon Nol had "vehement objections" to the part of the American proposal that called for Sihanouk's assassination. Dismissing the idea, "He doubted that either he or the U.S. Army would be able to control the popular uprising" he felt would develop from such an attempt, whether it was "successful or otherwise, and denounced the idea in strong language." However, Thornton continues, General Lon Nol had a counter-proposal: "to lead a coup when Prince Sihanouk left the country on one of his periodic rest cures" in France.

> It was felt by the General and his advisors that by confronting the Prince with a fait accompli when he was cut off from direct access to his resources they could discourage him from attempting to mount a counter-coup, to them a very real and frightening possibility based on their assessment of the profound support he enjoyed among most

Cambodians, excepting themselves. The General stressed that he had requested originally only overt U.S. military support for a possible coup ... [i.e. not covert assistance in an assassination attempt].

Lon Nol's counterproposal was duly relayed to the NSC whose response Thornton, perhaps unrealistically, found

> surprisingly cool considering the original carte blanche authorization. Officially, General Nol was to be told that while the U.S. would support in principle the accession to power of a Phnom Penh regime more sympathetic to U.S. interests in the region, the U.S. would have to base a decision for commitment of U.S. forces in support of such a regime on the circumstances which obtained at the time the new regime came to power. Unofficially, he was to be told that, although he could in fact expect the requested support, he must understand that the U.S. was sensitive to international criticism on this point, so that he must be prepared for a show of vacillation and great reluctance on our part to his initial, public requests for military assistance. The General indicated an understanding of this problem and an eagerness to go forward on these terms."

Thornton recalled that General Lon Nol also "expressed great interest in the possibility of using Khmer Krom cadre infiltrated into key Army units stationed in Phnom Penh, but insisted that he must first have discussions" with their commander (Son Ngoc Thanh). "A meeting was arranged and took place a few weeks later just inside the Cambodian border. The General and the Khmer Krom commander reached an agreement and the process of infiltration began shortly thereafter." This accords nicely with the account of T.D. Allman, who discussed this matter with Son Ngoc Thanh in 1971.[31]

Whether or not the details of Thornton's recollection were accurate, his account did, indeed, describe with considerable accuracy much of what actually transpired – both the execution of an anti-Sihanouk coup by Lon Nol's group and the antecedent condition for its feasibility – the infiltration of Khmer Serei and other Khmer Krom military elements into strategic units of Lon Nol's army and the Phnom Penh police. According to Sihanouk, Lon Nol gave himself credit for these "rallies" of Khmer Serei, portraying them as "a triumph for his propaganda efforts to win over the traitors."[32] Lon Nol may also have been able to convince Sihanouk that the best way of controlling his old nemesis, the Khmer Serei (whom reportedly the US had ceased to fund after diplomatic relations had been resumed with Phnom Penh in mid-1969), was to incorporate them into much larger existing units of the regular Cambodian army and capital police. It should be emphasized that the Khmer Serei were not the only Khmer Krom whose backing Lon Nol was counting on. Also very important in his calculations was support from the numerically fewer, but better-trained, Khmer Krom incorporated into US Special Forces units in South Vietnam, in whose recruitment Son Ngoc Thanh had also played a major role.[33] In view of the crucial role played by these "rallied" Khmer Serei in the coup of March 1970, it would seem appropriate that Daniel Roy should designate them as a "Trojan Horse."[34]

As for Lon Nol's expectation of US support for a coup, once Son Ngoc Thanh had secretly agreed to have his troops ostensibly "rally" to Sihanouk and be incorporated in the Cambodian army, it would have been clear to Lon Nol that he could count upon American backing. It must be understood that until the very eve of the coup Sihanouk believed Lon Nol to be absolutely loyal to him and also assumed that there could be no collusion between such long-term enemies as Lon Nol and Son Ngoc Thanh. But, of course, Lon Nol had known for at least a decade that this Son Ngoc Thanh and his Khmer Serei had been supported by the United States as an instrument of its anti-Sihanouk policy. So once he had decided to break with Sihanouk, despite an undoubted lingering antipathy towards Son Ngoc Thanh, it made sense for him to align himself with this lifelong rival of the prince in a common American-supported effort to oust him from his leadership of Cambodia. William Colby, the ex-director of the CIA, has acknowledged: "Lon Nol may well have been encouraged by the fact that the U.S. was working with Son Ngoc Thanh ... the obvious conclusion for him, given the political situation in South Vietnam and Laos, was that he would be given United States support."[35] Moreover, Son Ngoc Thanh was so important to the US army's recruiting effort for the roster of its Special Forces that he was supplied with a US helicopter and used it in his visits to US Special Forces (CIDG) camps, and as the ex-CIA head, William Colby, stated, "This certainly gave him the mark of U.S. approval."[36]

Clearly when Lon Nol met with Son Ngoc Thanh and found him ready to provide his troops he would naturally assume that the US supported his plans for a coup. According to Milton Osborne, who had discussions about this matter with Son Ngoc Thanh's brother Son Thai Nguyen (then a Senator in the South Vietnamese government), it was in September 1969, about a month after Sihanouk appointed him prime minister, that Lon Nol initiated negotiations with Son Ngoc Thanh.[37] T.D. Allman, who interviewed Son Ngoc Thanh in 1971, writes that he was told: "Only after I was able to provide assurances that the U.S. would send the Khmer Krom troops ... did Lon Nol act." He further states that Lon Nol's brother, Lon Non, "who played a crucial role in the coup, said the same thing: 'We would not have done what we did', he told me, 'had we not been absolutely sure President Nixon would support us.'"[38]

Whatever Henry Kissinger's denial, there is no doubt that he and senior US army commanders knew about the coup in advance. Thus a key member of his own National Security Council, Roger Morris (who subsequently resigned over Kissinger's Cambodian policies), writes: "It was clear in the

White House that the CIA station in Phnom Penh knew the plotters well, probably knew their plans, and did nothing to alert Sihanouk. They informed Washington well in advance of the coup."[39] According to William Shawcross, the deputy US army commander in South Vietnam, General William Rosson "confirms that the United States commanders were informed several days beforehand that a coup was being planned" and that "American support was solicited."[40] And further down the command chain, a Green Beret captain, Forrest Lindley, in charge of several companies of Special Forces made up of South Vietnamese upland minorities, states that in mid-February 1970 he was ordered to send two of his companies from their camp in the Central Highlands to the nearby Special Forces camp at Bu Prang. He was informed his montagnards were to replace Khmer Serei forces there that had been incorporated into the Special Forces that were being ordered to move into Cambodia, where there was going to be a change in government favorable to the United States.[41] As we will see, these troops were shifted in time to be poised to play an important role in the first stages of the coup against Sihanouk. Great secrecy attended US military operations at this time, as was evident in a confidential instruction from MACV's Saigon headquarters the morning after the coup, entitled "Guidance Concerning Discussion of Current Situation in Cambodia," which stated that

> In view of the sensitivity of the situation, all members of this command are enjoined to refrain from making any comments, prognostications, or speculations concerning the situation, its impact on Republic of Vietnam or U.S. forces ... Comments concerning GVN or RVNAF [South Vietnam Airforce] relationships with the Cambodians against NVA forces *in Cambodia* are also to be avoided.[42]

Not only were Khmer Serei and US Mike (Mobile Strike) forces pre-positioned in Cambodia before the coup. There is also the high probability that the US made available a substantial amount of military supplies to Lon Nol's group shortly before its launching. Here one must note the strange story of the US army's transport *Columbia Eagle*. While ostensibly carrying a load of munitions to the port of Sattahip in Thailand, the *Columbia Eagle* was reported by Army spokesmen to have been "hijacked" just over 100 miles from the Cambodian coast by two armed members of its American crew, referred to as "bearded hippies," and diverted by these "mutineers" to the Cambodian port of Sihanoukville, arriving there three days before Sihanouk's ouster.

According to Pentagon sources as reflected in the press,[43] the *Columbia Eagle* was a former World War II liberty ship of approximately 10,000 tons under charter to the US Military Sea Transportation Service. As the ship, loaded with "bombs and other arms," was steaming through the Gulf of Siam south of Cambodia, two of its crew of thirty-nine, Clyde W. McKay Jr and Alvin L. Glatkowski, produced pistols and demanded that the captain, Donald A. Swann, order the crew to abandon ship or else the two would detonate a bomb and blow up the ship. Acquiescing to the threat, Swann advised the crew of the danger and ordered them to leave the ship, whereupon twenty-four of the crew lowered two lifeboats and pulled away. (The lifeboat with an engine pulling the second were both seen about eight hours later by another US army munitions ship that was following behind and the twenty-four crew members were later picked up by another American munitions freighter, the *Rapphannock*, and taken to Sattahip.) Neither Captain Swann nor any of the few journalists covering the event was ever reported to have explained why he and twelve other members of the crew stayed aboard if they thought there was a real possibility of the ship being blown up, or if they actually believed that the two mutineers were prepared to kill themselves along with the crew that remained on board.

Soon after the lifeboats had pulled away from the ship, its engines revved up and it proceeded toward the Cambodian port of Sihanoukville. A US Coast Guard vessel, the *Mellon*, responding it was said to the ship's radio alert that the *Columbia Eagle* had been seized by armed men, soon reached the ship and followed a short distance behind, and US planes monitored it from above. An order on 17 March to the *Mellon* by the commander of the Pacific Fleet, Admiral John Hyland, to take over the *Columbia Eagle* by force was quickly rescinded by his superior Admiral John S. McCain, commander-in-chief Pacific, but that evening the US assistant secretary of defense, Daniel Z. Henkin, denied that McCain had issued any such order. It seemed appropriate for the *New York Times* to report: "Officials said that there appeared to be considerable confusion and something of a communications breakdown in relaying the known information to Washington," and that "there were indications that the Defense and State Departments were at odds as to the character of the *Columbia Eagle*'s seizure."

The treatment of the two "hijackers" was also confusing. Their request to the Cambodian government for political asylum was promptly granted. (By this time, the coup against Sihanouk had taken place and Lon Nol headed the government in Phnom Penh.) Initially, at a time when Captain Swann was still being held incommunicado by Cambodian authorities, the hijackers were detained in reasonable comfort in a Cambodian navy officers' quarters on the river edge of Phnom Penh and then in one of the city's hotels – meals and lodging at the government's expense.[44] On 8 April Cambodian authorities released the *Columbia Eagle*, and when on its way back to California it reached the US naval base at Subic Bay in the Philippines on 13 April, its captain filed mutiny charges against the two men. But two days later a US Coast Guard spokesman there stated that no formal charges would be filed against them. Then on 4 July they were reported to have been transferred to a prison ship (presumably in the Mekong river port area of Phnom Penh), where they were held in rather loose custody along with five other prisoners including the half-brother of

Sihanouk's wife. They were reportedly able to walk most of the ship's deck, send out for liquor and were permitted to visit restaurants in the company of guards. It was on such an occasion in October that Clyde McKay apparently eluded his guards and dropped out of sight. Glatkowski reportedly suffered a nervous breakdown, and on 6 September was transferred from his loose confinement to a mental hospital in Phnom Penh. The US embassy on 24 September was said to be considering asking for his extradition for medical treatment in the United States, but to be concerned that the move would be criticized as an illegal extradition from a country with which the US had no extradition treaty.[45]

On 14 December The Associated Press reported that Glatkowski "walked into the United States Embassy in Phnom Penh and surrendered to American authorities," while McKay was said to have disappeared.[46] A few days later US government marshals flew Glatkowski to Los Angeles where he was booked in the county jail without bail, with the US attorney explaining that he had been returned secretly "to maintain the safety of the prisoner."[47] Having already been indicted by a federal grand jury (presumably in absentia) on charges of mutiny, assault and "transporting kidnapped persons in foreign commerce,"[48] Glatkowski's prospects could hardly have been enhanced when it was reported that, in the course of a hearing which determined that he was mentally competent to stand trial, two psychiatrists testified that "he had taken LSD up to 150 times and engaged in a homosexual relationship with his alleged accomplice." (The brief press report gave no indication as to how these psychiatrists had ascertained this.) On 2 March 1971 Glatkowski pleaded guilty to hijacking the *Columbia Eagle*, and the US district court judge imposed a ten-year sentence on him for mutiny and five years for assault, the terms to run concurrently. The whereabouts of McKay, this report noted, were still unknown.[49] (I have been unable to trace what happened to McKay, or how long Glatkowski stayed in jail.)

In assessing the veracity of the Pentagon's account of this incident, it would be irresponsible not to take into consideration the brazen mendacity of its top officials, together with Nixon and Kissinger, in denying their "Menu" bombing campaign of areas inside Cambodia's eastern border begun just a year previously. The only motivation Captain Swann, and later the Pentagon, offered for the "hippies" mutiny was that it was to protest the US role in the Vietnam War. The two mutineers allegedly warned the captain that this was simply the first of many similar mutinies aboard such munitions transports designed to impede the war effort in Vietnam. Later, on shore and under detention (though not held incommunicado as was Captain Swann) by officials of the newly installed Lon Nol government, the two hijackers elaborated on their world view. They told an American correspondent that, though they were themselves not members of the antiwar Students for a Democratic Society (SDS), they admired its anti-Vietnam War objectives and that their mutiny should be regarded as "an S.D.S. plot more than anything else," adding that they hoped Cambodia would become a hijackers' paradise. When asked about the future, they responded that if they left Cambodia in the immediate future they would probably go to Cuba.[50]

If more was needed to discredit and establish the exotic character of the two hijackers, they later obliged by making statements from a prison ship where they were held along with five other political prisoners. Their words were reported by the Associated Press (and carried on 4 July by the *New York Times*) including:

> I am a Marxist. I believe in the Marxist way of life ... You know that political power grows out of the barrel of a gun ... If the United States gets me, they will sentence me to death or at least make life not worth living. I won't go back until the present form of government in the United States is overthrown.

It is this sort of overkill – so out of character and baffling for the families of the young "hijackers," as reporters in the United States discovered,[51] that inclines one to ask whether the two men were, for whatever reason, trying to reinforce the Pentagon's explanation for their ship's diversion. Lame as that rationale may have seemed (and still does), it is difficult to come up with any other even semi-plausible explanation for the propitiously timed arrival of an American munitions ship on the eve of a coup that risked resistance and possible civil war.

It was this question, of course, which underlay the request of the few interested newsmen who insisted upon being shown the *Columbia Eagle*'s cargo. Finally on 8 April, the very day of the ship's departure from Sihanoukville, the *New York Times* (9 April 1970) reported: "a small group of newsmen was then taken down into one of the vessel's five holds in a move to demonstrate that none of the munitions ship's cargo had been unloaded in Cambodia." According to the London *Times* correspondent, they were allowed just one hour on board so that "it was impossible to verify the cargo meticulously," and in fact they were permitted to examine just one of its five holds and none of its deck cargo. The one hold they were able to examine contained crates with napalm canisters, and they were left with assurances from the ship's captain that the contents of the other four holds were identical and that he was carrying away the cargo "exactly as it arrived."[52]

But the really central question is, of course, why when the *Columbia Eagle* steamed out of Sihanoukville three weeks after the coup, it turned east and headed back to the United States, some 8,000 miles away, rather than proceeding just another 200 miles to Sattahip in Thailand to where its cargo of munitions was allegedly destined.[53] As reported by the *New York Times* (9 April 1970), the only reason offered for the ship's immediate return to the United States was that the Lon Nol government had set this as a condition for granting permission for the ship to leave Cambodian waters. Is it reasonable to believe that this shaky new government, so critically dependent on the support and goodwill of Washington, would have been disposed, much less able, to exact such an onerous demand on the US military?

Because the dramatic events attending Lon Nol's coup and its aftermath soon overshadowed and absorbed the attention of the few correspondents who initially reported the "hijacking," the event was never sufficiently probed in the international press, although the bizarre account of the ship's odyssey did not go entirely unnoticed. Noting that after Sihanouk's ouster the *Columbia Eagle* became "a forgotten issue," the *Far Eastern Economic Review* quoted one diplomat as saying: "it was the sort of thing that only happens in novels about coups d'état in banana republics in Central America. If you'd dared to have included it in a serious plot, it would have made such a book unbelievable."[54] The few journalists then based in the area and subsequent chroniclers have tended either to back away from reporting a subject that they had insufficient opportunity to investigate and ignored it in their writings, or simply accepted the army's official explanation, bizarre as that was. To challenge the army's explanation, all they would have had to do was later ask why after leaving Cambodia the ship did not continue to its officially stated original destination in Thailand, but rather reversed course. After touching very briefly at Manila, it proceeded directly back to San Francisco, where, together with Long Beach, it had originally taken on its military cargo. During the quarter of a century that has elapsed since this episode serious authors have apparently not been sure enough of their ground to mention it, or else, as the army's public relations staff must have hoped, passively accepted its version.

Sihanouk left Phnom Penh for his biennial medical cure in France on 7 January 1970. It seems probable that Lon Nol would have mounted his coup earlier after Sihanouk's departure had he not been thrown off stride by a serious auto accident that had sent him too to France for medical attention in late October of 1969, from where he did not return until 18 February 1970. During his absence, as mentioned earlier, he left governance primarily in the hands of his co-conspirator, Vice-Prime Minister Sirik Matak.

After Sihanouk arrived in France he had discussions with Lon Nol before the latter's return to Cambodia in mid-February. Sihanouk has written that he then still had full confidence in Lon Nol's loyalty to him and assumed that if there were any action against him Lon Nol could be counted upon to use the army to repress it.[55] There could hardly have been a greater earnest of this trust than his acceptance of Lon Nol's plan to secure the "rallying" of the Khmer Serei to the government and its incorporation into the national army. Presumably when the two met in France Sihanouk told Lon Nol of his plans to visit Moscow and Beijing in an effort to obtain their support in applying pressure on Hanoi and the NLF to reduce the border activities in Cambodia.

By the time Lon Nol returned to Cambodia two of three essential conditions for the coup were in place. First, he knew that the Nixon administration backed the move, and that once Sihanouk was ousted it would promptly recognize and support his successor regime. Second, the process of incorporation and strategic placement of some 2,000 Khmer Serei in the army and capital police was completed.[56] The third essential condition was the propitiously timed entrance into Cambodia of units of ethnically Khmer Krom "Mike Force" from US Special Forces based in South Vietnam. This last requirement, of course, had to await Lon Nol's return and direct oversight.

Soon after Lon Nol's return, and while Sihanouk was yet in France, another essential pre-condition for the move against Sihanouk was begun by Lon Nol and Sirik Matak. This was their successful maneuver to remove three Sihanouk loyalists from pivotal posts in the power structure he had left in place on his departure for France. A campaign was mounted to discredit Colonel Oum Mannorine, head of army ground defense, and Colonel Sosthène Fernandez, head of public security, through charges of smuggling – well founded at least with respect to the latter, but hardly greater in degree than in the case of Lon Nol himself. Through skillful maneuvering and application of pressure in the National Assembly beginning on 26 February, charges were leveled against these two Sihanouk loyalists, culminating in the Assembly's session of 16–18 March, during which they were ousted from their key positions. This campaign apparently helped pave the way for the less dramatic, but even more important removal from authority of the chief-of-staff of the armed forces, General Nhek Tioulong, a man of proven loyalty to Sihanouk, on the basis of his health and having reached the age limit for his position.[57] These moves eliminated the three most important impediments to Lon Nol's uncontested use of the army for his political objectives. And with this accomplished, it was presumably easy for Lon Nol to insert his brother, Lon Non, as chief of the capital's police, a force, it will be remembered, that had already been infiltrated by some of the "rallying" Khmer Serei.

The campaign against these key figures was undoubtedly sufficient to alert Sihanouk to the prospect of a move under way against him. Any uncertainty would probably have been dissipated upon learning that on 8 March, Lon Nol had organized demonstrations against the NLF and Hanoi in Cambodia's Svay Rieng province (the so called "parrot's beak" that jutted into South Vietnam close to Saigon).[58]

According to Henry Kamm, then the *New York Times* correspondent covering Cambodia, and Jean-Claude Pomonti, Southeast Asia correspondent for *Le Monde*, in arranging these demonstrations Lon Nol relied on US Mike Forces who had crossed over from South Vietnam, of whom sixty were then trucked to Phnom Penh where they played a leading role in the much larger and more important demonstrations there organized by the army three days later outside the North Vietnamese and NLF embassies.[59] These culminated in elements from the large crowd led by soldiers in mufti from these same Mike Force Khmer Krom[60] – driving out the embassies' occupants and sacking the buildings.[61] T.D. Allman, who was in Phnom Penh at the time, wrote: "the demonstration was hardly spontaneous. Few of the students and civil servants would have shown up had they not been ordered, and they undoubtedly had no idea that the ultimate result of their demonstration would be the ousting of Sihanouk."[62]

The next day, 12 March, according to Shawcross, the CIA received a report entitled "Indications of Possible Coup in Phnom Penh," informing Washington that the demonstrations were planned by Sirik Matak and Lon Nol. "Sirik Matak," it said, "decided to adopt a showdown policy against Sihanouk's followers" and the army had been put on alert "to prepare ... for a coup against Sihanouk if Sihanouk refused to support the current government or exerted pressure upon the government."[63] That same day,[64] Lon Nol and Sirik Matak made a series of moves they could hardly have even contemplated without backup assurances from the United States. They served notice on the North Vietnamese and NLF embassies canceling all trade agreements, again closed the port of Sihanoukville to shipments destined for their troops, and, rashest of all, gave them an ultimatum to remove all their troops from Cambodian soil within seventy-two hours.[65] It seems likely that only a promise of Mike Force units and additional Khmer Serei elements – which did indeed arrive soon after[66] – or an undertaking to give immediate recognition to their new government once Sihanouk was ousted – which did promptly ensue – would have been sufficient to embolden Lon Nol and Sirik Matak to throw down the gauntlet so defiantly. Any rational[67] assessment of their conduct would suggest that they had been given assurances that, if the supplement of Mike Force and Khmer Serei troops were not sufficient to protect their new regime against the reaction of NLF and Hanoi forces, they could count upon the intervention of additional US military muscle to save them. And, of course, just seven weeks later, after Lon Nol's augmented forces made several largely disastrous probes into Vietnamese Communist border base areas and it was clear that they were being overwhelmed by these Vietnamese troops, that is precisely what President Nixon ordered.

The last act in the coup occurred on 18 March, as Sihanouk was leaving Moscow for Beijing. With armored cars ringing the General Assembly building, its deputies, both pro- and anti-Sihanouk, meekly supported a motion of no confidence in Sihanouk, and in effect formally registered his loss of power to Lon Nol and Sirik Matak.

By the time he left Moscow on 18 March Sihanouk had been unable to win any promise that it would try to influence the North Vietnamese or NLF to reduce their operations in Cambodia's border area. He flew on to Beijing on a similar mission, but though his reception there was much warmer he was equally unsuccessful. Indeed, unbeknown to him, soon after his arrival in

Beijing and while he was attempting – again unsuccessfully – to secure such support, a secret Chinese mission was in Phnom Penh. Arnold Isaacs, the former *Baltimore Sun* correspondent, who was well informed about this period, has written that the objective of the Chinese mission was to induce the Lon Nol government to permit the North Vietnamese and NLF the same conditions for sanctuary use and internal supply that they had possessed under Sihanouk and "give propaganda support to Vietnam's liberation." The quid pro quo was that China would "consider that 'the matter between Sihanouk and the Khmer government was nothing more than an internal problem' with which Peking would not concern itself."[68] Essentially then, if these conditions were met the Chinese were prepared to deal with the Lon Nol government on the same basis as the United States – that is they would regard the Lon Nol government as simply an extension of the previous government that Sihanouk had led, with no need for formal recognition.[69] Isaacs notes that this unsuccessful mission remained on in Phnom Penh until Nixon's invasion; less than a week later, on 5 May, Beijing broke diplomatic relations with Phnom Penh. On that same day Sihanouk announced in a broadcast from the Chinese capital the formation of a Chinese-supported national front, the Royal Cambodian Government of National Union, that incorporated representatives of the still small Khmer Rouge.

In Cambodia, in the meantime, Lon Nol's army embarked during April upon a pogrom against the country's 400,000 Vietnamese minority, about half of whom fled to Vietnam,[70] and many thousands were killed. Whether or not encouraged by the Indonesian officers who were advising him, as Shawcross indicates, Lon Nol sought to unleash the traditional hatred of Cambodians for Vietnamese as a means to compensate for lack of peasant support.[71] And certainly, as had been the case in Indonesia in 1965–6, the army took the lead in organizing and conducting the killings. After Lon Nol's new army volunteers suffered heavy casualties in engaging Vietnamese Communist forces, anti-Vietnamese feelings intensified. Even in Phnom Penh and its environs, where many Vietnamese had lived for generations, Chandler writes: "In May 1970, acting on orders from overwrought superiors and panicky themselves, army and police units rounded up and killed thousands of Vietnamese civilians." He concludes that "the massacres brutalized the conduct of South Vietnamese troops coming to the aid of his government in 1970–71 and eroded the small fund of good will that the regime had earned in other countries."[72]

The massacre of thousands of Cambodian citizens of Vietnamese ethnicity was not the only violence. In addition, Western correspondents themselves witnessed some of the widespread brutal repression by Lon Nol's army against ethnic Cambodians – peasants and townspeople – who, outraged at the ouster of Sihanouk staged large, unarmed protest demonstrations. These continued for several weeks, and the loss of life was considerable.[73]

Within two days of Sihanouk's ouster, the South Vietnamese airforce commenced strikes into sanctuary areas, that were followed on 27 and 28 March by cross-border penetrations of tank-supported infantry of up to three battalions.[74] Apparently still hoping that Sihanouk might return, Vietnamese Communist forces, despite provocative small-scale Cambodian army probes against their sanctuary areas, initially took no offensive actions, and did not begin attacking Cambodian army posts until 29 March.[75] Soon they commenced arming and training Khmer Rouge forces, something they had also refrained from during Sihanouk's rule.

On 29 March, the White House announced that for the first time American troops were permitted to cross the Cambodian frontier "in response to enemy threats." Whereas the term "protective reaction" had previously applied to cross-border air and artillery actions, it was now explained that "border crossings by ground troops 'possibly could occur' at the initiative of field commanders." Evidently it was this new departure and reports of American shelling and gun-ship attacks across the frontier that brought Lloyd Rives, the clearly unbriefed US chargé d'affaires in Phnom Penh, to cable the State Department on 4 April:

> I would appreciate information and guidance. Despite requests, I have received virtually no info from Saigon about what is happening along frontier (perhaps there is no frontier; perhaps there is no info). Are US and ARVN forces shelling or otherwise in action on Cambodian territory? Have rules of engagement been changed?"[76]

It is unclear whether Rives received a satisfactory answer. He appears often to have been, even more than Secretary of State Rogers, kept outside of the "loop" controlled by Nixon, Kissinger, the senior US military and usually Secretary of Defense Melvin Laird. But after American correspondents sighted a US army officer on the Cambodian side of the frontier, the Pentagon came up with its own elegant public explanation. Its spokesman on 9 April stated that US military advisers had been given permission for "protocol" visits across the frontier, but these were merely to "exchange pleasantries and protocol greetings and not to carry on any substantive discussions or to make any plans or commitments."[77]

On 30 March Chargé Rives had cabled Washington: "I do not believe Lon Nol Govt will ask us directly for military ... or economic aid in the near future unless it is in desperate straits."[78] It very soon was in that condition. Under pressure of US and South Vietnamese air attack, cross-border shellings, and probes by battalion-sized South Vietnamese forces as well as now aggressively hostile Cambodian troops, the Vietnamese refused to limit themselves to the enclaves to which they had confined themselves during Sihanouk's rule. They now began dispersing westward, engaging Cambodian forces that stood in their way. Their progress was rapid, provoking a sense of "national emergency" when by 22 April some of their units had reached to within fifteen miles of Phnom Penh,[79] whose only effective defense rested with an outer perimeter manned by troops from the Khmer Serei and Khmer Krom Mike Forces.

This was clearly an unexpected development for the White House and US military leaders in Saigon and Washington.[80] The priority for them now began to shift from eliminating the Vietnamese border sanctuaries to rescuing an increasingly beleaguered Lon Nol government. At first it was hoped that a massive airborne delivery of weapons, additional Khmer Krom soldiers (some 4,800 of whom were assigned to guarding Phnom Penh),[81] and if possible the introduction of Thai and Indonesian troops would be sufficient to rescue the Lon Nol regime. The Cambodian army used Soviet and Chinese rather than US rifles, and a crash program was mounted to airlift these AK-47s and SkS rifles into Phnom Penh from stocks that had been captured in Vietnam, the first shipment of which arrived on the night of 22 April.[82] Apparently a considerably larger number of such weapons was provided by the Indonesian army on the understanding that it would be reimbursed with modern US equipment.[83]

Though the training of Cambodian soldiers abroad soon expanded beyond Indonesia to Thailand, South Vietnam, Malaysia, Taiwan and Australia,[84] the effort to bring Thai and Indonesian troops ("volunteers") into Cambodia to defend the Lon Nol regime was ultimately unsuccessful. In response to a request from Lon Nol for 12,000 regular troops, the Thai government, "after a brief debate between hawks and doves in the cabinet" agreed to send an undisclosed number of troops, recruited from Thailand's Cambodian minority for the defense of Phnom Penh, with an initial contingent of about 1,200 men.[85] This was not, of course, meant to be unrequited support. Thai privates in the 14,000 man contingent Bangkok sent on behalf of the American effort in Vietnam were then receiving a monthly "overseas allowance" from the United States amounting to $39 in addition to their regular pay of $26, while Thai majors were being given $180 on top of their regular monthly pay of $98. In Laos, where the situation and expectations were presumably considered more analogous to Cambodia, privates in the twenty-five Thai battalions of the CIA's "Secret Army" (Armée Clandestine) were being paid by the US an allowance of 300 per cent over and above their regular pay. (One of the most closely held secrets at the time was the fact that Philippine "allies" and especially Koreans fighting in South Vietnam were paid appreciably more – Korean privates being rewarded with twenty times the pay they received in Korea.)[86]

It was the recently disclosed information of the nature of these hitherto secret payments that now brought the US Senate to take a position effectively halting the move to fund the entry of Thai troops in support of Lon Nol's government. The chairman of the Foreign Relations Committee, Senator J. William Fulbright, argued "It is time to stop making mercenaries out of allies, and allies out of mercenaries," and introduced in the Senate a unanimously backed motion on 20 August 1970 barring the use of

American funds to pay for contingents of foreign troops fighting in support of the governments of Cambodia and Laos. Specifically targeted "was the use of American funds to pay the bills of the 5,000-man 'volunteer' force Thailand [had] been considering sending to help the Lon Nol Government in Cambodia."[87] With no promise of financial reward, it was predictable that soon after the American Senate made known its position, the Thai government lost interest in the idea of contributing troops to the defense of Lon Nol's government.

Presumably this same financial consideration was a significant factor in weakening the efforts of the faction in the Indonesian army that urged sending troops to support Lon Nol.[88] Their campaign had already been undercut by Indonesia's astute civilian foreign minister, Adam Malik, who thought the idea foolish and probably disastrous. He was temporarily able to block the proposal by arguing to President Suharto, who appears to have initially supported this interventionist faction, that such a move would destroy Indonesia's claim to nonaligned status. But the proponents of intervention, including General Ali Murtopo, head of Opsus (Special Operations), continued to press their case, arguing now not for direct financial reward from the United States but for repayment in the form of a re-equipment of the Indonesian armed forces with modern US arms. That formula clearly had appeal for Suharto and several other generals. And it enjoyed support not only from some quarters in the American military, but apparently also from the US ambassador to Indonesia, Marshall Green, who, according to a former senior officer of Indonesia's crack Siliwangi division, had earlier been a vigorous proponent for sending a Siliwangi brigade to fight on the American side in Vietnam. Also, according to this officer, a persistent advocate of sending Indonesian troops to Cambodia was the US navy-supported Rand Corporation's Indonesia specialist, Guy Pauker.

To head off this gathering bandwagon, Adam Malik worked feverishly to provide a diplomatic alternative to military intervention. This was his plan, announced in mid-April, for an international "Djakarta Conference on Cambodia," with the aim of ending civil war there by a cease-fire, reinforcing the supervisory International Control Commission and the departure of *all* foreign troops from Cambodian soil – extending ultimately, when the conference was held 16–17 May, to American and South Vietnamese as well as Vietnamese Communist forces.[89] Though realistic enough to appreciate the utopian character of this official expectation, Malik was able by this gambit to outmaneuver and neutralize the hawkish Indonesian generals, arguing, as Weinstein notes, "that since Indonesia was engaging in sensitive diplomatic efforts with respect to Cambodia, nothing else should be done for the time being."[90] Equally important in convincing Suharto was Malik's argument that it would be grossly inconsistent for Suharto, in chairing the Jakarta conference of nonaligned states scheduled for mid-May (an event the Indonesian president looked forward to with pride), to be seen as so obviously aligning his country with American policy.

Malik's success in convincing Suharto of his view was evident when the Indonesian president, in the course of his speech at a state dinner in Washington on 26 May, hosted by President Nixon, urged that *all* foreign forces (meaning US and South Vietnamese as well as Vietnamese Communist troops) should be withdrawn from Cambodia.[91]

16　Invasion of Cambodia

Even before hope ended for strengthening Lon Nol's government by the introduction of Thai and Indonesian troops, its deteriorating prospects in Cambodia precipitated a critical American decision. On 19 April, just a month after Lon Nol's coup against Sihanouk, a senior *New York Times* correspondent reported from Saigon that ranking members of the US mission and military command "now harbor growing doubts about the capacity of the new government to control the Cambodian people and to stabilize the domestic political situation." He continued:

> As a result, the initial optimism that was prevalent among Americans here in the wake of the Cambodian coup d'état has given way to skepticism. A month after the event, the officials are tending to doubt that American interests are likely to be served after all.

These officials acknowledged that as a consequence of recent fighting "the North Vietnamese and Vietcong have now effectively secured their sanctuaries in eastern Cambodia," with a senior American commander observing: "At this point I think the best we can hope for is the equivalent of the military situation that prevailed before the coup. Our chances of making much real capital out of the situation seem to be diminishing rapidly."[1] And the threat was soon no longer confined to the border areas, for, starting on 13 April, "enemy forces had been detected moving westward into Cambodia from the border areas, cutting roads, blowing up bridges, harassing military posts and towns."[2]

The actual period of decision making for an invasion extended only over the second half of April 1970. By the middle of the month the situation had become sufficiently minatory for General Abrams, commander-in-chief of US forces in Vietnam, and the US ambassador to Saigon, Ellsworth Bunker, after meeting together, to send parallel recommendations to Washington that the US launch an attack against the "Fishhook" (a Cambodian territorial projection into South Vietnam), together with joint American–South Vietnamese attacks against other Communist Vietnamese border bases. But it was not until it was confirmed on 20 April that Saang, a provincial capital only 18 miles from Phnom Penh, had fallen that the extent of the deterioration of Lon Nol's position hit Nixon with sudden force. From then until the end of April he received daily briefings on the steadily worsening situation from Richard Helms, director of the CIA. Apparently the only one of the president's top officials who took a strong stand against an invasion, even if it was limited to the "Fishhook," was Secretary of State William Rogers, who was credited with delaying Nixon's decision by a day. It was Henry Kissinger, his national security adviser, with whom the president consulted most. Together with the military, Kissinger was apparently one of those most strongly in favor of an invasion – not merely by South Vietnamese troops supported by American air-power, as some of his advisers seemed to prefer, but for there also to be US ground force input.[3]

By 29 April 1970, when President Nixon ordered American troops to join the South Vietnamese forces in invading Cambodia, the commander-in-chief of Lon Nol's army recalls, "the capital of Phnom Penh was in effect surrounded on three sides by territory in the hands of the enemy."[4] Whatever Nixon's and Kissinger's explanatory rhetoric to the American public, the central reason for the invasions was not, as they publicly insisted, to facilitate the withdrawal of American troops from Vietnam but rather to save Lon Nol's desperate and tottering regime from collapse. As a team of senior *New York Times* correspondents who covered Washington and Cambodia concluded: "High [American] officials felt the whole rationale for defending South Vietnam would collapse if they acquiesced in a Communist take over of Laos and Cambodia." By the time Nixon made his decision to invade, it was evident "how intimately the survival of the Lon Nol regime had become linked in his own mind with American success in Vietnam."[5]

Le Monde's Indochina correspondent observed:

> The American–[South] Vietnamese military intervention came just in time to save the Phnom Penh government, which could have been overthrown by the Vietcong. If the Americans had not attacked their rear with a massive strike against their "sanctuaries" and also staged a frontal attack by landing the "Khmer Kroms" at Phnom Penh, they could easily have made a clean sweep of Lon Nol's army. They might not even have had to.[6]

This immediate threat to the capital, still standing bereft of protection by the hoped-for Thai or Indonesian troops, meant that at the outset of the US–South Vietnamese invasion the highest priority was given to flying in additional Khmer Krom Mike Force units for Phnom Penh's defense.[7]

It is likely, though as yet unproved, that in making his public announcement on 20 April that he would withdraw 150,000 more American troops by the end of the year, Nixon was already disposed to agree with the US military's persistent call for an invasion of easternmost Cambodia and realized that this move would be more readily acceptable to the American Congress and public if preceded by such a popular promise. In any case, the timing was propitious and made more plausible the rationale that he provided in his address ten days later when he justified the invasion as a means of protecting the process of US troop withdrawal from Vietnam.

Under sustained pressure for an invasion from General Abrams in Saigon, the president, though himself already clearly leaning in that direction, appeared to need further self-assurance. On the night of 25 April, in the company of only his close friend Charles ("Bebe") Rebozo and Henry Kissinger, he arranged to see, himself for the fourth or fifth time, the film "Patton," the story of the defiant, aggressive, and ultimately successful World War II tank-commanding American general. By the next day Nixon had made up his mind in favor of a joint American–South Vietnamese invasion, and so advised the National Security Council.[8] Over the next two days he devoted himself to writing a speech which he would deliver the night of 30 April to the American public to explain and justify the invasion that would then be in progress.

Without informing Congress, Nixon authorized an invasion, focused first on the "Parrot's Beak" of eastern Cambodia's Tay Ninh province by South Vietnamese troops, supported by US planes, artillery and advisers, which began on 29 April. This was followed the next day by an invasion by US forces alone, initially focusing on the "Fishhook" area some 50 miles to the north. Neither the American chargé in Cambodia nor Lon Nol were informed in advance of the invasions.[9] (The word "invasion" was apparently deemed to have too pejorative a connotation, and the White House enjoined officials to use instead the term "incursion," apparently assuming this had a less harsh meaning).[10]

Realizing his action would be highly controversial, Nixon had arranged for the mailing on the day of the attack to American newspapers and television stations of a set of answers to questions likely to be asked regarding it, and especially points in his speech, which, it was hoped, would respond to and placate their expectedly surprised audiences.[11]

The next day the United States Information Agency sent a one-and-a-half page cable to the embassy in Cambodia on "media guidance" in handling Nixon's address. In it there was absolutely no mention of Cambodia's people or their government. Its first and major point read: "His [Nixon's] decision to authorize US–SVN military action was taken to save American and allied lives imperiled by communist occupation of Eastern Cambodia … there should be no nuance of apology or hesitation on part of the USG [US Government]." The third and final paragraph of the "guidance" cable was entitled "Pike Pamphlet" and read

> Saigon now plans to issue Douglas Pike's new pamphlet, 'Viet Cong Strategy of Terror,' on or about May 11. This document will deserve full exploitation by our media once it is made public, and will be basic reference work in future output to keep before our audiences use of terror as

calculated Communist political policy in course of its aggressive designs against South Viet-Nam and Laos and Cambodia."[12]

Addressing his television audience on the evening of 30 April, Nixon treated the American public to a forcefully delivered deception, calculated to persuade it that American lives and the continuing withdrawal of American forces from Vietnam and his "Vietnamization program" were all now suddenly threatened by greatly increased aggressive enemy actions based across the border in Cambodia. The speech incorporated egregious distortion and outright lies concerning the existing situation and the American record in Cambodia. Among them: American policy since the 1954 Geneva Agreement "has been to scrupulously respect the neutrality of the Cambodian people" and "For five years neither the United States nor South Vietnam has moved against these enemy sanctuaries because we did not wish to violate the territory of a neutral nation."

The central thrust of Nixon's address was that the withdrawal of 150,000 American troops from South Vietnam "over the next year," which he had promised some two weeks before – and that he knew was one element in his Vietnam policy that *was* popular with the American public – was now jeopardized by heightened aggressive Vietnamese Communist forces based in the Cambodian cross-border sanctuaries. The invasion he had just launched was "indispensable for the continuing success" of his withdrawal program. Involved in his decision was "the opportunity for 150,000 Americans to come home in the next 12 months." The invasion was "not for the purpose of expanding the war into Cambodia, but for the purpose of ending the war in Vietnam." The American and South Vietnamese thrusts into Cambodia would "attack the headquarters for the entire Communist military operation in South Vietnam ['COSVN' (Central Office for South Vietnam)]." (Much larger American forces had been fruitlessly searching for this still elusive, constantly shifting, target when it was located in South Vietnam and it was never found, nor would it be; and some reports at this time indicated that with the recent South Vietnamese probes into the sanctuaries it had been moved back into South Vietnam.) "To go to the heart of the trouble" meant "cleaning out major North Vietnamese- and Vietcong-occupied territories, these sanctuaries which serve as bases for attacks on both Cambodia and American and South Vietnamese forces in South Vietnam."

"If when the chips are down the world's most powerful nation – the United States of America – acts like a pitiful, helpless giant, the forces of totalitarianism and anarchy will threaten free nations and free institutions throughout the world." Referring then to Woodrow Wilson and his "great decision which led to victory in World War I," to "Dwight D. Eisenhower" and his "decisions which ended the war in Korea and avoided war in the Middle East," and to "John F. Kennedy [who] in his finest hour made the great decision which removed Soviet missiles from Cuba," it was now, Nixon averred, incumbent for him to act.

> I would rather be a one-term president and do what I believe is right than to be a two-term president at the cost of seeing America become a second-rate power and to see this nation accept the first defeat in its proud 190-year history.

Nixon stipulated that American troops would penetrate no more than 21.7 miles into Cambodia and would remain no more than two months. He did keep to his two-month schedule, but US ground force penetration was somewhat deeper than he had announced, and US air-power ranged over the whole country, not only continuing the B-52 bombing that had commenced in mid-March 1969 but now also providing tactical jet and helicopter support to Cambodian troops and the South Vietnamese forces whose invasion had preceded the American one by a day. And though it was originally understood that the invading South Vietnamese armed forces would remain no more than six months, in fact they stayed on for fourteen. And soon after his troops had crossed into Cambodia, South Vietnam's president, Nguyen Van Thieu, made clear that his troops would not be bound by restrictions as to the area and duration of their operation. He announced: "We have no deadline, no limits. We will move on intelligence. When there is a target, we will strike it." Noting that he had already supplied some 4,000 American-trained ethnic Cambodian troops (presumably the Mike Force contingents), he said "he expected that more would have to be sent to Phnom Penh to bolster the position of the Lon Nol Government." Then with a candor Nixon could hardly have relished, he said that the next six months would be critical for the war as well as for "political leaders," and continued: "If Lon Nol and Cambodia stand for the next six months ... then I think Mr. Nixon will win the Congressional elections this year and be re-elected in 1972, because then the operations will have proven a success."[13]

As is well known, the public and congressional reaction to Nixon's invasion was deep, intense and widespread. In an unbriefed and outraged Senate, John Sherman Cooper, a Republican, and Frank Church, a Democrat, announced they were drafting an amendment precluding the use of any funds already appropriated by Congress for military operations in Cambodia. Though finally passing the Senate on 30 June, the amendment was turned down by the House.[14] A stronger "end-the-war" amendment to a military sales bill (encompassing Vietnam as well) by Senators George McGovern and Mark O. Hatfield, even more worrisome to the administration, on 25 June failed in both houses but picked up considerable support. Nevertheless, while these amendments were being debated, on 22 June the Senate voted to terminate the Johnson administration's Tonkin Gulf Resolution, which had provided the major "legal" foundation for Nixon's, as well as his predecessor's, Indochina military involvement.

When I was invited down to Washington by a bipartisan group of senators a week after Nixon's speech to prepare a rejoinder and a critique of the questions and answers the White House had sent out to the media, I found that they and a good many other members of Congress were seething with anger at both the invasion Nixon had ordered and his and Kissinger's duplicitous demeanor in the period leading up to it.[15] The anger of some was compounded because they were convinced the two had calculatedly misinformed them right up to the invasion as to the likelihood of deeper involvement in Cambodia.[16] Some 250 foreign service officers in the State Department signed a protest statement, and an angry, and apparently sympathetic, Secretary Rogers refused the White House's request for their names. Four of Kissinger's senior aides resigned in protest against both the invasion decision and his having misled them in the process of arriving at it.

Universities and colleges around the country exploded with student and faculty protest, with about a third of them closing or having many classes suspended, and suffering physical disruption, including destruction of ROTC premises in some. Many students joined approximately 100,000 protesters who descended on Washington in a show of their opposition to what Nixon had done. Student anger sometimes triggered violent reaction from citizens who regarded their protest as unpatriotic. On 3 May at Kent State University in Ohio the Governor, James Rhodes,

> taking his cue from Nixon and [Vice President] Agnew, declared that he would "eradicate" rioters and demonstrators there – "They're worse than the Brown Shirts and the Communist element and also the nightriders and the vigilantes. They're the worst type of people we have in America."[17]

The next day the National Guard that he had sent to the campus to control rioting by unarmed antiwar students fired on and killed four of the protesting students and wounded fifteen others.

According to the report of the President's Commission on Campus Unrest, led by two distinguished heads of academic institutions, even before the Kent State affair there had been some twenty new student protest strikes daily against the Cambodian invasion: during the four succeeding days there were a hundred or more each day. "By the end of May ... nearly one third of the approximately 2500 colleges and universities in America had experienced some kind of protest activity." Rioting that led to the police killing two black students and wounding twelve others at Jackson State College in Mississippi on 14 May was attributed by the commission to severe racial problems.[18] (But protest against the war may well also have been a factor.)

On 6 May, in an episode that the press did not report and the potential of which was known to only a few, Cornell University, too, narrowly escaped serious bloodshed. A large number of students planned to make a peaceful march down the hill to the town of Ithaca, wishing thereby to symbolize their outrage against the attack on Cambodia. Fortunately, the very worried Tompkins county district attorney, Matthew McHugh, telephoned the university's administration to warn that several hundred people from the surrounding hills had learned of plans for the march and had begun to assemble in downtown Ithaca with their shotguns "to teach the students a lesson." Only the wisdom and skill of two highly respected antiwar student leaders, who immediately understood the danger of such a confrontation, persuaded the march's organizers to call it off shortly before it was scheduled to begin, thereby averting the virtual certainty of bloodshed.[19]

The 31,000 American and 43,000 South Vietnamese troops that Nixon ordered into Cambodia cleared the Vietnamese Communist forces from only a few of their border sanctuaries and, of course, never found that will-o'-the-wisp of COSVN. They did, however, manage to drive some of the Communist forces much deeper into Cambodia – which military intelligence had not anticipated. This reportedly infuriated Lon Nol, who argued that the US should have positioned a blocking force behind (to the west of) the sanctuaries to prevent such a deployment.

The *New York Times* Washington correspondent, Tad Szulc, reported six weeks after the invasion began that high officials in the Nixon administration now acknowledged that "in its decision to move into Cambodia, the White House completely misjudged the Communist political and military response." It had

> disregarded estimates of Communist intentions that both the State Department and the Central Intelligence Agency began to provide in early April on the consequences of the overthrow of Prince Norodom Sihanouk ... Instead, the officials said, the White House seemed to have accepted the judgements of the Joint Chiefs of Staff and of General Creighton W. Abrams ... The military judgement was said to have been that the North Vietnamese and the Vietcong were unable to conduct major new operations in Cambodia and Laos while pursuing the war in South Vietnam ... the White House accepted the military judgement that the enemy would concentrate on fighting for the sanctuaries or, if he lost them, to be too weakened and too far from North Vietnamese supply centers to react offensively.[20]

Nothing could better describe the miscalculations of the White House and the US military than Chargé Rive's frantic telegram sent to Washington two and a half days after Nixon's 30 April address.[21]

> Since noon 2 May Cambodian military positions along route 1 at Neak Louong ... and Kampong Trabek ... and town of Banam ... have fallen. III Corps armoured squadron has halted at position about 12 kilometers west of Svay Rieng ... The town of Takeo [some 30 miles into Cambodia] has been encircled and cut off from Ang Tassom. Two battalions have been holding out for three nights of continued attack and suffering from heavy losses. Two para [parachute] battalions in Ang

Tassom unable to break through enemy defensive line ... Generals request US/ARVN air strikes on enemy positions around Takeo Town ... Also request helicopter-lift of 2 Khmer Krom Special Forces battalions scheduled for delivery Phnom Penh nights 3 and 4 May to make rendezvous with two para battalions attempting to move from Ang Tassom. This movement requested Asap.

Rives recommended against meeting any of these requests, except perhaps air attacks against VC/NVA fire bases around Takeo because:

If credence is to be given President's recent speech, as well as to his overall policy, we must draw a line somewhere. Movement of troops beyond Svay Rieng, helicopter-lift of troops to Takeo area and attack in support [of] latter's defenders would only appear [to] accomplish exactly what USG's critics fear, i.e. get USG further involved into hopeless morass. There is no rpt no guarantee that any of requested moves will do other than push enemy toward Phnom Penh or elsewhere into Cambodia without really resolving issue or stopping VC/NVA.

Rives concluded by urging that he be instructed to inform the Cambodian military that their requests were denied or else that Lon Nol be told "exactly how much he can expect from the USG [government]." The Cambodian government, he concluded, "seems to be becoming truly conscious [of] its weakness and desirous [to] fall into our arms but I am convinced we must stop somewhere, even if Lon Nol govt threatened."

The unhappy chargé had yet to appreciate that the hubris of those who had ordered the invasion would not risk the ridicule that such early exposure of their fallibility could have incurred. (It is, I think, worth noting that the Nixon administration's long record of duplicity and misinformation concerning the situations in Cambodia, Laos and Vietnam had the long-term consequence that in subsequent years there was a tendency by Congress and the public to be initially skeptical of and discount any US government reports as to the atrocities of the Khmer Rouge.)

Having been completely bypassed in Nixon's decision to invade Cambodia and long jaundiced as to the reliability of the US military's reporting on Vietnam, the Senate Foreign Relations Committee sent two former National Security Council staffers, James Lowenstein and Richard Moose, to Cambodia a few days after the invasion to determine what was actually happening. On 6 May through the US Phnom Penh embassy they cabled the Senate Foreign Relations Committee a report (based on their meeting with Prime Minister Sirik Matak, the foreign minister and army chief-of-staff) that presumably left Chargé Rives feeling vindicated but evidently had no influence in keeping Nixon even within the limits of the objectives described in his 30 April address. Among the points they made were the following:

During past 24 hours North Vietnamese and Viet Cong (NVA/VC) had taken towns of Kratie, Senmoram and Banam ... and advanced to within 18 miles of Phnom Penh.

At Banam NVA/VC had handed out arms to ethnic Vietnamese thereby virtually tripling their strength. This occurring also in other areas with result earlier estimate of enemy strength ... must be raised ...

US and ARVN [South Vietnamese Army] forces have been asked to move deeper into Cambodia along Route 1 beyond Svay Rieng. [Cambodian Government] would favor ARVN advance to clear highway as far as Phnom Penh.

US/ARVN presence along Cambodian border is pushing NVA/VC deeper into Cambodia. Enemy believed planning to take everything east of Mekong. Infiltrating toward Phnom Penh increasing and capital will be in danger of falling within few days ...

Cambodians think US will produce what is necessary to save Cambodia and that it will arrive within ten days.[22]

Vietcong (NLF) and North Vietnamese forces quickly moved deeply into Cambodia, while maintaining some of their border area concentrations. They soon cut vital roads, such as that linking the capital to the port of Sihanoukville, and took a number of strategically located towns, including Kratie; but they had no incentive to capture Phnom Penh. The name of the game for them was still the military struggle inside Vietnam. To occupy Phnom Penh would require a diversion of too many troops from their priority contest there. Moreover, with a US naval blockade of Sihanoukville and the Mekong river, the other major route for imports to the capital, it would have been impossible for them to feed such a large urban population. Their own most essential supply needs were met by seizing Cambodian army stocks and, together with their Pathet Lao allies, capturing the key southern Laotian towns of Attopeu (which they took the day after the South Vietnamese army invaded Cambodia), and Saravene, which they captured on 9 June. By taking over these key Laotian towns and their environs they were able to expand the Ho Chi Minh trail network sufficiently to significantly increase their capacity to move military supplies into northeastern Cambodia.[23]

As for the American military in Vietnam, though they managed to eliminate most of the major Communist border sanctuaries, this was at the cost of considerably increasing the territorial responsibility of the US and South Vietnamese military. After these invasions, Cambodia no longer provided the United States and South Vietnam with a neutralist flank flawed only by scattered Communist border sanctuaries. What had previously been a state whose presence helped contain the war in Vietnam now became a broad military and political battlefield dominated not by Cambodians, but by American, South Vietnamese, NLF and North Vietnamese forces. And as for Nixon's vaunted program of "Vietnamization," there were now appreciably fewer South Vietnamese troops to take over from departing Americans when domestic political pressures brought the president to resume his withdrawal schedule later in the year. With some of Saigon's most seasoned troops now absorbed into battle areas inside Cambodia for a total of fourteen months, the number of its soldiers available to replace the American soldiers Nixon had promised to withdraw were that much fewer. And the pillaging and raping that these South Vietnamese forces visited on the Cambodian population during their long sojourn in the country was probably, next to the American bombing, the most important factor in pushing peasants into the arms of the Khmer Rouge.

Within a year of Sihanouk's ouster, especially after Lon Nol suffered a severe stroke in February of 1971, it had become clear that this firmly American-backed leader had become militarily incompetent and politically had alienated almost all of the elements that had earlier backed him.[24] His military dependency on Khmer Serei and Khmer Krom Mike Force troops had been critical from the outset of his rule. And this was initially reflected when Lon Nol's military tribunal cleared Son Ngoc Thanh of all charges of treason leveled against him in Sihanouk's reign,[25] and Lon Nol appointed this former nemesis as his "special counselor" and deputy premier in August 1970.[26]

In retrospect, it may be difficult to appreciate how highly American military and diplomatic personnel had regarded the Khmer Krom troops and their confident expectations of the consequences of infusing them into the Cambodian army. The intelligence branch of US forces in Vietnam and the American embassy in Phnom Penh respectively portrayed these Khmer Krom additions to the Cambodian army as providing its "backbone" and "most effective part ... and constituting its mobile strategic reserve."[27]

Whereas initially Khmer Krom Mike Forces apparently moved into Cambodia in no more than company strength, during 1970 a total of eight battalions were deployed there.[28] While in Vietnam these Mike Forces had operated only at platoon or company strength; in Cambodia, where they frequently encadred existing units, their officers assumed battalion and even regimental commands. And following the coup, additional Khmer Krom were recruited from South Vietnam's Mekong Delta, trained by US Special Forces and encadred into Cambodian army units. An additional group of about 1,000 relatively poorly trained men usually identified as KKK (Khmer Kambodja Krom) or "White Khmer," who had previously at least nominally supported Sihanouk and operated as an irregular force on both sides of the border, sometimes addicted to banditry, was also incorporated into the Cambodian army as a brigade during 1971.[29] The deputy assistant chief of intelligence for US forces in Vietnam informed me that as of mid-1971 approximately 15,000 Khmer Krom trained by US Special Forces had been infused into the Cambodian army, and that some (less-trained) South Vietnamese Army popular force Khmer Krom units from the Mekong Delta had also been incorporated, the total for which he did not specify.[30] A month later Son Ngoc Thanh told me that he himself had recruited more than 10,000 of these Khmer Krom Mike Forces, some of whom had been introduced into Cambodia before the coup, with the first major contingent having arrived in April 1970 and a second in June, with other smaller additions following. He said that he had recently recruited an additional 2,500 Khmer Krom in the Delta that were currently being trained for entry into Mike Force, and that he could easily arrange for the recruitment of another 10,000.[31] These Khmer Krom additions, *Le Monde*'s Jean Paul Pomonti wrote, were expected to form "the nucleus of the new Cambodian army."[32]

During the next year and a half the performance of the Khmer Krom military components of the army continued to eclipse its poorly trained and less experienced regular units, the disparity in quality having become even greater with the forced draft program (financed by the United States) that undertook to more than quadruple the size of the Cambodian armed forces. As the relative effectiveness of Khmer Krom units grew, Son Ngoc Thanh's support to Lon Nol's government became even more crucial. With this in mind, it is all the more understandable why Lon Nol, now bearing the title of "President," on 18 March 1972 – precisely two years after the coup against Sihanouk – appointed Son Ngoc Thanh as both premier and foreign minister[33] – the same offices he had occupied in 1945 during the last months of the Japanese occupation.

Three months later an increasingly demented and authoritarian Lon Nol staged and won a long awaited and very fraudulent election. The American embassy, despite the internal protest of its chief political officer, made no protest at the blatant corruption and ruthless intimidation by Lon Nol that accompanied the election, nor did it raise any objection to his assertion to the electorate that if he did not win all American aid would cease. (Shawcross notes that "If the embassy insisted on visibly fair electoral procedures," the victory of In Tam [the uncorrupt and popular minister of interior who had the courage to run against Lon Nol] "would be possible, and then Lon Nol could be gently retired.") Lon Nol won this rigged election, prompting In Tam to suggest that Americans "stew in Lon Nol's juice."[34]

On the basis of this "mandate" and American acquiescence to the way it was achieved, Lon Nol now turned on Son Ngoc Thanh and forced his resignation, along with those of Lon Nol's three other strongest rivals – General In Tam, Sirik Matak (his former partner), and Chen Heng, who pending the election had occupied the now largely powerless office of chief-of-state. But Lon Nol was still so dependent on the Khmer Serei and Khmer Krom Mike Force soldiers that were supporting his government that he appointed one of Son Ngoc Thanh's chief lieutenants to serve as premier and kept as ministers two others that Thanh had appointed in the cabinet.[35]

On my return to Phnom Penh in August of 1971, I had found the city choked with refugees, its population, according to Long Boret, the acting prime minister, having nearly tripled since the coup against Sihanouk – reaching approximately 1,800,000.[36] I found broad consensus among those with whom I talked that most of the refugees had fled from the approximately half of the country now dominated by North Vietnamese, NLF (Vietcong) forces and the Khmer Rouge maquis whom they had begun to arm shortly after Sihanouk's ouster. The general consensus among those with whom I talked was that the major cause for the influx of refugees was the American bombing of the part of the country the Lon Nol government no longer occupied. Much of this area, as was the case by now in considerable areas of Laos and Vietnam, had become a sort of free-fire zone.

Shawcross writes:

> There were fewer controls and restraints on targeting in Cambodia than in Vietnam. The South Vietnamese Air Force ... considered Cambodia an open field, and although most American pilots were, as a rule, more careful, several have testified that almost anything in Cambodia constituted a legitimate target ... By now, [Operation] Menu was a recognized procedure, not merely a geographic area ... it meant that the falsification of Cambodian bombing reports was now accepted as normal.
>
> The main area of the new [post-30 April 1970] extended bombing was known as Freedom Deal. Originally a box of Northeastern Cambodia between the border and the Mekong, it was gradually pushed southward and westward into more heavily populated areas, as the fighting spread. Bombing outside Freedom Deal was reported as being inside, and bombing in populated areas inside as being in wild, uninhabited places ... In the eastern half of the country, B-52 missions were controlled (and targets were selected) by the Seventh Air Force in Saigon. West of Freedom Deal – west of the Mekong river, in effect – B-52 strikes could be requested by the Cambodians.[37]

In August 1971, I found the American ambassador, Emory Swank, a deeply troubled and bitter man. He complained to me that his embassy's role in coordinating the US bombing, which he appeared to deplore, was an operation lacking even suitable maps, and that for some areas the embassy was even dependent on grossly outdated ones from the French period. Thus, it could often not be ascertained whether or not a village occupied the area at which air strikes were being directed.[38] Initially the major input of the US Phnom Penh embassy was to vet the plethora of air strikes requested by the Cambodian army west of the Mekong, but in February 1973, an embassy panel "became responsible for bombing strikes in all parts of the country except the eastern Freedom Deal area, which was still a virtual free fire zone."[39]

Shawcross states that, in judging the plethora of requests from the Cambodian military for air strikes, the embassy's bombing panel had available only outdated maps of a scale of 1:50,000. He cites the complaint of pilots of the US 8th Tactical Fighter Wing that the maps they had to use "lacked sufficient detail and currency to pinpoint suspected enemy locations with some degree of confidence" and that they had asked for up-to-date maps with a scale of 1:5,000 – ten times as large – but did not get them. If fighter pilots had this much difficulty in being accurate, it can be imagined how blind the pilots of the much-higher-flying B-52s must have been in delivering their almost daily loads of bombs.

The bombing that I had found to be the major reason for the stampede of refugees into Phnom Penh in August 1971 continued to be the major cause for the exodus from the countryside to the capital and to the few smaller towns controlled by the Lon Nol government. Indeed, until the bombing finally ended in August 1973, Shawcross writes, "the refugees tended to cite American bombing as the main reason for flight."[40] Ben Kiernan cites a State Department study from as early as 25 September 1970 stating that Lon Nol's own intelligence had observed that "aerial bombardments against the villagers have caused civilian loss on a large scale" and that peasant survivors were turning to the Cambodian Communist Party (Khmer Rouge) for support. He also notes a report of 2 May 1973 by the CIA's director of operations regarding bombing consequences in Cambodia's Southwest Zone who reported that the Khmer Rouge (CPK) had launched a new recruiting drive.

> They are using damage caused by B-52 strikes as the main theme of their propaganda. The cadre tell the people that the Government of Lon Nol has requested the airstrikes and is responsible for the damage and the "suffering of innocent villagers" ... The only way to stop "the massive destruction of the country" is to ... defeat Lon Nol and stop the bombing. This approach has resulted in the successful recruitment of a number of young men ... Residents ... say that the propaganda campaign has been effective with refugees and in areas ... which have been subject to B-52 strikes.[41]

Shawcross observes that the Nixon administration's "justification for bombing Cambodia had been to protect Americans in Vietnam," and that "since October 1970 the Congress had included in every military appropriation bill a proviso expressly forbidding bombing in Cambodia except for that purpose" and that, even though "by the end of March 1973 there were no American troops left in Indochina, [s]till the bombing of Cambodia increased." Not until 10 May 1973 did the House of Representatives join the Senate to block any funds from the Supplemental Appropriations Bill for the bombing of Cambodia. But in fact Nixon persisted in the bombing until 15 August 1973, by which time he could claim responsibility for American planes dropping a total of 539,129 tons of bombs on the country since his initially secret bombing began on 18 March 1969 – well over three times the total dropped on Japan during World War II.[42] (Some 104,000 tons of this amount was accounted for by the "secret bombing" that endured from 18 March 1969 to 30 April 1970.)[43]

It should not be assumed that initially the bombing generated only refugees who flocked directly to the Khmer Rouge standard. Many saw themselves as returning to Sihanouk, whose post-coup alliance with the Cambodian Communists the Chinese government had insisted on and nurtured. But as late as August 1971, General In Tam, then minister of security and internal affairs and the senior Cambodian leader who enjoyed most respect locally as well as with the American embassy, estimated at no more than about 10,000 the total Cambodian anti-Lon Nol Government insurgents. (This did not, of course, include the considerably more numerous Vietcong and North Vietnamese troops.) Of this 10,000 he reckoned no more than about 4,000 were actual Khmer Rouge, and the balance – apparently made up of several components, some led, he said, mostly by ex-secondary school teachers – he referred to by a Cambodian term, which at my urging he somewhat embarrassedly translated as "Khmer striving against being under American occupation."[44]

By the time the Khmer Rouge captured Phnom Penh on 17 April 1975, of course, the situation had radically altered; and though not yet the monolith it became under the man later known as Pol Pot, the Khmer Rouge, despite severe internal divisions, completely dominated the opposition forces, and no room remained for non-Communist insurgents.[45]

Notes

Foreword

1 Jayne S. Werner, "George McT. Kahin: A Tribute," *Bulletin of Asian Scholars*, 32 (October–December 2000) is superb, as is "George McT. Kahin," written by one of Kahin's most distinguished students, Benedict Anderson, for the 2000 *Cornell Necrologies*, available from the Dean of Faculty Office, Day Hall, Cornell University, Ithaca, New York 14853. Werner's essay has a list of Kahin's publications and his congressional testimonies and statements. A completely footnoted manuscript of this Foreword is deposited in the George McT. Kahin Papers at Cornell University's Olin Library. Those papers are presently closed. The author deeply appreciates the encouragement and help of Audrey Kahin in researching this essay, and the most helpful comments of Mark Selden.

2 During the 1969 Cornell crisis, a powerful, wealthy member of the university's Board of Trustees flew George, Professor Fred Marcham, and me from Ithaca to his magnificent home on New York City's Sutton Place that overlooked the East River. This trustee knew we opposed the university's policies, and he most hospitably listened to our views over a wonderful meal. As we three got into his limousine for the trip back to the airport, I joked to George, "I think I just found my price." George was appalled. He remained silent all the way to LaGuardia as I lamely tried to explain that I hoped my price was at least a little higher than that.

1 The Indonesian revolution

1 As to MacArthur's intention to reestablish Dutch government, see his *Reminiscences* (1985), New York: De Capo Press (Time), p. 256, and the statement of the former chief of intelligence of his Far Eastern Command, General Charles A. Willoughby, before the Committee on Un-American Activities, US House of Representatives, 16 December 1957, Washington DC: US Government Printing Office (1958: 13–14). After stating that "If MacArthur had had his way, the Borneo campaign [carried out under his orders by the Australian army under General Blaney] would have been extended to include the recapture of Java and the Netherlands East Indies," he then quotes MacArthur directly as having stated: "I had planned to move immediately on to Java with the Australian troops and restore the Dutch Government under Van Mook, which would have rapidly brought law and order there as it had done in New Guinea."

2 I am as guilty as anyone for having in previous writings given such short shrift to the full statement and limiting its reproduction to only the final proclamation statement, issuing from both Hatta and Sukarno, following Sukarno's actually quite significant preamble.

3   Address of Insinjur [Engineer] Sukarno in announcing the PROCLAMATION OF INDONESIA'S INDEPENDENCE on 17 August 1945, lodged in the archives of the Republic's Ministry of Foreign Affairs, Yogyakarta, as of September 1948, when a copy was given to me by Haji Agus Salim, Minister of Foreign Affairs (translation into English as it had been earlier rendered by its staff).

It has been my assumption that the full text of Sukarno's statement – and not just the spartan few lines attributed to both him and Hatta – was withheld from the contemporary press either because the Japanese still had that medium firmly under control or else because it was believed by the Indonesians that publication of the rest of the statement would provoke a harsh Japanese reaction, which it almost surely would have. The Japanese army and its Kempeitei certainly had much less tolerance for any assertive Indonesian nationalism than did the head of Japan's naval presence in the Indies, Admiral Maeda, who, on the basis of his other supportive actions, might well have encouraged the assertive tone of Sukarno's full statement.

4   The Committee of Good Offices was set up after the first Dutch "police action" of July 1947 "to assist in the pacific settlement of [the] dispute between Indonesia and the Netherlands." It was made up of representatives from Belgium, Australia and the United States, see George McTurnan Kahin, *Nationalism and Revolution in Indonesia* (1952), Ithaca NY: Cornell University Press, pp. 216–18.

5   See below.

6   *Modern Indonesia Project*, Interim Reports Series (1957, 1962), Ithaca NY: Cornell Southeast Asia Program, p. 34.

7   Discussions with the writer, New York, September–October 1962.

2   Communism and the Republic

1   According to the photographer of the ANTARA news agency (in a report submitted in Yogyakarta on 8 October), who had accompanied Musso, Sjarifuddin, Harjono and Wikana, they departed Yogyakarta on 7 September, arriving in Surakarta the same day before proceeding on to Madiun the next day and arriving in Kediri on 10 October. He stated that Setiadjit joined them in Kediri, but he made no mention of Suripno, who presumably went with some of the other leaders in another car.

2   Discussions with Sukarno, Muntok, Bangka, 1–3 May 1949.

3   Discussions with Hatta, Muntok, Bangka, 4 May 1949.

4   Discussions with Hatta, Muntok, Bangka, 2, 4 May 1949.

5   Musso was shot and killed on 31 October; Sjarifuddin and Suripno were captured on 1 December and shot later that month at the time of the Dutch attack.

6   Those with a serious interest in these matters should read Selosoemardjan's classic study, *Social Changes in Jogjakarta* (1962), Ithaca NY: Cornell University Press, keeping in mind that during the revolution and for several years afterwards the Sultan of Yogyakarta, with Selosoemardjan as his advisor and chief lieutenant in agrarian matters, pioneered the changes in the agrarian sphere adopted by the Republic.

7   He was clearly implying Sjahrir's Socialist Party (PSI) and his judgment were vindicated when national elections were finally held in 1955.

3   The Dutch attack on Yogyakarta

1   According to Air Commodore Soejono, who was deputy chief-of-staff of the airforce at the time of the Dutch attack (as well as concurrently head of the

Republic's airforce on Sumatra), in a series of interviews I had with him in Jakarta in August 1995, Yogyakarta's Maguwo airfield was practically unde-fended when the Dutch attacked, its one machine gun having been taken over a few days before by a senior army officer for use in Surakarta. Implicit in his cate-gorical statement that no defense at all was put up at Maguwo was severe criticism of Chief-of-Staff Air Marshal Suriadarma (subsequently voiced by many Indonesians) who was responsible for such plans. Soejono says that there were forty-seven air cadets quartered in a dormitory at Maguwo and that the Dutch killed them all.

2 There were two witnesses to this shooting, both of whom I interviewed. The bodies were recovered by the Indonesian Red Cross, whose autopsy found that these nine people had been shot at close range by a pistol.

3 Report from Col. D.R.A. van Langen on Visit of Sultan Hamid II of Pontianak to Jogja, 10–11 January 1949, file no. 3070, Inventarisen van de Persoonlijk Archief van S.H. Spoor, 2.21.036.01 (Algemeen Rijksarchif, The Hague [here-after ARA]).

4 I described the situation in East Indonesia rather extensively in my book *Nationalism and Revolution in Indonesia* and in the September 1949 issue of the journal *Pacific Affairs*.

5 Dr Charles O. Van Der Plas had entered the Dutch civil service (Binnenlands Bestuur) in 1908. Influenced by Snouk Hurgronje, he studied Islam and Arabic and was consul in Jeddah. He was an influential adviser for indigenous affairs to the colonial regime and later governor of East Java. He returned with the British immediately after the Japanese capitulation as representative of the Netherlands Indies Civil Administration (NICA) and again became governor of East Java. His jurisdiction also covered Madura where he established a separate state. He was a legendary figure among Indonesians with a reputation for political cunning, shrewd intelligence and a keen understanding of Indonesian society.

6 A. Arthur Schiller, *The Formation of a Federal Indonesia* (1955), The Hague: Van Hoeve, p. 193.

7 *Nationalism and Revolution in Indonesia*, p. 235.

8 Schiller, *Formation of Federal Indonesia*, p. 79.

9 Those wishing to learn more about this generally neglected island, and especially its socioeconomic and political history, should read Mary Somers Heidhues's superb study, *Bangka Tin and Muntok Pepper* (1992), Singapore: Institute of Southeast Asian Studies.

10 The KRIS was regarded as one of the ablest of the irregular armed organizations and was made up of the considerable number of Sulawesians then on Java. Ventje Sumual, son of a Christian Minahassan sergeant in the KNIL (Dutch colonial army), had a well-deserved reputation as an effective Republican officer.

11 Numbering between one-and-a-half and two battalions. I had an opportunity to talk to a senior officer of one of these Mobrig battalions soon after the attack of 9 January.

4 The Dutch transfer sovereignty

1 For a full discussion of the agreement, see George McT. Kahin, *Nationalism and Revolution in Indonesia* (1952), Ithaca NY: Cornell University Press, pp. 421–32.

2 For a perceptive evaluation of Australian policy, see the review by Frances Gouda (in *Indonesia* 67 (April 1999): 193–200) of the collection of official Australian government documents pertaining to Australia's role in the Dutch–Indonesian dispute edited by Philip Dorling and David Lee, *Australia and Indonesia's Independence* (3 vols: 1994, 1996, 1998), Canberra: Australian Government Publishing Service.

3 The Darul Islam (Islamic State) movement had grown up in West Java as a protest against the concessions made by the leaders of the Indonesian Republic under the Renville Agreement of 1948. Headed by Kartosuwirjo, it had an independent government and was an aggressive political force opposed to both the Republic and the Dutch. For a fuller description of the Darul Islam at the time, see *Nationalism and Revolution*, pp. 326–31.

4 Sumitro's letter of 29 August 1949 from The Hague to Palar, Soedjatmoko and Sudarpo in Washington.

5 Alastair Taylor, *Indonesian Independence and the United Nations* (1960), Ithaca NY: Cornell University Press, p. 444.

6 *Ibid.*, n. 58, p. 243,

7 *Ibid.*, n. 17, p. 444.

8 *Ibid.*, p. 244.

9 Sumitro's letter of 15 September 1949 from The Hague to Palar, Soedjatmoko and Sudarpo.

10 Taylor, *Indonesian Independence*, pp. 240, 482.

11 For the Indonesian calculations, see "Memorandum of the Indonesian Delegations" attached to Sumitro's letters dated 15 December 1949 and 7 October 1949 to Sudarpo, Palar and Soedjatmoko. For a fuller breakdown of the debt and its apportionment between the Netherlands and the new Indonesian government see E.P.M. Tervooren, *Statenopvolging en De Financiele Verplichtingen van Indonesie* (1957), The Hague: Martinius Nijhof, especially pp. 111–12, 341–69 and 163–87 for an analysis of the proceedings.

12 For the Cochran proposal, see *Officiele Bescheiden Betreffende de Nederlands-Indonesische Betrekkingen 1945–1950* (1996), vol. 10, The Hague: Insituut voor Nederlandse Geschiedenis, pp. 197–8.

13 *Ibid.*, p. 387. In the "internal debt" category, 1,352 million guilders was debt owed the Java Bank, 529 million was Treasury bills, 978 million currency in circulation and 100 million "obligations to be taken over from the Republic of Indonesia." Taylor, *Indonesian Independence*, p. 482. Taylor's calculations usually indicate a US$ to guilder rate of approximately 3 to 1. Under the exchange rate at that time the Dutch guilder was actually worth US$0.378, and I have used that figure for my calculations. Cochran asserted that this agreement involved a reduction of the external debt by 2 billion Ned. guilders (p. 179), an assertion that is open to question. See Taylor, *Indonesian Independence*, p. 248 and Tervooren, *Statenopvolging*, pp. 183–7.

14 C. Smit, *De Indonesische Quaestie: De wordingsgeschiedenis der souvereinteitsoverdracht* (1952), Leiden: E.J. Brill, pp. 280–1.

15 Thus in Sumitro's report of 15 December 1949, written and sent to Palar, Sudarpo and Soedjatmoko just after he had returned from attending a meeting of the KNIP in Yogyakarta where he had assisted Hatta in defending especially economic and financial aspects of the Round Table Conference Agreement, he wrote

> for your information Hatta's health is very poor. This is not generally known yet but as a matter of fact the doctor has prescribed that he rest for at least two months, which under the present circumstances is of course impossible. In view of this, he could not attend the sessions himself and had to have a group of people who could prepare the government's answer on the many criticisms against the RTC agreements.

16 Robert J. McMahon gives this *New York Times* report the prominence it deserves. See his *Colonialism and Cold War* (1981), Ithaca NY: Cornell

University Press, p. 256, for this and his book generally for an excellent account of the American role in the Dutch–Indonesian dispute.

17 The Indonesian delegation recognized this as being a central objective of the Netherlands' negotiators from the outset of the Round Table Conference, as was reflected in Sumitro's letters of 29 August and 19 October 1949 to Palar, Sudarpo and Soedjatmoko.

5 McCarthy, Lattimore and Cochran

1 A copy of the first of these memoranda, "The United States and the Situation in Indonesia" which I submitted in June 1949 can be found in the General Records of the State Department (RG 59) at the National Archives.

6 Return to Indonesia

1 I did not know of this at the time, only learning about it many years later thanks to documents retrieved under the Freedom of Information Act.

2 Allison notes this in his book *Ambassador from the Prairie* (1973), Boston: Houghton Mifflin, p. 308.

3 An extensive account of the PRRI rebellion, and the American involvement in it, may be found in the book my wife, Audrey, and I jointly authored, *Subversion as Foreign Policy: The Secret Eisenhower and Dulles Debacle in Indonesia* (1995), New York: New Press. For the concurrent and allied Permesta rebellion, see Barbara S. Harvey's excellent account in her *Permesta: Half a Rebellion* (1977), Ithaca NY: Cornell Modern Indonesia Project, Monograph Series.

4 Ithaca NY: Cornell University Press, 1956.

5 Howard Jones, *Indonesia: The Possible Dream* (1971), New York: Harcourt Brace Jovanovich, p. 49.

6 Yani made similar statements to Colonel Benson, the US military attaché during his farewell call on 7 June 1965. Yani stated that the US was the "only nation since independence that has openly supported rebellion" and that Sukarno believed that the "imperialists intend to kill him" – the imperialists including not only the Americans but also the British. See Amemb to Secstate, Djakarta 2650 6–7–65 (National Archives).

7 For further discussion of the Church committee's aborted investigation into alleged CIA involvement in assassination attempts against Sukarno and Sihanouk, see below, ch. 15, and Kahin and Kahin, *Subversion as Foreign Policy*, pp. 114–15.

7 Struggle over Malaysia

1 For an excellent recent assessment of British policy in this period, and the threats posed by the radical opposition party in Singapore, see Matthew Jones (2000) "Creating Malaysia: Singapore security, the Borneo territories, and the contours of British policy, 1961–63," *Journal of Imperial and Commonwealth History* 28(2): 85–109.

2 Indeed, the Tunku apparently imposed two conditions on his willingness to join with Singapore in a Malaysia federation: an arrest program in Singapore and the simultaneous accession of the Borneo territories, see *ibid.*: 101, citing Singapore (Selkirk) to CO (Sandys), No. 13, 5 January 1963, PREM 11/4346 (PRO).

3 It is interesting to note the remarks of Robert Trumbull, who was *New York Times* correspondent in Southeast Asia, with excellent relations to the British in Singapore and Malaya. When I spoke with him in Manila on 30 July 1963, he

said that approximately one month before the Tunku's speech of 27 May 1962, where at a Press Club luncheon the Tunku outlined the Malaysia proposal, Trumbull had met with the Deputy High Commissioner who spoke of the idea of a Malaysian confederation.

4 I must disclaim any suggestion that I am a Brunei specialist, but so little that is accurate has been written about its modern history, especially that of the early 1960s, that I feel an obligation to make this brief mention of it. Brunei has been all too neglected by scholars interested in Southeast Asia, and I know of none that treat the 1960s except the anthropologist Donald Brown and D.S. Ranji Singh, who devotes a few chapters to the period in his *Brunei 1839–1983: The Problems of Political Survival* (1991), Singapore: Oxford University Press.

5 Note, however, a couple of brief pieces: Michael Leifer, "Decolonisation and international status: the experience of Brunei," *International Affairs* April 1978: 240–52, and Michael Leigh, *Brunei: Independence for Whom?*, Parliament of the Commonwealth of Australia, 1984, Current Issues Brief, No. 1.

6 Azahari had formed his Partai Rakyat in 1956 with a vision of "enlarging the Brunei sultanate to include all of its former territory in Sarawak and Sabah." Stanley S. Bedlington, *Malaysia and Singapore* (1978), Ithaca NY: Cornell University Press, p. 107; Singh, *Brunei*, pp. 169–70.

7 In June 1962 the Philippine government had lodged a formal claim to most of North Borneo, based on the inherited claims of the Sultan of Sulu.

8 Approximately 400 men from Brunei did cross to Indonesian Borneo prior to the revolt and received some military training, between 100 and 150 of them returning to fight in the revolt.

9 According to Michael Leigh, these troops possessed "an almost mystical aura of ruthless effectiveness, an aura that is of great value to the Sultan in the event of his being challenged by elements from within his own armed forces or broader society." Leigh, *Brunei*, p. 7.

10 One should note, however, that there had been a considerable decline in oil production in the period before the revolt and a consequent increase in loss of jobs of those who would in relative terms have been the better educated. But although the income from oil declined (by 34 per cent between 1956 and 1963) the accumulated surplus continued to rise (in gilt-edged securities in London), as did the interest on this surplus. This amount was sufficient for Brunei to live on the interest without touching the capital. Interview with Joseph S. Gould, UN Economic Adviser to the Government of Brunei, June 1963.

11 Their attitudes also came through loud and clear in British embassy reporting from Jakarta, which has recently been declassified. With respect to Nasution's attitude, see the confidential report of 29 July 1963 (FO371/175249) which noted that "over the question of Malaysia every piece of information we have seems to show that Nasution is among its strongest opponents, even to the point of spite-fulness," and the Annual Report for 1963 (FO371/175244 36513) which noted that Nasution had become "one of the most rabid advocates of the anti-Malaysia cause." As late as 23 May 1965, Ambassador Gilchrist in a Confidential Report of a Meeting with Dr Hatta, stated that "Hatta emphasized that he had been against Malaysia long before Subandrio and Soekarno had adopted such a line ... Malaysia was a bad conception, giving the Chinese a bridge-head in South East Asia, whence they would come to dominate the whole of Malaysia" (FO371 180343 36513).

12 Telegram No. 410 Jakarta to Secretary of State, 1 September 1961, pp. 3–4. Actually two of the major leaders on Sumatra – Mohd. Natsir of the Masjumi party and Colonel Dahlan Djambek – were still in the hills then. Djambek was killed on 13 September and Natsir subsequently surrendered.

13 This account is based upon my discussions with Ichsan in Manila on 31 July and 2 August 1963. I regard Ichsan as one of my most reliable informants, and I've seen nothing in any other account that contradicts this.

14 Manila to Secretary of State, no. 156, 2 August 1963, 1 p.m. 4 pp. (National Archives). The cable was signed by Stevenson, though the information I had supplied had been given to Howard Jones, who passed it on to him. No mention of Jones was made in the cable.

15 Under the settlement on West Irian finally reached between the Dutch and Indonesians in August 1962, the Dutch agreed to transfer the territory to an interim UN administration which would hand it over to the Indonesians six months later, with the Indonesians agreeing to hold an "act of free choice" before the end of 1969 to see whether the Irianese wished to remain in Indonesia.

16 Roger Hilsman, *To Move a Nation* (1967), New York: Doubleday, p. 399.

17 Howard Palfrey Jones, *Indonesia: The Possible Dream* (1971), New York: Harcourt Brace Jovanovich, p. 284.

18 This judgment is based upon anecdotal evidence as gleaned from a small number of British colonial officials, but I would expect that if considerations of career, postings and pay could be eliminated it would be the judgment of most colonial officials in these territories, and indeed most had felt the pace of decolonization in these relatively backward areas to be too rapid, with a good many preferring a separate Borneo state, rather than a fusion of their territories with Malaya or Malaya and Singapore.

19 Jones, *Indonesia: The Possible Dream*, p. 287 and Hilsman, *To Move a Nation*, p. 403.

20 Hilsman, *To Move a Nation*, p. 403.

21 Sandys left for Kuala Lumpur on 23 August, having written to the Australian prime minister the previous day: "I am off to Kuala Lumpur tomorrow to hold the Tunku's hand. I am afraid he has rather lost his nerve just lately." CRO to Canberra (Sandys to Menzies), 22 August 1963, No. 1571, PREM 11/4349 (PRO).

22 Hilsman, *To Move a Nation*, p. 404.

23 Matthew Jones, "From the Manila summit to the creation of Malaysia: August–September 1963" (typescript), citing Telegram Kuala Lumpur to DOS, 17 September 1963, No. 253, and Kuala Lumpur to DOS, 18 September 1963, No. 259, POL 25–3 MALAYSIA, RG 59, DSR, USNA.

24 Frederick P. Bunnell, "Guided democracy foreign policy," *Indonesia* 2 (October 1966): 63.

25 Hilsman, *To Move a Nation*, p. 409.

26 By the time Jones wrote a book concerning his stewardship as ambassador seven years later, his outrage at this provocation had considerably subsided, and his attitude towards Sukarno had become generally more critical. That book, *Indonesia: The Possible Dream*, written after his retirement from the diplomatic service under a fellowship from the Hoover Institution on War, Revolution and Peace, reflects considerably less understanding of Sukarno's personality and actions than Jones manifested while ambassador. Nevertheless, I view Jones as one of the ablest of the American ambassadors sent to Indonesia.

27 Hilsman, *To Move a Nation*, p. 404.

28 My conversation with Ichsan, Sukarno's chef de cabinet, Manila, 2 August 1963, as conveyed to Ambassador Jones and by him to Ambassador Stevenson. Ichsan's remarks are incorporated in Stevenson's telegram to the Department of State later the same day.

29 Interview with Sukarno, Bogor, 20 July 1963.

8 Cornell and the coup

1 See Chapter 9.
2 We did manage to visit the country for a couple of months in 1985 by entering at the Medan airport, which at that time was not yet computerized. As we were in the midst of a large group of foreign tourists, the immigration officer apparently did not think it worth consulting his book for people on the black list and we were passed through with the others.

9 Opposition to the Vietnam War

1 Discussions with Tran Van Do, 14 January 1970.
2 With respect to the promised election and its expected outcome, see my book *Intervention: How America Became Involved in Vietnam* (1986), New York: Alfred A. Knopf, especially pp. 59, 62, 88–90, and relevant endnotes.
3 Credit for organizing the National Teach-In should, as I recall, go primarily to Professor Marshal Sahlins and colleagues of his in the Department of Anthropology at the University of Michigan.
4 According to Kai Bird's biography of the Bundy brothers, "Only in retrospect did MacBundy realize that Johnson had rushed him off to Santo Domingo not because there was any pressing need for his presence on the island, but 'to keep me away from all those wild men'" – presumably the Teach-In participants. Kai Bird, *The Color of Truth* (1998), New York: Simon & Schuster, p. 320.
5 This did not, however, mean that there was no opposition, as I discovered after I requested my investigative dossier from the Office of Security at the State Department. Amongst the papers there I found an undated memo that read as follows:

> It is noted that KAHIN has been extremely vociferous of late in opposing the Administration's policy in Viet-Nam. In the NY Times of 5/17/65, reprinted in the Congressional Record of 5/18/65, he was indicated to have been the leader in presenting the opposition's position at the National Teach-In held in Washington in mid-May. In view of this anti-Administration policy stand, it might be wise to check with the requesting Bureau … to see if they still wish to employ him as a consultant. If a decision is made to employ this bird, who has been quite troublesome in the past, there is a possibility of some repercussions from Pennsylvania Ave.

6 The proper translation was "Institute for the Propagation of the Faith." With most of its leaders Mahayana Buddhists, it was the most active and politically significant component of the United Buddhist Association of Vietnam.
7 When the underground Buddhist organization introduced me to Trinh Dinh Thao at his large villa just outside Saigon, he was regarded as one of South Vietnam's leading attorneys and counted among his clients the Japanese embassy. In mid-1945, during the last half year of Japan's occupation, he had served as minister of justice in Emperor Bao Dai's Tran Trong Kim cabinet. In 1954, 1959 and 1965 he had been arrested because of participation in groups advocating a peace settlement between Saigon and Hanoi. He was still advocating such a settlement when I talked with him on 16 January 1967. With the formation of the NLF-sponsored Provisional Revolutionary Government in June 1969, he emerged as vice-chairman of its Advisory Council.
8 In Saigon I met with Philip Habib, head of the embassy's political section and widely – and justifiably – regarded as Ambassador Lodge's hatchet man. He

acknowledged that General Walt and another marine corps general had indeed encouraged Tri Quang to believe that the American government supported him in his Buddhist Struggle Movement, and said "They had no business doing so." It was readily evident that Habib had nothing but contempt for the Buddhist leaders (interview, Saigon, 12 January 1967).

And, of course, Lodge had shifted 180 degrees from his attitude towards Tri Quang of three years before when it was convenient for him that the Buddhists opposed Ngo Dinh Diem.

10   Casualties and pacification, 1966/7

1   After his tour in Vietnam ended in 1968, Negroponte became US delegate to the Paris peace talks on Vietnam. He later served as US ambassador to Honduras (1981–5), Mexico (1989–93) and the Philippines (1993–6). In 2001 the Bush administration appointed him US ambassador to the United Nations.
2   Two months later, on 21 February 1967, Fall was killed by a booby trap when he was accompanying a marine sweep in the northern part of South Vietnam in the "Street without Joy," of which he had written earlier.
3   General Thi, immensely popular in I Corps area and with good relations with the Buddhist political activists, had been the dissident general most feared by Ky and Thieu. Following strong American pressure, culminating in an 11 March 1966 letter from General Westmoreland (of which I have a copy) "inviting" him to the United States to use "our medical facilities for a complete physical examination," he had felt obliged to leave Vietnam for the United States.
4   See the *New York Times*, 18 September 1967.
5   For details as to the extra allowances paid Korean troops and the various additional subventions paid the Korean government for the use of its troops in Vietnam, see George McT. Kahin, *Intervention: How America Became Involved in Vietnam* (1986), New York: Alfred A. Knopf, pp. 335–6.

11   Possibilities for peace, 1971

1   George did not have time to write this chapter. He just left a note stating his intention to include a section on our 1971 trips to Vietnam, and so I have reconstructed this brief account on the basis of the notes we took at the time (Audrey Kahin).
2   His views of the talks were reflected in a number of articles, for example, two of those published in the *New Republic*: "Impasse at Paris" and "Going Nowhere in Paris," *New Republic*, 12 October 1968, 26 December 1970.
3   *Washington Post*, 3 July 1971. In conversations with George, the village officials evidenced strong antipathy against this district head, Major Vo Van Dai, and repeated many of the things mentioned in this article.
4   Duong Van Minh had led the generals that threw out Diem in 1963. But the following year the United States, particularly elements in the Pentagon and General Paul D. Harkins, head of the US Military Assistance Command in South Vietnam, got rid of him at least in part because he indicated he wanted to explore negotiating possibilities with the enemy and that he was opposed to bombing the north.
5   Interview with a candidate from Danang for the Lower House elections, who was backed by the Buddhists (Saigon, 26 July 1971).
6   Interview with members of the student union of Van Hanh University (Saigon, 23 July 1971).
7   *International Herald Tribune*, 12 November 1971.

12   North Vietnam, 1972

1   Bernard Fall, *The Two Viet-Nams: A Political and Military Analysis* (1963), New York: Praeger (rev. edns 1964, 1966).
2   For more on Chu Van Tan, see the book by the former OSS agent in northern Vietnam, Archimedes L.A. Patti, *Why Vietnam?* (1980), Berkeley: University of California Press, especially p. 493.
3   This neglect of political prisoners held by the Saigon government was reiterated in the Paris Agreement, finally signed 27 January 1973, where paragraph c of Article 8, Chapter III leaves resolution of "the question of the return of civilian personnel captured and detained in South Vietnam" in the hands of "the two South Vietnamese parties" (Saigon and the PRG) themselves.
4   See Seymour M. Hersh, *The Price of Power: Kissinger in the Nixon White House* (1983), New York: Summit Books, pp. 614–15.
5   Officially fifteen B-52s were shot down, six more were seriously damaged, and eleven other aircraft (probably F-4s) were also downed. But privately the losses acknowledged were considerably higher. (Hanoi claimed to have shot down thirty-four B-52s.) A total of forty-four more American pilots were captured.
6   For the fullest discussion of the agreement, see Gareth Porter, *A Peace Denied: The United States, Vietnam, and the Paris Agreement* (1975), Bloomington: Indiana University Press.
7   For Nixon's pledge of economic assistance, see Nayan Chanda, *Brother Enemy: The War After the War* (1986), San Diego: Harcourt Brace Jovanovich, p. 153; Gabriel Kolko, *An Anatomy of War* (1985), New York: Pantheon Books, p. 447; and Marilyn Young, *The Vietnam Wars: 1945–1990* (1991), New York: Harper Collins, p. 279.

13   Cambodian neutrality and the United States

1   Henry Kissinger, *White House Years* (1979), Boston: Little Brown, p. 463.
2   Herbert De Ribbing was a retired (1963) Swedish career diplomat who had subsequently served on several United Nations conciliation missions and was appointed by it on 15 August 1966 to head its Cambodia–Thailand reconciliation mission. He was away when I was in Phnom Penh on this visit, and his deputy, Dr James Frederik Engers, a Dutch historian who had been with the UN's secretariat since 1946, was then in charge of the mission.
3   This was a body set up under the 1954 Geneva Agreements to monitor their proper implementation, with a staff made up of equal numbers of Canadians, Indians and Poles.
4   Noel Deschamps was as at this time dean of the Phnom Penh diplomatic corps, having served there for five years. Though it was to his Australian embassy that the United States had turned to represent American interests when Sihanouk severed diplomatic ties with Washington in 1965, he was privately critical of many aspects of US policy towards the country.
5   Interviews with Ambassador Noel St Clair Deschamps, Phnom Penh, 3 and 9 August 1967.
6   Interviews with M.K.L. Bindra and Dr J.F. Engers, Phnom Penh, 10 and 12 August 1967.
7   The foregoing account is based upon Son Ngoc Thanh's approved brief biographical statement (mimeo), Ministry of Information, Phnom Penh, 1971; my own interview with him there in August of 1971; Roger M. Smith, *Cambodia's Foreign Policy* (1965), Ithaca NY: Cornell University Press, pp. 25–8; and David P. Chandler, *The Tragedy of Cambodian History: Politics, War and Revolution since 1945* (1991), New Haven: Yale University Press, pp. 18–20.

8 Chandler, *Tragedy of Cambodian History*, p. 23.
9 During which he earned a law degree in Poitiers.
10 Michael Leifer, *Cambodia: The Search for Security* (1967), London: Pall Mall Press, p. 39. See also Donald Lancaster, *The Emancipation of French Indochina* (1961), London: Oxford University Press, p. 238.
11 Chandler, *Tragedy of Cambodian History*, p. 58.
12 Leifer, *Cambodia*, pp. 40–1.
13 Chandler, *Tragedy of Cambodian History*, p. 63.
14 *Ibid.*, p. 64.
15 Smith, *Cambodia's Foreign Policy*, p. 46. See also *Foreign Relations of the United States, 1952–1954, Vol. XIII: Indochina, Pt 1* (1982), Washington: US Government Printing Office, pp. 475–7, and 488–9 for Sihanouk's disappointment at the lack of American support.
16 Chandler, *Tragedy of Cambodian History*, p. 68
17 Leifer, *Cambodia*, p. 50.
18 Gravel edn, *The Pentagon Papers*, Vol. I, p. 160.
19 Leifer, *Cambodia*, pp. 65–6.
20 Chandler, *Tragedy of Cambodian History*, pp. 81–2.
21 Lancaster, *Emancipation*, p. 358.
22 See Leifer, *Cambodia*, pp. 55–9; Smith, *Cambodia's Foreign Policy*, pp. 68–70; and Leszek Buszynski, *S.E.A.T.O.: The Failure of American Security* (1983), Singapore: Singapore University Press, pp. 18 ff.
23 For more details on the Bandung Conference, see above Chapter 6. The following account is drawn from my personal records of the conference (at which I was present), the most important of which is the unpublished verbatim account now deposited with the John M. Echols Collection on Southeast Asia in Cornell University's Kroch Library, and is available in its Rare Book Room. Most of the information included here, however, can be found in my little book, *The Asian–African Conference: Bandung, Indonesia, April 1955* (1956), Ithaca NY: Cornell University Press.
24 Smith, *Cambodia's Foreign Policy*, pp. 91–5; and Leifer, *Cambodia*, pp. 72–4.
25 Smith, *Cambodia's Foreign Policy*, pp. 102–5; and see also Leifer, *Cambodia*, pp. 74–5.
26 Chandler, *Tragedy of Cambodian History*, p. 81.
27 Son Ngoc Thanh himself gives 1958 as the year of the Khmer Serei's establishment in his approved biographical statement. That date tallies with Laura Summers' findings in the Khmer Serei documents held in the locked press of the John M. Echols collection of Cornell University's Kroch Library. Sihanouk gives 1956 as the date of the Khmer Serei's creation, stating that it was then installed under Son Ngoc Thanh in Thailand with "the financial and material support of the American CIA." Norodom Sihanouk, *Chroniques de guerre ... et d'espoir* (1979), Paris: Hachette/Stock, p. 234. It is, of course, quite possible that covert American support was going to Son Ngoc Thanh and his followers as early as 1956, two years before the actual establishment of the Khmer Serei, and if so that may be what Sihanouk is here alluding to.
28 Smith, *Cambodia's Foreign Policy*, p. 127, citing a report of the International Commission for Supervision and Control in Cambodia.
29 Chandler, *Tragedy of Cambodian History*, p. 98.
30 *Annual Review of Events for 1958*, British Embassy in Phnom Penh to Selwyn Lloyd, Foreign Office, 23 January 1959, p. 6. FO 371, File #14434 (Public Records Office).
31 Smith, *Cambodia's Foreign Policy*, p. 127.
32 *Ibid.*, p. 128. See also William Shawcross, *Sideshow: Kissinger, Nixon and the Destruction of Cambodia* (1979), New York: Simon & Schuster, p. 54

33 British Embassy to Selwyn Lloyd (FO371/14434), p. 1.
34 Chandler, *Tragedy of Cambodian History*, p. 98.
35 Martin F. Herz, *A Short History of Cambodia* (1958), New York: Praeger, p. 83. Chandler also writes of Dap Chhuon ruling Siem Reap as his "personal fief.", *Tragedy of Cambodian History*, p. 101. Herz had served in the US embassy in Phnom Penh from 1955 through most of 1957. He was appointed country director for Cambodia and Laos in January 1968 and was posted to Saigon seven months later as political counselor with the rank of minister. Shortly after this, at his initiative, I had a long and difficult discussion with him, during which in a most hectoring fashion he sought to disabuse me of my critical attitude towards the South Vietnamese government. He was clearly the most ardent Cold War hawk of any of those I met in our Saigon embassy. He retired from the foreign service in the late 1970s, after having served as ambassador to Bulgaria.
36 Chandler, *Tragedy of Cambodian History*, p. 101.
37 "Synopsis of Intelligence and State material reported to the President", 31 December material reported 2 January 1959. The only other countries dealt with in this brief report (of just over one page) were Japan, India, Cuba and USSR–Iran.
38 Chandler, *Tragedy of Cambodian History*, p.102. Sihanouk alleged that the plan called for the removal of all the northern provinces of Cambodia, and not just Siem Reap, and "their merger with the southern provinces of Laos, to form a new secessionist state which would have been immediately recognized by the USA. The right-wing Laotian, Prince Boun Oum of Champassac, is said to have agreed to this. This was to be a starting point from which to take over the whole of Cambodia." *My War with the CIA: The Memoirs of Prince Norodom Sihanouk as related to Wilfred Burchett* (1973), London: Penguin, p. 109.
39 John Prados, *Presidents' Secret Wars: CIA and Pentagon Covert Operations Since World War II* (1986), New York: William Morrow, p. 299.
40 Discussions with Hugh S. Cumming, Jr, Washington DC, 27 December 1975.
41 For the fullest account, see Charles A. Stevenson, *The End of Nowhere: American Policy Towards Laos Since 1954* (1972), Boston: Beacon Press.
42 For a full account of this intervention, see Audrey and George Kahin, *Subversion as Foreign Policy* (1995), New York: New Press.
43 Almost three decades later it was evident that sensitivity concerning this period had by no means diminished when on 11 August 1987, US documents relating to 13 February and 23 February 1959 were withdrawn from these files for what was stipulated as their constituting "Security-Classified Information."
44 Phnom Penh (Garner) to British Foreign Office, No. 132 (Cypher/OTP), 27 February 1959.
45 Chandler, *Tragedy of Cambodian History*, p. 103. See also Shawcross, *Sideshow*, p. 54.
46 Evan Thomas, *The Very Best Men* (1995), New York: Simon & Schuster, p. 190. Thomas, Washington bureau chief of *Newsweek*, was given unusual access to some relevant CIA documents and to the papers of Richard Bissell.
47 Sihanouk claimed that a second member of the American embassy was also involved in the Dap Chhuon affair. British Embassy Phnom Penh to Foreign Office, No. 158 (Cypher/OTP), 20 March 1959.
   On the involvement of the CIA and Matsui see Chandler, *Tragedy of Cambodian History*, pp. 103–4; Smith, *Cambodia's Foreign Policy*, p. 164 and Milton Osborne, *Sihanouk: Prince of Light, Prince of Darkness* (1994), Honolulu: University of Hawaii Press, pp. 110–11.
48 Chandler, *Tragedy of Cambodian History*, p. 105.
49 Phnom Penh to British Foreign Office (Garner) No. 132, 27 February 1959.

50 Sir H. Caccia (Ambassador to Washington) to Foreign Office (Cypher/OTP), No. 215, 23 January 1959.
51 Saigon (Parker) to Foreign Office, No. 38, 30 January 1959.
52 British Embassy,The State Department apparently refused to participate directly in the plot, as they believed it was unlikely to succeed. See memo from Herbert F. Keppard 2/2/59 and memo from Walter Robertson, 22 April 1959 in State Department Lot files 63D 73. Phnom Penh (F.F. Garner) to Heppel, Foreign Office, 11 February 1959.
53 FO 371, Folder 144353, 20 April 1959 (Old # DU 14345/4/G). (Remarks by Butler and Appel.)
54 *Ibid.*, Secret Letter (20 April 1959) R.W. Parker, British Embassy, Saigon to D.F. MacDermot, Foreign Office.
55 FO 371, Folder 144353, 29 April 1959, Secret Letter: R.W. Parker, British Embassy, Saigon to D.F. MacDonald, Foreign Office.
56 F.F. Garner (Phnom Penh) to R.P. Heppel (Foreign Office), 16 October 1959 (1011/59).
57 Thus, the CIA's Biographic Register (Office of Central Reference) notes on p. 3 that South Vietnamese general Nguyen Khanh had in March 1960 "reportedly refused to allow the training of Cambodian dissident military forces in his area of responsibility." (General Khanh then had a reputation of being one of the most independent-minded South Vietnamese generals.)
58 See Leifer, *Cambodia*, p. 143. Sihanouk's fears had probably already been aroused by the assassination in April 1963 of the strongly neutralist Laotian foreign minister, Quinim Pholsena.
59 *Ibid.*, pp. 144–5; and Smith, *Cambodia's Foreign Policy*, pp. 199–200. Chandler states that the two captured Khmer Serei "were under the misapprehension that they could travel to Phnom Penh to discuss Khmer Serei policies and Son Ngoc Thanh's political ambitions with Sihanouk at the national congress." Chandler, *Tragedy of Cambodian History*, p. 130.
60 Chandler, *Tragedy of Cambodian History*, pp. 134–5.

14 Cambodia and the Vietnam War

1 Chargé d'affaires Leslie Fielding to Gordon Walker, Foreign Office, 15 January 1965, "Cambodia Annual Review for 1964," FO 371/ 180466 (36585).
2 Hal Kosut (ed.), *Cambodia and the Vietnam War* (1971), New York: Facts on File, pp. 20–1.
3 *Ibid.*, pp. 25–7.
4 *New York Times*, 12 July 1970, p. 4.
5 This training was witnessed in December 1967 by a seasoned member of the American Friends Service Committee (letter from him to senior AFSC personnel, a copy of which they sent to me).
6 William Shawcross, *Sideshow: Kissinger, Nixon and the Destruction of Cambodia* (1979), New York: Simon & Schuster, p. 65.
7 *New York Times*, 28 January 1970.
8 By January 1962 MAAG (Military Assistance Advisory Group) strength in South Vietnam had increased to "over 3,000" men, of whom 805 were listed as advisers "in the special program under CIA control," *The Pentagon Papers*, Gravel edn, Vol. II, p. 454.
9 National Security Action Memorandum No. 162 of 19 June 1962 stipulated:

> More Special Forces personnel will be assigned [by the Department of Defense] to support CIA covert operations where acute insurgency situations exist ... the Department of Defense will increase its capability to fund,

support, and conduct wholly or partly covert paramilitary operations under the criteria of NSAM [National Security Action Memorandum] 57 which distinguishes responsibilities of the Department of Defense and CIA: Where such an operation is to be wholly covert or disavowable, it may be assigned to CIA, provided that it is within the normal capabilities of the agency. Any large paramilitary operation wholly or partly covert which requires significant numbers of militarily trained personnel, amounts of military equipment which exceed normal CIA-controlled stocks and/or military experience of a kind and level peculiar to the Armed Services is properly the primary responsibility of the Department of Defense with the CIA in a supporting role.

The Pentagon Papers, Gravel edn, Vol. II, p. 683

10 The White House, Memorandum For Mr Bundy; "The New Year in Asia," 7 January 1966, p. 12.
11 In a memo for McGeorge Bundy, entitled "Two Weeks in Asia" dated 7 December 1965, James Thomson reported: "Lodge's approach to Ky for suspending GVN aid to Son Ngoc Thanh was favorably received. Ky stated that the GVN stand down would also apply to furnishing weapons to Thanh." (Ky, of course, was not the most reliable of clients, and in any case he was probably at this time subject to rather different marching orders from MACV.)
12 Directorate of Intelligence, Central Intelligence Agency, "The Situation in South Vietnam (24–30 September 1964)," pp. 9–10. Since so few CIA documents bearing on these Cambodian matters have ever been released, one naturally is curious why this one was declassified. Perhaps by releasing it the Agency's assessment officers wanted to distinguish themselves from the field activists, or at least in retrospect (the document having been declassified in 1978) to demonstrate that on these Cambodian issues they had been sensible.
13 Airgrams American Embassy, Phnom Penh to the State Department, 31 December 1964 and 5 March 1965 (US National Archives, College Park, Maryland). The broadcast also mentioned that a wealthy Thai-domiciled banker, Songsak, described as "Son Ngoc Thanh's adviser," had attended a meeting of the Khmer Serei Central Committee on 25 February.
14 FO 371/180467, foreign office covering note of 24 February 1965 to several reports from Ambassador Leslie Fielding in Phnom Penh.
15 Phnom Penh [Ambassador Fielding] to Foreign Office, 22 April 1966, FO 367/186236.
16 The strength of Cambodia's armed forces as of April 1965 was reckoned by the US embassy in Phnom Penh at: Army 31,549; Navy 1,398; and Airforce 1,387 (Airgram to State, 16 April 1965, p. 4).
17 *New York Times*, 4 May 1965. With respect to the involvement of US advisers in these cross-border probes, see also David Chandler, *The Tragedy of Cambodian History: Politics, War and Revolution since 1945* (1991), New Haven: Yale University Press, p. 143.
18 In these operations emanating from Thailand it claimed that twenty-three Cambodians had been killed, sixty-four wounded and thirty-three kidnapped, with another fifty killed and 133 wounded from land mines planted inside the Cambodian frontier. Don Noel, "Cambodia and Thailand," p. 1, Phnom Penh, 1 March 1967, report to the Alicia Patterson Fund. Noel, a reporter on leave from the *Hartford Times*, had been in Cambodia for approximately five months on a fellowship from the Patterson Fund.
19 Chargé d'affaires Leslie Fielding to Mr Stewart (Foreign Office and Whitehall Distribution), "Cambodia: Annual Review for 1965," 11 January 1966, p. 2.
20 Telegram No. 9903 of 10 December 1965 from Foreign Office to Washington, FO 371/180474. James Thomson evidenced similar concerns on behalf of the State Department in his 7 December memorandum to McGeorge Bundy, where

he noted: "State's Cambodia experts have been alarmed in recent days at pending decisions that might bring intentional U.S./GVN attacks against Cambodian territory. Their chief point is simply that so far (a) there appears to be no major increase in the limited Communist use of Cambodian territory, and (b) there is absolutely no evidence – and never has been – of Cambodian government tacit or overt support for such Communist use of Cambodian territory."

21 Telegram No. 3479 of 27 December from Sir P. Dean to Foreign Office, FO 371/180474.

22 Foreign Office attachment of 29 December 1965 (signed by J.E. Cable) to telegram from Ambassador Fielding of 28 December, FO 371/180474.

23 Don Noel, "The Commission and the Cong," p. 2, Phnom Penh, 7 March 1967, report to the Alicia Patterson Fund.

24 Interviews with Ambassador Deschamps, Phnom Penh, 3 and 9 August 1967. William Shawcross, writing after more pertinent data had become available twelve years later, described the same scenario, but in much bolder strokes. He stated that members of the royal family as well as Lon Nol and many senior army officers were involved in the traffic. He also asserted that "in 1966 Chou En-Lai personally asked Sihanouk to allow supplies to be brought into the port of Sihanoukville" for the Vietnamese Communists, and suggested that two-thirds go to them and the other third to Sihanouk. (Unfortunately he does not provide any documentation as to his source.) Shawcross, *Sideshow*, p. 64. With respect to military supplies reaching the NLF and North Vietnamese forces via Sihanoukville, Seymour Hersh noted that during 1966–70 US military analysts consistently estimated the amount as greater than did the CIA, and on the basis of captured documents asserted in May 1970 that the total for that period was 23,000 tons as against the CIA's estimate of 6,000 tons, Seymour Hersh, *The Price of Power: Kissinger in the Nixon White House* (1983), New York: Summit Books, p. 200n.

25 Interview with Ambassador (Airforce) Lt General Budiardjo, Phnom Penh, 2 August 1967. FULRO was established in 1963 or 1964 by upland tribal groups (Rhade, Bahnar, Jarai, Bru and others) in reaction to their discriminatory and repressive treatment by the Saigon government. It sought to end Saigon's rule and was able spasmodically and temporarily to secure some attributes of autonomy from a grudging South Vietnamese government. Sihanouk permitted its units sanctuary in Cambodia, and later some received at least indirect support from US Special Forces, which recruited a sizable number of its members. According to John Prados, it enrolled as many as 7,000 armed men and was strong enough in December 1965 to capture and briefly hold two South Vietnamese provincial capitals. Apparently FULRO elements remained a significant military factor in South Vietnam's Central Highlands until at least 1970. Further detail can be found in Prados's *The Hidden History of the Vietnam War*, pp. 80–7.

26 Chandler, *Tragedy of Cambodian History*, p. 172.

27 *Ibid.*, pp. 172–3; and Shawcross, *Sideshow*, pp. 68–70.

28 The initial stage of the campaign was known as "Operation Breakfast."

29 Shawcross, *Sideshow*, pp. 28–35.

15 Coup against Sihanouk

1 The number of students attending government secondary school rose from 4,200 in 1955 to 33,021 in 1965 and 83,000 in 1967. The number receiving university education rose from 116 in 1955 to 2,571 in 1963 and 7,400 in 1967. *Area Handbook for Cambodia* (1968), Washington: US Government Printing Office, p. 111. (Statistics are drawn from an official Cambodian government source.)

2 *Ibid.*, pp. 288–9.

3 Laura Summers (1986) "The sources of economic grievance in Sihanouk's Cambodia," *Southeast Asian Journal of Social Science* 14(1): 27.

4 For the fullest accounts of the Samlaut uprising, see Ben Kiernan, "The Samlaut rebellion, 1967–68," in Ben Kiernan and Chantou Boua (eds), *Peasants and Politics in Kampuchea, 1942–1981* (1982), London: Zed Press, pp. 166–205; and David Chandler, *The Tragedy of Cambodian History: Politics, War and Revolution since 1945* (1991), New Haven: Yale University Press, pp. 163–7.

5 According to Ambassador Deschamps, a substantial amount of foreign exchange was being lost to the government in 1966 and 1967 as a consequence of its purchase by Cambodian-domiciled Chinese merchants alone (i.e. quite apart from whatever role the Cambodian army was playing), who sold it to both the Vietnamese Communists and the Saigon government, the foreign exchange earned being thereby denied the Phnom Penh government (interviews Phnom Penh, 3 and 9 August 1967).

6 Summers, "Sources of Economic Grievance," p. 22.

7 Chandler, *Tragedy of Cambodian History*, p. 188.

8 T.D. Allman, "Anatomy of a coup," *Far Eastern Economic Review*, 9 April 1970, p. 1.

9 I have long been convinced that an important reason for Sihanouk having received such a bad press in the West was the experience (which I shared) of correspondents and other writers who flew between Saigon and Bangkok in the 1960s. Many of these flights were obliged to stop in Phnom Penh, with a lay-over of an hour or more. Passengers had the option of remaining aboard the plane (usually a DC3) and sweltering as it sat on the tarmac or entering the pleasantly cool airport lounge where the quid pro quo was to endure one of Sihanouk's dreadful movies.

10 Interview with Andrew Antippas, political officer US embassy, Phnom Penh, 24 August 1971. Before being posted to Phnom Penh in July 1970 he had served for two years as "Cambodia watcher" in the political section of the embassy in Saigon.

11 Seymour Hersh, *The Price of Power: Kissinger in the Nixon White House* (1983), New York: Summit Books, p. 176. T.D. Allman, who followed developments in Cambodia closely at this time, observes "By the beginning of 1969, Sihanouk's own Minister of Defense, General Lon Nol, was plotting to overthrow him." *Unmanifest Destiny* (1984), New York: Dial Press, p. 337.

12 *Washington Post*, 18 April 1970.

13 Chandler, *Tragedy of Cambodian History*, p. 190.

14 The conventional wisdom in the diplomatic community apparently placed Chau Seng on the moderate non-Communist left, and this accorded with my impression in a discussion with him in Phnom Penh in early August 1967. He was later imprisoned and executed under the Khmer Rouge.

15 Daniel Roy, "Le Coup de Phnom-Penh," *Le Monde Diplomatique*, April 1970, p. 12. Roy had served for several years with the title of Sihanouk's press attaché.

16 Interview with airforce Lt General Budiardjo, Jakarta, 22 May 1971. General Dharsono was one of the most powerful officers in the Indonesian army and had been strongly anti-Sukarno.

17 William Shawcross, *Sideshow: Kissinger, Nixon and the Destruction of Cambodia* (1979), New York: Simon & Schuster, p. 120.

18 *Newsweek* (Periscope), 25 May 1970.

19 Arrangements for this training involved input by General Dharsono, then ambassador to Thailand and formerly commander of West Java's Siliwangi division, which maintained the Lembang base. This operation apparently bypassed General Ali Murtopo and his special operations group, which had its own

connection with Lon Nol, and was arranged through General Sumitro's Kopkamtib (Operations Command to Restore Order).

20 Henry Kissinger, *White House Years* (1979), Boston: Little Brown, p. 463.
21 Hersh, *Price of Power*, p.183.
22 Shawcross writes that *privately* Kissinger amended his position, raising the possibility of US intervention at a lunch in 1977 with a group of European journalists where, "he defended his role in the whole Cambodian drama and said that the United States had not been involved in Sihanouk's overthrow, 'at least not at the top level' " (*Sideshow*, p. 122).
23 Richard Hall, a former member of the Australian Secret Intelligence Service (MO9), clearly understood that the American military played the major role, but, I believe, he attaches too much importance to the "old boy network of Cambodian soldiers trained in the U.S.," and by writing of the US military "bypassing" the CIA in organizing the coup suggests that the Agency was more out of the loop than it actually was. Richard Hall, *The Secret State: Australia's Spy Industry* (1979), Stanmore, New South Wales: Cassell Australia, p. 133.
24 Upon the completion of this assignment he received a glowing commendation (of which I have a copy) referring to his contribution that "significantly enhanced the United States' efforts in the Republic of Vietnam" and to his "outstanding intelligence" and a knowledge "far in excess of that required by, or expected of, a Yeoman First Class" during his tour of duty there.
25 Among them, T.D. Allman, Seymour Hersh and Ben Kiernan.
26 Hersh, *Price of Power*, p. 180n.
27 Hearings, Subcommittee on Foreign Assistance and Economic Policy, 6 March 1975.
28 See Chapter 6, pp. 157.
29 Hersh, *Price of Power*, p. 180n.
30 All the quotations in the following account are from copies of the exchange of correspondence in late 1979 between Thornton and the editor of *The Economist*, Andrew Knight, which I have in my possession, together with Thornton's supporting data.
31 Allman writes: "Son Ngoc Thanh ... himself confirmed that, through him, Lon Nol had requested, and the CIA had approved, a U.S. pledge to send the Khmer Krom troops to support Lon Nol in the event he overthrew Norodom Sihanouk." Allman, *Unmanifest Destiny*, p. 339. Thornton's reference to the infiltration of the Khmer Serei is also consistent with my own discussion with Son Ngoc Thanh in Phnom Penh, 25 August 1971.
32 Sihanouk, *My War with the CIA* (1973), Harmondsworth: Penguin Books, p. 39.
33 The former commander-in-chief of the Cambodian army under Lon Nol writes: "During the 1963–65 period, U.S. Special Forces in South Vietnam expanded their Civilian Irregular Defense Group (CIDG), an indigenous paramilitary force composed mostly of Montagnards serving under U.S. control, by recruiting ethnic Cambodians to form additional light guerrilla companies. These 'Khmer Krom' units were primarily deployed at border CIDG camps in the RVN's MR-3 and MR-4." Lt General Sak Sutsakhan, *The Khmer Republic at War and the Final Collapse* (1980), Washington DC: US Center of Military History, p. 55.
34 Roy, "Le Coup de Phnom-Penh," *Le Monde Diplomatique*, April 1970.
35 Shawcross, *Sideshow*, p. 122.
36 *Ibid.*, p. 65.
37 Milton Osborne, "Effacing the 'God-King': internal developments in Cambodia since March 1970," in Joseph Zasloff and Alan Goodman (ed.), *Indochina in Conflict* (1972), Lexington MA: D.C. Heath, p. 61.
38 Allman, *Unmanifest Destiny*, pp. 342–3.

39 Roger Morris, *Uncertain Greatness: Henry Kissinger and American Foreign Policy* (1977), New York: Harper & Row, p. 173.

40 Shawcross, *Sideshow*, p. 120.

41 Discussion with Forrest Lindley, Washington DC, 6 March 1975. Tad Szulc and Seymour Hersh in subsequent interviews with Lindley received corroborative information. See Hersh, *Price of Power*, p. 178; and Tad Zulc, *The Illusion of Peace* (1978), New York: Viking Press, pp. 242–3. Figures for the total assigned strength of the three companies at Bu Prang show a substantial increase between January and March 1970 – from 272 to 398 men (Camp Information Data, Bu Prang, Kien Duc District, Quang Duc Province USASF Det. A-236, Apt William L. Palmer, Det. Commander, US National Archives, College Park Maryland).

42 Emphasis in the original. COMUSMACV to VMAC, 19 March 1970, CZCQFA 328, BT 4996.

43 The following account is drawn from the *Los Angeles Times*, the *New York Times*, the *Washington Post* and the *Virginian Pilot* (a Norfolk VA paper which took a keen interest in the affair) during the period mid-March to December 1970. For brief, and superficial accounts, see 30 March 1970 editions of *Newsweek*, p. 36, and *Time*, p. 17. The tonnage of the ship and of its cargo was disparately reported in these newspapers.

44 *New York Times*, 26 March 1970, p. 16.

45 *Ibid.*, 25 September 1970, p. 2; see also *Far Eastern Economic Review*, 2 April 1970.

46 AP report carried in the *Virginia Pilot*, 15 December 1970, p. A20.

47 UP report carried in the *Virginia Pilot*, 20 December 1970, p. A14.

48 *New York Times*, 16 December 1970, p. 3.

49 *Ibid.*, 3 March 1971.

50 *Ibid.*, 26 March 1970, p. 16.

51 See for example, *Washington Post*, 19 March 1970, pp. A25–6

52 *The Times* (London), 9 April 1970, p. 8.

53 Whether or not the ship rode higher in the water on the eve of its departure from Sihanoukville than when it arrived was a matter of dispute among reported eyewitnesses, and tended to obscure the fundamental question of where it went.

54 2 April 1970, p. 7.

55 Sihanouk, *My War with the CIA*, p. 23.

56 This figure was given to me by Son Ngoc Thanh (interview, Phnom Penh, 25 August 1971).

57 Daniel Roy, "Le Coup de Phnom-Penh," *Le Monde Diplomatique*, April 1970, p. 13. See also Chandler, *Tragedy of Cambodian History*, pp. 195–6, who places the date of the Assembly's action later. These moves alone could have triggered the rash statements vowing retribution that Sihanouk was alleged to have made in the hearing of personnel at Cambodia's Paris Embassy and forwarded by them to Phnom Penh. (For this, see Shawcross, *Sideshow*, p. 119.) The fact that Colonel Fernandez re-emerged in a position of major importance within a few months of Sihanouk's removal (in charge of Cambodia's Military Region 2, according to Colonel Crego) suggests that he arrived at an understanding with Lon Nol when he was removed as head of internal security.

58 Shawcross, *Sideshow*, p. 117 and Sihanouk, *My War with the C.I.A.*, pp. 21–2.

59 Discussions with Henry Kamm and Jean-Claude Pomonti, Bangkok, 18 July 1971. According to them, the demonstrations outside the embassies followed contingency plans which Sihanouk had helped draft a year before, but which now went much further (i.e. the sacking) than had then been envisaged. See also T.D. Allman, "Anatomy of a Coup," *Far Eastern Economic Review*, 9 April 1970, p. 19.

60 Allman refers here to "a team of 45 trained soldiers in civilian dress" (*ibid.*). A correspondent from *Time*, H.D.S. Greenway, reported meeting with "an organizer of the mob that sacked the North Vietnamese and Provisional Revolutionary Government [NLF] embassies" who identified himself as a leader of the Khmer Krom troops "trained by the U.S. Special Forces as mobile strike forces [Mike Forces]," *The Atlantic*, July 1970, p. 34.

61 For the sacking of the embassies, see Chandler, *Tragedy of Cambodian History*, p. 194; and Allman, "Anatomy of a Coup," p. 19.

62 Allman, "Anatomy of a Coup," p. 19.

63 Shawcross, *Sideshow*, pp. 118–19; see also Chandler, *Tragedy of Cambodian History*, p. 195.

64 Note that Phnom Penh time is eleven hours ahead of Washington time.

65 Chandler, *Tragedy of Cambodian History*, p. 195; Shawcross, *Sideshow*, p. 118; and Szulc, *Illusion of Peace*, p. 242.

66 Henry Kamm, then the *New York Times* correspondent covering Cambodia.

67 While it is true that within a year of this challenge Lon Nol began to show frequent signs of irrationality, this was not evident at the time, nor was this quality then or later evident in the demeanor of his partner, Sirik Matak.

68 Arnold Isaacs, *Without Honor: Defeat in Vietnam and Cambodia* (1984), New York: Random House (Vintage Books), p. 201. Isaacs is here quoting Cambodia's then Colonel Sak Sutsakhan who later became head of Lon Nol's armed forces and the Khmer Republic's last chief of state (*ibid.*: 197).

69 With respect to the US position on recognition, see Cable: Secretary of State Rogers to Phnom Penh, 21 March 1970, p. 3.

70 Isaacs, *Without Honor*, p. 205. As of 5 June 1970, 87,000 of these Cambodian Vietnamese had fled to South Vietnam and another 75,000 were being held in Phnom Penh in what Dr Phan Quang Dan, the South Vietnamese minister of state known for his honesty, termed "concentration camps" (*New York Times*, 6 June 1970).

71 Shawcross, *Sideshow*, pp. 132–3.

72 Chandler, *Tragedy of Cambodian History*, p. 203.

73 There were numerous reports in the American press. For an account of one of these bloody repressions by government troops at the bridge leading into Phnom Penh, see the report of the *Time* correspondent H.D.S. Greenway in *The Atlantic*, July 1970, p. 34.

74 *New York Times*, 28 March and 1 April 1970.

75 Isaacs, *Without Honor*, p. 200.

76 Cable: Rives to Secretary of State, 4 April 1970, p. 2.

77 *New York Times*, 10 April 1970.

78 Cable: Rives to Secretary of State, 30 March 1970, p. 2.

79 *New York Times*, 23 April 1970.

80 *Ibid.*, 14 June 1970.

81 *Ibid.*, 2 July 1970. By 5 May over 2,000 Mike Force Khmer Krom were positioned for the defense of the capital (*ibid.*, 6 May 1970).

82 Cable: Rives to Secretary of State, 23 April 1970; and *New York Times*, 23 April and 30 May 1970.

83 *Newsweek*, 4 May 1970, p. 21. See also Jean-Claude Pomonti and Serge Thion, *Des courtesans aux partisans* (1971), Paris: Gallimard, p. 220.

   According to airforce Lt General Budiardjo, the Indonesian government did not insist that the quid pro quo be in modern US weapons, and it was equally interested in the US slowing up its release of rubber and tin stocks so that the price of these Indonesian exports on the world market could benefit (interview, Jakarta, 22 May 1971). With respect to Indonesia's supply of arms, see also Bernard Gordon, "Cambodia's Foreign Relations: Sihanouk and After," in

Joseph J. Zasloff and Allan E. Goodman (eds), *Indochina in Conflict* (1972), Lexington MA: D.C. Heath (Lexington Books), p. 161.

84 See Melvin Gurtov, "Security by Proxy: The Nixon Doctrine and Southeast Asia," in Mark W. Zacher and R. Stephen Milne (eds), *Conflict & Stability in Southeast Asia* (1974), New York: Anchor Press/Doubleday, p. 214, n. 35, for the reference to the US House of Representative hearings containing this information which were held 14–23 March. It was noted in these hearings that 360 Cambodians were then being trained in Indonesia. For Malaysia, see also Gordon, "Cambodia's Foreign Relations," p. 162.

85 *New York Times*, 7 and 8 June 1970.

86 For this and additional details concerning the payment of third-country troops on the US side in Vietnam and Laos, see George McT. Kahin, *Intervention: How America Became Involved in Vietnam* (1986), New York: Alfred A. Knopf, pp. 334–6; see also *New York Times*, 21 August 1970.

87 *New York Times*, 21 and 22 August 1970.

88 This, and the account that follows, are based primarily on my discussions during the spring of 1970 in Ithaca and Washington DC with Indonesia's then ambassador to the United States, Soedjatmoko Mangoendiningrat, one of Foreign Minister Malik's strongest supporters; with Idrus Nasir Djajadiningrat, head of the North American desk of the Indonesian foreign office, Jakarta, 28 January 1971; and with Colonel Daan Jaaja, formerly senior officer in the Siliwangi division, Jakarta, 30 May 1971.

Franklin Weinstein notes: "Beginning in 1968 there was discussion [in Indonesia] of proposals, some of them emanating from the United States, that Indonesia send substantial armed forces to Vietnam as part of an American-sponsored 'peacekeeping force' following the withdrawal of U.S. troops. Reportedly the plan had some backing for a time among a small group of army officers who hoped that Indonesia might be rewarded for such a role in Cambodia after the 1970 coup against Sihanouk" (Franklin B. Weinstein, *Indonesian Foreign Policy and the Dilemma of Dependence: From Sukarno to Soeharto* (1976), Ithaca NY: Cornell University Press, p. 35), see also Harold Crouch, *The Army and Politics in Indonesia* (1978), Ithaca NY: Cornell University Press, p. 336.

89 In addition to Indonesia, the conference was attended by Australia, Japan, Laos, Malaysia, New Zealand, the Philippines, Singapore, South Korea, South Vietnam and Thailand.

90 Franklin Weinstein, "The Uses of Foreign Policy in Indonesia," PhD dissertation, Cornell University, 1972, p. 640n.

91 *New York Times*, 27 May 1970. If there had been any ambiguity, Suharto reinforced his position the next day in a speech at the National Press Club by indicating that "other foreign troops" must be prevented from replacing Americans after their scheduled departure on 30 June. He was referring specifically to South Vietnamese and Thai troops (see Szulc, *Illusion of Peace*, p. 298).

16   Invasion of Cambodia

1 Terence Smith in the *New York Times*, 20 April 1970.

2 *New York Times*, 20 June 1970.

3 This account is drawn from those of Tad Szulc, who has probably the most detailed and best informed coverage of its decision-making period (Tad Zulc, *The Illusion of Peace* (1978), New York: Viking Press, pp. 245–70), and from the 20 June 1970 report in the *New York Times*.

4 Lt General Sak Sutsakhan, *The Khmer Republic at War and the Final Collapse* (1980), Washington DC: US Center of Military History, p. 67.

5 This team's report was written by Hedrick Smith in collaboration with Max Frankel and incorporated reports written by William Beecher, Henry Giniger, Henry Kamm, Sydney H. Schanberg, Robert H.Semple Jr, Neil Shehan, Terrence Smith, James P. Sterba and Tad Szulc. Occupying almost a full page of the 30 June 1970 edition of the *New York Times*, it was one of the fullest and most accurate coverages of this period of American involvement in Cambodia. It will be referred to from here on as the "Hedrick Smith Report."

6 Jean-Claude Pomonti, "Cambodia: the plunge into commitment," *Le Monde*, Weekly Selection, 3 June 1970, p. 4.

7 Jean-Claude Pomonti and Serge Thion, *Des courtesans aux partisans* (1971), Paris: Gallimard, p. 231.

8 Szulc, *Illusion of Peace*, p. 258; see also Hedrick Smith who apparently then thought it had been only Nixon's second viewing.

9 Cable: Rives to Secretary of State, "Top Secret," 1 May 1970. Rives pointed out he had received notice by a cable just ten minutes before Nixon's 30 April (Washington time) speech and the balance in a second cable half an hour later. "Therefore unable discuss with Lon Nol prior President's speech."
   The official reason for the delay in informing Lon Nol was that the Phnom Penh cable office was closed. The Hedrick Smith report, however, notes that, though Lon Nol had agreed to deeper South Vietnamese raids into Cambodia, including the Parrot's Beak, "his consent was not sought for the Fishhook [initial focus of the American invasion]. The White House believed if he said 'no' it was in trouble; if he said 'yes' he might be."

10 Nevertheless, *The New Webster's Dictionary* (1981) (College Edition), New York: Delair, gives as its first definition for "incursion," "a hostile, often sudden invasion of territory."

11 I learned of this when a group of Senators asked me down to Washington to prepare a critique of Nixon's speech and of the answers to the hypothetical questions provided in these mailings. This first mailing (dated 30 April) was twenty-two double-spaced pages and should not be confused with the more polished eight-page single-spaced version "Questions and Answers" dated simply May 1970 that was later circulated by the State Department's Office of Media Services.

12 Cable: Phnom Penh (Priority) for Carrigan from Oleksiw (drafted by Dean Koch/USIA/IAF), 5/1/70, received in Phnom Penh, 2 May, local time.

13 *New York Times*, 9 May 1970.

14 At the end of May the Senate approved part of the Cooper–Church amendment ending funds for support to the Cambodian government after 1 July 1970 – the date Nixon had promised the withdrawal of all US troops from Cambodia, see Szulc, *Illusion of Peace*, pp. 302–3. Szulc points out that "in May 1974 – fifteen months after the signing of the [Paris] agreement [providing for an end to US involvement in the Vietnam war] – there were still 9000 American civilians in South Vietnam, most engaged directly or indirectly in supporting Saigon's armed forces, especially in aviation" (*ibid.*: 676).

15 Those inviting me were Senators Alan Cranston, Charles E. Goodell, Mark O. Hatfield, Harold E. Hughes, and George McGovern. They informed me that the endeavor had the blessing of Senator Fulbright, with whom I'd previously worked with respect to Vietnam. I worked all out for five days, with important help from my wife, Audrey, and my only graduate student then specializing on Cambodia, Laura Summers, who both accompanied me to Washington. Many thousand copies of our product were promptly mailed out to the media. I've never known if this effort accomplished much. The few letters I received from recipients were positive and appreciative, but invariably ended on the note:

"Why didn't you get this material to us sooner, when it would have done more good?"!

16 A few days before the invasions Secretary of State Rogers had given the clear impression to a House sub-committee that no invasion was in prospect, saying "We recognize that if we escalate and get involved in Cambodia our whole [Vietnamization] program is defeated." Some Congress members tended to believe he was being honest but had been by then cut out of the decision-making loop by Nixon and Kissinger. On 27 April, I attended a dinner hosted by the Brookings Institution for a group of distinguished visiting Japanese officials at which Kissinger spoke and, in answering questions, asserted there would be no increased American involvement in Cambodia.

17 Quoted in William Shawcross, *Sideshow: Kissinger, Nixon and the Destruction of Cambodia* (1979), New York: Simon & Schuster, p. 153.

18 For this and fuller details regarding the Commission, see William Appleman Williams, Thomas McCormick, Loyd Gardner and Walter LaFeber, *America in Vietnam: A Documentary History* (1985), Garden City NY: Anchor Books, pp. 287–90.

19 Shortly after McHugh's warning I was summoned to a meeting of the university's deans. I had been invited to this meeting because I was regarded as having influence with students as a result of my opposition to the Vietnam War and a well-received recent address condemning the Cambodian invasions. (All attending the meeting except the dean of the Law School appeared to be sympathetic to the students.) It was agreed that I should be given a chance to contact the two especially influential student leaders, with whom I had good rapport, and I was fortunately able to make almost immediate contact with them. I found that they already had reservations about the wisdom of the planned march but that strong momentum had built among second echelon student leaders for the march and that they felt they could not stop it unless they could be assured of some plausible positive alternative. We settled on presenting the key activists with a plan that these two leaders and I had actually discussed in somewhat tentative terms over the previous month with respect to the Vietnam War. Thanks to the persuasive abilities of these two leaders and the good sense of the antiwar students, this alternative plan was accepted and the march was called off not very long before it was scheduled to begin. The plan called for Cornell students to carry out well-prepared lobbying in Washington against the Indochina war. Each of the students would target a congressional representative from his or her district and begin lobbying the representative approximately three weeks later after the beginning of summer recess. In the interim, knowledgeable faculty and graduate students would work with the students to help brief them so far as possible on the voting record, constituency base, and whatever information local and national newspapers would reveal as to their representatives' attitude towards the war. Fortunately many of the most committed students embraced this program and nearly 100 mostly well-prepared students did spend part of the summer lobbying against the war. It's impossible to know how effective they were, but at least some of them felt they had made a positive impact.

20 *New York Times*, 14 June 1970.

21 Cable: Rives to Secretary of State, NODIS, 3 May 1970, 9:57 am.

22 Cable: Rives to Secretary of State, 6 May 1970. "Please deliver soonest Carl Marcy, Senate Foreign Relations Committee, by 6 May. From Lowenstein and Moose."

23 See Charles A. Stevenson, *The End of Nowhere: American Policy Towards Laos Since 1954* (1972), Boston: Beacon Press, p. 233. It will be recalled that the Ho

Chi Minh trail complex was no single track, but a web of them sometimes, as in southern Laos, extending up to fifty miles in breadth (*ibid.*: 234).

24 See especially David Chandler, *The Tragedy of Cambodian History: Politics, War and Revolution since 1945* (1991), New Haven: Yale University Press, pp. 211–15; and Shawcross, *Sideshow*, pp. 187, 204, 208, 228–31.

25 Brief reference to the trial is found in the Ministry of Information's fact sheet on Son Ngoc Thanh that it gave me in August 1971.

26 See Milton Osborne, "Effacing the 'God-King': internal developments in Cambodia since March 1970," in Joseph Zasloff and Alan Goodman (eds), *Indochina in Conflict* (1972), Lexington MA: D.C. Heath, p. 62.

27 These were respectively the characterizations of these Khmer Krom by L.H. Askew, deputy head of the political section of the American embassy (interview, Saigon, 25 July 1971), and Andrew Antippas, political section, US embassy, Phnom Penh (interview, 24 August 1971).

28 This is according to Lt General Sak Sutsakhan, *The Khmer Republic at War*, p. 55.

29 Interview with Andrew Antippas, Phnom Penh, 24 August 1971.

30 Interview with Colonel Crego, Saigon, 28 July 1971.

31 Interview with Son Ngoc Thanh, Phnom Penh, 25 August 1971. He said that there were about another 20,000 Khmer Krom in the South Vietnamese army but that they were mixed in the same units as ethnic Vietnamese, and that it would be impossible to get Saigon to release them. When later in speaking with US embassy personnel I expressed my surprise at his candor, they said that because of the knowledge I had shown about this subject he had presumably concluded that I was working for an American intelligence agency.

32 Jean Claude Pomonti, "Cambodia: Signs of Internal Collapse," *Le Monde*, Weekly Selection, 10 June 1970.

33 *New York Times*, 19 March 1972.

34 Chandler, *Tragedy of Cambodian History*, pp. 221–2, and Shawcross, *Sideshow*, pp. 231–3.

35 Interviews with Nom Kimney, Cambodian ambassador to Thailand, Bangkok, 14 June and 17 August 1971. Then acting premier, Long Boret regarded Nom Kimney as the ablest and most knowledgeable of Cambodia's ambassadors (interview, Phnom Penh, 25 August 1971).

36 Interview with Long Boret, Phnom Penh, 23 August 1971. Highly regarded for his honesty, Long Boret had earlier served as a member of the parliament's finance committee and then had represented Cambodia in the Manila-based Asian Development Bank from 1969 until May 1971 when he was called by Sirik Matak to come and take over the post of minister of information. Shawcross writes that "the CIA reported that Phnom Penh's population doubled to 1,200,000 within the first months of the war. By the end of 1971, the Cambodian Ministry of Health estimated that more than two million of Cambodia's seven million people had been displaced" (Shawcross, *Sideshow*, p. 222).

37 Shawcross, *Sideshow*, pp. 214–15.

38 Interview with Ambassador Emory Swank, Phnom Penh, 24 August 1971. I later learned upon reading Shawcross's *Sideshow* that the embassy, particularly in the person of Thomas O. Enders, the deputy chief of mission, served as a sort of interface, vetting requests for air strikes by Cambodian or South Vietnamese officers and US air power.

39 Shawcross, *Sideshow*, p. 271.

40 *Ibid.*, p. 319.

41 Ben Kiernan, *The Pol Pot Regime* (1996), New Haven: Yale University Press, pp. 20 and 22.

42 Shawcross, *Sideshow*, pp. 271–2, 277 and 297.

43 Szulc, *Illusion of Peace*, p. 273.
44 Interview with General In Tam, Phnom Penh, 24 August 1971.
45 Those interested in this later period will find good coverage in the above-cited books by Chandler, Isaacs, Kiernan and Shawcross and in Nayan Chanda's excellent study, *Brother Enemy: The War After the War* (1986), New York: Harcourt Brace.

Index